Data Privacy and Competition Law in the Age of Big Data

OXFORD DATA PROTECTION AND PRIVACY LAW

Series Editors

CHRISTOPHER KUNER
Affiliated Professor of Law, University of Copenhagen

GRAHAM GREENLEAF
Professor of Law and Information Systems, University of New South Wales

The aim of this series is to publish important and original books on legal issues of data protection and privacy. This includes many different areas of law, including comparative law, EU law, human rights law, international law, privacy on the Internet, and others. Prospective authors are welcome to submit proposals for the series, as outlined on the series website: global.oup.com/academic/content/series/o/oxford-data-protection-and-privacy-law-odppl/

Data Privacy and Competition Law in the Age of Big Data

Unpacking the Interface Through Complexity Science

SAMSON Y. ESAYAS
BI Norwegian Business School

OXFORD
UNIVERSITY PRESS

OXFORD
UNIVERSITY PRESS

Great Clarendon Street, Oxford, OX2 6DP,
United Kingdom

Oxford University Press is a department of the University of Oxford.
It furthers the University's objective of excellence in research, scholarship,
and education by publishing worldwide. Oxford is a registered trade mark of
Oxford University Press in the UK and in certain other countries

Published in the United States of America by Oxford University Press
198 Madison Avenue, New York, NY 10016, United States of America

British Library Cataloguing in Publication Data

Data available

Library of Congress Control Number: 2024932021

ISBN 978–0–19–889142–0

DOI: 10.1093/oso/9780198891420.001.0001

Printed and bound by
CPI Group (UK) Ltd, Croydon, CR0 4YY

For every soul born into meagre beginnings: may this book serve as a testament to the courage to defy the odds of a poor start!

Foreword

For well over a century, competition law in its modern form has functioned as a prominent regulatory broker and breaker of large-scale business mergers, acquisitions, and other market machinations. The same cannot be said for data privacy law. While competition law has long been a legal giant in terms of economic impact, data privacy law has been, for most of its lifespan, little more than a legal 'sidekick' in market terms. Only in the past decade or so has it become a mainstream regulatory force capable of packing a powerful punch above the corporate belt.

The increasing market impact of data privacy law is due largely to the intensifying reliance by business and state actors on exploitation of personal data to drive productivity and profitability. Other factors have played a role as well, not least the weaponization of data privacy law with more powerful sanctions and enforcement mechanisms—a strategy partly inspired by competition law. This is most evident in the strengthened sanctions regime of the European Union's General Data Protection Regulation (GDPR). Although the machinery of that regime is still not firing with the efficiency that many actors expected, it is starting to bite, aided in large part by the willingness of the Court of Justice of the European Union to dismantle well-entrenched, profitable business practices in defence of fundamental human rights. The Court's recent landmark judgment in the *Meta Platforms* case (C-252/21) is especially telling on this point.

A key issue going forward concerns the relationship of competition law and data privacy law as market regulators. Although both rule sets have, to a significant degree, complementary, mutually reinforcing objectives, each comes to the regulatory task with different doctrines, methodologies, mindsets, and heritage. How will competition law—chronologically, the 'senior' legal heavyweight in this context—receive the emergence of data privacy law as a 'junior' counterpart? To what extent will they face off, eyeing each other, as it were, with suspicion? Will they engage in 'turf wars'? Or will they join hands and collaborate?

It is to be hoped that the answer to the latter question is affirmative. Fortunately, the aforementioned judgment of the Court of Justice in *Meta Platforms* helps push the answer in that direction by emphasizing that national competition authorities (NCAs) and data protection authorities (DPAs) are under a 'duty of sincere cooperation' with each other pursuant to Article 4(3) of the Treaty on European Union. Further, the judgment divides up central elements of the 'turf' over which these authorities may battle: NCAs must defer to the line taken by DPAs (or the Court) as to whether certain conduct accords with the GDPR, but NCAs may draw their own findings in respect of the application of competition law. The judgment accordingly goes a long way in dampening the potential for conflict between both sets of authorities, at least within the European legal framework. This is welcome as we need both sets of laws and their attendant regulatory authorities—along with those from consumer law—operating as a well-functioning 'tag team'.

Nonetheless, significant questions remain, not least whether the doctrines and methodologies of each rule set can properly cope with current market realities. Are they truly fit for purpose in light of the enormity of economic and data-processing power held by a handful of corporations with extremely deep pockets? Is there doctrinal and methodological baggage they ought to offload if they are to curb abuse of such power?

It is with these questions that this book deals. As intimated, they are important questions. Samson Esayas tackles them with flair and dexterity. This is no mean achievement as they are also large questions. In tackling them, Samson Esayas shows not only mastery of two massive, complex bodies of regulation in a cross-jurisdictional perspective but also the ability to utilize important insights from non-legal disciplines, particularly economics, systems theory, and complexity science. Obviously, this requires prodigious talent.

Earlier testimony to this talent is that the doctoral thesis upon which the book builds was awarded the King of Norway's Gold Medal for outstanding research in 2021. This is a highly esteemed prize amongst young academic researchers in Norway.

Ultimately, the best testimony to Samson Esayas's abilities, not just as a scholar but also as a policy entrepreneur, is the basic message of this book: we need to advance a polycentric regulatory strategy fostering synergy between competition law and data privacy law, and we need to imbue both sets of laws with a holistic systemic focus that is sensitive to emergent and non-linear risks. In my view, this message potentially speaks to many other areas of legal regulation as well.

Lee A. Bygrave
Oslo
November 2023

Table of Contents

PART III: HARNESSING COMPLEXITY TO UNDERSTAND THE INTERFACE

Table of Cases

EUROPEAN COURT OF HUMAN RIGHTS

COURT OF JUTCIE OF THE EUREOPAN UNION/GENRAL COURT

EUROPEAN COMISSION DECISIONS

EU MEMBER STATES

UNITED KINGDOM

UNITED STATES

Table of Legislation

EUROPEAN

EU MEMBER STATES

US LEGISLATION

List of Abbreviations

A29WP	Article 29 Working Party
AEC	as efficient competitor
AEPD	Agencia Española de Protección de Datos
AG	Attorney General/Advocate General
AGCM	Autorità Garante della Concorrenza e del Mercato (Italian Competition and Consumer Protection Authority)
AI	artificial intelligence
API	application programming interface
ATT	App tracking transparency
B2C	business-to-consumer
BA	British Airways
CERRE	Centre on Regulation in Europe
CJEU	Court of Justice of the European Union
CLES	Centre for Law, Economics and Society
CMA	UK Competition and Markets Authority
CML Rev	Common Market Law Review
CNIL	Commission nationale de l'informatique et des libertés
CPI	Competition Policy International
CPU	central processing units
CRM	customer relationship management
CSLI	cell-site location information
DDBM	data-driven business model
DG	Directorate General
DNT	Do Not Track
DMA	Digital Markets Act
DoJ	US Department of Justice
DPA	data protection authority
DPIA	Data Protection Impact Assessment
DSA	Digital Services Act
ECHR	European Convention of Human Rights
ECtHR	European Court of Human Rights
EDPS	European Data Protection Supervisor
EEA	European Economic Area
EU	European Union
EUMR	European Union Merger Regulation
FCA	French Competition Authority
FLoC	Federated Learning of Cohorts
FTC	US Federal Trade Commission
GC	General Court

GCLC	Global Competition Law Centre
GDPR	General Data Protection Regulation
GPS	global positioning system
GWB	German Competition Act
HHI	Herfindal–Hirschman Index
HTTP	Hypertext Transfer Protocol
ICO	UK Information Commissioner's Office
ICOMP	Initiative for Competitive Online Market Place
IDFA	identifier for advertisers
IE	Internet Explorer
IETF	Internet Engineering Task Force
iOS	iPhone operating system
IoT	Internet of Things
IP	Internet protocol/intellectual property
ISO	International Organization for Standardization
ISP	internet service provider
ITP	intelligent tracking prevention
J	Journal
JV	joint venture
LJ	Law Journal
L Rev	Law Review
ML	machine learning
MOS	mobile operating systems
NCA	National Competition Authority
NIST	US National Institute of Standards and Technology
NOx	nitrogen oxides
NSA	National Security Agency
OECD	Organisation for Economic Co-operation and Development
OEM	original equipment manufacturer
OS	operating system
OUP	Oxford University Press
PETs	privacy-enhancing technologies
PSN	professional social networks
SCR	selective catalytic reduction
SMEs	small and medium enterprises
SSO	standard-setting organization
TACA	Trans-Atlantic Conference Agreement
TEU	Treaty on European Union
TFEU	Treaty on the Functioning of the European Union
TPE	tracking preferences expression
UP	University Press
VLOPs	very large online platforms
W3C	World Wide Web Consortium
WEF	World Economic Forum

Introduction

I. WhatsApp Privacy Got to Do with Competition?

The idea for this book was conceived in 2014. It was triggered by my curiosity at Facebook's acquisition of the messaging service WhatsApp. Unlike many messaging services, WhatsApp championed an ad-free business model with no or minimal data collection—that is until it was acquired by Facebook. For as long as I can recall, I had resisted Facebook's persistent request to provide my mobile phone number. When I got wind of the acquisition, I thought Facebook might use the merger as a backdoor to obtain my number. I wasn't wrong. As I later learned, Facebook had, indeed, integrated my number from WhatsApp. Facebook started nudging me to confirm and log in to Facebook using my number. This triggered a question: had competition authorities been at all concerned about the issue of privacy and the possibility of Facebook obtaining users' mobile numbers (following the merger) without their (informed) consent? Intrigued, I began to do some research, eventually stumbling upon the European Commission's decision on the matter.

I was pleasantly surprised to find that the word 'privacy' was mentioned 15 times in the decision. Even more surprising was the Commission's stance on data privacy. It noted that data privacy could be considered an element of product quality or innovation and might potentially be degraded by a merger. This was encouraging as it reinforced my interest and my hunch that privacy ought to be of interest for competition law. Yet, the Commission's analysis did not go far enough to address my intuitive concerns. Drawing a line between the two legal regimes, the Commission remarked that 'Any privacy-related concerns flowing from the increased concentration of data . . . do not fall within the scope of the EU competition law but within the scope of the EU data protection rules.'[1] The remark did not sit well with me and triggered more questions. Specifically, I pondered the feasibility of such an either/or approach in a world where users' data has become a key resource for many digital services and consumers rarely pay a monetary price for these services, instead exchanging their personal data for access. This curiosity sparked a deeper

[1] Case M.7217 *Facebook/WhatsApp* decision of 3 October 2014. The Court of Justice of the European Union (CJEU) expressed a similar view in an earlier decision; see Case C-238/05 *Asnef-Equifax v Asociacion de Usuarios* ECLI:EU:C:2006:734, para 63.

Data Privacy and Competition Law in the Age of Big Data. Samson Y. Esayas, Oxford University Press.
 DOI: 10.1093/oso/9780198891420.003.0001

inquiry into the interface between data privacy and competition laws, culminating in the conception of this book that chronicles my journey.

Fast forward to 2023. The interface between data privacy and competition law has become salient in several high-profile cases both at the Commission and member state levels. A case in point is the Bundeskartellamt's widely publicized Facebook investigation. The social media giant was found to have abused its dominance in the market for social networks by imposing unfair privacy terms, in breach of EU data privacy rules.[2] It is notable that the agency used data privacy law as a benchmark in assessing what constituted abuse under German competition law. The European Commission's recent probes into Facebook and Google similarly shone a spotlight on how these tech giants use data and the risk that such practices may violate EU competition law.[3] Markedly diverging from its earlier perspective in the *Facebook/WhatsApp* merger, the Commission now underscores the importance of considering user privacy and adhering to EU data privacy rules when addressing competition issues in the advertising sector.[4]

The culmination of this issue was evident in the recent Court of Justice of the European Union (CJEU) decision *Meta v Bundeskartellamt*. This decision highlighted the vital role of data privacy rules in competition assessment, especially when examining whether a dominant undertaking's conduct is based on competition on the merits.[5] The CJEU stressed that, given the critical role of personal data in the digital economy, 'excluding the rules on the protection of personal data when investigating an abuse of a dominant position would overlook the reality of this economic development and could jeopardize the effectiveness of competition law within the European Union'.[6] This perspective is a marked departure from both the Commission's approach in *Facebook/WhatsApp* and the CJEU's earlier stance in *Asnef* regarding the role of data privacy rules and their importance for competition assessments. However, the importance of data privacy for competition has taken an unexpected turn.

Recent debate has centred on whether digital incumbents can engage in potentially anticompetitive practices under the pretext of enhancing users' privacy. A case in point is Google's Privacy Sandbox initiative, which aims to remove third-party trackers from Chrome and replace them with its set of Privacy Sandbox tools. Although this seems a positive step for users' privacy, it has triggered increased scrutiny from competition authorities. The European Commission is investigating whether this would restrict competition in the advertising market and constitute

[2] Bundeskartellamt, *Background Information on the Facebook Proceeding* (2017) 4.

[3] European Commission, 'Commission Opens Investigation into Possible Anticompetitive Conduct by Google in the Online Advertising Technology Sector' (22 June 2021) (European Commission, 'Investigation into Google's Online Advertising'); European Commission, 'Commission Opens Investigation into Possible Anticompetitive Conduct of Facebook' (4 June 2021).

[4] European Commission, 'Investigation into Google's Online Advertising' (n 3).

[5] Case C-252/21 *Meta Platforms Inc v Bundeskartellamt* ECLI:EU:C:2023:537.

[6] ibid para 50.

a breach of EU competition law.[7] Similarly, the UK Competition and Markets Authority (CMA) has indicated that Google's actions could amount to abuse of a dominant position and has secured commitments to mitigate the competition concerns.[8]

Although late to the party, momentum is also building across the Atlantic. The US Federal Trade Commission (FTC) has initiated a lawsuit against Facebook, accusing it of illegal monopolization as a result of its acquisition and sidelining of competitors. These actions are considered to harm consumers by diminishing the level of privacy and increasing exposure to advertising.[9] Similarly, the US Department of Justice (DoJ) has accused Google of monopolizing the search market, engaging in actions detrimental to consumers 'by reducing the quality of search (including on dimensions such as privacy, data protection, and use of consumer data), lessening choice in search, and impeding innovation'.[10] In a recent antitrust lawsuit, Texas accused Google of 'privacy fixing', an accusation equivalent to price fixing or forming a cartel but in the field of privacy.[11] These developments show the increased interface between data privacy and competition rules and the need for a dialogue between the two sets of rules and their respective enforcement agencies.

The book cuts to the heart of these issues, offering a timely and comprehensive account of the interface between EU data privacy and competition laws. To this end, it draws insights from system theory, complexity science, informatics, and economics to identify the shifts entailed by the commercialization of personal data and big data, showing how these shifts affect the application of data privacy law and competition law, including their interface. Using emergent properties as an analytical framework, the book exposes the similarity in the mechanics of application of the two legal regimes (ie their atomized approach) and shows how this gives rise to challenges in light of the shifts entailed by the commercialization of personal and big data.

Further, the book provides a comprehensive analysis of the intersection (tensions and convergence) between data privacy and competition law entailed by the increased attention to personal data and data privacy in competition assessments. The book argues that the interface presents an opportunity to enhance the efficacy of both sets of rules. Competition law can enhance the efficacy of data privacy rules by tackling macro-level harms to data privacy in the form of privacy fixing

[7] European Commission, 'Investigation into Google's Online Advertising' (n 3).

[8] Case 50972 *Decision to Accept Commitments Offered by Google in Relation to Its Privacy Sandbox Proposals* Competition and Markets Authority 11 February 2022.

[9] Case 1:20-cv-03590-JEB *Federal Trade Commission v Facebook, Inc* in the United States District of Columbia, filed 19 August 2021.

[10] Case 1:20-cv-03010 *US Department of Justice v Google LLC* in the United States District Court of Columbia, filed 20 October 2020.

[11] Civil Action 1:21-md-03010-PKC *State of Texas v Google LLC* in the United States District of New York, filed 14 January 2022.

and reductions in choice resulting from mergers or platform bans on privacy-enhancing services. Similarly, data privacy law can provide competition law with the necessary tools and normative guidance needed to address new forms of anticompetitive conduct through harms to data privacy. Thus, the book is essential for scholars, policymakers, and legal professionals seeking to understand the key challenges, discern when to deploy data privacy law or competition law, depending on the situation, and when the two legal systems need to join forces to address the challenges.

While the above developments at the interface of competition law and data privacy highlight the growing importance of the issues, they also present unique challenges. As one of the anonymous reviewers pointed out, these are the types of changes that necessitate a book rewrite. This has made the writing process demanding, with constant changes on both the enforcement and legislative fronts. The conception and subsequent passage into law of the Digital Markets Act called for an overhaul of previous analyses and the addition of new sections. The final text, which underwent three rounds of review at Oxford, is markedly different from the initial 2020 draft and even further removed from the original PhD dissertation that was submitted in October 2019. However, one certainty remains: these multiple rounds of revision have made the writing process engaging and the book more compelling. As Beth Luey states in *Revising Your Dissertation*, acknowledging that 'your first book will not be a revision of your dissertation takes a good deal of courage'.[12] This has been true in my case: what follows is not a revised dissertation but a transformed text.

II. Reorientating Data Privacy and Competition Law to a Complex Economy

One notable transformation has been the advancement of the theoretical framework, grounded in systems thinking and complexity science, used to unpack the nexus between data privacy and competition law. Both systems thinking and complexity science offer a broader lens to contextualize how the changes and challenges stemming from the commercialization of personal data fit into and underpin the larger narrative of the increased complexity of the digital economy, marked by the multiplicity of actors and their interactions. The quest to accumulate extensive and diverse data sets is driving organizations to expand into novel product sectors and to acquire entities with rich troves of personal information, leading to the emergence of multiproduct ecosystems. Such ecosystems generate value by bringing together multiple actors and markets and fostering a web of economic interactions.

[12] Beth Luey, 'What Is Your Book About?' in Beth Luey (ed), *Revising Your Dissertation: Advice from Leading Editors* (University of California Press 2007) 40.

Moreover, personal data plays a crucial role in linking different markets, enabling personalization of both production and distribution. The multiplicity of actors and the web of economic links generate feedback loops and lead to outcomes characterized by non-linear and emergent effects. These are the defining features of complex systems.[13]

Despite this complexity, the mindset that permeates current regulation, especially in data privacy and competition law, still relies on a dated model that emphasizes isolated units of analysis and additive rather than emergent and non-linear effects.[14] This model is reflected in two approaches in the application of data privacy law and competition law. The first relates to their atomized approach, namely their reliance on isolating a specific component as the target of regulation—whether a relevant market in competition law or a specific processing operation in data privacy—even when dealing with a system comprising several intertwined components. The second manifestation of the outdated paradigm is the prevailing either/or mentality in the application of data privacy law and competition law. Both approaches falter in the face of the complexity entailed by the commercialization of personal and big data.

Specifically, the atomized approach may potentially overlook broader, system-wide privacy and competitive harms, which I refer to as emergent risks. These emergent risks may stem from the cumulative processing operations or from various practices in seemingly different relevant markets within the comprehensive ecosystem. These risks are 'emergent' in the sense that they may exist independently of, and hence may not be attributed to, individual processing operations or a relevant market. Similarly, maintaining the either/or mentality becomes increasingly challenging amidst increasing interface (convergence and conflicts) between these legal systems, missing opportunities for synergy.

In light of these challenges, the book underscores the importance of three insights from complexity science: (1) its use of a system-level unit of analysis, (2) its emphasis on interconnections that lead to non-linear and emergent outcomes, and (3) its adoption of a polycentric approach to navigate such complexity. In this regard, Chapters 2 and 3 discuss the need for a systems-level analysis and accounting for emergent effects. Chapters 4–7 highlight the potential harms faced by consumers as data producers and the adverse effects that may result from new forms of power (eg panopticon power) stemming from managing interconnections. I show how complexity thinking may be embraced by paying more attention to data- and privacy-related harms in competition law.

[13] Steven Johnson, *Emergence: The Connected Lives of Ants, Brains, Cities, and Software* (Penguin 2001).

[14] See Samson Esayas, 'The Important Role of Emergence in Conceptualizing the Challenges of New Technologies to Private Law' (2023) 31 European Private Law Review 779; Nicolas Petit and Thibault Schrepel, 'Complexity-Minded Antitrust' (2023) 33 Journal of Evolutionary Economics 541.

Furthermore, by discussing the intersection between data privacy and competition law and highlighting areas for cooperation between the two legal regimes, the book points to the need for a polycentric regulatory system better able to navigate complex economic landscapes. This system suggests the formation of a network of legal regimes that operate synergistically and supplement one another as well as a collaborative structure among various legal authorities. The call for a polycentric approach aligns well with the central argument of this book, which emphasizes the need to move beyond the either/or mentality and embrace a synchronized approach that draws on the perspectives of both data privacy and competition law.

The evolution of the theoretical framework was largely due to the guidance and encouragement of the initial anonymous reviewers and Konstantinos Stylianou. Konstantinos provided invaluable support throughout the final stages of the writing process and was generous with his time. His suggestion to weave the discussion through the lens of systemic thinking and complexity science was crucial in ensuring cohesion. I would also like to express my gratitude to the BI Norwegian Business School for providing me with the time, resources, and support, over the past four years, to transform what began as a PhD dissertation into a book of Oxford University Press (OUP) calibre. I thank my colleagues at BI's Department of Law and Governance for their encouragement, intellectual insights, and support during the lengthy writing process.

I wish to extend my sincere gratitude to Professors Lee Bygrave and Inger Ørstavik at the Department of Private Law, University of Oslo, for their support and guidance during the writing of the PhD dissertation. Thank you to my colleagues at the Norwegian Research Centre for Computers and Law, University of Oslo—Tobias Mahler, Dag Schartum, Kevin McGillivray, Tommy Tranvik, and Arild Jansen—for their mentorship, friendship, and invaluable advice on both personal and professional fronts. I thank Katherine Llorca for copyediting sections of the book. At OUP, I extend my gratitude to Peter Daniell for propelling a slow-moving project to its conclusion, to Christopher Kuner for his encouragement during moments of frustration, and to Paulina dos Santos Major for her outstanding editorial support. I am also grateful to have had the opportunity to utilize the excellent facilities and interact with inspiring individuals at Harvard University's Berkman Klein Center during the later stages of the book's writing. Special thanks to Sandra Cortesi, Patrick Goulart Soares, and Elisabeth Sylvan for their hospitality and support.

Finally, special thanks goes to my mother, Kiros, who taught me the value of hard work. To my wife Selam, and my daughters Markan and Amrah, thank you for sharing the joys and pains of this journey. Your love and unwavering support have been my solace whenever the going was tough.

All legal instruments, references, and websites are up to date as of 1 November 2023.

PART I

DATA PRIVACY AND COMPETITION LAW IN THE AGE OF BIG DATA

Data privacy law and competition law are often viewed as two regimes pursuing distinct objectives with fundamental differences in their material scope and in the harms they seek to address. Thus, the conventional approach has been to treat these two regimes separately. Where there are attempts to discuss these two regimes in tandem, the discussions are still nascent and rather narrow in scope. This book connects data privacy law and competition law, exposing both the interface and the dichotomies between these legal regimes in addressing the challenges resulting from the commercialization of personal data and big data. This connection occurs at two levels: at the macro level, where the similarities between data privacy law and competition law are highlighted using the concept of emergent properties (Part II); and, at the micro level, where the points of interface are addressed from both empirical and normative perspectives and then contextualized within the macro level using insights from complexity science (Part III).

Part I, consisting of Chapter 1, lays the groundwork for the analysis in the rest of the book by highlighting key socio-economic and technological changes. Three key socio-economic and technological shifts associated with the commercialization of personal data and big data are identified: a shift in the significance of data as a key resource, a shift in how information is understood and used, and a shift in the organization of markets. All three shifts are crucial to understanding the current regulatory challenges, including the intersection between data privacy law and competition law. The chapter subsequently examines how these socio-economic and technological changes underscore the need to address the interface between the two legal regimes.

1

Data Privacy and Competition Law in the Age of Big Data

I. The Commercialization of Personal Data

The digital economy is characterized by the collection of vast quantities of information that is analysed and exploited by businesses for their commercial ends, a phenomenon commonly referred to as 'big data'. Massive amounts of data about consumers—where they are, what devices they use, what they purchase, and different aspects of their online behaviour and interests—are collected every day. Together with progress in data mining and analytics technology, this enables companies to gain insights from new and existing data sets, leading to the emergence of companies whose core business models are built around the monetization of personal data. Descriptions of personal data as the 'new oil', 'new asset class', 'lifeblood of businesses', and 'new currency' of the digital economy encapsulate the pivotal role that personal data plays in this economic landscape—spurring new business models, serving as a key source of revenue, and unlocking a range of benefits for consumers in exchange for their data.[1]

At the heart of the business models of companies such as Google and Facebook is the detailed collection and analysis of consumer data, often without consumers fully comprehending how their data is used. Among other things, the availability of such vast amounts of data enables these companies to create detailed profiles of consumers and deliver online advertising with remarkable precision. This ad-based business model has allowed these companies to achieve extremely high turnovers and propelled them to the top of the hierarchy of the world's most valuable companies, displacing their predecessors in the oil and gas industry. In addition to data's importance for targeted advertising, personal data is instrumental in improving the quality of many digital services, increasing the profitability of services via personalized pricing, developing new products/services, and making better decisions. The growing importance of personal data for commercial purposes, coupled with the plunging cost of storage, is creating a drive for 'digital land

[1] See World Economic Forum and Boston Consulting Group, *Unlocking the Value of Personal Data: From Collection to Usage* (World Economic Forum and Boston Consulting Group 2013).

Data Privacy and Competition Law in the Age of Big Data. Samson Y. Esayas, Oxford University Press.
 DOI: 10.1093/oso/9780198891420.003.0002

grab', shifting the priorities of organizations towards collecting and harnessing as much personal data as possible.[2]

Consumers are also benefiting from the commercialization of personal data, receiving better and more useful ads and a broad array of content, products, and services at no monetary cost. Once highly expensive services, such as navigation tools, are now *gratis*, a notable feature of digital services. Google reportedly offers over 100 services, of which more than 70 are 'free'. These services generate enormous social and economic benefits for users. The value that Europeans and Americans derive from 'free' services, such as Internet search or online map services, is estimated to be worth USD 280 billion annually.[3] All users are asked for (in exchange for access to these services) is their personal data—preferences, contacts, location, and online behaviour and interests.

Overall, the commercialization of personal data is unlocking significant benefits for businesses, individuals, and the public. However, as shown throughout this book, developments associated with the commercialization of personal data—especially the desire to amass personal data to gain a competitive edge, the pivotal role of personal data in generating value (turnover), and the prevalence of zero-price services—generate significant challenges linked to data privacy and competition policy.

On the one hand, the unprecedented scale of data collection has exposed consumer privacy to greater risks than ever before. Even more disconcerting is the danger of a 'race to the bottom' in privacy protection, where non-compliance with data privacy rules and the acquisition of data through illegitimate and deceptive mechanisms become a source of competitive advantage.[4] On the other hand, there are emerging competition concerns that control over data and related network effects can provide dominant companies with a competitive advantage, potentially resulting in barriers to market entry and unlawful leveraging of data collected in one domain to gain market power in another. Moreover, in recent years, privacy concerns have increasingly permeated competition law discussions, particularly in instances where data-rich companies aim to merge.[5] This, in turn, ushers in a new challenge for two hitherto separate domains of law, that is data privacy law and competition law.

In light of these developments, the challenge lies in striking a balance between the economic benefits derived from the commercialization of personal data, on the one hand, and the negative impacts on privacy and healthy competition, on the

[2] White House, *Big Data: Seizing Opportunities, Preserving Values* (Executive Office of the President 2014) 54.

[3] The Economist, 'The Superstar Company: A Giant Problem', *The Economist* (17 September 2016).

[4] See European Data Protection Supervisor (EDPS) Preliminary Opinion, *Privacy and Competitiveness in the Age of Big Data: The Interplay between Data Protection, Competition Law and Consumer Protection in the Digital Economy* (2014).

[5] See Case M.7217 *Facebook/WhatsApp* decision of 3 October 2014; Case M.8124 *Microsoft/LinkedIn* decision of 6 December 2016.

other. This book offers a critical, in-depth examination of how the collection, analysis, and commercialization of personal and big data present challenges for data privacy and competition law. It provides a novel, interdisciplinary insight by integrating elements from emergent properties and complexity science to expose the interface between data privacy law and competition rules, elucidate the challenges, and seek potential solutions.

II. Key Socio-Economic and Technological Shifts from Big Data

This book is premised on the idea that developments associated with big data and the commercialization of personal data give rise to a problem that requires a response from data privacy law and competition law. Thus, it is crucial to understand the key shifts resulting from the commercialization of personal data and big data to address the challenges effectively. Drawing insights from the literature on informatics, business, and economics, this section identifies three key socio-economic and technological shifts associated with the commercialization of personal data and big data. First, the exponential growth in the amount of data and related advances in data analytics have elevated the role of data, particularly personal data, to a key resource. Second, society has moved from a narrow and static view of data to one embracing secondary and innovative uses. Finally, the organization of the market is evolving. Single products/services are being replaced by ecosystems comprising several integrated products/services, where personal data plays a crucial role in coordinating activities across the different markets. As the subsequent sections and chapters show, these shifts pose significant challenges for data privacy law and competition law and are essential in understanding the intersection of the two fields of law.

A. Shifts in the Amount and the Importance of Data Use

The Organisation for Economic Co-operation and Development (OECD) identifies the dependence on data, particularly big data, as a defining characteristic of the digital economy.[6] This is exemplified by the fact that many of the world's most valuable companies, including Google and Facebook, derive over 85 per cent of their value from knowledge-based capital, primarily data, rather than physical assets.[7] This illustrates the importance of data as a key resource that powers innovation, competitiveness, and growth in the digital age. The reference to the digital

[6] OECD, *Addressing the Tax Challenges of the Digital Economy* (OECD Publishing 2014) 89.
[7] OECD, *Data-Driven Innovation: Big Data for Growth and Well-Being* (OECD Publishing 2015) 22.

economy as the 'data-driven economy' or 'big-data economy' further underscores the paramount importance of data in today's society. Underlying the increased importance of data for the economy are three shifts. These include the exponential growth in the amount of data and advancements in data analytics technology—referred to as the 'twin revolutions'—as well as the prominence of business models that rely on data as a key resource.

1. Exponential Growth in Data Generated

The word 'big' in big data suggests that size is of the essence. As Mayer-Schönberger and Cukier explain, big data 'refers to things one can do at a large scale that cannot be done at a smaller scale'.[8] Thus, the exponential growth in the amount of data generated is a central characteristic of big data. According to Eric Schmidt, the former CEO of Google, the amount of information created from the beginning of civilization to 2003 was five exabytes, but by 2010 this amount was produced every two days, and there are indications that the amount of data generated is doubling every two years.[9] The exponential growth in the amount of data generated is driven by two factors: the digitization of information and the migration of most social and economic activities onto the Internet.

Digitization is the process of converting analogue data into a digital format (bits comprising zeros and ones) for processing by computers and other capable devices. With the ubiquity of digital devices, such as smartphones, data can be captured easily in a digital format and shared instantly. Thus, digitization facilitates the production and storage of sizeable data in a short period, with less effort, and at low cost. In 2000, only one-quarter of the world's data was digital, but by 2013, over 98 per cent of stored data was digital.[10] Crucial in this development is the ability to capture activities in the physical world through ubiquitous and networked sensors, a development widely known as the Internet of Things (IoT). The IoT is a term used to describe a network of objects equipped with sensors and the ability to generate and process information about the physical and virtual world through interactions with intelligent services. For example, a refrigerator or car with embedded sensors can be managed through a smartphone app. The IoT is often confused with big data. This is partly because the more the IoT becomes a reality, the more data can be digitized and fed to the big data economy. While the IoT plays a crucial role in enabling big data, it goes beyond just data; it is also about devices and interconnectivity.

[8] Viktor Mayer-Schönberger and Kenneth Cukier, *Big Data: A Revolution That Will Transform How We Live, Work, and Think* (Houghton Mifflin Harcourt 2013) 6.

[9] See Marshall Kirkpatrick, 'Google, Privacy and the New Explosion of Data', *Techonomy* (4 August 2010). The National Institute of Standards and Technology (NIST), *Big Data Interoperability Framework: Volume 1, Definitions*, Special Publication 1500-1 (NIST 2015) 13.

[10] Mayer-Schönberger and Cukier (n 8) 8–9.

Another notable factor contributing to the rapid expansion of data volume is the transition of social and economic activities to the digital realm. Combined with the growing number of connected devices, this shift allows for the continuous tracking of people's digital footprints, such as website clicks, searches, purchases, social media posts, and locations. The rapid decline in the cost of data storage, with the average cost per gigabyte falling from USD 56 in 1998 to USD 0.05 in 2012, further incentivizes the accumulation of data. Greater storage capacity at a cheaper cost erodes the desire to discard data.

The outcome of these developments is *voluminous* information about people, objects, and their interactions. Such data is often raw and unorganized, gathered from a *variety* of sources (and formats), including devices (mobile, PC), sensors, Internet transactions, email, video, click streams, and other digital and physical sources. This has led to most definitions of big data focusing on its size and variety.[11] However, the discussion on size extends beyond the sheer *volume* and *variety* of data; it also encompasses the concept of data 'completeness' and the decision to use all available data instead of just a sample.[12] Regardless of the amount of data analysed, the data often represents a sample of the population; for example, using social media posts to analyse people's mood is still a sample because not everyone is on social media. Thus, 'completeness' should be approached more in terms of whether the increase in volume opens possibilities to 'extract new insights or create new forms of *value*'.[13] This implies that a core tenet of big data is that the size creates *value*, which is lacking in small data samples.[14]

The increase in the volume and variety of data has regulatory implications that are relevant for data privacy and competition law. From a data privacy perspective, these developments raise concerns about the accuracy and reliability of the data collected, the indiscriminate and excessive collection of personal data (data creep), and the potential to re-identify individuals from seemingly anonymized data. Furthermore, one notes the growing literature and case law from the United States looking at whether the *volume* and *variety* of data create a 'reasonable expectation' of privacy in situations that are traditionally outside the protection of the Fourth Amendment.[15] These discussions are also relevant in the European Union (EU) context and are addressed in more detail in Chapter 2.

In the EU, even the idea of big data seems to conflict with one of the core principles of data privacy, namely the data minimization principle, which limits the

[11] See Andrea De Mauro, Marco Greco, and Michele Grimaldi, 'What Is Big Data? A Consensual Definition and a Review of Key Research Topics' International Conference on Integrated Information (IC-ININFO 2014), AIP Conference Proceedings 1644 (2015) 97–104.

[12] Mayer-Schönberger and Cukier (n 8) 28.

[13] ibid 8.

[14] ibid 76.

[15] See David Gray and Danielle Citron, 'The Right to Quantitative Privacy' (2013) 98 Minnesota Law Review 62. Orin Kerr, 'The Mosaic Theory of the Fourth Amendment' (2012) 111 Michigan Law Review 311.

collection of personal data to the minimum necessary to achieve one's purpose. Given that big data is founded on the idea that data size (volume) creates *value*, a minimalist approach to data collection comes into direct conflict with the value-creation process. As Koops has noted, the rise of big data practices marks both the failure of the data minimization principle and its limited importance moving forward.[16] Additionally, the overwhelming amount of data collected and generated from numerous sources creates an information overload for data subjects, hindering their ability to make informed choices. Moreover, the desire to increase both the scale and scope of data is a significant driving force behind many data-driven mergers, spurring novel regulatory questions in competition law, especially at its interface with data privacy. Issues that arise include whether data accumulation may lead to increased market power and whether and how privacy issues should be incorporated into merger assessments.[17]

2. Pervasive Power of Data Analytics

The increasing availability of advanced data analytic tools is another trend in the realm of big data. Data analytics, sometimes referred to as data mining, enables the identification of patterns and interrelations among facts, concepts, and entities. Big data analytics offers two major capabilities: (1) the extraction of insights and valuable information from large and unstructured data sets, including the capacity to make inferences and predictions; (2) real-time monitoring and tracking.[18] The idea that data is 'the new oil' emphasizes the importance of refining tools to extract value and knowledge from the data. However, conventional analytical tools face challenges in processing data in various formats (such as text, multimedia, and raw data from sensors) that come from multiple and dispersed sources, and in large quantities.

The quest for better data analytics solutions has led to the scaling of data analytics both vertically and horizontally. Vertical scaling enhances data-processing power by providing faster processing capabilities and has seen significant advances in recent times. However, the hallmark of big data is horizontal scaling, that is the ability to utilize distributed computing resources to generate valuable insights from massive unstructured data. The definition from the US National Institute of Standards and Technology (NIST) emphasizes this shift and characterizes big data as data sets with high volume, variety, and velocity that 'require a *scalable architecture* for efficient storage, manipulation, and analysis'.[19]

[16] Bert-Jaap Koops, 'The Trouble with European Data Protection Law' (2014) 4 International Data Privacy Law 250, 256.

[17] See discussions in Chapters 4–7.

[18] See James Manyika and others, *Big Data: The Next Frontier for Innovation, Competition, and Productivity* (McKinsey Global Institute 2011) 33.

[19] NIST (n 9) 20.

Thus, big data practices mark a fundamental shift from a single server (ie monolithic) system with vertical scaling to a distributed system with horizontal scaling. This shift offers several advantages, including lower costs, increased reliability, and scalability of processing power through the addition of new computers. Not only are these analytical tools powerful and sophisticated, but they are also affordable to a wide range of actors, including small businesses.

The above developments in data analytics have several regulatory implications. From a data privacy standpoint, these analytical tools enable the inference of intimate personal details from innocuous data and raise concerns of transparency as it relates to automated decisions.[20] The distributed nature of the resources and computing power creates a global ecosystem with activities and actors distributed across various jurisdictions, leading to questions about cross-border data transfer and access by foreign law enforcement. Data analytical tools, such as pricing algorithms, can also be used to coordinate market behaviour in violation of competition law.[21] The level of transparency required of such algorithms can be a point of contention between data privacy law (which demands more transparency) and competition law (where such transparency could lead to the restriction of competition).

3. From Data-Informed to Data-Driven Businesses

Data and information have always been crucial to the market or the economy at large. The question is what makes the role that data plays in today's economy unique and subject to greater regulatory scrutiny. In addition to the changes associated with size, there exists a shift in the significance of data as a driver of innovation and competitiveness. In this regard, one can distinguish between companies that use data to inform their business (big data-informed) and those that run their business using data (data-driven business models). The former encompasses companies that use data to improve their marketing strategies and tailor their services. For example, bricks-and-mortar retail stores may use consumer data and data analytics to inform decisions regarding product inventory, consumer behaviour, and marketing strategies, thus allowing them to offer targeted discounts and improve their product placement and customer experience.

Conversely, a data-driven business model (DDBM) is one 'that relies on data as a key resource'.[22] In management literature, a business model represents a roadmap outlining how a company creates and delivers value to its target market, including the key resources needed and the key activities performed to deliver the value

[20] See, eg Lilian Edwards and Michael Veale, 'Enslaving the Algorithm: From a "Right to an Explanation" to a "Right to Better Decisions"?' (2018) 16 IEEE Security & Privacy 46.

[21] See Ariel Ezrachi and Maurice Stucke, *Virtual Competition: The Promise and Perils of the Algorithm-Driven Economy* (Harvard UP 2016).

[22] Philipp Hartmann and others, *Big Data for Big Business? A Taxonomy of Data-Driven Business Models Used by Start-Up Firms* (Cambridge Service Alliance 2014) 6.

proposition (whether goods or services).[23] Hartmann and colleagues have conducted comprehensive research on this subject, identifying six core components constituting a business model and the specific attributes for each component as they pertain to a DDBM.[24]

In the context of this book, the features of DDBMs pertaining to key resources and key activities are of greater relevance. In a conventional firm, key resources encompass personnel, technology, distribution channels, and brand. For service-orientated companies, the principal resource is typically personnel, while for product distributors, it is their distribution channels. As the name suggests, for data-driven businesses, the crucial resource is data.[25] This aligns with the current trend of companies listing data as an asset on their balance sheets.[26] The World Economic Forum (WEF) posits that personal data represents a new asset category and an essential resource for many digital companies.[27] Nevertheless, data or personal data may not be the sole resource for DDBMs. They might also possess intellectual property or patent rights concerning data analytics tools and ownership of hardware, such as server farms.

Within the big data landscape, three categories of personal data can function as key resources: volunteered, observed, and inferred data.[28] The term 'volunteered data' refers to information willingly provided by consumers, such as during purchases or participation in surveys. Observed and inferred data, on the other hand, are collected without the consumer's full awareness. Observed data is collected in the background (eg location data, browsing history, search history, and cookie data[29]), whereas inferred data comprises a new set of data generated from, and in combination with, volunteered and observed data. This may involve inferring a person's age, sexuality, or gender based on their browsing behaviour or Facebook 'Likes'.[30]

The key activities of DDBMs are 'gathering, organizing, selecting, synthesizing, and distributing' data.[31] The two most prominent examples of DDBMs are Google and Facebook, which use data—especially personal data—as their primary resource or asset. Similarly, the main source of their revenue is providing access to

[23] Mark Johnson, Clayton Christensen, and Henning Kagermann, 'Reinventing Your Business Model' (2008) 86 Harvard Business Review 57, 60.

[24] Hartmann and others (n 22) 7.

[25] ibid.

[26] Vincenzo Morabito, *Big Data and Analytics: Strategic and Organizational Impacts* (Springer 2015) 75 (indicating that more than 20 per cent of large companies do so).

[27] WEF, *Personal Data: The Emergence of a New Asset Class* (WEF 2011) 5.

[28] WEF, *Rethinking Personal Data: Strengthening Trust* (WEF 2012) 18.

[29] A cookie is a small text file placed on the user's device or web browser by websites. It captures information about the websites visited by the user, items looked at or saved, time spent on the website, and the operating system of the users' device.

[30] Zeynep Tufekci, 'Algorithmic Harms beyond Facebook and Google: Emergent Challenges of Computational Agency' (2015) 13 Journal on Telecommunications & High Technology Law 203, 210.

[31] Hartmann and others (n 22) 9.

their customer data, whether to advertisers or application developers. In 2021, advertising accounted for over 90 per cent of Google's and 95 per cent of Facebook's revenue.[32]

The distinction between data-informed and data-driven business models carries significant regulatory implications. This is because most competition policy arguments involving personal data are driven by the understanding that data, especially personal data, constitutes a key asset or resource for many digital platforms. For instance, discussions over whether there is a market for 'input data used for advertising purposes', separate from the service market for advertising, are based on the premise that data, including personal data, is a key input or resource in providing advertising services (see Chapter 4). Similarly, recent initiatives from certain EU member states and the European Commission to amend merger notification thresholds,[33] on the basis of not only turnover but also data, highlight the importance of data as a key asset. Commenting on the subject, Commissioner Vestager stated, 'it's not always turnover that makes a company an attractive merger partner. Sometimes, what matters are its assets. That could be a customer base or even a set of data.'[34]

Furthermore, the notion that (personal) data is a key asset or resource is crucial to the intersection between data privacy and competition law. For instance, questions about whether data privacy may be considered when evaluating mergers are motivated by businesses' desire to acquire and integrate new data assets that may be useful in the provision of certain services. The desire to collect and amass personal data also raises novel competition issues: does the accumulation of personal data create barriers to entry? Would mandating access to data allay these concerns? This, in turn, raises questions about the limits imposed by data privacy law and how to strike a balance between privacy and competition interests. Moreover, as personal data has become a key resource in the provision of many digital services, data privacy rules have taken centre stage, both as competitive constraints and as barriers to market entry, which need to be accounted for in competition analysis (see Chapters 4 and 7).

[32] Alphabet Inc FORM 10-K, 'Annual Report for the Fiscal Year 2021 the Pursuant to Section 13 Or 15(D) of the Securities Exchange Act of 1934' (2021) <https://www.sec.gov/Archives/edgar/data/1652044/000165204422000019/goog-20211231.htm#i0ef93c820da04204a9c5a49f49a3b2eb_130>; Meta Platforms, Inc FORM 10-K, 'Annual Report for the Fiscal Year 2021 Pursuant to Section 13 Or 15(D) of the Securities Exchange Act of 1934' (2021) <https://www.sec.gov/Archives/edgar/data/1326801/000132680122000018/fb-20211231.htm>.

[33] For example, some of the amendments to the German Act against Restraints on Competition include a new substantive test that clarifies the need to consider access to data in assessing the competitive impact of mergers and in assessing market power of multi-sided platforms.

[34] European Commission, 'Refining the EU Merger Control System', speech by Commissioner Vestager (10 March 2016).

B. Paradigm Shift in Knowledge Creation and Decision-Making

Big data practices also involve a shift in mindset with regard to how information is used. Three shifts are especially noteworthy. The first is society's transition from the static view of data, where data is collected for a specific purpose or one-time use, to innovative and secondary uses, such as basic reuse, combining different data sets, and multi-use collection. The key to creating value in big data is to capture information and convert it into reusable data form.[35] The second shift relates to society's desire to loosen up its fixation on 'exactitude' or understanding 'a phenomenon down to the inch'.[36] The most valuable big-data decisions are based on predictions, which include applying mathematical models to vast quantities of data to predict the likelihood that a person wants to buy something. The third shift, linked to the second, is a trend towards decision making based on correlation rather than causality.[37] Historically, the dominant discourse in knowledge creation has been to describe events through cause and effect. In contrast, big data practices are primarily based on establishing correlation—that is, how closely two occurrences are related—without questioning why this is the case. This shift to correlation allows for easier automation of decisions.

These shifts are pivotal in fuelling the prevalence of ad-driven business models. These models rely heavily on predictive analytics derived from vast data sets to deliver targeted advertisements. Inferences may be drawn about a visitor to a specific website, such as their economic status, potential interest in buying certain products, or a preference for reading particular books. These decisions prioritize a 'general direction' over exactness and causality, valuing imprecision and correlation. Furthermore, the emergence of complex, algorithm-driven ad-trading markets—characterized by multilayer data sharing and combination and currently attracting intense scrutiny under data privacy and competition law—are fuelled by these very correlations and the subsequent capacity to automate decision-making processes.

The shifts in knowledge production, decision making, and data use have significant regulatory ramifications. For example, they present significant challenges in applying key data privacy principles under the EU regime, including the purpose limitation and data minimization principles, and in protecting the rights of individuals against automated decisions. Additionally, these shifts open new avenues for anticompetitive behaviour, as companies try to leverage their dominance by repurposing data collected in one area to gain market power in another. The issue of such data repurposing from one market to another is addressed in several ongoing cases involving Google, Facebook, and Amazon. Such data repurposing can also violate data privacy rules, which raises the question of whether, and to what extent,

[35] Mayer-Schönberger and Cukier (n 8) 96.
[36] ibid 13.
[37] ibid 7.

breaches of data privacy rules can contribute to breaches of competition rules or represent a deviation from competition on the merits (see Chapter 7).

C. Shifts Related to the Organization of Markets: Multi-Sided and Ecosystems Markets

Another trend relates to the change in the organization of markets, particularly the prevalence of multi-sided and ecosystem markets. Many of the actors that have (personal) data as their key resource bring together two or more groups of customers to transact or exchange information. These actors are referred to as two-sided or multi-sided markets or platforms.[38] While it remains unclear exactly how such platforms should be defined, this section avoids the complexities of these debates[39] by focusing on the key attributes of two-sided or multi-sided platforms that have implications for the interface between data privacy law and competition law. According to Evans and Schmalensee, a business model is multi-sided if it brings together at least two distinct but interdependent customer groups in a manner that benefits both or at least one of the customer groups.[40] The benefit can be manifested in the form of indirect network effects, where the demand of one customer group is impacted by the number of customers in the other group, or by reducing the costs of finding and interacting with each other.

While multi-sidedness is not entirely new to the digital economy, the provision of multiple money-free services, often in exchange for personal data, is a recent phenomenon. In the traditional multi-sided markets, such as ad-supported TV, consumer data had little to no role to play, whereas in the digital economy, the role of data in intermediation is significant. Moreover, this collection of personal data places online platforms in a different position towards their users compared with traditional media, creating new sources of power and avenues for extraction (see more in Chapter 3).

Another development, partly underpinned by multi-sided platforms, is the rise of ecosystems.[41] Broadly speaking, ecosystems refer to multi-actor and multi-product complementarities that are not fully hierarchically controlled.[42] In this

[38] See Jean-Charles Rochet and Jean Tirole, 'Platform Competition in Two-Sided Markets' (2003) 1 Journal of the European Economic Association 990; David Evans and Richard Schmalensee, 'The Industrial Organization of Markets with Two-Sided Platforms' in David Evans (ed), *Platform Economics: Essays on Multi-sided Businesses* (Competition Policy International (CPI) 2011).

[39] See, eg Evans and Schmalensee (n 38). Lapo Filistrucchi, Damien Geradin, and Eric Van Damme, 'Identifying Two-Sided Markets' (2013) 36 World Competition Law and Economics Review 33.

[40] Evans and Schmalensee (n 38) 2.

[41] Many ecosystems are built on platforms, including software platforms like Xbox and operating systems like Android, which are both multi-sided and ecosystems. But not all multi-sided platforms can be considered ecosystems, as ecosystems require an element of 'generic supermodular complementarity'. See Michael Jacobides, Carmelo Cennamo, and Annabelle Gawer, 'Towards a Theory of Ecosystems' (2018) 39 Strategic Management Journal 2255.

[42] ibid 2264.

sense, ecosystems exemplify a distinct organizational form; they are alternatives to vertical integration or supply-chain arrangements. Although there is some disagreement as to the salient features of an ecosystem, two elements are widely considered central: modularity and non-generic complementarity.[43] Modularity allows for bundling of independently produced complementors into a package to be consumed by a customer. This modularity occurs through a coordination by an orchestrator, which is sometimes referred to as a lead organization. The orchestrator bears responsibility for the development of the common value proposition and establishes the rules of interaction. This is typically achieved using standards and platform interfaces such as application programming interfaces (APIs) and software development kits.[44] However, a critical element of this modularity is that the complementors have autonomy in deciding on the design and price of their respective products. In addition, modularity entails that the customer has the possibility to customize the products by choosing among the complementors.

Another fundamental aspect of ecosystems involves the necessity for bundled products to exhibit either distinct or non-generic supermodular complementarities. Two products (A and B) are described as unique complementarities if 'A doesn't function without B', whereas the two products are non-generic supermodular complementarities if 'more of A makes B more valuable'.[45] As these types of complementarities create added value, they require a well-defined structure of relationships and alignment, which can be fostered by the orchestrator. This implies that one need not have ecosystems to coordinate and bundle products that are generic complementarities, which can easily be done by the customer. For example, although electricity is essential to produce many products and services, there is no need to establish a coordination and alignment structure as it can be purchased in generic terms in markets.[46]

Thus, ecosystems enable the offer of complex interdependent products or services with limited coordination by the orchestrator but without centralized command. An example is the Android ecosystem, which comprises the Android mobile operating system (MOS), Google Play, and Google's popular apps such as search, YouTube, and maps, as well as millions of other apps. Although the MOS, Google Play, Google search, and YouTube are independent services, they are offered as a bundle to smartphone manufacturers with the aim of creating the 'Google experience'. Additionally, these products are either unique or non-generic supermodular complementarities. For example, an app or an app store will not function without the MOS, making these products unique complementors. Moreover, the apps, app store, and MOS are supermodular complementarities because more apps in

[43] ibid 2255.
[44] ibid 2258.
[45] ibid 2261–62.
[46] ibid 2262.

the app store increases the value of both the app store and the MOS. Customers, whether smartphone manufacturers or users, also have the possibility to customize the bundles, for example by choosing which apps to install on their devices.

One of the main drivers behind ecosystem development, especially those based on platforms, is the ability of the orchestrator to extract value from the interaction between the complementors. The power to set the rules of the ecosystem gives the orchestrator the ability to 'harvest information about their competitors (panopticon power)', gather information about consumers and shape their behaviour, or monetize the customer's attention or data through customization and advertising (intermediation power).[47]

Both multi-sided and ecosystem markets have several characteristics with significant regulatory implications. These include the existence of indirect network effects, the prevalence of zero prices, and the potential for cross-subsidization across different markets, which raise several regulatory issues, most notably in relation to competition law. For example, the conventional measures for market power (ie market share and price above marginal cost) become difficult to apply in a digital world where products and services are offered for free or at very little cost.[48] In this context, data privacy has become a crucial factor in determining the level of market power that a company can exert. This is reflected in the increasing recognition by competition authorities that data privacy can serve as a non-price competition parameter, and companies can exert market power on the 'free' side by reducing the level of privacy on offer.[49] From a data privacy viewpoint, multi-sided platforms and ecosystems occupy a unique position with their ability to collect, use, and generate massive amounts of personal data when mediating interactions. This raises questions about information asymmetry, transparency in processing personal data, and the effectiveness of consent-based regulation, to mention just a few.

Importantly, and as shown in Chapter 3, ecosystems present a systemic problem to the application of competition rules that rely on identifying and isolating 'the relevant market' as the target of regulation. The important role that personal data plays in coordinating activities across the different markets of an ecosystem means that this systemic problem extends to data privacy law, as illustrated in Chapter 2. This is because the application of the current rules requires that one distinguish the different services for which data is collected (processing activities) and relate each item of personal data to one particular service (processing activity). The multiplicity of products and their interconnection through data use blurs the lines between the different processing activities and relevant markets, thereby complicating the attribution of individual data to a particular processing operation and of

[47] Michael Jacobides and Ioannis Lianos, 'Ecosystems and Competition Law in Theory and Practice' (2021) 30 Industrial and Corporate Change 1199, 1205.

[48] David Evans, 'Antitrust Economics of Free' (2011) Spring Competition Policy International <https://papers.ssrn.com/sol3/papers.cfm?abstract_id=1813193>.

[49] See *Microsoft/LinkedIn* (n 5).

competition harms to a relevant market. Moreover, the current approaches in both legal regimes may potentially overlook the privacy risks that arise when companies engage in multiple processing activities. They may also overlook the competition harms stemming from multiple and systematic practices in seemingly distinct relevant markets within the comprehensive ecosystem.

III. Imperatives for Addressing the Interface between Data Privacy Law and Competition Law

Addressing data privacy and competition law under one umbrella may be seen as unusual, as these two regimes are thought to pursue distinct objectives. Typically, data privacy law concentrates on tackling demand-side issues—challenges that emerge from the consumption of goods and services such as information asymmetry and are therefore internal to the individual. On the other hand, competition policy primarily focuses on addressing supply-side concerns—problems that arise from the production or delivery of goods and services and that are thus external to the individual. The conventional approach has been to treat these two regimes separately.[50] This book argues that the above socio-economic and technological changes associated with big data demand a re-examination of the interaction between data privacy law and competition law. As this section demonstrates, while the two legal frameworks ostensibly pursue different objectives (Section A), there is increased interaction between them due to the commercialization of personal data. This suggests that there is a pressing need to address their interface.

A. Objectives of EU Data Privacy Law and Competition Law

Despite ongoing debates about its boundaries and theoretical foundations,[51] the primary goal of EU data privacy law is to accomplish two main objectives. The first of these is the protection of the fundamental rights of individuals, particularly their right to the protection of their personal data, which is enshrined in Article 8 of the Charter of Fundamental Rights of the European Union.[52] This right has

[50] Some even insist that these two regimes should be kept apart. See Maureen Ohlhausen and Alexander Okuliar, 'Competition, Consumer Protection, and the Right [Approach] to Privacy' (2015) 80 Antitrust Law Journal 121; Giuseppe Colangelo and Mariateresa Maggiolino, 'Data Accumulation and the Privacy–Antitrust Interface: Insights from the Facebook Case' (2018) 8 International Data Privacy Law 224.

[51] See Lee Bygrave, *Data Protection Law: Approaching Its Rationale, Logic and Limits* (Kluwer Law International 2002).

[52] Regulation (EU) 2016/679 of the European Parliament and of the Council of 27 April 2016 on the Protection of Natural Persons with Regard to the Processing of Personal Data and on the Free Movement of Such Data, and repealing Directive 95/46/EC OJ L119/1, Article 1(2).

been part of the EU's constitutional framework since 2009, and Article 16 of the Treaty on the Functioning of the European Union (TFEU) explicitly recognizes each person's right to data protection. Privacy is another fundamental right that data protection rules aim to safeguard. The roots of the right to data protection can be traced back, in part, to the right to privacy as recognized under Article 8 of the European Convention on Human Rights (ECHR), which upholds an individual's right to respect for their private and family life, home, and correspondence. The European Court of Human Rights (ECtHR) has interpreted this right to include the protection of personal data.[53] Thus, the rules on data protection reinforce the right to privacy.

The second objective of EU data privacy rules is to promote the free flow of data between member states. Article 1(3) of the General Data Protection Regulation (GDPR) prohibits restrictions on the 'free movement of data within the Union ... for reasons connected with the protection of natural persons with regard to the processing of personal data'. This provision aims to prevent excessive divergence in the level of data protection, which can harm cross-border trade between member states and hinder the realization of the 'internal market'.

The two objectives are interrelated because an adequate and harmonized level of data protection is deemed necessary to achieve the free movement of data. This dual aim also imposes an upper ceiling on the level of protection that member states can provide. Thus, a competition or market-based approach to privacy could be seen as a way of breaking through the upper ceiling by encouraging firms to provide even higher levels of privacy than those guaranteed by the rules.

The objectives of EU competition law are more controversial than those of data privacy.[54] Generally, competition rules are seen as part of the larger policy instruments aimed at achieving the goals of the Union, as outlined in the Treaty on European Union (TEU). Some of these goals include establishing an internal market, promoting sustainable development based on a competitive social market economy, and ensuring an open market economy with free competition.[55] Competition rules advance these interests, but they are particularly central to the realization of the single market. Protocol No 27, annex to the Lisbon Treaty, specifies that the internal market, as described in Article 3 of TEU, should encompass a system for ensuring that competition is not distorted.[56] These treaty provisions capture the main goals of EU competition policy, namely the integration of the

[53] App no 10454/83 *Gaskin v UK* ECHR:1989:0707, para 37.

[54] See, eg Ioannis Lianos, 'Some Reflections on the Question of the Goals of EU Competition Law' in Ioannis Lianos and Damien Geradin (eds), *Handbook on European Competition Law: Substantive Aspects* (Edward Elgar 2013); Ariel Ezrachi, 'The Goals of EU Competition Law and the Digital Economy' (Oxford Legal Studies Research Paper No 17/2018, 2018)< https://ssrn.com/abstract=3191766>.

[55] Consolidated Version of the Treaty on European Union OJ C326/01 [2012] Article 3(3).

[56] Consolidated Version of the Treaty on European Union—Protocol (No 27) on the Internal Market and Competition OJ C115/09 [2008].

single market and ensuring effective and undistorted competition. These goals are concretized in several treaty provisions and regulatory instruments, such as TFEU, Articles 101 and 102 and the Merger Regulation (EUMR).[57] The case law and practice dealing with these provisions clarify the general policy prescriptions contained in the treaty provisions.

Article 101 prohibits coordinated behaviour between undertakings that restrict competition resulting from agreements, decisions by associations of undertakings, or concerted practices. Article 102 focuses on unilateral conduct by undertakings holding a dominant position in relevant markets and prohibits abuse of dominance in the internal market. The Merger Regulation establishes a framework for controlling 'concentration', which broadly encompasses the merger of at least two independent undertakings into a single entity and the acquisition of control of one undertaking by another.[58] The Regulation prohibits a 'concentration which would significantly impede effective competition, in the common market or in a substantial part of it, in particular as a result of the creation or strengthening of a dominant position'.[59] These three areas are commonly known as matters of antitrust, and the Court of Justice of the European Union (CJEU) has interpreted these instruments as pursuing various objectives, such as economic welfare, protecting the structure of the market, economic actors' freedom to compete, fairness, and facilitating market integration.[60]

In *T-Mobile*, the CJEU suggested that Article 101 'is designed to protect not only the immediate interests of individual competitors or consumers but also to protect the structure of the market and thus competition as such'.[61] The Court further insisted that, to find restriction of competition under Article 101, it is not necessary to demonstrate negative effects on final consumers 'in terms of supply or price'.[62] This stance has been reiterated in the context of Article 102.[63] These decisions demonstrate that the structure of the market and the process of competition as such are protected. A harm may be found—at least in relation to some practices—from the mere foreclosure of competitors or when competitors' access to the market is made difficult. However, such an approach has been criticized for protecting non-efficient competitors and condemning practices that do not harm consumer welfare.

[57] Council Regulation (EC) 139/2004 of 20 January 2004 on the Control of Concentrations between Undertakings OJ L24/1.

[58] European Union Merger Regulation (EUMR), Article 3(2) (defines control as the legal or factual 'possibility of exercising decisive influence on an undertaking').

[59] ibid Article 2(3).

[60] See Lianos (n 54). For an empirical study of these objectives, see Konstantinos Stylianou and Marios Iacovides, 'The Goals of EU Competition Law: A Comprehensive Empirical Investigation' (2022) 42 Legal Studies 620.

[61] Case C-8/08 *T-Mobile Netherlands* ECLI:EU:C:2009:343, para 38.

[62] ibid paras 36–39; Case C-202/07 P *France Télécom SA v Commission of the European Communities* ECLI:EU:C:2009:214, paras 62–63.

[63] Case C-52/09 *TeliaSonera Sverige* ECLI:EU:C:2011:83, paras 21–24.

Such critiques appear to have motivated the European Commission to adopt a 'more economic approach' in relation to Article 102. This approach views competition law as a means to achieve to consumer welfare and efficiency, restricting its application to situations where concrete harms to consumer welfare can be shown in terms of negative effects on price, quality, choice, or innovation.[64] The CJEU has endorsed this approach in various instances, asserting that the main function of EU competition law is to prevent 'consumer harm', which must be assessed in terms of negative effects 'on the price, quantity or quality of the goods and services'.[65] The Court recognizes that 'not every exclusionary effect is necessarily detrimental to competition' and that merit-based competition may result in the foreclosure or marginalization of less efficient competitors, which are 'less attractive for consumers in terms of price, choice, quality, or innovation'.[66] These judgments clarify that harm to consumers cannot be assumed from the foreclosure of less efficient competitors.

Another important and undisputed objective of EU competition law is promoting market integration. Article 3(1(B)) of the TFEU designates the EU as having exclusive competence in establishing the competition rules necessary for the functioning of the internal market. EU competition law pursues the internal market objective by prohibiting practices, such as restrictions on parallel trade, that have the effect of isolating one national market from another. According to the CJEU, such restrictions 'frustrate the Treaty's objective of achieving the integration of national markets through the establishment of a single market'.[67]

More controversial is the issue of fairness as an objective of EU competition law.[68] This aspect is reflected in decisions that interpret the competition rules as promoting 'equality of opportunity' and a fair distribution of outputs.[69] Fairness is also viewed as an overarching value and the desirable outcome of a competitive market.[70] Additionally, the European Commission has taken into account other policy considerations, such as media pluralism, employment policy, cultural

[64] European Commission, 'Guidance on the Commission's Enforcement Priorities in Applying Article 82 of the EC Treaty to Abusive Exclusionary Conduct by Dominant Undertakings' [2009] OJ C45/7, para 19; Paul Nihoul, 'The Ruling of the General Court in Intel: Towards the End of an Effect-Based Approach in European Competition Law?' (2014) 5 Journal of European Competition Law & Practice 521, 522.

[65] Case C-209/10 *Post Danmark AS v Konkurrancerådet* EU:C:2013:172, para 20; Case C-67/13 P *Groupement des cartes bancaires* ECLI:EU:C:2014:2204, para 51.

[66] *Post Danmark AS v Konkurrancerådet* (n 65) para 22.

[67] Case C-501/06 P and others *GlaxoSmithKline Services Unlimited v Commission* ECLI:EU:C:2009:610, para 61.

[68] Lianos (n 54) 28–35; Ezrachi (n 54) 12.

[69] See Case C-49/07 *MOTOE* ECLI:EU:C:2008:376, para 51; Lianos (n 54) 28–35.

[70] European Commission, 'Fairness and Competition', speech by Commissioner Vestager at Global Competition Law Centre (GCLC) Annual Conference (25 January 2018). Fairness is also seen as a concept that connects data privacy and competition laws. See Harri Kalimo and Klaudia Majcher, 'The Concept of Fairness: Linking EU Competition and Data Protection Law in the Digital Marketplace' (2017) 42(2) European Law Review 210.

policy, environmental policy, and public health when enforcing Article 101 and the merger rules.[71]

In summary, EU competition laws are applied to promote consumer welfare, protect the structure of the market, and support single market integration. These are overlapping goals, but they may occasionally be in conflict. For example, while there is significant overlap between the protection of consumer welfare and of the structure of the market, the latter encompasses a broader range of considerations than the consumer welfare standard. Similarly, while the integration of the single market has a welfare-enhancing dimension, its protection may be in tension with a consumer welfare standard that focuses on efficiency and price.[72] Moreover, the single-market imperative may lower the threshold for intervention in domains such as vertical agreements, licensing, and online sales.

B. Increased Interface from the Commercialization of Personal Data

From the above discussion, it is evident that data privacy and competition law have fundamental differences in relation to the harms they seek to redress, with the latter primarily focusing on economic harms and the former less so. These two sets of rules also differ in their material scope. While data privacy rules apply to the processing of personal data by any entity, competition rules apply to firms engaged in economic activity. Additionally, the methods of application and enforcement of the rules differ substantially.[73] Despite these differences, data privacy and competition law share common objectives, requiring coherent application where their objectives intersect. For instance, competition rules aim to ensure that consumers have a broad range of choices, whereas data privacy law—especially the rules on transparency—aim to ensure that consumers make informed choices based on accurate information. This implies that a weakening of competition may negatively affect privacy protection because, when users are dealing with monopolies, they may be forced to accept privacy policies on a take-it-or-leave-it basis. In this case, the notion of information control becomes 'illusionary'.[74]

Additionally, both sets of rules aim to protect consumers from exploitation due to unequal bargaining power. For example, Recital 43 of the GDPR specifies that consent cannot be used as a legitimate ground for processing data 'where there is a

[71] See, eg Case IV.F.1/36.718 *CECED* decision of 24 January OJ L187/47, paras 55–57; Case IV/34.252 *Philips-Osram* decision of 21 December OJ L378/37, para 27.

[72] Simon Bishop and Mike Walker, *The Economics of EC Competition Law* (Sweet & Maxwell 2010) 7.

[73] For example, unlike EU competition rules, the Commission does not have extensive competence to act under data protection law.

[74] See Christopher Kuner and others, 'When Two Worlds Collide: The Interface between Competition Law and Data Protection' (2014) 4 International Data Privacy Law 247, 247.

clear imbalance between the data subject and the controller'. This imbalance may arise when users deal with monopolies. Data privacy rules—particularly the requirements that personal data must be processed 'fairly and lawfully' and consent must be 'freely given'—could be seen as aiming to protect data subjects from 'abuse by data controllers of their monopoly position'.[75] Similarly, competition rules aim to prevent companies from abusing their market power, or dominance, to the detriment of consumers. Thus, both legal regimes are mutually reinforcing.

Moreover, some provisions of EU data privacy law go to the heart of competition policy. A case in point is the data portability right, which aims to reduce switching costs between providers and, thus, facilitate competition—including in the field of privacy. One implication of the economic nature of the rights is that a breach by a dominant undertaking may have effects that go beyond the harm to fundamental rights and disrupt the competitive process, with potential implications for competition law (see Chapter 7, Section IV.A for more on this). This implies that, in some instances, data privacy and competition rules need to work hand in hand to ensure their effective enforcement.

The need for synchronized application of the two sets of rules is even more urgent in light of the commercialization of personal data and big data. First, as many of the digital services are provided without monetary payment but in exchange for personal data, competition authorities have come to recognize data privacy as an element of non-price competition.[76] This development further reinforces the complementary nature of the rules. As noted above, the recognition of data privacy as a competition parameter may incentivize firms to provide a higher level of data privacy than that mandated by the rules. Importantly, given that data privacy focuses on privacy harms internal to the individual, the recognition of data privacy as a competition parameter helps address broader macroeconomic harms to data privacy, which result from harms to the competitive process or to market structure. For example, agreements among companies to restrict innovation that could enhance users' data privacy are not captured by data privacy rules (see Chapter 6). The same goes for the competitive harms arising from the foreclosure of firms that try to use data privacy as a value proposition, such as removal of anti-tracking and ad-blocking applications from dominant platforms (see Chapter 7). In this sense, competition law becomes instrumental in ensuring that companies do not conspire or use their market power to limit choices or stifle innovation that enhances users' data privacy. This, in turn, can incentivize competition and innovation in data privacy.

[75] Lee Bygrave, *Data Privacy Law: An International Perspective* (OUP 2014) 147.

[76] See *Microsoft/LinkedIn* (n 5). Case 50972 *Decision to Accept Commitments Offered by Google in Relation to Its Privacy Sandbox Proposals*, Competition and Markets Authority 11 February 2022 (CMA, *Decision to Accept Google's Commitments*).

Second, and related to the above, the recognition of data privacy as a parameter of competition creates opportunities for the coherent application of the two fields of law. Specifically, to the extent that data privacy is a parameter of competition for firms, data privacy rules could provide normative guidance on the dimensions of privacy that are relevant to competition and on what constitutes a reduction in the level of data privacy.[77] This seems to be the approach adopted by competition agencies in Germany and Italy, which have resorted to data privacy violations to establish abuse under competition law.[78] In Germany, Facebook was found to have abused its dominant position by imposing unfair privacy terms in breach of data privacy rules. In Italy, Google was accused of abusing its dominance by preventing users from exercising their data portability rights under the GDPR. As shown in Chapter 7, this is not unprecedented in the EU context, where other legal norms, such as intellectual property, play a similar role in the application of competition law.

Third, as personal data has become a key resource in the provision of many digital services, data privacy rules have moved centre stage, both as a competitive constraint and as a barrier to market entry. With the increased importance of data for competition, concerns have arisen regarding the accumulation of personal data (eg following a merger) and the extent to which this can give rise to, or perpetuate, market power by creating barriers to entry. In response to this, competition authorities have started to factor in the constraints that data privacy rules impose on merging firms' ability to combine data and thereby limit the potential market power from the accumulation of such data.[79] In the ongoing investigation of Google, the European Commission has highlighted the competitive significance of data privacy regulations in the advertising market, emphasizing the need for both sets of rules to 'work hand in hand' to ensure every market player upholds user privacy uniformly.[80]

Moreover, the commercialization of personal data creates tensions between data privacy law and competition law. For instance, competition agencies use data-related measures to address competition concerns in digital markets that benefit from data-driven network effects.[81] Dominant undertakings also use data privacy

[77] See Chapters 4, 5, and 7.

[78] Bundeskartellamt, *Case Summary: Facebook, Exploitative Business Terms Pursuant to Section 19(1) GWB for Inadequate Data Processing* (2019); Italian Competition and Consumer Protection Authority (AGCM), 'Investigation Opened against Google for Abuse of Dominant Position in Data Portability', (14 July 2022) <https://en.agcm.it/en/media/press-releases/2022/7/A552>.

[79] See Case M.9660 *Google/Fitbit* decision of 17 December 2020, para 408.

[80] See European Commission, 'Commission Opens Investigation into Possible Anticompetitive Conduct by Google in the Online Advertising Technology Sector (22 June 2021) (European Commission, 'Investigation into Google's Online Advertising').

[81] See 'Communication from the Commission on Building a European Data Economy' COM(2017) 9 final; Autorité de la Concurrence and Bundeskartellamt, *Competition Law and Data* (2016) <https://www.bundeskartellamt.de/SharedDocs/Publikation/DE/Berichte/Big%20Data%20Papier.pdf?__blob=publicationFile&v=4>.

improvements or obligations to justify potentially anticompetitive practices. Google's Privacy Sandbox initiative exemplifies this. It aimed to eliminate third-party trackers from Chrome and replace them with its own set of Privacy Sandbox tools. While this appears to benefit user privacy, it has attracted increased scrutiny from competition authorities.[82] These developments highlight the increased tensions that may emerge and raise a crucial question of how to balance privacy and competition interests.

Careful examination of the interaction between data privacy law and competition law is therefore imperative to effectively tackle the challenges stemming from the commercialization of personal data. For instance, the European Data Protection Supervisor (EDPS) has called for a holistic approach to the application of data privacy law and competition law, emphasizing that the lack of a clear framework for their interaction undermines the effectiveness of competition law enforcement and reduces the incentives for developing privacy-enhancing services.[83] Many scholars also share this sentiment, especially in light of the concerns related to big data. Bygrave, for instance, notes that we are only at the early stages of potential 'cross-fertilization' between these two fields and that the dialogue between them warrants 'considerably more cultivation'.[84]

This book provides a critical and comprehensive analysis of the interface and the dichotomy between these legal regimes in addressing the challenges stemming from the commercialization of personal data and big data. The analysis lays the foundation for understanding when to deploy data privacy law or competition law, depending on the situation, and when the two legal systems need to join forces to address the challenges. This, in turn, should contribute to a more holistic approach to addressing the issues that lie at the intersection. It should also ensure that enforcement of the relevant rules is coherent and coordinated, leveraging the unique strengths of each system.

IV. The Book's Argument and Contribution

The developments associated with the growing commercialization of personal data—and particularly the increasing attention paid to personal data and privacy in competition assessments—have led to greater interface between data privacy and competition rules. However, the conventional approach has been to treat these two regimes separately. While there is a substantial body of literature examining their logics, their application, and the challenges entailed by recent technological

[82] See European Commission, 'Investigation into Google's Online Advertising' (n 80); CMA, *Decision to Accept Google's Commitments* (n 76).

[83] EDPS Preliminary Opinion (n 4) 6.

[84] Lee Bygrave, 'Legal Scholarship on Data Protection: Future Challenges and Directions' in Elise Degrave and others (eds), *Law, Norms and Freedoms in Cyberspace* (Larcier 2018) 498.

advances, much of this work is siloed.[85] Where there are attempts to discuss these two sets of rules in tandem, such discussions are still nascent and rather narrow in scope.[86]

A considerable portion of the work exploring the intersection between data privacy law and competition law focuses on the role that data plays as a source of market power or an essential facility, highlighting the ensuing tension between the two legal regimes.[87] While this is an important part of the intersection, it leaves many other significant intersection points unexplored. This book adopts a broader perspective, offering an in-depth analysis of the intersection, not just as it results from data-related competition remedies but also engaging with the increased attention given to personal data in competition assessments. Taking a broader perspective sheds light on how the commercialization of personal data is changing the role that data privacy law plays in the competitive process (eg as a competitive constraint and as a barrier to market entry) and what this means for the interplay between the two sets of laws. This book further enriches the discussion by providing a detailed account of data privacy as a non-price competition parameter, noting the ways in which this amplifies the intersection between data privacy and competition rules. Specifically, it outlines various theories of harm that might serve to incorporate privacy into merger assessments and address privacy-related anticompetitive practices in light of Articles 101 and 102 of the TFEU—an analysis that has been missing from the existing literature.

Another significant departure for this book is its utilization of emergent properties and complexity science as a fresh analytical lens and theoretical framework to examine the interface, identify gaps, and propose potential solutions. The use of these analytical frameworks makes it possible to connect data privacy law and competition law. This connection occurs on two levels: at the macro level, where the similarities between data privacy law and competition law are highlighted using the concept of emergent properties, and at the micro level, where the points of interface from both empirical and normative perspectives are addressed and contextualized within the macro level using insights from complexity science, as shown in Chapter 4.

85 See, eg Koops (n 16). Ira Rubinstein, 'Big Data: The End of Privacy or a New Beginning?' (2013) International Data Privacy Law. See Mayer-Schönberger and Cukier (n 8) 15–16; Maurice Stucke and Allen Grunes, *Big Data and Competition Policy* (OUP 2016); Ania Thiemann and Pedro Gonzaga, *Big Data: Bringing Competition Policy to the Digital Era* (OECD 2016).

86 Peter Swire, *Submitted Testimony to the Federal Trade Commission Behavioral Advertising Town Hall on Google/DoubleClick* (2007) <https://www.europarl.europa.eu/meetdocs/2004_2009/documents/dv/testimony_peterswire_/Testimony_peterswire_en.pdf>; Francisco Costa-Cabral and Orla Lynskey, 'Family Ties: The Intersection between Data Protection and Competition in EU Law' (2017) 54 Common Market Law Review 11; Stucke and Grunes (n 85); Inge Graef, *EU Competition Law, Data Protection and Online Platforms: Data as Essential Facility* (Kluwer Law International 2016).

87 See Graef (n 86); Beata Mäihäniemi, *Competition Law and Big Data: Imposing Access to Information in Digital Markets* (Edward Elgar 2020).

At the macro level, the book leverages the concept of emergent properties to expose substantial similarities in the mechanics of application of data privacy and competition law. More specifically, both adopt an atomized approach, which relies on isolating a specific component as a target of regulation when dealing with a system composed of multiple components. The application of data privacy rules is predicated on the ability to identify and isolate the individual processing operation based on a specific purpose and distinct legal basis, as well as on attributing data to the individual processing operation. Similarly, the application of competition rules focuses on identifying and assessing the impact of conduct on properly defined and well-delineated relevant product/service markets. Both approaches are predicated on the assumption that there are well-delineated processing activities based on specific purpose (in the case of data privacy rules) and well-delineated relevant product/service markets (in the case of competition law).

Drawing insights from emergent properties, the book argues that this atomized approach poses significant challenges to the application of both sets of rules in light of the shifts entailed by the commercialization of personal data and big data practices. From a data privacy perspective, the book highlights two shifts, namely the tendency to process personal data for a panoply of purposes and aggregate data across these processing activities. These changes align with Zuboff's two mechanisms of surveillance capitalism: rendition based on breadth and depth.[88] Closely related to these changes, and of particular relevance to competition law, is the shift from offering a single product/service to offering ecosystems comprising several integrated products/services with personal data taking centre stage in coordinating activities across the different markets.

These developments give rise to a systemic problem, common in the application of data privacy and competition rules. The lines between the different processing activities and relevant markets are blurred, thereby complicating the attribution of individual data to a particular processing operation and competition harms to a relevant market. Further, the atomized approach may potentially overlook emergent privacy risks from the totality of processing operations and emergent competitive harms from multiple and systematic practices in seemingly different relevant markets within the comprehensive ecosystem. These risks are 'emergent' in the sense that they exist independently of, and hence may not be attributed to, individual processing operations or a relevant market.

By discussing the common challenge, the book reveals several ways the two sets of rules can complement each other in addressing the underlying challenges. For example, in order to help address some of the challenges to data privacy law, the book draws from the special responsibility regime under competition law where companies with a dominant position have a special responsibility and are subject

[88] Shoshana Zuboff, *The Age of Surveillance Capitalism: The Fight for a Human Future at the New Frontier of Power* (PublicAffairs 2019) chs 8–9.

to closer scrutiny than other firms. This means that certain restrictions apply only to entities with a dominant position. The book argues that data privacy would benefit from a similarly tiered framework that imposes enhanced responsibilities based on a holistic view of the processing activities and data-aggregation practices. Anchoring the holistic approach in the special responsibility regime allows data privacy law to leverage the existing work of competition authorities in imposing enhanced responsibilities. This enhanced responsibility regime would be crucial in addressing some of the emergent privacy risks. Additionally, scaling data privacy responsibilities based on the scale and scope of data-processing operations could partially mitigate the disproportionate disadvantage that data privacy rules place on smaller entities.

At the micro level, the book shows that the commercialization of personal data has led to an increased interface between data privacy and competition rules from both an empirical and a normative perspective. Empirically, the commercialization of personal data has led to increased attention to personal data and data privacy in competition assessments, thus increasing the points of convergence and conflict between the two sets of rules. As outlined in Section III.B, competition authorities have started to recognize the significance of data as a source of market power and of data sharing as a remedy to address some of the competition concerns in digital markets. Relatedly, competition authorities have come to recognize data privacy as an element of non-price competition, and harms to privacy are featuring prominently in competition law enforcement. This increased attention to personal data and data privacy has normative implications and opens competition law up to greater influence from data privacy law. As briefly noted in Section III.B and expounded upon in Chapter 4, these developments elevate the importance of data privacy rules in regulating the competitive process—as a competitive constraint, as a barrier to market entry, and as a source of normative guidance in addressing data- and privacy-related harms.

The book further provides a macro level context for these discussions by drawing on insights from complexity science. Specifically, it illustrates how the shifts brought about by the commercialization of personal data—particularly the tendency to process data for a plethora of purposes and the emergence of multi-product ecosystems—give rise to a complex economic landscape. This landscape is characterized by a multitude of actors, a network of interactions, and non-linear, emergent outcomes. In light of these developments, the book underscores the importance of three insights from complexity science: (1) its use of a system-level unit of analysis, (2) its emphasis on interconnections that lead to non-linear and emergent outcomes, and (3) its adoption of a polycentric approach to navigate such complexity. Chapter 8 brings to the fore how these insights inspire and are woven throughout the discussions in the book. In essence, the emergence of multi-product, complex systems underpins all discussions in the book. Chapters 2 and 3 underscore the need for a systems-level analysis that takes account of emergent harms. Chapters 4–7 then go on to explore the growing intersection between data privacy law and competition law, advocating for a polycentric regulatory approach.

The book argues that the interface presents an opportunity to enhance the efficacy of both sets of rules. Competition law can enhance the efficacy of data privacy rules by tackling macroeconomic harms to data privacy in the form of privacy fixing, reduction in choice from mergers, or platform bans of privacy-enhancing services/apps. On the other hand, data privacy law can provide competition law with the necessary tools and normative guidance needed to address new forms of anticompetitive behaviour caused by harms to data privacy.

V. Method and Analytical Framework

The issues examined in this book touch upon legal, technological, and socio-economic considerations. As such, they require both an internal and external inquiry into law. The internal inquiry is conducted by adopting a legal dogmatic method, systematically presenting and examining the theoretical foundations of EU data privacy law and competition law, including how existing laws are applied and interpreted. The internal inquiry requires that the core objectives of both sets of rules be set out, their relationship described, and any possible contradictions explored.[89] The discussion also delves into the assumptions, values, and interests that underpin both sets of rules. Discussion of the 'atomized approach' used in the application of data privacy and competition rules (in Chapters 2 and 3) and the limitations of such an approach are primarily based on the doctrinal method.

The book then takes an external view, examining the law as a social construct that requires consideration of the context in which it is applied, be that economic, technological, or historical.[90] This can be described as a law-in-context method. This method is used to identify the socio-economic and technological changes associated with big data and how these extra-legal considerations affect the application and effectiveness of data privacy law and competition law. Accordingly, the book draws on insights from a variety of disciplines, including systems theory, complexity science, informatics, economics, the literature on disruptive innovation, and management to highlight the extra-legal considerations relevant to the interface between data privacy law and competition law.

The use of these external disciplines serves two purposes: heuristic and auxiliary.[91] The heuristic use entails the adoption of material or concepts from other

[89] See Section III of this chapter.

[90] Paul Chynoweth, 'Legal Research' in Andrew Knight and Les Ruddock (eds), *Advanced Research Methods in the Built Environment* (Wiley-Blackwell 2008) 30.

[91] Bart van Klink and Sanne Taekema, 'On the Border: Limits and Possibilities of Interdisciplinary Research' in Bart van Klink and Sanne Taekema (eds), *Law and Method: Interdisciplinary Research into Law* (Mohr Siebeck 2011) 3–4.

disciplines to substantiate claims or answer a question of law; however, the claims derived from other disciplines need to be 'justified within the discipline of law, on the basis of recognizable legal concepts, to be recognized as a legal argument'.[92] The use of the concept of emergent properties in Chapters 2 and 3 is an example. Insights from systems theory and complexity science are used to conceptualize data privacy and competition risks as emergent properties, but these risks are justified based on interests recognized within data privacy law (such as autonomy, information self-determination, and transparency) and within competition law (harm to consumer welfare). In this way, systems theory and the concept of emergent properties serve as a source of argumentation or inspiration.

Another use of external disciplines is auxiliary, where developments in other disciplines give rise to a problem requiring a legal response.[93] In this type of research, materials derived from other disciplines serve as a necessary contribution to the legal arguments, and the claims made in a legal context must be valid in light of both the legal and auxiliary disciplines. The book examines issues external to the legal framework—big data and the commercialization of personal data—but which are perceived as demanding a legal response. Thus, material from the fields of informatics, business, and economics is drawn upon to highlight the socio-economic and technological developments related to the commercialization of personal data, thereby serving an auxiliary purpose. Accordingly, Section II highlighted three key socio-economic shifts and characterized big data as both a technology and a social and economic force.

These socio-technical and economic changes are subsequently used as a point of departure for identifying possible gaps in the application of data privacy and competition rules. Drawing on elements from emergent properties,[94] the book shows how the changes brought about by the commercialization of personal data affect the application of the rules (see Chapters 2 and 3). Methodologically, the concept of emergent properties serves four purposes. First, it is used to understand the *modus operandi* of EU data privacy and competition rules, characterizing their application as 'atomized' in nature. In this sense, the concept provides a lens for highlighting the underlying assumptions behind the application of the rules. Second, the concept is used to identify changes entailed by the commercialization of personal data and highlight how these changes create complexities or emergent risks that challenge the plausibility of the assumptions underlying the current rules. Third, the concept informs the discussion on how to understand emergent behaviour (risk) in data privacy law and competition law. Specifically, the concept provides a framework for looking at multiple processing activities or multiple

[92] ibid.

[93] ibid 4.

[94] For more on this, see Samson Esayas, 'The Important Role of Emergence in Conceptualizing the Challenges of New Technologies to Private Law' (2023) 31 European Private Law Review 779.

cross-market practices as a single complex and a way of examining the privacy and competition interests that emerge in such a complex. Finally, the concept indicates a potential way forward: a holistic, systems-level perspective to data privacy law and competition law. In this sense, the concept enables the marriage of the theoretical foundations and assumptions identified through the internal inquiry into law (legal dogmatics) and the socio-technical changes and the resultant gaps examined using the law-in-context method.

PART II

EMERGENT PROPERTIES IN DATA PRIVACY LAW AND COMPETITION LAW

Part II, which consists of Chapters 2 and 3, explores the idea of emergent properties in the application of EU data privacy law and competition law. Using emergent properties as a lens, this part exposes substantial similarities in the mechanics of their application, leading to a systemic problem common to both legal regimes. This problem relates to their similarly atomized approaches, namely their tendency to isolate a specific component as the target of regulation when dealing with a system comprised of several components. The application of data privacy rules is predicated on the ability to identify and isolate the individual processing operation (based on a specific purpose and a distinct legal basis) and to attribute data to the individual processing operation. Similarly, the application of competition rules focuses on identifying and assessing the impact of conduct on properly defined and well-delineated relevant product/service markets. Drawing insights from emergent properties, the book argues that this atomized approach poses significant challenges to the application of both sets of rules in light of the shifts entailed by the commercialization of personal data and big data practices.

From a data privacy perspective, the book highlights two shifts, namely the tendency to process personal data for a panoply of purposes and the aggregation of data across these processing activities. Closely related to these changes, and of particular importance to competition law, is the shift from offering single products/services to offering ecosystems comprising several integrated products/services, with personal data taking centre stage in coordinating activities across the different markets. These developments blur the lines between the different processing activities and relevant markets, thereby complicating the attribution of individual data to a particular processing operation and a competition harm to a relevant market. Further, the atomized approach may potentially overlook emergent privacy risks from the totality of processing operations and emergent competitive harms from multiple and systematic practices in seemingly different relevant markets within the comprehensive ecosystem. These risks are 'emergent' in the sense that they exist independently of, and hence may not be attributed to, individual processing operations or a relevant market.

In light of these challenges, the discussion underscores the need for a holistic, system-level perspective in the application of both data privacy law and competition law. Chapter 2 advocates a holistic approach in data privacy law that imposes enhanced responsibilities based on the totality of processing activities and data-aggregation practices to deal with emergent privacy risks. The holistic approach is akin to regulation under competition law, in which companies with a dominant position are subject to special responsibilities. Chapter 3 calls for a holistic approach to the application of competition law. The holistic approach would consider competitive fields and power dimensions that go beyond specific relevant markets, thus acknowledging the potential for dominant digital players to stifle competition through multiple actions across various markets and targeting several players.

Using the lens of emergent properties, the discussion aims to show the substantial similarities in the mechanics of application of European Union (EU) data privacy law and competition law. It insists on their similarly atomized approaches, the challenges they both encounter when addressing the commercialization of personal data, and the need for a holistic approach to address these challenges. It shows how the concept of emergent properties offers a unifying framework for understanding the challenges posed by big data when enforcing both legal regimes. There are two particularly important takeaways from the discussion on emergent properties in this context. First, although the idea of 'one thing at a time' is a useful guiding principle in life, it may prove inadequate in a world where the line between one thing and another is unclear. Importantly, data privacy law and competition law must recognize the prospect that the sum of fully compliant behaviours may still engender non-compliant conduct or actions deviating from the intended spirit of the law.

2
The Idea of Emergent Properties in Data Privacy Law

'The whole is more than the sum of its parts.'[1]

I. Atomized Approach to Data Privacy Law

A legal regime can be described as atomized if, in dealing with a system built from several components, it focuses, as a matter of law or practice, on isolating a specific component of the system as the target of regulation as opposed to the system as a whole. In the context of European Union (EU) data privacy rules, this issue of atomized approach arises when an entity processes personal data for multiple purposes. The use of the term 'purposes' (plural) under Article 6(1(b)) of the 1995 Directive[2] or Article 5(1(b)) of the General Data Protection Regulation (GDPR)[3] implies that personal data can be collected for more than one purpose. In such cases, the Article 29 Working Party (now the European Data Protection Board) requires that 'each separate purpose should be specified in enough detail to be able to assess whether collection of personal data for this purpose complies with the law' and '*the data quality requirements must be complied with separately for each purpose*'.[4] This represents an atomized view of the processing and implies that when an

[1] This quote is often attributed to Aristotle, although others are also credited for it. See Daniel Solove, *Understanding Privacy* (Harvard UP 2008) 117.

[2] Directive 95/46/EC of the European Parliament and Council of 24 October 1995 on the Protection of Individuals with Regard to the Processing of Personal Data and on the Free Movement of Such Data OJ L281/31 (the Directive).

[3] Regulation (EU) 2016/679 of the European Parliament and of the Council of 27 April 2016 on the Protection of Natural Persons with Regard to the Processing of Personal Data and on the Free Movement of Such Data, and repealing Directive 95/46/EC OJ L119/1 (GDPR).

[4] Article 29 Data Protection Working Party (WP203), 'Opinion 03/2013 on Purpose Limitation' (2013) (WP203) 12 and 16 (emphasis added). The Working Party was an independent group established under Article 29 of the 1995 Directive, comprising the national data protection authorities (DPAs), responsible for ensuring the consistent application of data protection rules and providing guidance to the European Commission on various issues concerning data protection. While the guidance was issued in relation to the 1995 Directive, it remains relevant to the GDPR (n 3) insofar as the content of the provisions has not changed. This is consistent with the opinion of Advocate General (AG) Bobek in *Fashion ID*, who stated that if the key terms in the GDPR remain the same as in the Directive (n 2), the interpretations would not differ. In that case, the AG relied on the Working Party's opinion under the 1995 Directive in interpreting the GDPR. See Case C-40/17 *Fashion ID GmbH & Co KG v Verbraucherzentrale NRW* ECLI:EU:C:2018:1039, Opinion of Advocate General Bobek, paras 83–100.

Data Privacy and Competition Law in the Age of Big Data. Samson Y. Esayas, Oxford University Press.
© Oxford University Press 2024. DOI: 10.1093/oso/9780198891420.003.0003

entity processes personal data for multiple purposes, each processing must comply with the data privacy principles separately, in light of the specific purpose and the relevant legal basis.

The main argument in this chapter is that this atomized approach is inadequate in an era where companies process personal data for manifold purposes and data is combined across several processing activities. This inadequacy partially stems from an underlying assumption within the atomized approach, which posits that there exist well-delineated, distinct processing activities serving distinct purposes, with every piece of data fitting into those delineated individual boxes of processing activities. However, in light of the increasing commercialization of personal data, this assumption is a half-truth at best. The processing of personal data for multiple purposes, along with its combination from the various sources, blurs the lines between the different processing activities, thereby complicating the attribution of individual data to a particular processing operation.

Furthermore, the account of the atomized approach partially signifies that as long as the individual processing is compliant, the data privacy rights of individuals are not endangered. However, as shown throughout this chapter, this may not always be the case. Drawing insights from the concept of emergent property, the chapter argues that when entities process personal data for a wide array of purposes and combine data across these processing activities, there are privacy risks that may exist independent of and/or in combination with the individual processing activities. These include overexposure of the individual and losses of transparency, accountability, and practical obscurity. But before discussing these risks, it is essential to explain the atomized approach.

The compliance assessment lifespan for a certain processing activity commences by determining the specific purpose of collecting personal data.[5] On determining the purpose, one needs to find an appropriate legal basis from among the six alternative legal grounds under Article 6 (or Article 9(2) for sensitive personal data) of the GDPR that suits the specified purpose.[6] The determination of the purpose and relevant legal basis creates a set box for that processing activity, as shown in the

[5] Indeed, one might contend that this does not accurately represent real-world practices. As elaborated in Chapter 1, numerous big data applications involve determining the purpose of processing after conducting a comprehensive analysis of the data in conjunction with other data sets. This method challenges the conventional model of establishing a specific purpose beforehand; see Lokke Moerel, *Big Data Protection: How to Make the Draft EU Regulation on Data Protection Future Proof* (Tilburg University 2014) 7. However, this claim aligns with the overarching argument that current data privacy rules are inadequate for dealing with emerging data-processing practices.

[6] Article 6 of the GDPR (n 3) provides that personal data may be processed only if (1) the data subject has given consent, (2) processing is necessary for the performance of a contract, (3) processing is necessary for compliance with a legal obligation, (4) processing is necessary for protecting the vital interests of the data subject or another natural person, (5) processing is necessary for the performance of a task carried out in the public interest or in the exercise of official authority, and (6) processing is necessary for the purposes of the controller's legitimate interests.

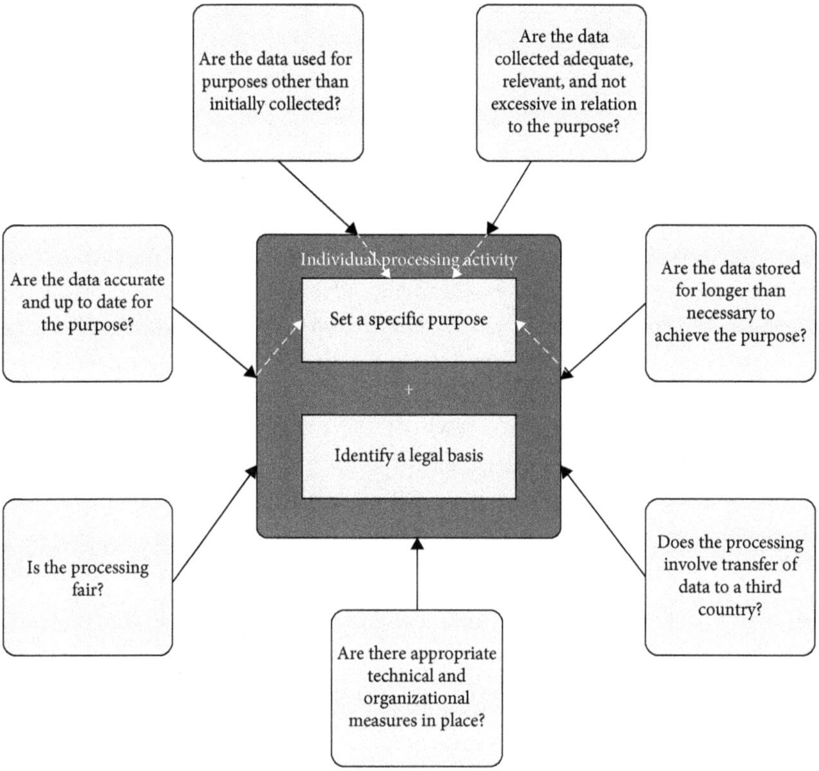

Figure 2.1 Atomistic view of data-privacy compliance assessment
Source: author.

middle of Figure 2.1, which becomes the epicentre of the application of the core data privacy principles.[7]

A regulator or internal auditor who is interested in assessing the compliance of the specific processing activity should be able to identify the specific purpose for which the personal data was collected. Moreover, the regulator or auditor should determine if there is a legitimate legal basis and this suits the specific purpose; the data collected is the minimum necessary for the purpose; the data collected is accurate and up to date for that purpose; the personal data is not stored for longer than necessary to achieve the purpose; and the processing of such data is fair (ie it does not exceed the reasonable expectations of individuals). The assessment should also consider whether appropriate technological and organizational measures are in place to protect personal data from 'unauthorised or unlawful

[7] These include the lawfulness, fairness, and transparency principle, Article 5(1(a)); the purpose limitation principle, Article 5(1(b)); the data minimization principle, Article 5(1(c)); the accuracy or data quality principle, Article 5(1(d)); the storage limitation principle, Article 6(1(e)); and the principle of integrity and confidentiality, Article 5(1(f)).

processing and against accidental loss, destruction or damage' (integrity and confidentiality),[8] as well as whether the processing involves a transfer of personal data to a third country—in which case, the requirements on international transfer demand compliance.[9] Figure 2.1 depicts this atomized way of assessing compliance with the rules.

When personal data is processed for multiple purposes, this process is repeated for each distinct purpose. These distinct processing activities may be based on different purposes and different legal grounds under Article 6 (Article 9(2)) or based on different, unrelated purposes with the same legal ground.[10] For example, personal data may be processed for marketing purposes (and using consent as a legal basis), for processing payment (and using the 'performance of a contract entered into with the data subject' as a legal basis), or for taxation purposes (and using compliance with legal obligations as a legal basis). Alternatively, personal data may be processed under the same legal basis but for different purposes. For example, consent can be used to process personal data for both marketing and research purposes.

Each of these processing activities, based on a specific purpose and distinct legal basis, forms a set box, as represented in the middle of Figure 2.1. Therefore, when personal data is processed for multiple purposes, each box should comply with the data privacy principles separately.[11] In the figure, these principles are represented by the questions embedded in the boxes attached to the central box. To apply the principles to each box, one must identify the different set boxes based on the specific purpose, distinct legal basis, and the data that belongs to each box. This represents an atomized view of processing where the focus is on the individual processing based on a specific purpose and distinct legal basis, with little regard for the total number of processing activities and data-aggregation practices. However, this approach leads to systemic gaps in the application of data privacy rules in light of the commercialization of personal data, which has resulted in the processing of personal data for a wide range of purposes and aggregation of data across multiple processing activities. Therefore, this chapter underscores the need for a holistic approach to address the risks associated with the totality of processing activities and data-aggregation practices.

Before proceeding further, it is important to note two points of caution. First, in most cases, the purpose limitation principle will not allow data aggregation across different processing activities that serve distinct purposes. Aggregation counts as processing under the EU rules and therefore requires an independent legitimate basis when conducted on processing operations based on distinct purposes.

[8] GDPR (n 3), Articles 5(1(f)) and 32.
[9] ibid Articles 45–49.
[10] For discussions on 'related' processing operations, see WP203 (n 4) 16 and examples in Annex 3.
[11] The Working Party makes it clear that 'If personal data are processed for several purposes, all requirements of Article 6 apply to each purpose separately'; ibid 16.

In other words, if an entity aggregates data across different processing activities without a legitimate basis, it violates the rules. However, this is complicated by the reliance of many entities on consent as a legal basis for processing data, including the aggregation practices. Once the user consents to such aggregation practices, the line between the different individual processing activities and the data in each box becomes blurred, complicating the application of the data privacy rules to a specific box.

The second point relates to the flexible tools that data protection authorities (DPAs) have to consider the relevant interests under each circumstance. There is some evidence that the authorities are not restricted to looking at the individual processing activities and do account for the overall privacy interests of individuals.[12] In this regard, it is worth mentioning the flexibility that some principles, such as the fairness principle, provide in terms of looking beyond the individual processing activities. However, these kinds of encouraging moves towards a holistic approach need to be strengthened by relevant tools and a theoretical framework for their consistent application.

The aim of this chapter is to contribute to achieving this objective. To this end, the chapter draws from the concept of emergent property to shed light on how to understand a system involving several processing operations as a single complex. The motivation for using the concept of emergent property in data privacy law is twofold. First, the growing importance of personal data for commercial purposes is fuelling the desire to collect and amass as much personal data as possible, both through legitimate (eg acquisitions) and illegitimate (eg deliberate deception) mechanisms, leading to the emergence of companies processing personal data for a panoply of purposes. Second, big data practices represent substantial value in repurposing, recombining, and multi-purposing personal databases. A salient example is Google's aggressive expansion into a wide range of new product domains, encompassing email, searches, map services, video sharing, social networks, mobile operating services (MOS), payment services, and more. A 2013 investigation by the Spanish DPA reveals that Google collects personal data through nearly 100 consumer-facing products or services.[13]

Moreover, since their inception, Google and Facebook have acquired over 150 and 50 companies, respectively. Companies also combine data across these different processing activities based on separate purposes.[14] This growth in the number of processing operations and the combination of data across these operations creates

[12] See Agencia Española de Protección de Datos (AEPD), 'The AEPD Sanctions Google for Serious Violation of the Rights of the Citizens' (19 December 2013) <https://www.personuvernd.is/media/frettir/frettatilkynning-AEPD_en.docx>.

[13] See ibid 1.

[14] Google's 2012 change of privacy policy is a good example. See Google Official Blog, 'Updating Our Privacy Policies and Terms of Service' (24 January 2012) <https://googleblog.blogspot.ca/2012/01/updating-our-privacy-policies-and-terms.html> accessed 6 February 2024.

a complex system that necessitates examination in its entirety. In light of these developments, the focus on individual processing activity overlooks the fact that the totality of personal data collected based on separate purposes and/or the combination of data across these processing activities could be a source of concern for the individual (eg overexposure) or society at large (eg loss of practical obscurity), as explored in Section IV.

Based on discussions about emergent property, this chapter calls for a holistic approach grounded on enhanced responsibility to certain entities, considering different factors such as the totality of the processing activities and data-aggregation practices. The holistic approach is akin to the regulation under competition law, where companies with a monopoly or dominant position are subject to special responsibilities. The chapter emphasizes that data privacy will benefit from a comparable tiered framework that imposes enhanced responsibilities based on the holistic view of the totality of the processing activities and data-aggregation practices. The objective is not to condemn the atomized approach but rather to highlight instances where the current approach might benefit from a complementary approach rooted in a holistic view.

At this juncture, it is important to highlight whether the reform that led to the adoption of the GDPR alters the paradigm in relation to the above problem. The answer is both yes and no. It is no because, although the reform was primarily aimed at aligning the rules with new business practices, the architecture of the rules, including the core principles and the atomized nature of their application, remains unchanged.[15] However, the Regulation has introduced measures that give the regulatory authorities additional tools for dealing with the identified problem, including scalable penalties for breach and the Data Protection Impact Assessment (DPIA). More particularly, the Regulation opens the door—*albeit* for predominantly economic reasons—to conduct DPIA-encompassing operations beyond 'a single project' (ie processing activity).[16] Moreover, subject to notification of the European Data Protection Board, DPAs can include additional processing operations that could be subject to the DPIA.[17] Thus, with an open eye to a holistic approach, these tools should give greater flexibility to address the concerns outlined in this chapter.

Throughout this chapter, Google and Facebook serve as examples to illustrate some of the challenges, but they are by no means the only entities engaged in the relevant practices. Moreover, none of these examples are meant to deny the

[15] See Peter Hustinx, 'EU Data Protection Law: The Review of Directive 95/46 EC and the Proposed General Data Protection Regulation' (*European Data Protection Supervisor*, 2014) 28 <https://edps.europa.eu/sites/default/files/publication/14-09-15_article_eui_en.pdf> accessed 6 February 2024 (noting that 'in spite of all innovation—there is also a lot of *continuity* (in the Regulation). All the familiar basic concepts and principles will continue to exist').

[16] GDPR (n 3), Recital 39.

[17] ibid Article 35(4).

enormous social and economic benefits that those companies bring to users at (seemingly) no cost.

The remainder of the chapter is structured as follows. First, the concept of emergent property and its relevance in relation to data privacy discussions are explained. Second, the chapter applies the concept to explain the challenges posed by the commercialization of personal data and big data in relation to data privacy. Third, the chapter examines the privacy interests that emerge with such practices. Finally, the potential way forward in dealing with the identified challenges is discussed.

II. Emergent Properties

The idea of emergence offers an alternative to scientific inquiry based on reduction, which entails breaking down a phenomenon into its components and examining them individually.[18] Physics is a prime example of a reductionist discipline. Although the scientific importance of reduction is not disputed, it is argued that reduction is less helpful for studying certain things, such as the behaviour of human groups (how a group behaves cannot necessarily be explained by the behaviours of individual members). Thus, emergence fills this gap by studying this phenomenon as a collective whole. Simply put, while reduction explains Xs as 'nothing more than Ys', emergence explains Xs as 'something over and above Ys'.[19] Emergence is discussed in different forms and emergent property is one of them.[20] At its core, emergent property emphasizes the notion that 'the whole is more than the sum of its parts', with the 'whole' representing the 'emergent property'. While the concept of emergent properties is widely used across many fields,[21] there is no distinct classification of it as a theory, methodology, or any other category. It is discussed as an independent theory, as part of a larger theory of complexity, or as a methodology.[22]

Notwithstanding the lack of consensus on its significance, the concept of emergent property has been central to general systems thinking. In this context, the concept provides a framework for understanding how complex systems emerge from the interaction of simpler elements and emphasize that the properties of the system cannot be fully understood by examining each component in isolation.[23]

[18] Paul Davies, 'The Physics of Downward Causation' in Paul Davies and Philip Clayton (eds), *The Re-Emergence of Emergence: The Emergentist Hypothesis from Science to Religion* (OUP 2006) 35.

[19] Robert Van Gulick, 'Reduction, Emergence and Other Recent Options on the Mind/Body Problem. A Philosophic Overview' (2001) 8 Journal of Consciousness Studies 1, 16.

[20] Philip Clayton, 'Conceptual Foundations of Emergence Theory' in Davies and Clayton (eds) (n 18) 2 (discussing four kinds of emergence).

[21] Despite the lack of a clear definition, the concept of emergent property is prevalent in many domains, such as biology, ecology, geophysics, and social science disciplines, including economics. See Eric Bonabeau, Jean-Louis Dessalles, and Alain Grumbach, 'Characterizing Emergent Phenomena (1): A Critical Review' (1995) 9 Revue internationale de systémique 327, 336.

[22] Harold Morowitz, *The Emergence of Everything: How the World Became Complex* (OUP 2002) 1, 10

[23] Systems theory and emergent properties share a focus on systems and the interactions among their components, acknowledging that complex behaviours can emerge from these interactions. Both

This thinking enables systems engineers to look beyond the properties of individual components in a system and understand the system as a single complex.[24] Complexity is particularly essential in characterizing the emergent property 'because emergence can be considered as an increase in the complexity of a system'.[25]

From a general systems perspective, a complex can emerge in three forms.[26] First, a complex can arise from the summation of its component parts, that is *summative* complex. Second, it can emerge from the *special characteristics* of the components.[27] Third, the complex can result from the *interrelations* of the components.[28] As shown in Figure 2.2, these distinctions are important in drawing comparisons of how a complex emerges in data privacy law.

Despite the close association, there is, nevertheless, a distinction between a mere increase in complexity and a complex system that displays emergent properties.[29] A system may be described as complex if it is 'built on multiple agents dynamically interacting in multiple ways, following local rules and oblivious to any higher level of instruction'.[30] But that, by itself, does not necessarily create emergent behaviour. In his seminal work on the topic, Johnson uses a semi-intelligent billiard example to illustrate the distinction. The billiard has motorized balls that interact based on specific rules. The balls are designed to follow these rules: (1) swerve left

concepts also embrace a holistic approach, understanding the system as a collective whole. Nevertheless, general systems theory has a broader scope, focusing on structures, relationships, and interdependence between elements in a system, including non-complex systems where reductionist approaches are still relevant. See Lars Skyttner, *General Systems Theory: Problems, Perspectives, Practice* (World Scientific 2005). It is worth noting that some scholars emphasize the importance of reductionism and modularity in understanding and building complex systems. For instance, Simon's 'architecture of complexity' underscores the need to break down complex systems into hierarchical subsystems to better comprehend their behaviour. However, he concedes that in the face of complexity, even a devoted reductionist may need to be 'a pragmatic holist'. Similarly, Baldwin and Clark highlight the role of modularity in effectively managing complex systems and enhancing their adaptability to change. See Herbert Simon, 'The Architecture of Complexity' (1962) 106 Proceedings of the American Philosophical Society 467; Carliss Baldwin and Kim Clark, 'Modularity in the Design of Complex Engineering Systems' in Dan Braha, Ali A Minai, and Yaneer Bar-Yam (eds), *Complex Engineered Systems: Science Meets Technology* (Springer 2006).

[24] Misha Hebel, 'World-Views as the Emergent Property of Human Value Systems' (1999) 16 Systems Research and Behavioral Science 253, 253.

[25] Eric Bonabeau, Jean-Louis Dessalles, and Alain Grumbach, 'Characterizing Emergent Phenomena (2): A Conceptual Framework' (1995a) 9 Revue internationale de systémique 347, 347.

[26] Ion Georgiou, 'The Idea of Emergent Property' (2003) 54 Journal of the Operational Research Society 239, 240.

[27] 'For example, a complex may be constituted by one poodle, one Dalmatian and one Alsatian. This complex is understood as being of three elements belonging to the species 'dogs'; it is thus a complex of dogs': ibid.

[28] 'For example, a complex may be constituted by a palomino stallion, his mare and their pony. This complex is thus one of a family of palomino horses': ibid.

[29] Both complex and complicated systems have several interacting components, but there are crucial differences. In contrast to merely complicated systems, a complex system is characterized by distinct properties that arise from the relationship between the components including emergence, nonlinearity, spontaneous order, adaptation, and feedback loops. See Steven Johnson, *Emergence: The Connected Lives of Ants, Brains, Cities, and Software* (Penguin 2001) 18.

[30] ibid.

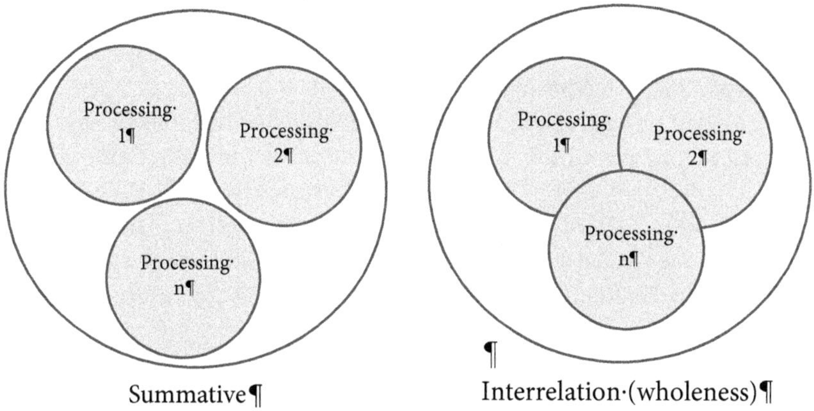

Figure 2.2 Summative and interrelation (wholeness) aspects
Source: author.

when hitting a solid-coloured ball, (2) speed up after touching the three-ball, and (3) stop when they hit the eight-ball. These rules allow the balls to explore the space of the table and alter their movements and speed based on their interaction with other balls. While this system represents a basic form of complex behaviour, it does not yet display emergent behaviour.[31]

For emergence to occur, the interaction based on local rules must lead to 'some kind of discernible macrobehaviour' or 'global structure—a structure that you wouldn't necessarily predict from the rules'.[32] In the billiard example, if the rules cause the balls to cluster into two groups, one even-numbered and another odd-numbered, this will represent emergent behaviour because the low-level rules produce high-level sophistication. This occurs because 'the balls are not programmed explicitly to cluster in two groups, they are programmed to follow much more random rules'.[33] In short, emergence arises when 'agents residing on one scale start producing a behaviour that lies one scale above them: ants create colonies; urbanities create neighbourhoods; simple pattern recognition software learns how to recommend new books'.[34] Thus, emergence entails something more than just an increase in complexity.

The literature on emergent property varies in terms of what characterizes the emergent property, such as its composition, structure, or functionality.[35] Van Gulick distinguishes between three levels of emergence—namely specific value, modest emergent properties, and radical emergent properties.[36] In specific-value

[31] ibid.
[32] ibid 32 and 90.
[33] ibid 19.
[34] ibid 18.
[35] Timothy O'Connor, 'Emergent Properties' (1994) 31 American Philosophical Quarterly 91, 91.
[36] Van Gulick (n 19) 17.

emergence, the whole and constituent parts share the same features, but the whole differs in type or value.[37] The summative complex falls under this category, but some argue that specific-value emergence should not qualify as an emergent property.[38] Modest types of emergence occur when the whole exhibits features that are different in kind from those of its constituent parts.[39] In radical emergence, the whole is different in kind from the features of its constituent parts, and its 'nature and existence is not necessitated by the features of its parts [or] their mode of combination'.[40] The existence of real cases of radical emergence is subject to debate; thus, the most commonly discussed emergent property is emergence of the modest kind.[41]

It is beyond the purview of this chapter to delve into the details of the characterization outlined above. This is because, first, the idea of emergent property is used as a lens for examining data privacy challenges; in other words, the main arguments put forth, although examined through a systems-thinking lens, can stand independently of the concept of emergent property.[42] Furthermore, despite its origins in systems thinking, the idea of emergent property is also viewed as an epistemological theory that provides a foundation for construing knowledge of the whole in contexts other than systems.

Emergent properties have been used, for example, to explain the unforeseen consequences of interactions among different behaviours that form a system in a broader sense, such as a system of law.[43] A good example in this regard comes from laws that require automobile drivers to wear seatbelts while driving. The objective of such laws, not surprisingly, is to ensure the safety of drivers, mitigating injuries and deaths from accidents. Notwithstanding, such laws can lead to a collective behaviour that contradicts the intended objective. The compulsory seatbelt rules may not reduce the overall injuries or deaths from accidents because 'in wearing a seatbelt, drivers usually feel safer and willing to take greater risks'.[44] In this example, the property 'drivers usually feel safer and are willing to take greater risks' emerges, representing the emergent property. By regarding the system and its components as a single complex, emergence can help uncover hidden assumptions or unintended consequences of the collective interaction among the components or behaviours. This perspective enables the consideration of the potential collective behaviour and the more effective design of the system and its enforcement

[37] ibid.
[38] Jaegwon Kim, 'Being Realistic about Emergence' in Davies and Clayton (eds) (n 18).
[39] Van Gulick (n 19) 17.
[40] ibid.
[41] ibid 18; Kim (n 38) 192.
[42] That is, the concept is used as 'a way of seeing things which were previously overlooked or bypassed, and in this sense is a methodological maxim'; Ludwig Von Bertalanffy, 'The History and Status of General Systems Theory' (1972) 15 Academy of Management Journal 407, 424.
[43] Georgiou (n 26) 241.
[44] ibid.

machinery. Similarly, the concept of emergent property can provide a useful lens for explaining and understanding some of the challenges that result from entities processing personal data for manifold purposes and engaging in data-aggregation practices.

Accordingly, the concept serves four main purposes. First, as illustrated in Section I, the concept is used to understand the *modus operandi* of the EU data privacy rules and characterize their application as atomized. This characterization, in turn, lends support for highlighting the underlying assumptions behind the application of current data privacy rules, namely (1) it is possible to distinguish between different processing activities and relating every piece of personal data to a specific processing and (2) if each processing is compliant, the data privacy rights of individuals are not endangered. Second, as shown in Section III, the concept is used to identify data-processing practices that result in the emergence of a property and challenge the above assumptions in light of these developments. Parallels are drawn between the two data-processing developments resulting from the commercialization of personal data (namely the tendencies to process personal data for a panoply of purposes and aggregate data across these processing activities) and the 'summation' and 'interrelation' complexes under discussions of emergent property. This aims to highlight how these two developments give rise to complexes that do not exist when companies process data for a handful of purposes and in silos. The complexity, in turn, blurs the lines between different services (processing activities) and complicates the ability to attribute every piece of data to a specific processing. In this regard, the concept provides a framework for looking at multiple processing activities as a single complex.

Third, as demonstrated in Section IV, the concept is used for identifying the data privacy interests that emerge when entities collect data through a multitude of services and aggregate data across such services. These interests include, but are not limited to, overexposure of the individual and losses of transparency, accountability, and practical obscurity. These risks represent 'emergent properties' in the sense that the sum (ie the aggregated and accumulated data) contains risks that are not present in the individual data sets or processing operations. In this regard, the concept serves as a means for examining the privacy interests that emerge independent of, or in combination with, privacy interests in the individual processing activities and to demonstrate the inadequacy of the atomized approach to deal with the emergent risks. While data privacy rules, such as the purpose limitation principle, set restrictions on data combinations, entities can circumvent these restrictions, for instance by relying on consent, to expand their processing scope and combine data across these operations. Yet, even when confronted with complex systems featuring multiple processing activities and data aggregation across these services, the atomized approach remains overly fixated on the individual processing operations and neglects the potential system-level (emergent) risks not evident in the individual processing activities. Finally, the concept provides useful guidance on constructing the potential way forward (Section V). Informed by the discussion about emergent property, this section calls for a holistic, system-level view to address the emergent risks.

III. The Idea of Emergent Properties in Data Privacy

This section applies the discussions about emergent property to data privacy law. It starts by briefly reviewing developments in case law from both sides of the Atlantic that reflect some emergent property reasoning in relation to government processing of data. Then, it identifies business practices in processing personal data that lead to the emergence of a property. This is followed by a discussion on how to understand emergence for data privacy purposes.

A. The Emergence of Emergent Properties in Case Law

There have been recent decisions from the EU and US courts that reflect some emergent property thinking, although the discussions in the United States are a step ahead. In the EU, this line of reasoning is observed in the Court of Justice of the European Union (CJEU) judgment that invalidated the Data Retention Directive.[45] In that judgment, the Court emphasized the wide array of data about a private person that providers of electronic communication services or networks are required to retain, including data concerning

> the source of a communication and its destination, ... the date, time, duration and type of a communication, ... users' communication equipment, and ... the location of mobile communication equipment, the name and address of the subscriber or registered user, the calling telephone number, the number called and an IP address for Internet services.[46]

According to the Court, the collection and storage of such data constitute interference with the right to respect for private life and the fundamental right to the protection of personal data, which can only be derogated insofar as it is 'strictly necessary' in a democratic society.[47] Although the Court recognized the need to retain some data about individuals for purposes of law enforcement, the retention of such 'vast quantity of data' as required by the Directive goes beyond what

[45] Cases C-293/12 and C-594/12 *Digital Rights Ireland v Minister for Communications* ECLI:EU:C:2014:238, para 26.
[46] ibid para 26.
[47] ibid paras 37–40.

is strictly necessary in a democratic society.[48] This is because '[t]hose data, *taken as a whole*, may allow very precise conclusions to be drawn concerning the private lives of the persons whose data has been retained'.[49] The judgment, particularly the reference to 'taken as a whole', reflects emergent property reasoning in the sense that, although the retention of different sets of data individually may not violate the rights of individuals, collectively, they constitute a breach of the right to respect for private life and the fundamental right to the protection of personal data. The emergent property in this case is the breach of data privacy rights in the totality of the data sets retained, which does not exist in the individual data sets alone.

Across the Atlantic, the discussions are even more advanced. Following the 2012 decision of the US Supreme Court in *United States v Jones*,[50] concepts similar to emergent property—such as the *mosaic theory* and *quantitative privacy*—began attracting considerable attention in the US literature in relation to the Fourth Amendment.[51] The mosaic theory was initially articulated in *United States v Maynard* by the Court of Appeals for the DC Circuit, which was later reviewed by the Supreme Court decision under the name *Jones*.[52] In this case, the police—investigating a drug conspiracy involving the defendant, Mr Jones—installed a global positioning system (GPS) tracking device without a warrant[53] on the defendant's car to track his movements over the course of one month.[54] This tracking resulted in 2,000 pages of data, which were then used to coordinate the defendant's movements and convict him (and his associate, Mr Maynard) of drug conspiracy.[55]

Mr Jones appealed the decision to the DC Circuit Court on the grounds that the warrantless tracking via GPS had violated his 'reasonable expectation of privacy' under the Fourth Amendment.[56] One of the doctrines in assessing the right under the Fourth Amendment is the public disclosure doctrine, which precludes a reasonable expectation of privacy of an individual's movements in public spaces. This means the mere fact that the information is exposed to the public view precludes

48 ibid para 66.

49 ibid para 27 (emphasis added).

50 *US v Jones* 132 Supreme Court (2012) 945.

51 See, eg Orin Kerr, 'The Mosaic Theory of the Fourth Amendment' (2012) 111 Michigan Law Review 311, 311; Christopher Slobogin, 'Making the Most of United States v. Jones in a Surveillance Society: A Statutory Implementation of Mosaic Theory' (2012) 8 Duke Journal of Constitutional Law & Public Policy 12, 12; David Gray and Danielle Citron, 'The Right to Quantitative Privacy' (2013) 98 Minnesota Law Review 62. The US Constitution Fourth Amendment recognizes, 'The right of the people to be secure in their persons, houses, papers, and effects, against unreasonable searches and seizures, shall not be violated, and no warrants shall issue, but upon probable cause, supported by oath or affirmation, and particularly describing the place to be searched, and the persons or things to be seized.'

52 *US v Maynard* 615 Court of Appeals, Dist of Columbia Circuit (2010) 544.

53 In fact, the police had obtained a warrant to install a GPS, but violated the conditions for installing it within 10 days and within the district of Washington.

54 *US v Maynard* (n 52) 948.

55 ibid.

56 ibid.

protection under the Fourth Amendment (and the need for a warrant). Given that the GPS was tracking Mr Jones's movements on public roads, the government argued that Mr Jones had no reasonable expectation of privacy that would warrant protection under the Fourth Amendment.[57] However, the DC Circuit Court disagreed and found the following:

> [T]he totality of Jones's movements over the course of a month—was not exposed to the public: First, unlike one's movements during a single journey, the whole of one's movements over the course of a month is not actually exposed to the public because the likelihood anyone will observe all those movements is effectively nil. *Second, the whole of one's movements is not exposed constructively even though each individual movement is exposed, because that whole reveals more—sometimes a great deal more—than does the sum of its parts.*[58]

The decision shows that, although it may be legal for government to carry out a GPS tracking of single trips in public spaces, the aggregation of numerous trips over the course of a month becomes illegal because it reveals more private information than the individual constituent parts (individual trips or locations). In other words, individuals may not have a reasonable expectation of privacy for their single public movements, but an aggregation of these single public movements could create a reasonable expectation of privacy. The decision of the appellate court was reviewed by the Supreme Court on *certiorari* and resolved on the grounds of physical trespass due to the installation of the GPS on private property, that is the car.[59] Although the unconstitutionality of the mere installation precluded the Supreme Court from entertaining the issue of 'aggregation' in greater detail, Justices Alito and Sotomayor concurred with the DC Circuit Court's stance that citizens could invoke a reasonable expectation of privacy regarding aggregated data—ie the whole—despite the lack thereof in the individual trips that constitute the whole.[60] This stance is further confirmed by the Supreme Court in *Carpenter*.[61]

Carpenter is factually similar to *Jones* but addresses the third-party doctrine under the US Constitution. The US Supreme Court has historically held that information that an individual voluntarily hands over to a third party (eg to a telecom provider) is not protected by the Fourth Amendment.[62] This allows the government to obtain such information without a warrant supported by probable cause as

[57] The lower court accepted Mr Jones's challenge to track the location of the vehicle on Mr Jones's private premises without a warrant but considered the tracking on public roads as lawful, citing the Supreme Court decision in *United States v Knotts* 460 Supreme Court (1983) 277.

[58] *US v Maynard* (n 52) 558 (emphasis added).

[59] See *US v Jones* (n 50) 949.

[60] Justice Alito reasoned that short-term tracking of a person's public movements is not protected under the Fourth Amendment but a longer term could be: ibid 964 (Alito J concurring).

[61] *Carpenter v US* 585 Supreme Court (2018) 2217–21.

[62] See *Smith v Maryland*, 442 Supreme Court (1979) 735.

the Fourth Amendment requires. In this case, the defendant, Timothy Carpenter, was accused of robbery. In the course of the investigation, the police had obtained more than five months of location record, known as cell-site location information (CSLI), from his wireless carrier, without a warrant.[63] The request generated 12,898 location points in total, showing Carpenter's location during call origination and termination during this period.[64] Of those, four location points indicated that Carpenter was near the robbery sites.[65] The police used this data to charge Carpenter with robbery and carrying a firearm during a federal crime of violence. Given that the government can, under the third-party doctrine, access data in the hands of telecom providers, the question was, as in *Jones*, whether 'more is different'. More pointedly, the question was whether the warrantless obtention of cell-phone location data over the course of 127 days created a reasonable expectation of privacy that warranted protection under the Fourth Amendment.

In the lower courts, Carpenter moved to suppress the police's access to CSLI, claiming that the government's seizure of these records violated his Fourth Amendment rights. The District Court denied the motion, and the Sixth Circuit upheld the decision, citing the third-party doctrine under the US Constitution.[66] The Sixth Circuit held that although the content of personal communication is private, the metadata (ie information necessary to get that content from point A to point B) is not.[67] According to the Court, since CSLI records only provide information about which cell towers a phone connected to at specific times and that the defendants had voluntarily revealed their location data to the phone company, the subsequent seizure of that data was not in violation of the Fourth Amendment.[68] However, the US Supreme Court overturned the Sixth Circuit's decision and held that Carpenter had a reasonable expectation of privacy with regard to the CSLI data, even though the data was held by a third party.[69]

The Supreme Court distinguished between rudimentary tracking of an individual's movements and more sweeping modes of surveillance.[70] The Court recognized that the third-party doctrine allows the government to obtain a pen register from a phone company, which tells law enforcement the phone numbers an individual dialled, without triggering Fourth Amendment protections. Given that such pen registers have 'limited capabilities', it is unlikely that people have an actual expectation of privacy concerning the numbers they dial.[71] However, the

[63] The government obtained the records based on court orders under the Stored Communications Act, which, unlike the Fourth Amendment, does not require a finding of probable cause: *Carpenter v US* (n 61) 2210–11.
[64] ibid 2212.
[65] ibid 2213.
[66] *US v Carpenter*, 819 F.3d (6th Cir 2016) 880.
[67] ibid 887–88.
[68] ibid 884–88.
[69] *Carpenter v US* (n 61) 2216–21.
[70] ibid 2215.
[71] ibid 2216 (citing *Smith v Maryland* (n 62) 743).

Court differentiated CSLI data from pen register and likened the collection of CSLI data to GPS monitoring because of how detailed the information is and how effortlessly it can be compiled. In so doing, the Court emphasized the risks associated with the CSLI data as opposed to rudimentary tracking of an individual as follows:

> While the third-party doctrine applies to telephone numbers and bank records, it is not clear whether its logic extends to the *qualitatively* different category of cell-site records. After all, when Smith was decided in 1979, few could have imagined a society in which a phone goes wherever its owner goes, conveying to the wireless carrier not just dialed digits, but a detailed and comprehensive record of the person's movements.[72]

Accordingly, the Court considered that CSLI data was 'qualitatively different' from information in pen register because it could provide an 'intimate window into a person's life, revealing not only his particular movements, but through them his familial, political, professional, religious, and sexual associations'.[73] Because of the 'the unique nature of cell-site records', the Court declined to extend third-party doctrine to such data and held that the government was required to get a warrant.[74] The Court's reasoning echoes the claim in 'More Is Different' by Anderson, that a change in scale or quantity can transform into a qualitative change in terms of the behaviour of a system.[75] Overall, both the DC Circuit Court judgment in *Jones* and the US Supreme Court judgment in *Carpenter* recognize the emergence of a property (ie reasonable expectation of privacy) in the sum of individuals' public movements or third-party held data despite the absence of such a feature in the constituent parts.

The above discussion demonstrates the important role emergent properties can play in law. It provides a framework to conceptualize how complexity and emergence might arise in the legal context. More specifically, it shows how a change in scale or quantity can transform into a qualitative change that raises new legal questions. Moreover, the concept provides vocabulary with which to refer to the dangers of wrongfully attributing the properties of constituent parts to the system as a whole, known as the fallacy of composition. In this sense, the qualification handed down by the US Supreme Court in *Carpenter* to the longstanding third-party doctrine can be partly explained by emergence and the desire to avoid the fallacy of composition.

Furthermore, emergence offers valuable lessons on how to deal with attribution challenges arising from complex systems with multiple interacting components.

[72] *Carpenter v US* (n 61) 2216–17 (emphasis added).
[73] ibid 2222.
[74] ibid 2209, 2223.
[75] Philip Anderson, 'More Is Different: Broken Symmetry and the Nature of the Hierarchical Structure of Science' (1972) 177 Science 393, 393.

This can be achieved, in part, by studying the interacting components as a collective whole. In law, this implies giving legal recognition, where possible, to the whole (emergent privacy risks). The above judgments from the US Supreme Court are examples of legal recognition given to an emergent behaviour (ie risk) arising from the sum of fully compliant behaviours. Thus, compared to the concepts of mosaic theory and quantitative privacy, which are confined to the Fourth Amendment discussions and government surveillance,[76] the notion of emergence provides broader and richer vocabulary for the different forms of emergence, the associated risks, and the solutions for mitigating them. The concept can be readily adapted to contexts beyond constitutional privacy under the European Convention on Human Rights (ECHR) and the US Fourth Amendment.[77]

In this chapter, the goal is to examine the extent to which the notion of emergent properties could be useful to conceptualize some of the challenges to the application of EU data privacy law, not only in light of government practices but also regarding the processing of personal data by private entities. As shown in Section III.B, the discussions in Section II concerning the different forms of complexity (such as summative, interrelation) and different levels of emergence (specific value, modest, and radical) provide a useful framework for understanding how emergence should be approached under EU data privacy law. Moreover, the concept offers useful guidance on potential solutions to address the identified challenges. Section III.B discusses the emerging data-processing practices that are common across different businesses, which may lead to the emergence of a property.

B. Data-Processing Practices Leading to Emergence

Key considerations in driving the EU and the US courts to embrace emergent thinking are the volume and variety of data and the aggregation of such data. In the same fashion, the motivation for using the concept of emergent property in data privacy law could be attributed to two emerging data-processing practices. The first relates to the growth in the number of entities that process individuals' personal data for a panoply of purposes. The increasing value of personal data for commercial reasons creates the desire to collect and amass as much personal data as possible, both through legitimate and illegitimate mechanisms; this leads to the emergence of companies processing vast amounts of personal data for a wide array of purposes. The second, but related, development pertains to big data practices that represent substantial value in the repurposing, recombining, and

[76] See the limitations of mosaic theory in Kerr (n 51).

[77] See discussions in Chapter 3, where the concept is also used to discuss some of the competition law challenges. For a detailed discussion of the importance of emergence and its application in other legal domains, see Samson Esayas, 'The Important Role of Emergence in Conceptualizing the Challenges of New Technologies to Private Law' (2023) 31 European Private Law Review 779.

multi-purposing of personal databases. These developments represent the emergence of a property (ie complexity) that is overlooked under current data privacy rules. As elaborated further below, these respective developments can be compared with the summative and interrelation aspects of a complex in discussions about emergent properties.

In data privacy, the summative aspect as a complex emerges when entities engage in multiple processing activities based on separate purposes. In the digital economy, the volume and quality of the personal data controlled by companies is becoming a key source of revenue and market power. Data could be used to improve the quality of goods/services, improve targeted advertising, personalize pricing, develop new services, and make better business decisions. Moreover, personal data can be bought, sold, and traded.

Such growing importance of personal data for commercial purposes, coupled with the ever-sinking cost of storage, is creating a drive for a 'digital land grab', shifting the priorities of organizations to collect and harness as much personal data as possible to maximize their market position.[78] This desire is being pursued using legitimate grounds, such as expanding to new product sectors and acquiring entities with valuable personal information. Google's aggressive expansion to a broad array of new product areas is a case in point, with its more than 100 services, 70 of which are 'free'. This number is not only a result of legitimate acquisitions but also controversial practices of nudging users to consume the new product or subscribe to the service launched. When launching its social networks, individuals with a Gmail account were automatically given a Buzz account (now defunct), and later, a Google+ account.[79] The result is a large pool of processing activities involving data that is collected legally and controversially.

This development gives rise to a complexity that does not exist when entities process personal data for a single or handful of purposes. This can be likened to the *summative* complexity in emergent property, where the 'whole can be understood as the *summation* of processing activities based on separate purposes' ('sum' hereinafter). The summative aspect is possibly one that gives rise to scepticism from proponents of the emergent property, mainly because the emergence is quantitative (value) rather than qualitative (kind).[80] However, this is not always the case. In the article entitled 'More Is Different', Philip Anderson, a Nobel laureate and individual credited for his significant contribution to the writings on emergent property, indicates that a change in scale or quantity often transforms into qualitative change in the behaviour of a system.[81] In his view, the summation of less

[78] White House, '*Big Data: Seizing Opportunities, Preserving Values*' (Executive Office of the President 2014) 54.

[79] See US Federal Trade Commission (FTC), 'FTC Charges Deceptive Privacy Practices in Google's Rollout of Its Buzz Social Network' (30 March 2011) <https://www.ftc.gov/news-events/news/press-releases/2011/03/ftc-charges-deceptive-privacy-practices-googles-rollout-its-buzz-social-network>.

[80] Kim (n 38) 191–92.

[81] Anderson (n 75) 393.

complicated pieces into a system can result in a new type of behaviour that raises new questions.[82]

Section III.A discussed the manner in which the judgments of the DC Circuit Court in *Jones* and the US Supreme Court in *Carpenter* address the question of whether more of a compliant behaviour gives rise to non-compliant behaviour, encapsulated by the phrase 'more is different'. These rulings recognize a privacy interest, specifically a reasonable expectation of privacy, in the sum of individuals' public movements or third-party held data, even when such a feature is absent in the individual components. Similarly, this characterization of the summative complex holds true for data privacy because there are privacy interests independent of the individual processing when an entity processes personal data for multiple (*n* number of) purposes, irrespective of any actual aggregation. This means that processing data for a wide array of purposes paints a different risk picture compared to processing for a single or handful of purposes. In other words, the sum has features (risk) that are different in kind (qualitative change) from the features in the individual processing activities, meeting the criteria for the modest form of emergence as defined in Section II. The modest form of emergent property is one where the whole displays features that are different in kind from those of its constituent parts.[83] Furthermore, the potential for aggregation exists, leading to the emergence of a new property through the combination of data across different processing activities. This property (complexity) that emerges due to data-aggregation practices can be likened to the interrelation aspect.

Chapter 1 highlighted the trend towards aggregating and combining data, which is a hallmark of big data practices. The aim of these practices is to derive value from scale (volume) and scope (variety) of data, which is absent in smaller data sets. However, equally important is the societal change that accompanies big data practices, especially society's shift from the static view of data, where data is collected for a singular purpose or one-off use, towards innovative and novel secondary uses.[84] According to Mayer-Schönberger and Cukier, the underlying logic with big data practices is that 'the sum is more valuable than its parts, and *when we recombine the sums of multiple datasets together, that sum too is worth more than its individual ingredients*'.[85] Thus, big data practices represent substantial value in the repurposing, recombining, and multi-purposing of personal databases. Such a practice of collecting data for multiple purposes, together with combining such data across data sets, creates another complexity that is not present when the processing of personal data is done in isolation. This complexity can be compared to the *interrelation* aspect of emergent property, where the whole can be understood

[82] ibid 396.
[83] Van Gulick (n 19) 17.
[84] See Chapter 1. Also Viktor Mayer-Schönberger and Kenneth Cukier, *Big Data: A Revolution That Will Transform How We Live, Work, and Think* (Houghton Mifflin Harcourt 2013) 96.
[85] ibid 108 (emphasis added).

as the 'interrelation of data sets collected for separate purposes' (here, 'wholeness'). The interrelation aspect emphasizes the importance of interaction among data sets collected based on separate purposes.[86]

This aspect of emergent property (ie wholeness) was exemplified when Google changed its privacy policy in 2012. Prior to this, Google had collected individuals' personal data in offering different services (under different accounts), that is for separate purposes. However, in March 2012, Google took the initiative to consolidate all its services under one account. Before the consolidation, Google claimed that a user's data from, for example, YouTube, Gmail, and Search were kept separately, at least in theory. Following the consolidation, Google was able to integrate user data from YouTube, Gmail, and virtually all other services to create a more comprehensive profile of each user. This profile embodies the concept of emergent property, as it holds more value for Google than the individual profiles kept under separate accounts. Nevertheless, it also poses risks that did not exist when data was stored in the individual accounts. In Europe, different stakeholders, including the Article 29 Working Party, have voiced their concerns about this issue. Some of these concerns are discussed in Section IV.

In light of the above discussions, the idea of emergent property in the context of data privacy can be approached from two interrelated angles: the first angle is wholeness, which involves multiple processing activities based on separate purposes with interactive elements among them, such as aggregation. The second angle is the summative aspect, which represents the scope of the processing activities in which an entity undertakes, as measured by the sum, based on separate purposes without an actual interactive element among them, but with the potential to include such an element. Figure 2.2 depicts the conceptual distinction between these two angles.[87]

Generally, for the purposes of data privacy, emergent property can be approached as a way of looking at multiple processing activities (n) as a single complex, where an entity aggregates data across the processing activities or has the potential to do so. This perspective enables the examination of privacy interests that arise in such a complex, independent of, or in combination with, the privacy interests in the individual processing activities. The question that follows is: what are the privacy interests involved in the wholeness and sum? Specifically, what

[86] More generally, from an information science perspective, the interrelation can be approached in what is referred to as *mutual information*: 'Mutual information quantifies the information processes going on between two elements A and B: intuitively, there is mutual information between A and B if A and B are able to affect one another's behavior': Bonabeau, Dessalles, and Grumbach, 'Characterizing Emergent Phenomena (2)' (n 25) 364. Thus, an interrelation is considered to exist between two data sets collected for different purposes if new information, unbeknownst to the two data sets, can be derived from them or the data sets affect each other in any other way.

[87] Nonetheless, the distinction between the notions of wholeness and summative aspects remains relatively insubstantial, as it is customary for organizations to amalgamate data across processing activities or possess the potential to do so. Consequently, they are regarded as both wholeness and sum.

privacy interests are there when Google processes personal data through 100 separate purposes ($n = 100$) insofar as each processing activity is compliant? Section IV undertakes the task of answering this question.

IV. Privacy Interests in Wholeness and Sum

The term 'privacy interest' is used to denote the concerns and values that data privacy rules seek to protect.[88] While some of the concerns identified in this section are not new, current data privacy rules may not fully address them, necessitating further consideration. Others are existing concerns that are exacerbated by the emerging data-processing practices discussed above, and as such, efforts are made to link the concerns to these data-processing practices.

One may be tempted to argue that the larger the wholeness and sum become (number of processing activities based on separate purposes—n), the less individual privacy there is. This is especially true when data is combined across different processing activities. The retort to this argument is that if each processing is compliant with data privacy rules, there should be no need for concern about the wholeness and sum of the processing activities based on distinct purposes. This is a way of arguing that since all the parts of a system are compliant, so is the system as a collective whole. A judge in the DC Circuit Court made a similar argument in the *Jones* judgment, stating that '[t]he sum of an infinite number of zero-value parts is also zero'.[89] Put differently, the legitimacy of each activity (the constituent part of the whole) legitimizes the plurality (the whole). However, this reasoning succumbs to a well-known error in the discussions about emergent property, namely the 'fallacy of composition',[90] where the properties of the constituent parts of a system (compliance in this case) are erroneously attributed to the system as a whole. As Section III.A and the US Supreme Court decision in *Carpenter* demonstrate, the sum of fully compliant behaviours may contain emergent properties and so create a non-compliant behaviour. Thus, *Carpenter* overturns the fallacious argument that '[t]he sum of an infinite number of zero-value parts is also zero'.

It is important to note that the argument in this chapter is not that wholeness and sum always violates data privacy law. Rather, there are privacy interests that necessitate some regulatory oversight independent of, and/or in combination with, the individual processing activity, particularly where companies process personal

[88] For more, see Lee Bygrave, *Data Protection Law: Approaching Its Rationale, Logic and Limits* (Kluwer Law International 2002) especially ch 7.

[89] *United States v Jones*, 625 F.3d (DC Cir 2010) 766, 769 (Sentelle J dissenting).

[90] William Rowe, 'The Fallacy of Composition' (1962) 71 Mind 87, 87.

data through a wide array of services and the data is combined across these processing activities. The following sections discuss these privacy interests in more detail.

A. Protection against Overexposure of Individuals

This section examines how the practices of processing personal data for multiple purposes, together with data aggregation across processing activities, can lead to the overexposure of individuals. This overexposure undermines their personal autonomy, integrity, and dignity, which are interests that data privacy rules seek to safeguard.[91] More specifically, the interest in protection against overexposure is closely related to what Bygrave refers to as Group 2 interests, particularly 'non-transparency (i.e. a person's interest in avoiding being rendered transparent vis-a-vis other persons and organizations)'.[92]

The focus of the current rules on 'individual processing' activity means that they overlook the overexposure and transparency of the individual resulting from the totality of the data collected through various processing operations and combinations of data across these different processing operations. Again, with nearly 100 processing activities at its disposal, Google is a good example.

Apart from the personal information collected during product or service registration, as part of its YouTube service, Google collects data on users' video preferences, likes, and dislikes. As part of its Search, Google gains insights into the different interest of users, such as the products they are interested in purchasing or health concerns they may have. Google also has access to users' contact lists, locations, and schedules through services like Gmail, Groups, Calendar, and Maps. Android GPS tracks users' location even when no apps are running.[93] Credit card and bank information is accessible if an individual uses CheckOut or Google Wallet. Search, Gmail, Books, and Fitbit may contain health information. Browsing habits are monitored and recorded through Chrome. What users write (and think) is scanned from Gmail attachments, Google Drive, and Dropbox. Millions of mobiles run on Google Android. Through its Nest Cam, Google is promising users to look after their homes and families 24/7, even when they are away.[94] Through its Analytics service, Google collects the browsing habits of individuals from millions of third-party websites. The list goes on: there is hardly anything that Google does not do or plan to do.[95]

[91] See Bygrave, *Data Protection Law* (n 88) ch 7.

[92] ibid 150.

[93] The Norwegian Consumer Ombudsman, 'Out of Control: How Consumers Are Exploited by the Online Advertising Industry' (14 January 2020).

[94] Nest Cam website <https://nest.com/ie/camera/meet-nest-cam> accessed 7 February 2024.

[95] This includes smart fabric, contact lenses, and watches. See Zach Miners, 'Google's Project Jacquard to Make Smart Fabric for Smart Clothing, Levi's First Official Partner', *PC World* (29 May 2015).

Organizations may also resort to controversial methods of collecting data that provide valuable insights about consumers. For instance, the Google Street View Project accessed the communication of individuals transmitted over Wi-Fi networks in many countries, which led to fines and confiscation of properties in some cases, such as North Korea.[96] It is claimed that this access was deliberately designed to obtain data deemed instrumental for the success of Google Maps and self-driving cars.[97]

Thus, given the omnipresence of Google, even the usage of a fraction of these services creates a transparent data subject, an individual who exposes significant aspects of his or her life willingly to use the services. In using them, data relating to the usage of the services, clicks, and even cursor hovers over links, are monitored, recorded, analysed, and combined, often with little or no knowledge on the user's part. This collection of personal data through multiple channels and its combination overexposes individuals, threatening their personal autonomy, integrity, and dignity.

There is a growing consensus that the above practices amount to data-driven surveillance, with all its associated risks. Surveillance studies scholar David Lyon argues that big data practices amplify surveillance by rendering people's 'everyday lives increasingly transparent to large organizations'.[98] Omer further observes that these practices represent an omnipresent and indiscriminate form of surveillance, and there is no reason to treat it differently.[99] One expert described Google's main business as 'for-profit intelligence', conducting an 'espionage operation on a global scale'.[100] Google itself admits to the pervasive surveillance of individuals.[101] This is not limited to Google. Facebook accumulates troves of personal data by tracking every digital move of its users.[102] Unlike Google, Facebook has perfected the ability to solicit a wide array of data using simple features and make it appear as if all the data collected falls under the umbrella of a single service—justifying their processing using only one specific (and legitimate?) purpose. The dangers of surveillance are widely discussed elsewhere and need not be reiterated here.[103] The key point is that individuals are overexposed to private entities. Therefore, this

[96] See Mark Burdon and Alissa McKillop, 'The Google Street View Wi-Fi Scandal and Its Repercussions for Privacy Regulation' (2014) 39 Monash University Law Review 702.

[97] See Yasha Levine, 'Google's For-Profit Surveillance Problem', *Pando* (16 December 2013).

[98] See David Lyon, 'Surveillance, Snowden, and Big Data: Capacities, Consequences, Critique' (2014) 1 Big Data & Society, 4. Bruce Schneier, *Data and Goliath: The Hidden Battles to Collect Your Data and Control Your World* (WW Norton & Co 2015) 4.

[99] Omer Tene, 'What Google Knows: Privacy and Internet Search Engines' (2008) 4 Utah Law Review 1433.

[100] Yasha Levine, 'The Psychological Dark Side of Gmail: Google Is Using Its Popular Gmail Service to Build Profiles on the Hundreds of Millions of People Who Use It', *AlterNet* (31 December 2013).

[101] See Nick Saint, 'Google CEO: "We Know Where You Are. We Know Where You've Been. We Can More Or Less Know What You're Thinking About"', *Business Insider* (4 Oct 2010).

[102] Bernard Harcourt, *Exposed: Desire and Disobedience in the Digital Age* (Harvard UP 2015) 2–5.

[103] See, eg Neil Richards, 'The Dangers of Surveillance' (2013) 126 Harvard Law Review 1934; Paul Schwartz, 'Privacy and Democracy in Cyberspace' (1999) 52 Vanderbilt Law Review 1607.

section focuses on how this overexposure can give rise to problems from an EU data privacy perspective.

A central objective of the data privacy rules is allowing the individual to selectively self-disclose his or her information based on free choice, referred to as information self-determination, thereby preventing undue interference in his or her autonomy, integrity, and dignity. This ensures the protection of the individual from 'manipulation or control by others'.[104] However, the more exposed an individual becomes, the easier it is to 'force his obedience' and suppress the capacity to make free choices.[105] Such limitless knowledge of the individual transforms into a significant power imbalance, where entities (private and government) become 'omnipotent parents and the rest of society … helpless children', giving the entities the ability to define who they are and who they should become.[106] Overall, overexposure makes individuals powerless, turning them into predictable citizen-consumers who can easily be stimulated and nudged to serve profit-maximizing goals.[107] This reality undermines the essence of an individual's autonomy, integrity, and dignity, which data privacy rules—at least in the EU context—are meant to safeguard.[108]

It is important to note the link between the scope of the processing activity in which an entity is involved and the resulting exposure of individuals. The greater the number of processing activities due to the wide array of services or products, the more exposed the individuals become, especially if there is a possibility of combining data across these processing activities. This increased overexposure makes it more difficult for the individuals to control self-disclosure and exercise free choice. For example, one study claims that firms that offer diverse services (ie more economy of scope) find it easier to convince consumers to consent than new entrants and small and medium enterprises (SMEs) do.[109] It could be argued that the more services consumers use from an entity, the more they come to trust the company, making it easier for the company to obtain consent. However, this claim bears little relation to reality. According to a Eurobarometer survey, 63 per cent of Europeans do not trust online businesses like search engines.[110] Thus, concerning

[104] Bygrave, *Data Protection Law* (n 88) 133–34.

[105] Paul Schwartz and Joel Reidenberg, *Data Privacy Law* (Michie 1996) 39; Daniel Solove, 'Privacy and Power: Computer Databases and Metaphors for Information Privacy,' (2001) 53 Stanford Law Review 1393, 1396.

[106] Schwartz and Reidenberg (n 105) 39; Solove, 'Privacy and Power' (n 105) 1396.

[107] Julie Cohen, 'What Privacy Is for' (2012) 126 Harvard Law Review 1904, 1919.

[108] See discussions in Bygrave, *Data Protection Law* (n 88) 125ff. However, the danger of overexposure goes beyond just privacy interests. For example, Cohen (n 107) argues that overexposure and transparency can impair one's ability to freely tinker and experiment, which are essential for innovation and self-development.

[109] James Campbell, Avi Goldfarb, and Catherine Tucker, 'Privacy Regulation and Market Structure' (2015) 24 Journal of Economics & Management Strategy 47.

[110] Special Eurobarometer 431, 'Data Protection' (Directorate General for Communication 2015) 63 <https://dataeuropa.eu/data/datasets/s2075_83_1_431_eng?locale=en> accessed 13 February 2024.

digital services, an alternative explanation could be that when consumers use diverse services from a single entity, they become so dependent that they develop a sense of helplessness, rendering them incapable of withholding consent.[111] Even more significant is the claim by Schwartz and Reidenberg that the more the company knows the individual, the more ability it has to force the individual's obedience and suppress free choice.[112]

Experiments by Facebook highlight the power that such private entities have gained to impose social control over their users. Facebook triggered outcries for manipulating users' behaviours through two separate experiments.[113] Beyond the concerns of conducting the studies without users' knowledge,[114] the experiments demonstrated how easily the social network, with its deep knowledge of individuals' personal details, can influence users' moods and even their voting behaviours.[115] The first example suffices for our purpose. In the emotional contagion experiment, Facebook classified the moods conveyed by users' updates using an algorithm. Then, a user or group of users was shown updates on the Newsfeed conveying a specific mood. To do this, Facebook had to algorithmically suppress updates that did not convey the relevant emotion. In this way, Facebook was able to influence the users' moods, meaning that the more the users were exposed to updates conveying a positive mood, the more positive posts (and fewer negative posts) these users produced, and vice versa.[116] Similarly, omitting both positive and negative emotional content from the user's Newsfeed reduced the number of words the person subsequently produced.[117]

One could just look at the Facebook experiment as a well-intended study aimed at contributing to academic discussion. However, a closer look reveals a clear commercial interest in understanding the causal effect of one friend's mood (or a group of friends' moods) on another person's mood or behaviour. Such knowledge would be immensely valuable in terms of targeted advertising, allowing Facebook to show ads to users based on the actions and behaviours of their friends.[118] In

[111] ibid 7 (noting that a large majority of Europeans [71 per cent] 'say that providing personal information is an increasing part of modern life and accept that there is no alternative other than to provide it if they want to obtain products or services').

[112] Schwartz and Reidenberg (n 105) 39.

[113] Adam Kramer, Jamie Guillory, and Jeffrey Hancock, 'Experimental Evidence of Massive-Scale Emotional Contagion through Social Networks' (2014) 111 Proceedings of the National Academy of Sciences 8788.

[114] Interestingly, in their study on emotional contagion, the authors claim that users agreed to such experiments when they expressed their consent to use the service: see ibid. The authors later apologized for the possible misunderstanding and anxiety created due to the research results. See 'Facebook Emotion Experiment Sparks Criticism', (*BBC*, 30 June 2014) <https://www.bbc.com/news/technology-28051930> accessed 8 March 2024.

[115] Robert Bond and others, 'A 61-Million-Person Experiment in Social Influence and Political Mobilization' (2012) 489 Nature 295.

[116] Kramer, Guillory, and Hancock (n 113) 8788.

[117] ibid 8789.

[118] For example, it is common practice for Facebook to show products or services based on friends' 'likes'.

2018, Facebook added a new feature that allows users to prioritize posts from family and friends, yet another attempt to nudge users to reveal their social connections and gain insight into users' personal and family lives. One could not help but wonder if this new feature was connected to Facebook's earlier study on users' mood. While there is no evidence to support this theory, it is easy to suspect that Facebook is strategically seeking to understand which individuals users are most sensitive to and how to better influence them. Facebook seems to have realized that the more it knows the individual, the more it can influence and persuade the individual.

Despite the significant risks associated with the collection of vast amounts of personal data, through expansion into multiple processing operations (Google) or through simple features and persistent nagging for information (Facebook), data privacy law still focuses on addressing risks associated with the individual processing operation, without considering the broader scope and total number of processing activities undertaken by these companies. This narrow perspective fails to adequately address the risk of overexposure from data collection through a multitude of processing operations, which can undermine an individual's autonomy, integrity, and dignity.

Taking Google as an example, the focus on individual processing activity means that compliance with the data privacy rules, for example, in relation to Gmail, will be evaluated independently, as will be the processing of data in relation to Google Maps, YouTube, Search, and the remaining (nearly 100) Google services. This remains the case even though these services are consolidated into one account and the data collected is combined across them. This creates an institutional challenge as it becomes difficult for DPAs to draw the lines between the different processing activities based on a specific purpose and to attribute a set of data to a particular processing operation. The alternative is to try and find a purpose and legal basis under the umbrella of generic 'Google services', which essentially makes the purpose specification and limitation principle—and other principles that are built on it—ineffective, as is discussed in Section IV.B.

Furthermore, even assuming that DPAs can differentiate between distinct processing activities and assess the compliance of each processing operation, the atomized approach still overlooks the overexposure and related risks that emerge when entities are involved in multiple processing activities, where almost every use of the service generates personal data, and the data is combined across these processing activities. Thus, data privacy rules need to look beyond individual processing activities based on a specific purpose and encompass the full range of risks from the entirety of the data collected through expansion into a wide array of new product areas, acquisitions, and the combination of data from different sources. The holistic approach, discussed in Section V, addresses this need.

B. Loss of Transparency and Accountability

In addition to the risk of overexposure to individuals, the wholeness and sum of data collected also obscures the transparency and accountability of the entities that control the data. Specifically, current accountability and transparency mechanisms based on the purpose limitation principle begin to falter when entities merge data across various services based on distinct purposes. The purpose limitation principle is of fundamental importance for the general application of data privacy rules and their compliance.[119] This principle is central in the application of the core data privacy principles under Article 5(1) of the GDPR, as discussed in Section I. Both transparency and accountability are essential elements of the purpose limitation principle. Having a specific and explicit purpose for processing enables data controllers to be transparent about how they use personal data, both to regulators and data subjects, ensuring the accountability of entities processing personal data.

Transparency refers to the openness of entities processing personal data with both data subjects and regulators on what data is collected, for what purpose, and how they are used.[120] On the other hand, accountability relates to the responsibility of the parties, particularly the controller, to implement and demonstrate compliance with the data privacy principles enshrined under the GDPR.[121] However, the aggregation of data across different services or products obscures transparency in terms of what data has been collected, for which purpose(s), and whether the data is necessary for that (those) purpose(s). Similarly, assessing whether a certain reuse of data is compatible with original purposes becomes challenging. These challenges, in turn, make it difficult to hold the controller accountable for non-compliance with the rules. The following paragraphs discuss these issues in light of the two notions of the purpose limitation principle: purpose specification and compatibility.

1. Purpose Specification

The notion of purpose specification comprises of three aspects: specificity, explicitness, and legitimacy. Specificity emphasizes the need for a precise and sufficiently defined purpose for collecting of personal data that must be determined prior to, or at the latest during, data collection.[122] The explicitness requirement aims to ensure that the purpose is expressed unambiguously and communicated in an intelligible manner so that all relevant stakeholders can understand. Legitimacy requires

[119] WP203 (n 4) 4 (describing the principle as the 'cornerstone of data protection'); see also Lee Bygrave, *Data Privacy Law: An International Perspective* (OUP 2014) 153.

[120] See GDPR (n 3), Articles 12–14 and Recital 39.

[121] Thus, accountability implies an obligation to do the following: (1) adopt concrete and practical measures for the implementation of the core data privacy principles and do so in a verifiable manner, (2) ensure that these measures are effective, and (3) assume liability when the relevant measures are not taken or are ineffective.

[122] See GDPR (n 3), Recital 39.

that the purpose should not be contrary to the law, including both the GDPR and other applicable laws. Among other aims, having a specific, explicit, and legitimate purpose ensures the transparency and accountability of the controller to both regulators and data subjects on how the data is used.[123] This, in turn, ensures legal certainty and predictability. Additionally, purpose specification enables users to make informed decisions about their data, thereby strengthening users' control over their data. Article 12 of the GDPR further reinforces the transparency obligation by imposing an obligation on data controllers to provide data subjects with information regarding the categories of data under processing, the purpose of the processing, potential recipients, and the retention period of the data. However, when data is combined across multiple services based on separate purposes, the words 'specific' and 'explicit' start to lose meaning, and transparency becomes an inconvenience. This occurs because the outcome is either information overload or the deliberate use of vague terminology ('confusology').

In its opinion on purpose specification, the Article 29 Working Party made clear that the use of phrases like 'improving users' experience', 'marketing purposes', 'IT-security purposes' or 'future research' do not meet the specificity criteria.[124] Nevertheless, Google resorted to such vague terminologies in its privacy policy when consolidating its services under one account, leading to fines from the Spanish DPA. The DPA noted that despite the company processing data through nearly 100 services, it failed to provide adequate information about what data was collected and the purpose for which it was used.[125] The use of ambiguous language, such as 'improving users' experience', was particularly unhelpful to users and resulted in a policy that was 'indeterminate and unclear'.[126] This lack of clarity creates challenges in the enforcement of the rules.

In the absence of a sufficiently clear and explicit purpose for processing (in other words, a lack of transparency), users cannot exercise effective control over their data or provide meaningful consent. The French DPA's investigation found that Google's consolidated privacy policy was too vague to form a basis for meaningful consent.[127] This lack of clarity distorts the legal certainty and predictability envisioned by purpose specification. As noted by the German Constitutional Court,[128] in a world where 'individuals can no longer ascertain who knows what about them', the right to information self-determination remains elusive.

Furthermore, having a specific and explicit purpose provides evidence of the original purpose, a necessary prerequisite for ensuring accountability.[129] This is

[123] WP203 (n 4) 18.
[124] ibid 13.
[125] AEPD (n 12).
[126] ibid.
[127] Linklaters, 'EU-Coordinated Enforcement Action over Google's New Privacy Policy', 67 *Technology Media and Telecommunications* (January 2014) .
[128] German Constitutional Court on the Census Act 15 December 1983 (BVERFGE 65, 1), cited in Albrecht Philipp, *Hands Off Our Data* (Knaur Taschenbuch 2015).
[129] WP203 (n 4) 15.

because the existence of a specific and explicit purpose is essential for the regulators to assess compliance with the relevant principles, such as the legality of the processing; whether the data collected is the minimum necessary, relevant, and adequate for the specific purpose; whether the duration of the processing is necessary for the purpose; and whether the security measures are appropriate. Similarly, having a specific and explicit purpose allows data subjects to exercise their rights towards the controller. However, if the purpose of the processing is not distinctly and specifically conveyed to the relevant stakeholders, it becomes challenging for both regulators and individuals to hold entities accountable for noncompliance. If an entity consolidates 100 services in a single account and combines data across these services, any data collection or processing will be relevant for one service or another within an extensive array of purposes.

Two examples can be illustrative here regarding the accountability problems of aggregation. First, under the EU rules, the processing of sensitive personal data is subject to stricter requirements than that of non-sensitive personal data. For example, if consent is the basis for processing, for non-sensitive data, the consent must be 'unambiguous',[130] whereas 'explicit' consent is needed if it involves the processing of sensitive personal data per Article 9(2(a)). The latter is a higher standard than unambiguous consent is. The stricter requirements are not limited to consent as such, but the 'appropriateness' of the security measures pursuant to Article 32 need to be assessed in light of the sensitivity of the data. However, at the centre of the concept of emergent property is that, when combined, the data tells a story that one would not be able to glean from the individual components. Accordingly, the combination of non-sensitive personal data could give rise to the emergent property of sensitive personal data.[131] Such data can only be processed in line with the stricter legal requirements.

Despite the above, given that the sensitivity emerges at a later point than the initial collection or exists independently of the individual processing activities based on a specific purpose, controllers may continue to treat such data as non-sensitive and avoid complying with the stricter requirements. This is not a mere theoretical claim. Despite its apparent disclaimer for not using sensitive data to serve ads, Google was found to be in breach of the Canadian Health Privacy Law and fined for targeting people with health-care ads based on their search topics. Like the EU law, the Canadian law distinguishes between 'express consent', which is required when processing health (sensitive) data, as opposed to 'implied consent' in the case of non-sensitive personal data.[132] The case demonstrates that Google continued

[130] GDPR (n 3), Article 6(1[a]) cum Article 4(11).

[131] For discussions on how a combination of innocuous data could reveal intimate details and raise privacy concerns, see Internet Society, 'The Internet of Things: An Overview—Understanding the Issues and Challenges of a More Connected World' (2015) 26, <www.internetsociety.org/doc/iot-overview> accessed 7 February 2024.

[132] Office of the Privacy Commissioner of Canada, 'Report of Findings: Use of Sensitive Health Information for Targeting of Google Ads Raises Privacy Concerns' (14 January 2014) <www.priv.gc.ca/

to process sensitive personal data, which emerged from a combination of search queries, without complying with the stricter requirements.

Although this case seems to show that the current rules can capture the data-aggregation practices, its scope remains limited to the individual processing activity for search purposes. That the aggregation was limited to a single processing activity (ie Search) makes it easier to detect non-compliance. In other words, Google's breach was essentially related to the legal basis for the specific processing activity rather than arising from processing activities for multiple purposes. The atomistic nature of the rules' application means that it becomes more problematic when the sensitivity exists independently of the individual processing, that is when the sensitivity is a result of the combination of data from different processing operations. This is mainly due to the absence of a framework for looking at the totality of the processing activities and data-aggregation practices.

The second accountability-related problem arises where the rights and protections of individuals can vary depending on the legal basis used for collection. An example can be found in the GDPR's data portability right. One aspect of the data portability right is enabling the data subject to transmit personal data and other information provided by the subject from one automated processing system to another. An essential trigger of this right is that the legal basis for processing should be based on either *consent* (Article 6(1(a))) or *contract* (Article 6(1(b)))—meaning that processing based on the legitimate interests of the controller or vital interest of the data subject does not give rise to such right. When data initially collected with a diversity of legal bases is aggregated, this obscures the rights of the data subject that are linked to a specific legal basis. For example, in its reply to the French DPA's questionnaire, Google identified the use of one or more of Articles 6(1(a) (consent), 6(1((b) (contract), and 6(1((f) (legitimate interest of the controller) in processing personal data. While the data collected under the first two legal grounds is subject to the data portability rights, that collected under the third is not. When data collected through these different legitimate grounds is combined under one account, it may be challenging to distinguish which data is collected based on which legitimate ground and whether that data is subject to the data portability or any other rights. This can create difficulties in enforcing these rights.

2. Purpose Limitation (Compatible Use)

The notion of compatible use prohibits further processing of personal data for purposes incompatible with the original purpose. This principle is important because it ensures that the processing of data remains foreseeable and does not exceed the

en/opc-actions-and-decisions/investigations/investigations-into-businesses/2014/pipeda-2014-001> accessed 7 February 2024.

reasonable expectations of individuals.[133] Thus, the purpose limitation principle reinforces the principle of fairness. However, the combination of data across services makes it difficult to assess whether certain uses of data are compatible. This is related to the above-described challenge, that is that the notion of purpose specification becomes obscured, making it difficult to assess whether the reuse of data is incompatible with the initial purpose or every reuse of data becomes compatible owing to the large pools of purposes and their combinations.

Google-like consolidation initiatives seem to be a strategic evasion of data privacy principles. According to Google, the main goal of the consolidation into one account is using data collected in one service for providing another service. The difference between the pre-and post-2012 policies is all but clearly spelled out by Google. Before 2012, independent services and policies

> meant that we couldn't combine data from YouTube and search history with other Google products and services to make them better. So if a user who likes to cook searches for recipes on Google, we are not able to recommend cooking videos when that user visits YouTube.... We wanted to change that so we can create a simpler, more intuitive Google experience—to share more of each user's information with that user as they use various Google services.[134]

This assertion appears to resemble an overt admission of violating the purpose limitation principle. It is seemingly tantamount to stating that, prior to the 2012 policy change, Google adhered to the purpose limitation principle but ceased to do so afterwards. The most intriguing aspect of the claim is that, according to Google, the inability to merge data from disparate services primarily resulted from its policy not being formulated to execute this action, rather than the purpose limitation principle mandating such behaviour. Indeed, the further processing of data for another purpose alone does not constitute a breach of the compatibility aspect, and thus, the question arises as to whether the use of search data is compatible with the purpose of a YouTube search. Given that both services facilitate searching, there is room for arguing that the use might be compatible. However, as noted by the Spanish DPA, the combination and reuse of data collected from one service to another are not limited to Search and YouTube.[135]

In assessing whether the further processing of data is compatible with the original purpose, consideration must be given to different factors, especially the reasonable expectation to privacy of the data subjects.[136] However, the idea of having a consolidated privacy framework for 100+ different services is in tension with the

[133] Bygrave, *Data Privacy Law* (n 119) 153.
[134] See Google Official Blog (n 14).
[135] AEPD (n 12) 2.
[136] WP203 (n 4) 16.

reasonable expectations of data subjects associated with each processing. Given the different nature of the services, individuals have different expectations of security and privacy, which are often translated into the measures they are willing to take to protect their interests. An individual's privacy expectations may not be the same when he or she creates a YouTube account over an email account. Arguably, the individual will have higher expectations of privacy for the email services. This expectation is likely to have effects on the time and effort the individual is willing to invest in protecting his or her privacy and security, including the time and effort related to using strong passwords and selecting privacy preferences.[137] A combination of such accounts associated with different expectations of privacy and security into a single account confuses those different expectations and may result in the user settling for the lower standard of protection.[138]

Furthermore, the combination of data from across services opens the door for using the data for 'multiple purposes that are not clearly determined', violating the restriction on incompatible use. Particularly, the Spanish DPA emphasized the following:

> This combination of data across services that allows Google to enrich the personal information it stores, exceeds the reasonable expectations of the average user, who is not aware of the mass and transversal nature of the processing of their data. Acting in this way Google uses a sophisticated technology that exceeds the capacity of the majority of users to make conscious decisions about the use of their personal information so that, in practice, they lose control over it.[139]

The decisions from the Spanish and French DPAs may seem to suggest that the current rules can capture the data-aggregation practices, which apparently contradicts the claim in this chapter that the atomized approach is inadequate in light of the aggregation practices. In the above decision, the Spanish DPA was not referring to a breach related to a specific processing operation but to how the 'combination of data across services . . . exceeds the reasonable expectations of the average user' and how 'Google uses a sophisticated technology that exceeds the capacity of the majority of users to make conscious decisions'. Thus, the breach was attributed to the 'totality of the processing operations', rather than a 'single processing' activity. The

[137] During the 2012 consolidation initiative, Google was criticized for its failure to distinguish 'the innocuous content of search queries . . . from more intrusive types of data such as credit card details or data on telephone communications'; see Linklaters (n 127).

[138] See Scott Cleland, 'The Unique Google Privacy Problem: Why Google's Forced Integrated Privacy Policy Is So Problematic?' (25 October 2012) <www.precursorblog.com/?q=content/unique-google-privacy-problem-my-presentation-korean-privacy-council-seoul> accessed 7 February 2024 (commenting that 'Google's forced integrated privacy policy de-sovereignizes privacy policymaking and pushes the world towards lowest common denominator privacy standards').

[139] AEPD (n 12).

reference to 'reasonable expectations' of users implies that the Spanish DPA relied on the fairness principle to condemn Google's conduct.

The decision shows the flexibility of some of the principles, such as the fairness principle, for looking beyond the privacy concerns of individuals within the specific processing activities. However, it is questionable that the DPA intended to depart from the atomized approach. It is plausible that Google's bold move of consolidating its different processing activities into seemingly one processing activity under the umbrella of 'Google services' made it easier to apply the fairness principle under these circumstances. If this is true, a more systematic aggregation of data across several processing operations (and without consolidating them under one account) could go undetected. Even if the intention was to depart from the atomized approach, such encouraging moves towards a holistic approach need to be strengthened by relevant tools and a theoretical framework for their consistent application. The lack of a clear legal and theoretical framework for dealing with such aggregation practices is partly to blame for the uncertainty and uncanny situation that followed Google's announcement of consolidating its processing operations.

It is to be recalled that, after Google's consolidation announcement, the Article 29 Working Party asked that the company postpone the consolidation until it could evaluate the implications, which Google ignored.[140] This was followed by the first round of questions intended for Google to clarify its data-handling practices, on which Google provided clarification that the Working Party found unsatisfactory.[141] The second round of questions was issued, which was again met by unsatisfactory and repetitive answers from Google.[142] Even more, in a move exposing the inadequacy of the current rules in dealing with aggregation across different processing activities, Google questioned the legal basis for such a review by the Working Party and its ultimate aim.[143] In October 2012, the Working Party found Google to be in breach of EU data privacy rules and issued recommendations requesting the implementation of changes to its privacy policies and practices within four months.[144] Yet, Google stood firm, and in April 2013, the Working Party announced that Google had not implemented the requested changes. This led to fines by national DPAs, including the Spanish and French DPAs.[145]

Case closed, one might say. Google was penalized for its breach, and similar practices would be handled in the same manner. However, there was one problem. The future compliance dimension was overlooked because Google-like aggregations have a perpetual effect on compliance with the data privacy

[140] Initiative for Competitive Online Market Place (ICOMP), 'The Google Privacy Investigation in Europe: Two Years On' (2014).
[141] ibid.
[142] ibid.
[143] See Google France's 'Updated Letter Regarding CNIL'S Questioners' (20 April 2012) 4 <https://www.datatilsynet.no/globalassets/global/english/google_answer_cnil_april_20th_2012.pdf>.
[144] ICOMP (n 140) 1.
[145] ibid 2.

rules in that they distort the very foundation on which the transparency and accountability mechanisms are built. As noted in Section I, the enforcement of the current rules heavily relies on the ability to distinguish among different processing activities, relate every piece of personal data to a particular processing, and assess the compliance of each processing activity in light of the data privacy principles. In contrast, Google-like aggregation practices blur the lines between different processing activities and make it difficult to attribute every piece of data to a particular processing. Such practices obscure the transparency in terms of what data has been collected, for which purpose(s), and whether the data is necessary for that (those) purpose(s). Similarly, assessing whether a certain reuse of data is or is not compatible with the original purposes becomes highly challenging, making it almost impossible to hold entities accountable for non-compliance with the data privacy rules. The losses of transparency and accountability, in turn, make it difficult for individuals to understand and enforce their rights.

Thus, unless the measures taken prevent aggregation from happening or restore the independent processing activities, it is not clear how the atomized approach continues to regulate such companies when there is no longer a clear line between the different boxes based on specific and legitimate purposes and the data that belongs in those boxes. In fact, in light of the above decisions of the Working Party and the Spanish and French DPAs, Google has been in continuous breach of the data privacy rules since it consolidated its services, with no apparent recourse. Furthermore, in light of the business value that aggregation practices add and the diminished transparency and accountability for companies going forward, paying fines for data-aggregation practices could become a worthwhile investment. This implies that, in the absence of a sufficiently deterring and proportionate measure, such practices could become deliberate strategies for circumventing the application of the data privacy rules. That is where the special responsibility regime discussed in Section V may be helpful.

C. Loss of Practical Obscurity

In its broadest sense, practical obscurity represents the cost and practical difficulties one encounters in obtaining and compiling information on the private lives of individuals or, more generally, intruding on a person's privacy. Practical obscurity has served privacy extensively owing to the costs and difficulties associated with following and recording every footstep an individual takes. However, with the ubiquity of smartphones connected to the Internet 24/7 and the sinking cost of storage, companies can track and record every digital footprint through an individual's mobile and browsing habits. The more data that is collected, recorded, and combined, the more practical obscurity becomes a lost cause.

Google-like consolidation and aggregation initiatives are the main culprits regarding the continuous weakening of the importance of practical obscurity. In an era where the capacities of hackers and thieves are boosted by computing power, security breaches are not uncommon, even in industries that invest heavily in information security.[146] The consolidation of data across services in general and the single account for many data sets collected for different services do not fit well with information security best practices of 'isolation' and 'compartmentalizing information' in order to prevent catastrophic breaches.[147] This means that Google's one-account principle creates a single point of failure and vulnerability. A hacker who manages to gain access into a user's Google account can potentially access the user's email communications, search history, and calendar. Thus, the consolidation reduces the cost of obtaining a user's detailed profile and aggravates the effect that a single security breach can have on individuals' rights.

Maintaining anonymity and pseudonymity also becomes extremely challenging. In its 2012 policy, Google declared that

> we may replace past names associated with your Google Account so that you are represented consistently across all our services. If other users already have your email, or other information that identifies you, we may show them your publicly visible Google Profile information, such as your name and photo.[148]

This means that individuals who deliberately use different names and credentials for different accounts can no longer remain anonymous and are forced to be identified, although this is not necessary for accessing the services. Therefore, the consolidation represents a regression in the level of data security and further weakens practical obscurity.

The problem is exacerbated when government security agencies access the databases of several organizations simultaneously, a phenomenon partially exemplified by the PRISM program. PRISM permits government agencies to access user data from companies like Google, Facebook, Microsoft, and Yahoo!. Having reviewed the files obtained from Snowden, Greenwald reported that the programme grants the NSA direct access to the servers of the participating providers 'without having to request them from the service providers and without having to obtain individual court orders'.[149] As reported by the *Washington Post*, 'government employees cleared for PRISM access may "task" the system and receive results from an Internet company without further interaction with the company's staff'.[150] By

146 Tene (n 99) 1456.

147 Cleland (n 138).

148 Google Official Blog (n 14).

149 Glenn Greenwald, 'NSA Prism Program Taps into User Data of Apple, Google and Others', *The Guardian* (7 June 2013).

150 Robert Jr O'Harrow, Ellen Nakashima, and Barton Gellman, 'U.S., Company Officials: Internet Surveillance Does Not Indiscriminately Mine Data', *Washington Post* (8 June 2013).

accessing different data sets simultaneously, such agencies can generate a more detailed profile than what companies like Google can generate by combining data across their extensive range of services. If, as demonstrated earlier, the profile from private entities endangers individuals' data privacy rights through overexposure, access by government authorities to the databases of several companies that possess detailed profiles of individuals can only exacerbate the problem. Importantly, the capacity to access such profiles presents the possibility for governments to circumvent constitutional safeguards aimed at protecting privacy.

In an article entitled 'The Transparent Citizen',[151] Reidenberg cites a US example in which the federal government sought information about pornography and issued subpoenas to the five largest search engines, ordering them to log files for all user search requests during a specific period.[152] In the absence of such platforms, Reidenberg argues, the alternative would have been to wiretap a large part of the net traffic. For one, this would be a costly exercise for the government.[153] Even more so, it 'is something the government chose to avoid' because '[i]t would have faced strict legal constraints, namely the need for search warrants for each of the individual account holders'.[154] Thus, the circumvention of the constitutional safeguards (ie the need to obtain a search warrant) is facilitated by the loss of practical obscurity. The loss of practical obscurity, in turn, is facilitated by the accumulation of massive data about individuals within private entities, and more importantly, their practices of aggregation of data about individuals. Thus, the accumulation of massive data about individuals and aggregation practices by private entities not only makes it cheaper or even free for governments to engage in what could have been a costly conduct but also provides a way of circumventing the safeguards.[155]

The above example shows that having separate accounts with different service providers arguably involves some element of practical obscurity because the government had to issue a subpoena to each service provider to access the accounts. Similarly, even for the same service provider, one can argue that operating separate accounts has a privacy-protective feature in that governments, at least in most democratic states, would have to obtain a search warrant for accessing information in each account or at least justify the scope of their request to access all the accounts. This means, for example, that before Google's 2012 consolidation, a law enforcement agency that wanted to access someone's Gmail, Search, Google

[151] Joel Reidenberg, 'The Transparent Citizen' (2015) 47 Loyola University Chicago Law Journal 437.

[152] Except Google, the search engines did not even attempt to challenge this large-scale profiling of users; ibid 452.

[153] ibid.

[154] ibid. This is in part because of the third-party doctrine under the US Constitution (see Section III.A for more).

[155] Democracy Now, 'Data and Goliath: Bruce Schneier on the Hidden Battles to Collect Your Data and Control Your World' (13 March 2015) <www.democracynow.org/2015/3/13/data_and_goliath_bruce_schneier_on> accessed 7 February 2024 (noting that '[a]lthough the federal Privacy Act of 1974 (5 U.S.C. sec. 552a) places some restrictions on uses of personally identifiable information by federal agencies, access to the extensive services of these information brokers appears to be a way around the law').

Maps, and YouTube accounts had to undertake the task of justifying (*ex factum* or *post factum*) whether accessing all four accounts was necessary for the investigation. This creates a checkpoint for the judiciary to assess the proportionality of the interference in light of other interests. However, a subpoena after the 2012 consolidation could give law enforcement full access to someone's Google account—virtually every service the individual uses with Google. Individuals are even more exposed when governments can access several similar accounts from different service providers at once, as in the case of PRISM.

None of this is to deny that access to aggregated data increases governments' efficiency in their investigative actions and the need for governments to request such access from different providers. The argument is rather that, given the existence of privacy interests beyond the individual components, any access of this nature should be subjected to heightened regulatory or judicial oversight. This signifies that as the number of processing activities used to aggregate data increases, so should the safeguards against government interference.[156] Accessing one's Gmail is one matter; accessing a Google account is distinctly different. Similarly, accessing one's Google account may be disconcerting, but simultaneously accessing one's Google, Facebook, and Microsoft accounts represents an entirely separate issue. In the face of the increased desire by entities to collect, combine, and analyse as much personal data from various sources as possible, ensuring effective data privacy for individuals becomes extremely difficult. Confronting a system encompassing government, Google, Facebook, and Microsoft renders this task even more formidable.[157]

Such practices conflate the boundaries between state and economy, distorting the checks-and-balances mechanisms designed to ensure the state's adherence to the rule of law.[158] As the lines between governance, surveillance, commerce, and private life disappear, the constitutional safeguards for protecting privacy become easy to circumvent. These practices erode what Bygrave identifies as Group 2 data privacy interests, specifically encompassing the interests of rule of law and democracy.[159] Furthermore, the loss of practical obscurity is closely related to the interest of non-transparency, which includes the individual's interest 'in being able to act without being identified'.[160]

In recognition of the importance of practical obscurity for privacy, the US Supreme Court has made a distinction between information that is distributed across different sources and information centralized in one location.[161] According

156 See Slobogin (n 51) (having noted that the duration of surveillance will generate more private information, the author suggests scalable safeguards against such interference).

157 Harcourt (n 102) 188.

158 Reidenberg (n 151) 113 (noting that '[t]he transparency of personal information presents a basic challenge to the rule of law both in terms of the state's faithfulness to its ideals and in terms of individuals' respect for its principles').

159 Bygrave, *Data Protection Law* (n 88) 150.

160 ibid.

161 *US Dept of Justice v Reporters Committee* 489 Supreme Court (1989) 764.

to the Court, 'there is a vast difference between the public records that might be found after a diligent search of courthouse files, county archives, and local police stations throughout the country and a computerized summary located in a single clearinghouse'.[162] The implication of this decision is that the latter represents more risks than the former, warranting more oversight.

In applying Article 8 of the ECHR, the European Court of Human Rights (ECtHR) followed a similar approach in *Szabó and Vissy v Hungary*. The Court indicated that the need to upgrade the 'necessary in a democratic society' test under Article 8(2) to '*strictly necessary*' in *Klass*[163] was necessitated by 'the particular character of the interference in question and the potential of cutting-edge surveillance technologies to invade citizens' privacy'.[164] The Court further noted that '[g]iven the technological advances since the *Klass and Others* case, the potential interferences with email, mobile phone and Internet services as well as those of mass surveillance attract the Convention protection of private life even *more acutely*'.[165] The ECtHR emphasized that a government's accumulation of '*a detailed profile* ... of the most intimate aspects of citizens' lives may result in particularly invasive interferences with private life'.[166] Given the sophistication of the surveillance technology, the Court underlined that '[t]he guarantees required by the extant Convention case-law on interceptions *need to be enhanced so as to address the issue of such surveillance practices*'.[167] The existence of voluminous data from a wide range of sources, practices of aggregation across these sources, and a centralized access point for such data are among the main factors that necessitated the stricter application of the rules, particularly the 'necessity' test.

Both decisions recognize not only the dangers of the limitless collection of data about an individual but also the need for a more enhanced and stronger protection than in other circumstances. Constitutional and legislative measures with the aim of protecting privacy rights should be used for carefully examining the loss of practical obscurity and the overexposure of individuals and for devising appropriate approaches for mitigating the dangers through enhanced mechanisms. The argument in this chapter is that the enhanced mechanisms should not be limited to government actions and should extend to private entities. Section V details such an enhanced framework.

[162] ibid.
[163] App no 5029/71 *Klass v Germany* ECLI:CE:ECHR:1978:0906.
[164] ibid para 73 (emphasis added).
[165] App no 37138/14 *Szabó and Vissy v Hungary* ECLI:CE:ECHR:2016:0112, para 54 (emphasis added).
[166] ibid para 70 (emphasis added).
[167] ibid.

V. Towards a Holistic Approach: Enhanced Responsibility

The argument in this section is that, in light of the interests identified above, the atomized approach is inadequate and needs to be complemented by a holistic approach with enhanced responsibility for certain actors. This is akin to the regulation under competition law, where companies in a dominant position have a special responsibility and are subject to closer scrutiny and oversight than others.[168] This is based on the recognition that a dominant firm, because of its powerful position in the market, has the ability to distort competition and harm consumer welfare. Therefore, such entities shoulder a unique responsibility, restricting them from certain actions that might be permissible for non-dominant firms. While the precise boundaries of this responsibility are debated, the CJEU has underscored that its scope should be assessed based on the details of each case, including the degree of dominance and the nature of the conduct.[169] For instance, a dominant firm might have an obligation to avoid refusing to supply products or services without a valid reason, providing selective price reductions, or entering into certain contracts, especially if these actions are likely to impair genuine and undistorted competition.[170] The CJEU has further pointed out that, given their unique responsibility, a dominant undertaking's conduct might be deemed abusive under Article 102, even if such behaviour occurs in a market different from the dominated market, provided the two markets are closely related.[171] However, this special responsibility does not prevent dominant entities from competition on merits and defending their commercial interests when attacked.[172]

Data privacy law will benefit from a similar tiered regulatory framework that looks at imposing enhanced responsibilities based on the holistic view of the entire processing activities, data-aggregation practices, and their associated dangers. Thus, based on the holistic view of the processing activity, certain entities may be subject to more enhanced *ex ante* and *ex post* responsibilities, providing safeguards against the dangers of overexposure and the losses of transparency, accountability and practical obscurity.

The introduction of the GDPR has brought about changes that reflect a regulatory approach similar to competition law. This is evident from the significant penalties imposed for violations of data privacy rules, which are in line with fines typically associated with competition law. It is worth noting that these fines are

[168] See Case C-27/76 *United Brands v Commission* ECLI:EU:C:1978:22, para 65 (defining dominance as 'a position of economic strength enjoyed by an undertaking, which enables it to prevent effective competition being maintained on a relevant market, by affording it the power to behave to an appreciable extent independently of its competitors, its customers and ultimately of consumers'). See Case 322/81 *Nederlandsche Banden-Industrie Michelin NV v Commission* ECLI:EU:C:1983:313, para 57.

[169] Case T-83/91 *Tetra Pak v Commission* ECLI:EU:T:1994:246, para 115.

[170] ibid.

[171] ibid para 5.

[172] Case T-203/01 *Michelin v Commission (Michelin II)* ECLI:EU:T:2003:250, paras 55 and 97.

scalable, based on the worldwide annual turnover, as proposed in this section.[173] Moreover, competition law can help mitigate privacy risks arising from the aggregation of personal data across services. Specifically, to the extent that the accumulation of data is deemed to create market power or barriers to entry, competition law can restrict the combination of data across services.[174] This can address the privacy risks arising from wholeness and sum. For example, the Bundeskartellamt investigated Facebook for abuse of its dominant position in the market for social networks by imposing unfair terms and conditions on users.[175] The Bundeskartellamt held that Facebook abused its dominant position 'by making the use of its social network conditional on its being allowed to limitlessly amass every kind of data generated by using third-party websites and merge it with the user's Facebook account'.[176] Moreover, the agency found the integration of data from Instagram problematic from an antitrust perspective because it 'can transfer and safeguard market power, can exclude other market players and create barriers to market entry for competitors such as Snapchat'.[177] In February 2019, the Bundeskartellamt ordered Facebook to stop combining user data from third-party sources without users' 'voluntary consent'.[178]

According to the agency, the consent to combine users' data from third-party sources is not voluntary if it is a prerequisite to using Facebook's social network. The order seeks to preserve data silos by preventing Facebook from combining data from third-party websites and its subsidiaries unless users were given a genuine choice. This measure would certainly address the privacy risks discussed in Section IV resulting from the accumulation and aggregation of data, particularly the risks of overexposure and loss of practical obscurity.[179] Additionally, there are several ongoing investigations into the practices of Facebook and Amazon that address data uses, particularly the repurposing of data from one market to another market, which could help address the identified privacy risks if found to be in violation of competition law.[180] If successful, these efforts reinforce the purpose limitation

[173] See GDPR (n 3), Article 83.

[174] There is growing interest in using competition law for addressing issues related to big data. See Chapters 1 and 3–7.

[175] See Bundeskartellamt, 'Bundeskartellamt Initiates Proceeding against Facebook on Suspicion of Having Abused Its Market Power by Infringing Data Protection' (3 March 2016).

[176] Bundeskartellamt, 'Preliminary Assessment in Facebook Proceeding: Facebook's Collection and Use of Data from Third-Party Sources Is Abusive', (19 December 2017).

[177] Bundeskartellamt, *Decision in the Administrative Proceedings of Facebook (6th Division B6-22/16)* (2019) para 747.

[178] Bundeskartellamt, 'Bundeskartellamt Prohibits Facebook from Combining User Data from Different Sources' (7 February 2019); Bundeskartellamt, *Case Summary: Facebook, Exploitative Business Terms Pursuant to Section 19(1) GWB for Inadequate Data Processing* (2019).

[179] For detailed discussion of the implications, see Chapter 7, Section V.

[180] European Commission, 'Commission Sends Statement of Objections to Amazon for the Use of Non-Public Independent Seller Data and Opens Second Investigation into Its E-commerce Business Practices' (10 November 2020); European Commission, 'Commission Opens Investigation into Possible Anticompetitive Conduct of Facebook' (4 June 2021).

principle, a fundamental principle in the GDPR and central to discussions of the atomized approach and its associated limitations. The question of whether competition law can effectively tackle data-related will be discussed in upcoming chapters (see Chapters 4 and 7). Here, the focus is on examining how the layered approach, based on the special responsibility of entities with a dominant position, can be adapted as relevant to data privacy for dealing with the emergent data privacy risks identified above.

Recent legislative actions indicate a trend towards a tiered approach to regulation, where basic obligations apply to all actors, with additional, enhanced obligations tailored for specific actors. The Digital Services Act (DSA) is a prime example, where there are obligations that apply to all intermediaries, and additional obligations that apply to very large online platforms (VLOPs).[181] Similarly, the Platform-to-Business Regulation enforces lightweight transparency obligations on providers of online intermediation services, while the Digital Markets Act (DMA) introduces more extensive additional obligations for providers of 'core platform services' (gatekeepers) with a significant economic role in the EU market.[182] For example, the enhanced responsibility for VLOPs in the DSA is justified because they 'may cause societal risks, different in scope and impact from those caused by the smaller platforms' and thus should 'bear the highest standard of due diligence obligations, proportionate to their societal impact'.[183] The central argument in this section is that data privacy law should adopt a similar framework, imposing enhanced obligations for entities involved in data-processing operations that present higher risks.

The layered regulatory approach is not entirely new under data privacy, although it is based on a slightly different justification and framework. For example, under the EU data privacy rules, SMEs are exempted from certain obligations.[184] The main rationale behind the exemption is that SMEs will be deterred from entering the market if they are treated like established firms. Thus, the exemptions make it easier for the SMEs to compete with bigger players. However, research has shown that the current data privacy rules impose an undue burden on SMEs. According to one study, firms with more scope and economy of scale find it easier to obtain consent from users than SMEs do.[185] The underlying idea is that, when similar

[181] Regulation (EU) 2022/2065 of the European Parliament and of the Council of 19 October 2022 on a Single Market For Digital Services and amending Directive 2000/31/EC OJ L277/1 (Digital Services Act, DSA).

[182] Regulation (EU) 2022/1925 of the European Parliament and of the Council of 14 September 2022 on Contestable and Fair Markets in the Digital Sector and amending Directives (EU) 2019/1937 and (EU) 2020/1828 OJ L265/1 (Digital Markets Act, DMA); Regulation (EU) 2019/1150 of the European Parliament and of the Council of 20 June 2019 on Promoting Fairness and Transparency for Business Users of Online Intermediation Services OJ L186/57.

[183] DSA (n 181), Recital 76.

[184] For example, SMEs are exempt from recordkeeping obligations; see GDPR (n 3) Article 30(5).

[185] Avi Goldfarb and Catherine Tucker, 'Privacy and Innovation' in Josh Lerner and Scott Stern (eds), *Innovation Policy and the Economy, Volume 12* (University of Chicago Press 2012) 83.

standards of consent are applied across the board, the entities engaged in a smaller scale of processing suffer disproportionately. One possible explanation for the disproportionate costs of 'small and young firms' is the lack of scaling framework as the scope of the processing grows.[186] Given that the enhanced responsibility is primarily based on heightened privacy concerns as a result of the scale and diversity of the information-processing activity, it caters not only to the data privacy interests of individuals but also to the interests of SMEs.

In the context of data privacy, the proposal for enhanced responsibility can be compared with proposals calling for fiduciary duties of certain undertakings. In his book, Schneier writes,

> We need information fiduciaries. The idea is that they would become a class of organization that holds personal data, *subject to special legal restrictions and protections*.... Perhaps some types of business would be automatically classified as fiduciaries simply because of the large amount of personal information they naturally collect ... Fiduciary regulation would give people confidence that their information wasn't being handed to the government, sold to third parties or otherwise used against them.[187]

This argument for entities with fiduciary duties is in line with the competition law approach of special responsibility on monopolies and the enhanced responsibility put forth in this section. In fact, Google's chief economist compared Google to doctors and lawyers when justifying why users would entrust much of their data to the company.[188] The missing point in his analysis was that Google is not subject to similar secrecy obligations.[189]

The idea of scalable responsibility was picked up, *albeit* briefly, by the European Data Protection Supervisor (EDPS).[190] In discussing the interplay between consumer protection, data privacy, and competition law, the EDPS indicated that the responsibilities under the data privacy rules are incremental, depending on the volume, complexity, and intrusiveness of a company's personal data-processing activities.[191] Citing the ECtHR's decision in *MM v UK*,[192] the EDPS strengthened this argument and held that safeguards for protecting personal data should be commensurate with the sensitivity of the personal data being processed.[193] This

[186] ibid 83.

[187] Schneier (n 98) 205 (emphasis added).

[188] See Shoshana Zuboff, 'Big Other: Surveillance Capitalism and the Prospects of an Information Civilization' (2015) 30 Journal of Information Technology 75.

[189] See ibid.

[190] EDPS Preliminary Opinion, *Privacy and Competitiveness in the Age of Big Data: The Interplay between Data Protection, Competition Law and Consumer Protection in the Digital Economy* (EDPS 2014) 14.

[191] ibid 14.

[192] App no. 24029/07 *MM v UK* ECLI:CE:ECHR:2012:1113.

[193] EDPS Preliminary Opinion (n 190) 14.

incremental responsibility is considered to resemble the special responsibility of dominant undertakings under competition law.[194] Thus, there is some agreement on the need to impose enhanced responsibility on certain entities based on the privacy risks to individuals. However, the criteria used to designate such entities and the obligations to be imposed should be carefully tailored to situations where there are heightened data privacy risks.

This chapter does not provide detailed policy proposals regarding the enhanced responsibility regime. However, there are several measures that might be used to effectively tackle the privacy risks associated with processing of personal data for a panoply of purposes and the combination of data across these different processing operations.[195] For example, in situations where an entity engages in multiple processing operations based on different legal bases that are subject to varying obligations or rights, regulatory agencies could enforce the strictest compliance for all processing operations. Concretely, if an entity combines data from one set of processing operations (eg based on consent) that gives the user certain rights (eg data portability) with another processing operation (eg based on legal obligation) that does not give such rights, then users should be allowed to exercise the right for all the processing operations. This is similar to the approach suggested by the Commission in relation to the interaction of the GDPR and the regulation of free flow of non-personal data. The Commission maintains that if the non-personal data and personal data parts of a mixed data set are 'inextricably linked', then the GDPR's data protection rights and obligations apply to the entire data set, even if personal data represents only a small portion of it.[196] Such an approach of imposing the strictest obligation on the whole could mitigate the institutional challenge that arises from the combination of data across several processing operations, especially the difficulties encountered in attributing the data to a specific processing operation and determining whether the data is subject to the portability right.

One could also use the enhanced responsibility regime to impose measures aimed at addressing the emergent privacy risks. This could include the need to conduct DPIAs where entities engage in data-processing operations beyond a certain number and combine data across these operations. These obligations could easily be incorporated into Article 35(4) of the GDPR, where DPAs can establish a list of processing operations subject to the DPIA. Recital 92 of the GDPR underlines the need for the DPIA to go beyond a single processing activity in certain circumstances. Moreover, as noted in Section III.A, the ECtHR has upgraded the

[194] ibid.

[195] See Orla Lynskey, 'Grappling with "Data Power": Normative Nudges from Data Protection and Privacy' (2019) 20 Theoretical Inquiries in Law 189 (outlining different measures for addressing 'data power'). See also other suggestions, eg Inge Graef, Damian Clifford, and Peggy Valcke, 'Fairness and Enforcement: Bridging Competition, Data Protection, and Consumer Law' (2018) 8 International Data Privacy Law 200.

[196] See Guidance on the Regulation on a Framework for the Free Flow of Non-Personal Data in the European Union COM(2019) 250 final, 9.

'necessity' test under Article 8(2) of the ECHR to 'strictly necessary' in response to the increased risks posed by technological advancements and further noted that this strictness is 'acutely' needed in the current technological reality.[197] In this context, it is worth noting that Article 5(3) of the ePrivacy Directive uses the 'strictly necessary' test with regard to the placement of cookies on users' devices without their consent.[198] Similarly, once an entity is subject to the enhanced responsibility regime, the 'strictly necessary' approach could be applied to the legal bases outlined in Articles 6 or 9 of the GDPR that employ the 'necessity' test. Other measures could be considered, such as excluding consent or legitimate interest as legal grounds for combining data across multiple processing operations if the sum of these processing operations exceeds a certain threshold.

The approach adopted in the DMA seems in line with this suggestion. The DMA introduces enhanced data privacy obligations for large digital platforms, known as gatekeepers. Gatekeepers meeting certain thresholds must comply with the measures, including restrictions on certain uses of personal data, extended users' right of data portability, and increased transparency on consumer profiling.[199] For example, Article 5(2) prohibits gatekeepers from combining data across their services or from third-party services unless the end-user 'has been presented with the specific choice and has given consent' in line with the GDPR. While the relationship between the DMA and the GDPR needs further research, this provision seems to require gatekeepers, in addition to any legal ground they use for combining data, to obtain user consent. This means that for gatekeepers subject to the DMA, it is no longer sufficient to rely on 'legitimate interest' or 'contractual necessity' as a basis for combining data across services.

Furthermore, the DMA restricts the gatekeeper from requesting consent within a year after the data subject has declined or withdrawn his or her consent for the combination of data.[200] Apart from these and other data use restrictions under Articles 5 and 6, the DMA further extends the right to data portability under Article 20 of the GDPR both in terms of the type of data covered by this right and the type of access.[201] Regarding the type of data, the DMA allows portability of data generated by the user, as opposed to data provided by the user under the GDPR. Additionally, it allows users to be provided with continuous and real-time access to their data. These obligations could be applied to entities that meet the designed criteria for the enhanced responsibility regime under data privacy law. In the DMA, entities are designated as gatekeepers based on competition and economic considerations, such as turnover and number of business and end-users.[202] While these

[197] *Szabó and Vissy v Hungary* (n 165) para 54.

[198] For a detailed guidance on what the 'strictly necessary' test entails, see Article 29 Working Party, 'Opinion 04/2012 on Cookie Consent Exemption' (2012) (WP194) 4.

[199] DMA (n 182), Articles 5, 6, and 15.

[200] ibid Article 5(2(d)).

[201] ibid Article 6(9).

[202] ibid Article 3.

factors overlap with some of the data privacy concerns resulting from the processing of data for panoply of purposes and data-aggregation practices, they may need to be adjusted to better reflect those concerns. The following paragraphs will outline some relevant factors to be considered for the imposition of the enhanced responsibility regime under data privacy law.

Under competition law, the trigger for the special responsibility regime is the existence of market power and whether an undertaking occupies a dominant position, which is often determined by the undertaking's market share.[203] Relevant factors in such an assessment are the undertaking's turnover or volume of total sales. From a data privacy perspective, the discussion on the concept of emergent property can be informative in identifying different factors that can be considered in assessing whether enhanced responsibilities ought to be imposed. However, it bears mentioning that the goal is not to suggest a bright-line rule where the enhanced responsibilities are triggered; neither would it be practicable, given the sophistication with which modern business is conducted. Thus, the assessment needs to be conducted on a case-by-case basis, considering some of the factors identified here.

As discussed in Section III, emergent properties could be considered from a data privacy perspective by examining the sum and wholeness of the data. The summative perspective focuses on the scope and amount of information collected and processed based on different purposes that provide insight into different aspects of individual life. One factor that is indicative of the scope is the total number of processing activities an entity undertakes, which can easily be deduced from the services or products it offers. This resembles criteria of competition law that consider economies of scope and scale. These are the economic advantages for a business that could lead to a dominant position because of the diversity of the goods or services offered and the resulting cost advantages stemming from the scope of operations.

Under competition law, the special responsibilities regime is justified on the grounds that dominance opens up the potential for stifling competition in a market. Similarly, the scale of processing activities has a direct influence on the privacy interests of individuals in terms of their overexposure and the losses of accountability, transparency, and practical obscurity. As noted above, the greater the number of channels through which an entity collects data from individuals, the greater the risks to individuals' privacy and the harder it is to apply the purpose limitation principle. This, in turn, leads to a decrease in overall transparency and accountability. Moreover, the more data an entity collects and stores through various processing activities related to individuals, the greater the risk of

203 European Commission, 'Guidance on the Commission's Enforcement Priorities in Applying Article 82 of the EC Treaty to Abusive Exclusionary Conduct by Dominant Undertakings' [2009] OJ C45/7.

government surveillance. This is because governments can not only access comprehensive data about individuals in the possession of a single entity but also combine it with similar data from other service providers. Consequently, transparency and accountability diminish. To a certain extent, this shows the link between the total number of processing activities and privacy interests in the wholeness and sum, justifying the application of enhanced responsibility.

The idea is not to suggest a specific number that triggers the enhanced responsibilities; instead, the total number of processing activities could form one criterion for a case-by-case assessment. This means that a certain total number of processing activities can be used as a threshold for starting the assessment to determine whether the enhanced responsibilities should be considered. This minimum threshold would serve the same purpose as market share in the competition law assessment. Under competition law, market share provides a useful first step in the assessment of the dominant position, but other factors should be considered, including the nature of the market, entry barriers, and potential competition.

Similarly, the threshold based on total processing activities would bring an entity into the spotlight for further assessments to determine whether it should be subject to enhanced responsibilities. Certain entities would easily fulfil the criteria. For example, as noted above, the Spanish DPA investigation indicated that Google collects personal data using more than 100 consumer-facing products or services in Spain. This scale provides a strong indication that the enhanced responsibilities should be applied. The same approach is followed under competition law, where a market share of over 50 per cent is considered to provide strong evidence of dominance. However, the total number of processing activities should not be the only criterion that must be factored into the assessment. One reason for this is that focusing on the number may not capture entities that process personal data under the umbrella of one processing activity but manage to accumulate massive amounts of personal data either through interrogative techniques (persistent nudging of users to reveal more data)[204] or continuous usage of the services. A good example in this regard is Facebook.

Although Facebook could be considered a service under a specific purpose (ie providing Facebook services), this does not imply that the dangers of the wholeness and sum are minimal.[205] Thus, if the technology progresses enough to enable the measurement of the size or amount of personal information collected, it can constitute one factor in the assessment of whether the enhanced responsibilities should be considered.[206] However, in light of the lack of transparency by entities in

[204] Facebook is a good example because apart from the troves of personal information it collects through registration and browsing activity, it occasionally establishes new boxes asking users for more information, like 'Do you know a person outside of Facebook?', 'Current job?', 'Family relationship?', and not least, 'What is on your mind?'.

[205] See discussions in Harcourt (n 102) 2–5.

[206] This criterion is implicit in Schneier's (n 98: 205) proposal for fiduciary duties for some actors that control a 'large amount of personal information'.

terms of what information they collect and the current technological development, it may be difficult to impose obligations according to the amount of data an entity is processing. In this sense, the total number of processing activities provides relatively measurable criteria for assessment. Yet, more general criteria could still be used. For example, whether the entity engages in practices of continuous nagging for information could be considered. In addition, whether the use of the services involves the continuous generation of personal data about the users or just one-off collection should be assessed. Such features are undesirable because they either constitute nagging or are the root cause of the individual's overexposure or the losses of accountability, transparency, and practical obscurity.

The interrelation of various processing operations based on distinct purposes through aggregation is another significant aspect of emergent property. As noted in Section IV, most of the accountability and transparency challenges are associated with the practice of combining data across services. This indicates that the aggregation of data from different processing activities, in addition to the sum of processing activities, may be another factor to consider when applying enhanced responsibilities. However, while the existence of actual aggregation signals the need for enhanced responsibilities, its absence should not be taken to reach a contrary conclusion. Rather, the assessment should also consider the potential for the aggregation of data from processing activities based on distinct purposes. There have been several instances where companies, including Google and Facebook, have made assurances to their users that they would not combine data from newly acquired entities, only to subsequently violate those promises.

Beyond those factors dictated by the discussions on emergent property, considering other factors, such as the history of privacy breaches, could be relevant. The basis for the application of the special responsibilities for dominant undertakings under competition law is that these undertakings can become 'insensitive to the actions and reactions of competitors, customers and, ultimately, consumers'.[207] Similarly, if an entity is engaged in processing personal data for manifold purposes and has a history of repeated privacy breaches, it shows its insensitivity to compliance and individuals' rights in general. Such practices ought to warrant enhanced responsibilities. These factors are by no means exhaustive, and other relevant factors could be considered depending on the context.

The main issue in the application of the enhanced responsibility regime should be the adequate consideration of the privacy interests identified above, that is overexposure of individuals and the losses of accountability, transparency, and practical obscurity. However, none of this should imply that the proposal put forth is the only alternative for addressing the challenges. Moreover, it should not imply that the proposal is without challenges. For example, determining when the privacy

[207] Guidance on Article 102 Enforcement Priorities (n 203).

interests emerge independent of and/or in combination with the individual processing activities may not be an easy exercise. The aim of this chapter is rather to highlight the instances where the current rules could benefit from a complementary approach based on a holistic view. Moreover, the objective is to open the floor for further research on similar holistic approaches. This could look at what specific measures need to be considered in the enhanced responsibility regime and how they can mitigate the dangers.

VI. Conclusion

This chapter has shown that, when an entity processes personal data for multiple purposes, under the current EU data privacy rules, each processing must comply with the data privacy principles separately in light of the specific purpose and relevant legal basis. This represents an atomistic view of the processing—that is the assessment of compliance focuses on the individual processing based on a specific purpose and distinct legal basis, regardless of the total number of processing activities and data-aggregation practices across the different processing operations. In this sense, the EU approach is reductionist, and it relies on two underlying assumptions: (1) one is able to distinguish among the different processing activities and relate every piece of personal data to a particular processing and (2) if each processing is compliant with the data privacy rules, individuals' data privacy rights are not endangered.

By drawing lessons from the concept of emergent property, the chapter has challenged the assumptions and outlined the inadequacy of the atomized approach in light of emerging data-processing practices, where entities process personal data for a panoply of purposes, almost every use of a service generates personal data, and data is combined across the processing activities. First, although the idea of 'one thing at a time' is a useful guiding principle in life, it may not be suitable in a world where the line between one thing and another is unclear. In this regard, the atomized approach overlooks the growing tendency to combine data across databases, which makes it difficult to distinguish among processing activities based on separate purposes and associate certain data with a particular processing activity. Moreover, the concept of emergent property is used to show that, when entities process personal data for a wide array of purposes and combine data across different processing activities, there are privacy interests independent of and/or in combination with the individual processing activities. These include, but are not limited to, overexposure of the individual and the losses of transparency, accountability, and practical obscurity. The discussion through the lens of emergent property has allowed for bringing together issues of surveillance (dataveillance), problems associated with the 'notice and consent'-based regulation, and some rule-of-law concerns relating to big data.

Finally, comparisons were drawn from the concept of emergent property in suggesting that data privacy rules need to look beyond the individual processing activities based on a specific purpose and consider the totality of the data collected by entering into a wide variety of new product areas, acquisitions, or combinations of data from different sources. Where collecting data without any purpose, storing such data indefinitely and aggregating across datasets is a feature, not a bug, of the business models, an enforcement mechanism built on well-delineated processing activities based on a specific and legitimate purpose is bound to fail. It is time for data privacy rules to adapt to this reality by focusing on the bigger picture and a system-level view. It was noted that, with an eye open to a holistic approach, there are existing tools that give regulatory authorities flexibility to cater to the interests identified in this chapter. However, the main goal was not to advocate that the particular possibility sketched here is necessarily the best one available; rather, it was to spur thinking about complementary approaches that better correspond to the concerns about overexposure and the losses of transparency, accountability, and practical obscurity. We must seek to address these concerns, whether through the holistic approach advanced in this chapter or any other better option. As the following chapters show, the application of competition rules to the data privacy practices of firms with market power usefully dovetails with the call to increase the protection mechanisms.

3
Digital Ecosystems, Emergent Harms, and the Need for a Holistic Approach in Competition Law

I. Atomized Approach to the Application of Competition Law

In line with the definition adopted in Chapter 2, a legal regime can be described as atomized if, in dealing with a system built from several components, it focuses, as a matter of law or practice, on isolating a specific component of the system as the target of regulation as opposed to the system as a whole. In the context of European Union (EU) competition law, this arises from the practice of trying to isolate the relevant product/service market as a target of regulation even when dealing with comprehensive ecosystems comprising several integrated products/services. This outcome results from the importance that identifying and delimiting the relevant market occupies in the application of competition law.

Defining the relevant market is an essential first step in the application of competition law in many jurisdictions, including the EU and the United States.[1] In both jurisdictions, this step involves defining the relevant product/service market and its geographical reach. The objective of market definition is to identify the competitive constraints imposed on a firm's behaviour to increase price or reduce output. This is determined by identifying current and potential competitors that offer goods/services that are perceived by consumers as substitutes in terms of their intended uses, prices, and characteristics.[2] Thus, a relevant market comprises all substitutable goods/services in a geographical area with sufficiently homogenous conditions of competition.[3]

While market definition is just a means to an end, sometimes the means may determine the outcome. The importance of market definition is particularly noticeable in the application of Article 102 of the Treaty on the Functioning of the European Union (TFEU). As the application of this provision is predicated on

[1] See Richard Whish and David Bailey, *Competition Law* (9th edn, OUP 2018) 27. However, there are questions over its continuing importance. See Louis Kaplow, 'Why (Ever) Define Markets?' (2010) 124 Harvard Law Review 437.

[2] European Commission, 'Commission Notice on the Definition of Relevant Market for the Purposes of Community Competition Law' [1997] OJ C372/5 para 7.

[3] ibid paras 7–8.

Data Privacy and Competition Law in the Age of Big Data. Samson Y. Esayas, Oxford University Press.
 DOI: 10.1093/oso/9780198891420.003.0004

establishing dominance, defining the relevant market and its geographical scope is instrumental in estimating market shares (and thus dominance) in the market. How the market is defined therefore has a decisive bearing on the outcome of the case: a broader relevant market means that it is less likely there will be one actor with significant market power and less likely that an abuse of dominance will occur. Similarly, a narrowly defined market may result in a decision condemning conduct that would otherwise enhance consumer welfare. For this reason, market definition is considered 'the foundation stone' in competition law interventions.[4] The Court of Justice of the European Union (CJEU) has reversed some Commission decisions for want of a properly defined relevant market.[5]

At its core, market definition serves as a way of identifying the target of regulation and its boundaries. When defining the market, competition authorities or courts delineate the commercial field and market relations that are relevant in a case. Some authors have likened market definition to a tennis court, a tool demarcating the playing field to which competition law applies.[6] Once the relevant target of regulation is identified and its limits established, the resources of competition authorities are primarily expended on identifying behaviours, and their impact on the competitive process, within this zone.

Market definition helps shape the target of regulation in two ways.[7] First, it helps identify market actors and their relations, thus delimiting the problem that competition law aims to correct.[8] For example, in relation to Article 102, it is only when markets are properly defined that one may establish dominance and identify the conduct in question. In this sense, market definition determines the conduct that lies both inside and outside the target (inside or outside the tennis court). Thus, unless the target market is linked to other markets in traditional terms (vertical integration, ties), market behaviour that lies outside of the target market is mainly ignored.[9]

Second, market definition determines the commercial field upon which the competitive impact of a behaviour is to be assessed. Again, this means that unless other markets are related to the target market in the traditional sense, the impact of a behaviour is assessed predominantly in relation to the target market. Returning to the tennis court metaphor, 'If the behaviour affects issues that lie outside of the playing field, the line umpire signals an out and competition law does not apply.'[10]

[4] See Lapo Filistrucchi and others, 'Market Definition in Two-Sided Markets: Theory and Practice' (2014) 10 Journal of Competition Law and Economics 293, 294.

[5] See Case 6-72 *Continental Can v Commission* ECLI:EU:C:1973:22, para 32; also Whish and Bailey (n 1) 188.

[6] Viktoria Robertson, *Competition Law's Innovation Factor: The Relevant Market in Dynamic Contexts in the EU and the US* (Bloomsbury 2020) 3.

[7] For a discussion of the different functions of market definition, see ibid.

[8] Michael Jacobides and Ioannis Lianos, 'Ecosystems and Competition Law in Theory and Practice' (2021) 30 Industrial and Corporate Change 1199, 1204.

[9] Robertson (n 6).

[10] ibid 3.

This practice of identifying and delimiting the boundaries of the target of regulation works fine in many contexts but could be problematic when applied to platforms and ecosystems that bring together seemingly different product/service markets under one umbrella.[11] It is this practice of trying to isolate a component as the target of regulation in the face of several integrated components that is referred to as atomized in nature.

The main argument of this chapter is that this atomized approach is inadequate in light of the shifts entailed by the commercialization of personal data and big data practices. As noted in Chapters 1 and 2, one such shift relates to the tendency to process personal data for a panoply of purposes and to aggregate this data across processing activities. Closely related to these changes, and of particular relevance to competition law, is the shift from offering single products/services to offering ecosystems comprising several integrated products/services with personal data taking centre stage in coordinating activities across the different markets. Among other challenges,[12] these developments blur the boundaries between what were previously separate relevant markets and complicate the attribution of a competitive harm to a specific relevant market, making it difficult to enforce the rules.[13] Further, the atomized approach may potentially overlook emergent competitive harms from multiple and systematic practices in seemingly different relevant markets within the comprehensive ecosystem.

The aim of this chapter is to shed light on how multiple and systematic practices across several seemingly distinct relevant product/service markets could form a complexity, which gives rise to challenges in the application of competition law. Specifically, the chapter explores the extent to which competition law is equipped to deal with potential competitive harms from multiple cross-market and systematic practices, which, seen in silos, might seem innocuous but, when considered holistically, may cause lasting harm to competition. Further, given the possibilities for emergent competitive harms from multiple and systematic practices across markets, it is worth exploring whether competition law should entertain the prospect of establishing dominance and sanctioning abuse in an ecosystem comprising several markets, even when the concerned undertaking lacks dominance in each market separately. In addressing these issues, the chapter draws upon the notions of emergent properties and technological momentum.

[11] Jacobides and Lianos (n 8) 1207 (noting that 'the standard "relevant market" approach explicitly focuses on the average behaviour in one of the system's components (i.e., firms producing neatly separable, substitutable products) . . ., but fails to appreciate the dynamics of multi-product and multi-actor ecosystems'). For a US perspective, see Daniel Crane, 'Ecosystem Competition and the Antitrust Laws' (2019) 98 Nebraska Law Review 412.

[12] The challenges of market definition in relation to multi-sided markets have been widely discussed. See David Evans, 'Two-Sided Market Definition' in ABA Section of Antitrust Law (ed), *Market Definition in Antitrust: Theory and Case Studies* (ABA Book Publishing 2012); Filistrucchi and others (n 4).

[13] Jacobides and Lianos (n 8) 1200.

II. Potential Sources of Emergent Competitive Harms

One important way technological development can impact law is by increasing the complexity of the system regulated by law and creating an environment conducive to the formation of emergent properties. For example, new technologies can increase complexity and encourage the formation of emergent properties by enabling an action at a scale that was not possible previously. This change in scale may generate qualitative changes (emergent properties).[14] From a competition law perspective, the potential source of emergent risks can be pinned down to two key developments associated with the commercialization of personal data. First, one of the outcomes associated with the commercialization of personal data is the shift from offering single products/services to offering several integrated products/services, often under the rubric of 'multi-sided platforms' or ecosystems markets.[15] This shift has led to the emergence of companies that control multiple gateways to consumers—for example, app stores, mobile operating systems (MOS), and web browsers, which are important entry points to markets. This control of gateways gives platforms the power to set the rules of the game regarding who gets in, who gets promoted, and who gets demoted on their platforms, and it ultimately grants the power to 'control and cut off' the 'oxygen supply' of many digital players.[16]

Second, personal data plays a central role in coordinating activities across the different markets. Data collected in the context of a specific commercial activity can be instrumental in other markets. It may be used to provide targeted advertising for businesses, to improve the quality of certain digital services, and to develop new products/services. For example, the data that Google collects from Internet searches is used to improve the quality of search results, video recommendations on YouTube, and other Google services (Maps). Importantly, the data from search and other services enables Google to deliver online advertising in an extraordinarily precise fashion and thereby increase the effectiveness of advertisements. Further, the data collected across these services (Search, Maps, Calendar, YouTube, Gmail) can be a key competitive differentiator in the new arena of competition for digital assistants, allowing Google Home to plan a route or meetings easily, play the user's favourite music or videos on YouTube, or compose an email to a colleague.

The central role that personal data plays in creating value and the reliance of leading digital players on monetizing users' personal data via advertising leads to a conflict of interests with certain actors that rely on the infrastructure of the leading

[14] See discussions in Chapter 2, Sections II and III.

[15] Martin Schallbruch, Heike Schweitzer, and Achim Wambach, 'A New Competition Framework for the Digital Economy: Report by the Commission "Competition Law 4.0"' (European Commission 2019) 13. See also Chapter 1.

[16] Ariel Ezrachi and Maurice Stucke, *Virtual Competition: The Promise and Perils of the Algorithm-Driven Economy* (Harvard UP 2016) 145.

platforms to access consumers and data. One instance of a clear conflict of interest is between the leading platforms and businesses trying to improve users' control over their personal data and privacy, such as anti-tracking and ad-blocking services. This is because efforts to limit data collection and enhance user control over their data are in direct conflict with the business models of leading platforms, such as Google and Facebook, which rely on the tracking and monetization of personal data. These big platforms therefore perceive innovation and competition in the field of privacy as a threat to their businesses, which can, in turn, generate incentives to suppress such competition.[17]

In light of these two factors (the conflict of interests and the fact that leading platforms control multiple consumer gateways), it is no surprise to find that companies trying to compete on privacy and privacy-enhancing technologies (PETs) often fall victim to bans across several access points. The examples are ubiquitous. In 2013, Google removed a significant number of anti-tracking and ad-blocking apps from its Play Store, including four prominent apps: Adblock Plus, AdBlocker, AdAway, and AdFree.[18] Google also expelled Adblock Plus from the Chrome Web Store and removed its website from search results.[19] In 2015, Google removed Disconnect from its Play Store.[20] In 2017, Google banned AdNauseam from its Chrome Web Store.[21]

But providers of PETs are not the only victims of the increased importance of personal data for commercial purposes. Interestingly, the same development gives rise to incentives to cut access to data that is important for competition. There are several ongoing investigations into Amazon and Google for denying customers access to data.[22] These practices aim to preserve or extend the competitive advantage that leading platforms gain from having exclusive access to some data. This, together with the fact that leading platforms control several gateways for accessing data, means that they can deter competitors from collecting data across several markets or gateways. Again, with its data-driven business and control of several key gateways, Google is a good example. In this regard, the Commission has recently opened an investigation into Google's practice of restricting the ability of

[17] See Samson Esayas, 'Competition in (Data) Privacy: 'Zero'-Price Markets, Market Power, and the Role of Competition Law' (2018) 8 International Data Privacy Law 181.

[18] See Chris Velazco, 'Google Pulls Ad-Blocking Apps from Play Store for Violating Developer Distribution Agreement', *TechCrunch* (13 March 2013).

[19] ibid; Case COMP 40099 *Complaint of Disconnect, Inc*, unreported (June 2015), para 9.

[20] See *Complaint of Disconnect, Inc* (n 19).

[21] See AdNauseam, 'AdNauseam Banned from the Google Web Store' (5 January 2017) <https://adnauseam.io/free-adnauseam.html> accessed 7 February 2024.

[22] European Commission, 'Commission Sends Statement of Objections to Amazon for the Use of Non-Public Independent Seller Data and Opens Second Investigation intoIts E-commerce Business Practices' (10 November 2020) (European Commission, 'Statement of Objections to Amazon'); European Commission, 'Commission Opens Investigation into Possible Anticompetitive Conduct by Google in the Online Advertising Technology Sector (22 June 2021) (European Commission, 'Investigation into Google's Online Advertising')'.

third parties, such as advertisers, publishers, or competing online display advertising intermediaries, to access data across several markets.[23]

The Commission identifies three data access restrictions in the Android MOS, Chrome, and the market for display advertising.[24] First, Google places restrictions on these third parties preventing them from accessing data about user behaviour when providing display advertising services, while this same information is available to Google's own advertising services.[25] Second, Google has announced plans to stop making the advertising identifier available to third parties on Android. Third, Google plans to prohibit the placement of third-party 'cookies' on Chrome and replace them with the 'Privacy Sandbox' set of tools. Both the advertising ID and third-party cookies are important sources of user data for publishers and competing online display advertising intermediaries. The Commission is investigating the effect of these data access restrictions on online display advertising and online display advertising intermediation markets.[26] Both the bans on PETs and restrictions on data access are clear instances of how control over several gateways and the conflict of interest due to commercialization of personal data give rise to incentives to engage in multiple cross-market practices.[27]

These developments—particularly the fact that leading platforms control multiple gateways to consumers and their data and the potential conflicts of interest—could create emergent competitive harms that may elude competition law scrutiny. The control over several gateways gives them the ability to engage in multiple cross-market practices, which poses challenges to the atomized approach in competition law application.[28] This is because, in following the atomized approach, competition authorities focus on analysing the impact of a behaviour on properly defined and well-delineated markets, which may overlook emergent competitive harms from multiple and systematic practices in seemingly different relevant markets within the comprehensive ecosystem.

These risks are 'emergent' in the sense that they may exist independently of, and hence may not be attributed to, specific conduct in a relevant market. However, the source of emergent competitive harms is not limited to the multiplicity of actions across different markets (ie a cross-market problem related to market definition) but may also result from the systematic elimination of competition by targeting several players in the same market, over time and at critical moments.[29] Thus, as

[23] See European Commission, 'Investigation into Google's Online Advertising' (n 22).

[24] ibid.

[25] ibid.

[26] ibid.

[27] However, additional factors, such as the existence of competition between platform owners and customers, may create conflicts of interest that could result in harmful practices. See Lina Khan, 'Amazon's Antitrust Paradox' (2017) 16 Yale Law Journal 564.

[28] Schallbruch, Schweitzer, and Wambach (n 15) 6 (underscoring the need for competition law to find mechanisms that counter 'cross-market foreclosure strategies in the digital economy').

[29] See European Parliamentary Research Service, 'Online Platforms: Economic and Societal Effects' (2021) VIII <https://www.europarl.europa.eu/RegData/etudes/STUD/2021/656336/

the leading digital players compete by creating and optimizing comprehensive ecosystems (eg the 'Google experience'), and not just by offering a single product/ service, the practice of competition authorities should also adapt. Competition authorities need to consider not only cross-market practices but also the systematic elimination of competition by suppressing the momentum of services over time. By drawing lessons from the literature on technological momentum and emergent properties, the analysis in this chapter underlines the need to give due regard to emergent effects. Multiple and systematic practices may, when considered holistically, cause lasting harm to competition, even if these practices, when considered individually, fall short of the required standards for competition law intervention.

Before proceeding further, it is important to sound a note of caution. Market definition is a tool, and competition authorities are not necessarily deterred from considering the combined effects of several actions across different markets. Indeed, competition law authorities and courts have started to consider how combined actions across different markets may amount to an abuse of a dominant position.[30] A case in point is the Commission decision in *Google Android*. In this case, the Commission fined Google €4.34 billion for abusing its dominant position in the market for licensable MOS and app stores by imposing illegal contractual restrictions on Android device manufacturers and mobile network operators.[31] The Commission identified four abusive practices.

The first involved tying the Google search app to the Google Play Store; the second, tying Google Chrome to the Play Store and search app. According to the Commission, Google's contractual terms require original equipment manufacturers (OEMs) that wish to install Play Store on their devices to also pre-install Google Search and Google Chrome.[32] The third conduct relates to financial payments to large device manufacturers and mobile operators on the condition that they exclusively pre-install Google Search (exclusivity payments). The fourth involves a prohibition on device manufacturers that wish to install Play Store or Search in their devices from selling even a single device running a competing Android OS, such as Android Fork (antifragmentation agreement). The Commission held that these practices have cemented Google's dominance in general search, denied rival

EPRS_STU(2021)656336_EN.pdf> (emphasizing the need for more research 'on platforms' behaviour in ecosystems over time').

[30] See Case AT.40099 *Google Android* decision of 18 July 2018. Similarly, competition authorities also assess the impact of a behaviour in several related markets: Case C-67/13 P *Groupement des cartes bancaires* ECLI:EU:C:2014:2204.

[31] *Google Android* (n 30). The Commission identified the following four markets: (1) the worldwide market (excluding China) for the licensing of smart MOS, (2) the worldwide market (excluding China) for Android app stores, (3) the national markets for general search services, and (4) the worldwide market for non OS-specific mobile web browsers.

[32] ibid.

search engines the possibility to compete on merits, and have harmed further innovation in MOS.

Of particular importance to the argument in this chapter is the Commission's approach insofar as it combined multi-market practices into a single overall abusive strategy. In this regard, the Commission noted that 'the four different forms of conduct all pursue an identical objective of protecting and strengthening Google's dominant position in general search services' and 'constitute a single and continuous infringement of Article 102 TFEU'.[33] The Commission's approach deviates from the traditional approach based on specific relevant market and unifies different abuses under a single overall strategy.

Indeed, as mentioned in Section V, the Commission's approach is commendable and concurs with the argument in this chapter that a holistic approach is necessary. The Commission seems to recognize that when the practices are interconnected, an isolated view—driven by the definition of market—could potentially overlook the synergistic effects in terms of the associated harms. However, even this more comprehensive approach does not address the question of emergence, namely whether multiple practices, which are not illegal on their own, can, when taken as whole, constitute an illegal practice under Article 102.[34] This is because although the Commission viewed the different practices as having the same objective and as forming part of a single strategy, it also insisted that each infringed Article 102 on its own.[35] If each practice is individually illegal under Article 102, there is no room for emergent properties. Thus, the chapter fills this gap on emergence and illustrates how a pattern of conduct, taken as a whole, may eliminate effective competition in a relevant market even if the actions taken separately are not harmful to competition.

In order to address emergence, the chapter uses the ban on privacy-enhancing services by dominant platforms and the application of the essential facilities doctrine as a case study. The focus on the essential facilities doctrine is justified because it is often seen as an important tool to open digital markets, particularly in terms of access to platforms and user data.[36] Relatedly, and as shown in Section III, given the high threshold for condemning abuse, the doctrine is suitable for discussing emergent properties, meaning the potential for abuse of dominance arising from holistic view of multiple practices that, individually, are not considered abusive.

[33] ibid para 1340.

[34] See Section V for more on the potential and limitations of the Commission's approach in addressing emergent harms.

[35] *Google Android* (n 30) para 1339.

[36] See Inge Graef, *EU Competition Law, Data Protection and Online Platforms: Data as Essential Facility* (Kluwer Law International 2016); Nikolas Guggenberger, 'Essential Platforms' (2020) 24 Stanford Technology Law Review 237.

III. Digital Platforms and the Essential Facilities Doctrine

The essential facilities doctrine grants competitors rights of access to facilities of a dominant undertaking to the extent that these competitors depend on the facilities and cannot reasonably duplicate them. In its original form, the doctrine applied to physical infrastructure, such as rail roads and port facilities that connected consumers and producers of goods and services. Digital platforms have become the railroads of the modern economy.[37] In the same way as railroads, digital platforms (such as app stores, search engines, and e-commerce websites) are key gateways to consumers for millions of traders and content providers. This reality has led to claims that the essential facilities doctrine can be used to facilitate access to critical digital assets, such as app stores, ranking in search engines and data.[38]

Despite this, there are reasons to question the extent to which the doctrine, in its current form, can provide answers to concerns about access to platforms and data. For example, in its recent decisions involving digital platforms, the Commission was presented with an opportunity to apply the essential facilities doctrine but chose a different route.[39] This, in turn, raises questions about the continued importance of the doctrine in digital markets. This section explores the application of the essential facilities doctrine to digital platforms in light of these recent developments. It starts by highlighting the Commission's recent decisional practice involving digital platforms and some of the reasons that may explain why the Commission has backed away from applying the essential facilities doctrine. Further, the analysis insists that the addition of emergent property thinking could potentially help reinvigorate the doctrine's importance for digital markets.

As highlighted earlier, the focus on the essential facilities doctrine is justified because, given the high threshold for condemning abuse, this doctrine provides a platform to discuss the potential of emerging properties. Using the ban on PETs as an example, the discussion shows that the nature of ecosystem markets makes it possible for leading digital players to engage in multiple cross-market practices deterring access and targeting several actors. However, the atomized approach to competition law application, together with the strict requirements for applying the essential facilities doctrine, mean that those bans, seen in silos, might fail to meet the required threshold for intervention under Article 102. The discussions underscore the significance of accounting for emergent effects, highlighting that while a single instance of refusal to deal may not qualify as an abuse, a combination of several such practices could meet the required threshold. Furthermore, the discourse on PETs serves to elucidate the intersection between data privacy and competition laws, highlighting more specifically how competition law can reinforce data

[37] Guggenberger (n 36) 240.
[38] See ibid; Graef, *EU Competition Law* (n 36).
[39] Case AT.39740 *Google Search (Shopping)* decision of 27 June 2017; *Google Android* (n 30).

privacy law by preventing macro-level harms to data privacy through platform bans. Notwithstanding the emphasis on the essential facility and PETs bans, the insights derived from this chapter remain pertinent to scenarios wherein undertakings have the possibility to engage in multiple cross-market practices, regardless of the type of conduct and theory of harm employed.[40]

A. Recent Commission Practice and Evasion of the Essential Facilities Doctrine

The essential facilities doctrine is a contentious topic in competition law discussions. The doctrine requires dominant undertakings to share their important facilities with their competitors, which entails an interference with fundamental freedoms and rights, such as the right to conduct business, property rights, and freedom of contract.[41] Moreover, while forcing dominant undertakings to share essential facilities might increase short-term gains such as lower prices and more variety (static efficiency), it may also discourage dominant undertakings from investing in new facilities and enhancing existing ones (dynamic efficiency).[42]

Because the application of the doctrine entails severe interferences with the rights and freedoms of businesses, the CJEU has established a very high threshold for forcing companies to deal with competitors. The main principle is that dominant companies are free to choose who they trade with and how they dispose their property. However, the Court has recognized that there may be 'exceptional circumstances' that warrant intervention. For example, in *Magill*, the CJEU considered whether a refusal by three broadcasting stations to license copyright-protected material constituted an abuse. The refusal occurred after Mr Magill attempted to get access to the weekly programme listings of the stations in order to introduce a comprehensive television guide consisting of the weekly programme listings of all three channels.[43] The Court noted that, while exclusion is inherent in exercising one's intellectual property (IP) rights, such a right might be restricted under 'exceptional circumstances', particularly when the right is exercised in a manner that restricts competition.[44]

Specifically, the Court indicated that it is an abuse of dominance when a copyright is used to prevent the publication of a comprehensive weekly programme

40 This includes cases of leading platforms cutting access to data across markets, as Google stands accused of by the Commission, on the pretext of enhancing users' privacy.

41 See European Commission, 'Guidance on the Commission's Enforcement Priorities in Applying Article 82 of the EC Treaty to Abusive Exclusionary Conduct by Dominant Undertakings' [2009] OJ C45/7, para 75.

42 ibid para 75.

43 Joined Cases C-241/91 P and C-242/91 P *Radio Telefis Eireann (RTE) and Independent Television Publications Ltd (ITP) v Commission (Magill)* ECLI:EU:C:1995:98, paras 7–10.

44 ibid para 50.

listing, together with commentary, that was not available on the market at the time.[45] In this regard, the Court noted, first, that the stations were the only source of the information, 'which is the indispensable raw material for compiling a weekly television guide'.[46] Second, by refusing to supply the information, the broadcasting stations prevented the appearance of a new product for which consumer demand potentially existed.[47] Third, through their conduct, the stations 'reserved to themselves the secondary market of weekly television guides by excluding all competition on that market'.[48] Finally, the refusal was not justified by objective considerations.[49] The CJEU confirmed these four conditions for the refusal to license IP rights in its *IMS Health* judgment.[50]

This notwithstanding, the Court seems to apply a different legal test when it comes to tangible assets. The *Bronner* judgment, which related to a refusal to provide access to a nationwide newspaper home-delivery scheme, is a case in point.[51] Despite the reliance on *Magill*, the Court does not mention the 'new product' requirement. In the Court's view, in order for a refusal to be in violation of Article 102 of the TFEU, it is necessary to establish that (1) the input is indispensable to carry out the business, (2) the refusal is 'likely to eliminate all competition' on the part of the access seeker, and (3) the refusal is 'incapable of being objectively justified'.[52] This seems to imply that the 'new product' requirement is applicable only to the licensing of IP rights, which was confirmed by the General Court (GC) in *Microsoft*.[53] The Court also highlighted that the refusal to license entails a stricter legal test than other circumstances.[54]

Many scholars have tipped the essential facilities doctrine as an important tool for addressing the competition challenges in digital markets, particularly the need to facilitate access to platforms and data.[55] Despite its promise, the doctrine has had limited practical application. Recent decisions by the Commission suggest a reluctance to apply the doctrine to digital platforms, even in cases where it appears applicable. For example, in both Google cases (*Shopping* and *Android*), the Commission had the opportunity to apply the essential faciality doctrine but chose not to do so. Moreover, the Commission seems to be avoiding the doctrine even in what appear to be conventional essential facility cases. In the *LG* case, a Lithuanian operator and manager of train infrastructure removed 19km of railway, allegedly

45 ibid para 51.
46 ibid para 53.
47 ibid para 54.
48 ibid para 56.
49 ibid para 55.
50 Case C-418/01 *IMS Health v NDC Health* ECLI:EU:C:2004:257, para 38.
51 Case C-7/97 *Oscar Bronner GmbH & Co v Mediaprint Zeitungs-und Zeitschriftenverlag GmbH* ECLI:EU:C:1998:569.
52 ibid para 41.
53 Case T-201/04 *Microsoft Corp v Commission* ECLI:EU:T:2007:289, para 334.
54 ibid para 284.
55 See Graef, *EU Competition Law* (n 36); Guggenberger (n 36).

to prevent its biggest customer from switching to a competitor in the market for the transport of oil products.[56] The Commission found the practice in breach of Article 102,[57] but it avoided framing the issue as a refusal to give access to an essential facility, even though railroads were the genesis of the doctrine. This raises questions about the continued relevance of the essential facilities doctrine, particularly in addressing harms associated with digital platforms.

Before delving into the reasons, it is worth briefly highlighting how the two Google cases could have been approached as a refusal to deal based on the essential facilities doctrine. *Google Shopping* was the first opportunity to apply the essential facilities doctrine to digital platforms. Google was fined €2.42 billion for abusing its dominant position in the market for general Internet searches 'by giving illegal advantage' to its specialized search service, Google Shopping.[58] To achieve this, Google changed its search algorithms to promote results from its shopping service at or near the top of the general search results and demoted results from its competitors. According to the Commission, the conduct 'has the potential to foreclose competing comparison-shopping services, which may lead to higher fees for merchants, higher prices for consumers, and less innovation.'[59] Consequently, the Commission ordered Google to treat both its own and rival comparison-shopping services equally. *Google Android*, mentioned above, is another instance where the Commission had the possibility to apply the essential facilities doctrine.

While there is room for debate, some scholars argue that certain aspects of Google's behaviour could have been framed as a refusal to deal. For instance, in the *Shopping* case, the Commission could have framed the case as a refusal 'to give access to the prominent spots in the search results'.[60] This claim is supported by the remedy, which compels Google to grant access and actively assist its downstream competitors in securing the prominent spots. The imposition of such remedies requires demonstrating that Google Search is an essential facility. Thus, the Commission decision to introduce a new theory of harm on self-preferencing appears to be an attempt to escape the argument that the search engine was indispensable for competing shopping sites that could reach users via browser or app.[61]

Similarly, some of Google's conduct in the *Android* case could be framed as a refusal to deal. This argument is particularly applicable to the first two theories of harm, which involve tying of Google Play Store and Google apps (Search and Chrome). For example, Akman argues that tying the Google Play Store and Google apps is more akin to a refusal to deal where Google is refusing to supply the Play

[56] See Case AT.39813 *Baltic Rail* decision of 2 October 2017, paras 1–2.

[57] See also Case T-814/17 *Lietuvos geležinkelai AB v Commission* ECLI:EU:T:2020:545, para 93.

[58] *Google Search (Shopping)* (n 39).

[59] ibid para 593.

[60] See Pinar Akman, 'A Preliminary Assessment of the European Commission's Google Android Decision' (2018) 1 CPI Antitrust Chronicle Winter 7.

[61] Inge Graef, 'Rethinking the Essential Facilities Doctrine for the EU Digital Economy', (Tilberg Law and Economics Center (TILEC) Discussion Paper DP 2019-028, TILEC 2019) 14.

Store without the condition that OEMs pre-install Google Search and Chrome on their devices.[62] The Commission's remark that the Google Play Store is a 'must-have' for device manufacturers may be indicative of the path that should have been taken.[63] Further, despite choosing a theory of harm based on tying, the remedy focuses on the terms of trade, specifically the conditions under which the Play Store is licensed, rather than on breaking the tie.[64] Therefore, the behaviour constitutes a refusal-to-deal offence and should have been scrutinized using the strict test of the essential facilities doctrine.[65] Both Google cases raise the question of whether the Commission is evading the stringent requirements of the essential facilities doctrine by devising new types of abuses or expanding the scope of existing ones.[66]

There may be several reasons for avoiding the use of the essential facilities doctrine in the above cases. Some of these are factual, whereas others relate to the legal tests. The Commission's avoidance of the doctrine in *LG* seems driven by the specific factual context. The GC accepted the Commission's argument that it was not required to demonstrate that access to the train track was indispensable.[67] This is because LG was required, both under EU and national law, to grant access to the railway infrastructure and to ensure that the infrastructure was in good technical condition. Furthermore, the railway network belongs to the Lithuanian state and was built using public funds.[68] This means that the justification for employing the strictest requirements imposed on essential facilities, namely intervening in someone's property rights and freedom of contract, was not present in this case. The CJEU has affirmed this stance in *Slovak Telekom (ST)*.[69] Clearly, this argument does not apply to digital platforms. Thus, the legal hurdles associated with the essential facilities doctrine might better explain why the Commission backed away from using the doctrine in the *Google Shopping* and *Android* cases.[70]

[62] See Akman (n 60) 6–7.

[63] See ibid 7.

[64] Graef, 'Rethinking Essential Facilities' (n 61) 17.

[65] See Akman (n 60) 7.

[66] Graef, 'Rethinking Essential Facilities' (n 61) 12 (noting that in both *Google Search (Shopping)* and *Google Android*, the Commission imposed 'essential facilities-alike remedies ... [but] under lower standards of tying and non-discrimination').

[67] *Lietuvos geležinkelai AB v Commission* (n 57) paras 91–94.

[68] ibid para 94,

[69] Case C-165/19 P *Slovak Telekom as v European Commission* ECLI:EU:C:2021:239, paras 50–51.

[70] Another challenge pertains to the argument that the doctrine is not suitable to practices that seek to leverage market power across different markets, as opposed to vertically integrated markets where the dominant undertaking is present both upstream and downstream. While the absence of the dominant undertaking in the secondary market might explain why the doctrine is not applicable to *Google Android*, this reasoning does not hold for *Google Search (Shopping)*. In the latter, the primary concern was Google's attempt to leverage its power from general Internet search to specialized searches, which is a typical concern for the essential facilities doctrine. There are also problems with the argument regarding the necessity for the dominant undertaking to be present in the secondary market. If this requirement applies to cases where a refusal to license occurs, it conflicts with the 'new product' condition. Such an interpretation would prevent competition authorities from intervening in cases where access seekers plan to utilize the requested input to enter a new market. See Graef, *EU Competition Law* (n 36) 227. Moreover, the General Court (GC) rejected the claim that the absence of the dominant

For an input to be considered indispensable, it must be shown that there are no substitutable inputs, actual or potential, that could be used by the access seeker. According to the CJEU, even less advantageous alternatives must be considered.[71] In both Google cases, the access seeker had the possibility to use other alternatives, though these were clearly less advantageous. In the case of *Shopping*, websites had the possibility to reach users via their own website on a browser or by developing an app. In the *Android* case, while Google Play Store is the default app store, there are also other alternatives available, such as Amazon and Aptoide. In such cases, it may be difficult to succeed in showing that the requested input—Search in the case of *Shopping* and Google Play in the case of *Android*—is indispensable to the customer. This may explain why the Commission backed away from using the essential facilities doctrine.[72] The availability of alternative sources of supply and the difficulty in assessing whether and which data is 'indispensable' are also the main challenges in using the essential facilities doctrine to facilitate access to data that could be used to develop services.[73]

The Commission also argues that the indispensability test does not apply to cases where terminating the infringement does not necessitate imposing an obligation on the dominant entity to 'transfer assets or establish agreements with parties it has not voluntarily chosen to engage with'.[74] This line of reasoning has gained some traction in the EU courts. For example, in *ST*, the CJEU accepted the Commission's argument that it did not need to prove the indispensability of the input.[75] According to the CJEU, the conditions outlined in *Bronner* do not apply to a dominant undertaking that grants access to its infrastructure subject on less favourable terms.[76] The Court emphasized the need to distinguish such practices from an outright refusal to deal, where competition authorities compel the dominant undertaking to grant competitors access to infrastructure it uses for its own business.[77] This distinction is important because of the different impact these measures have on the right to property and freedom of contract of the undertaking. Whereas forcing an undertaking to grant access entails severe interference with the undertaking's rights, measures aimed at remedying the conditions of access are less detrimental.[78] The GC confirmed this assessment in its *Google Shopping* decision.[79]

undertaking in the secondary market has a bearing in the application of the essential facilities doctrine. See Case T-128/98 *Aéroports de Paris v Commission* ECLI:EU:T:2000:290, para 165.

[71] Case C-7/97 *Bronner* (n 51) para 43.

[72] See Inge Graef, 'Differentiated Treatment in Platform-to-Business Relations: EU Competition Law and Economic Dependence' (2019) 38 Yearbook of European Law 448, 476.

[73] See the Commission's argument in Case M.7217 *Facebook/WhatsApp* decision of 3 October 2014, paras 188–89; Graef, *EU Competition Law* (n 36).

[74] See *Google Search (Shopping)* (n 39) paras 650–51. However, this seems unconvincing. See Graef, 'Rethinking Essential Facilities' (n 61) 13–14.

[75] *Slovak Telekom* (n 69) paras 50–51.

[76] ibid para 50.

[77] ibid.

[78] ibid.

[79] Case T-612/17 *Google LLC v European Commission* ECLI:EU:T:2021:763, para 219.

The Court emphasized that Google's behaviour is not just about a unilateral refusal to offer a service to competitors but also about providing preferential treatment to its own comparison service.[80]

This has significant implications for digital markets, where many of the platform bans are not outright refusal to deal, instead imposing conditions that put these services at a disadvantage. This suggests that certain platform bans or restrictions on data access could be addressed using this more lenient test, without the need to show indispensability.[81] But even in such cases, discussions on the indispensability of an input could be used to provide further support for the anticompetitive effects of the bans. As the CJEU has noted, showing that an input is indispensable increases the likelihood that the conduct under investigation will have potentially anticompetitive effects in the market and will constitute abuse under Article 102 of the TFEU.[82]

Importantly, despite its limited application thus far, the essential facilities doctrine is seen as an important tool for promoting competition in an economy characterized by complexity. In their article on 'Complexity-Minded Antitrust', Schrepel and Petit outline some shifts that create complexity and pose challenge to exiting tools and methods of competition law application.[83] These shifts related to a global increase in the number of activities, and interactions between them, the transition from an industrial to a knowledge-economy, and the decoupling of information from matter.[84] To effectively deal with these changes, the authors propose a shift towards a more complexity-minded antitrust, which focuses on multi-level analysis, feedback loops, and uncertainty-increasing intervention.[85] Specifically, a complexity-minded antitrust would increase uncertainty in markets by introducing positive feedback loops that spur output. In abuse-of-dominance cases, this could be achieved by imposing a duty to deal on the dominant firm, requiring it to share inputs to support a new composition of output.[86]

Therefore, the essential facilities doctrine is particularly suited for the complex economy and will remain instrumental in ensuring access to facilities that are essential for effective competition in a rapidly changing environment. In a response to a question on whether the essential facility would still be relevant in the context of digital platforms, Commissioner Vestager responded that 'the analysis of a case involving a platform could include, where relevant, consideration of the concept of

[80] ibid.

[81] According to the Court, the granting of access by a dominant undertaking under less advantageous conditions would constitute abuse if the practices 'are able to give rise to at least potentially anticompetitive effects, or exclusionary effects, on the markets concerned'; see ibid para 50.

[82] ibid.

[83] See Nicolas Petit and Thibault Schrepel, 'Complexity-Minded Antitrust' (2023) 33 Journal of Evolutionary Economics 541.

[84] ibid 544.

[85] ibid.

[86] ibid 559.

"essential facilities" in an appropriate form'.[87] In *Microsoft*, the Commission and the GC may have deliberately tailored the application of the essential facilities doctrine to the particular market situation.[88] There are similar arguments for rethinking the application of the essential facilities doctrine to digital markets, particularly how the doctrine could be tailored to address the competition concerns as regards access to platforms and data.[89] For example, Graef puts forward two suggestions in relation to the presence of the dominant undertaking in the secondary market and the new product requirements.[90] Others have suggested the lowering of the threshold, at least in relation to some assets, such as data generated as a by-product of providing a service.[91]

These suggestions notwithstanding, one of the arguments of this chapter is that adding an emergent properties perspective into the analysis could help revitalize the essential facilities doctrine as it applies to digital markets. This emergent thinking is particularly important in assessing the indispensability of input and in analysing the elimination of effective competition in the secondary market.

B. Emergence, the Essential Facilities Doctrine, and PET Bans

Chapter 2 discusses how emergence can result from an increase in the complexity of a system, which may occur through quantitative changes or the combination of component parts (known as summative complex). However, it is important to note that a mere increase in complexity does not necessarily lead to emergence. For emergence to occur, the interaction between the component parts must lead to 'some kind of discernible macrobehaviour'.[92] In the context of a summative complex, this means that the 'sum' should display features that are different in kind (qualitatively) from those of its constituent parts. In his influential article 'More Is Different', Nobel laureate Philip Anderson highlights how the summation of less complicated pieces into a system can result in a new type of behaviour that raises new questions.[93]

[87] See European Parliament, 'Answer Given by Executive Vice-President Vestager on Behalf of the European Commission' (6 April 2020) <https://www.europarl.europa.eu/doceo/document/E-9-2020-000591-ASW_EN.html> accessed 7 February 2024.

[88] See Graef, 'Rethinking Essential Facilities' (n 61) 12.

[89] See ibid. For the US perspective, see Guggenberger (n 36) 305.

[90] Graef, *EU Competition Law* (n 36) 225 (suggesting that the new product requirement ought to be dropped in markets that are characterized by external market failure—eg switching costs—where the competition could be improved through price, better quality, or product variety).

[91] See Heike Schweitzer and others, 'Modernising the Law on Abuse of Market Power: Report for the Federal Ministry for Economic Affairs and Energy (Germany)' (2018) 5–6.

[92] Steven Johnson, *Emergence: The Connected Lives of Ants, Brains, Cities, and Software* (Penguin 2001) 19.

[93] Philip Anderson, 'More Is Different: Broken Symmetry and the Nature of the Hierarchical Structure of Science' (1972) 177 Science 393.

In competition law, the summative complex can arise in relation to two practices that are made possible by the commercialization of personal data, namely the possibility of engaging in multiple markets simultaneously (cross-market practices) and systematic practices targeting several actors within the same market. Regarding the cross-market practices, the discussion of the *Android* case above demonstrates that the Commission can account for several cross-market practices. However, *Android* does not tackle the question of emergence, that is whether multiple practices, which are not illegal individually, can, when taken as whole, become illegal under Article 102 of the TFEU. For example, this issue might arise in relation to the essential facilities doctrine where an undertaking refuses to provide access to several inputs, which independently may fail to meet the indispensability test. Then the question is whether multiple bans across different markets could, when taken as a whole, constitute an illegal practice under Article 102, even where each ban, considered separately, fails to meet the required threshold, especially the indispensability test. The other source of emergent harms is the potential to engage in systematic practices by targeting several players in the same market, over time and at critical moments. This raises the question of whether the totality of a firm's conduct targeting several actors might risk eliminating competition in a specific market without any particular conduct, on a specific platform, causing harm in and of itself. The following sections highlight these potential risks using the bans on PETs as an example.

1. 'More Is Different': Emergent Harms from Cross-Market Practices

As noted above, the commercialization of personal data has led to the emergence of companies that control several gateways to consumers and data, which gives these companies the ability to engage in multiple cross-market practices. This, in turn, poses challenges to the atomized approach in competition law application, namely the focus on analysing the impact of behaviour on properly defined and well-delineated markets. By focusing on properly defined relevant markets, competition authorities may overlook emergent competitive harms from cross-market practices. Given the strict test for its application, the essential facilities doctrine, particularly the indispensability requirement, serves as a good example of how emergent competitive harms could arise.

As discussed in Section III.A, the indispensability requirement is one of the hurdles in the application of the essential facilities doctrine to digital platforms. One possible explanation for the Commission's avoidance of the doctrine in *Google Shopping* and *Android* is the availability of alternative options for access seekers.[94] In the *Shopping* case, websites could potentially reach users via their own website on a browser or by developing an app. In *Android*, Google Play was not the only

[94] See Graef, 'Rethinking Essential Facilities' (n 61) 12.

app store for Android devices as there are other alternatives, such as Amazon and Aptoide. However, as demonstrated subsequently, the nature of ecosystem markets and the control over key gateways enable leading digital players to engage in multiple practices deterring access across several markets. This raises the question of whether an input, not indispensable on its own, can become indispensable where the dominant undertaking controls the existing alternatives and engages in conduct that undermines the use of these alternatives. If so, this would exemplify an emergent property, in which the sum has features (indispensability) that are different in kind (qualitatively) from the features of the individual inputs, thereby satisfying the requirements for a modest form of emergence.[95]

A closer look at a complaint filed by Disconnect against Google will help to drive this point home. Following its ban from the app store, Disconnect accused Google of abusing its dominant position in the app store market through 'discontinuance of supply, and unjustified discrimination' and 'the related exclusion of competing privacy and security technology' in breach of Article 102 of the TFEU.[96] The extent to which Article 102 of the TFEU can capture Google's conduct, particularly the 'discontinuance of supply', comes down to the question of whether the Google Play Store can be considered an essential facility.

According to the case law, for an input to be considered an essential facility, it must be shown that it is indispensable to the product/service offered by the access seeker.[97] In *Bronner*, the CJEU analysed whether a nationwide home-delivery scheme, which consisted in delivering newspapers directly to subscribers in the early hours of the morning, could be considered indispensable. According to the CJEU, the scheme would be 'indispensable to carrying on that person's business, *inasmuch as there is no actual or potential substitute in existence for that home-delivery scheme*'.[98] Thus, at the centre of the indispensability requirement lies the assessment of whether there are substitutable inputs, actual or potential, that could be used by the access seeker. Actual substitution is assessed in light of the existence of other methods. In this regard, the Court asked the national court to assess 'whether other methods of distributing daily newspapers, such as sale in shops or at kiosks or delivery by post, are sufficiently interchangeable' with the home-delivery

[95] See Chapter 2, Section II.

[96] See *Disconnect Complaint* (n 19) para 16. For the complaint to proceed, certain market definition questions must be addressed. These include determining the relevant upstream market and assessing whether Google Play Store holds a dominant position in it. This is a factual question and is beyond the scope of this section. However, it is worth noting that in its *Google Android* decision, the Commission defined a separate market for 'app stores for the Android mobile operating system'. The Commission found that Google Play Store accounts for over 90 per cent of app downloads on Android devices and holds a dominant position in the app store market for the Android MOS. The Commission also identified high entry barriers arising from network effects as a characteristic of this market. Therefore, the same approach could be used in the *Disconnect* case, where the relevant upstream market encompasses app stores for the Android MOS, and Google Play Store holds a dominant position in this market.

[97] See *Magill* (n 43) paras 52–53; *Bronner* (n 51) paras 44–45.

[98] *Bronner* (n 51) para 41 (emphasis added).

scheme.[99] The assessment of potential alternatives focuses on whether 'there are any technical, legal or even economic obstacles capable of making it impossible, or even unreasonably difficult' to duplicate the requested input.[100]

Taking the Disconnect example, determining actual substitution involves evaluating whether other methods are 'sufficiently interchangeable' with the requested input, which, in this case, is Google Play. App stores act as gateways for users to access content and services, with Google Play being the dominant gateway for Android devices. However, it is not the only means of accessing users. Other Android app stores, such as the Amazon Appstore, F-Droid, and Aptoide, can be used by apps to provide services. Additionally, users can download the app directly from Disconnect's website through a process called 'sideloading'. Furthermore, since most anti-tracking and ad-blocking apps are available as browser extensions, Disconnect can reach users through web browsers.[101] The question is whether these alternatives are 'sufficiently interchangeable' with Google Play.

These alternatives might not be as optimal for reaching consumers as the Play Store. First, alternative app stores like Aptoide are less well known and have a much smaller market share. Google Play has over three million apps, making it more appealing to consumers than any other competing Android app store, with the closest competitor being the Amazon Appstore with approximately 600,000 apps. The number of apps is important because it drives network effects: the more apps there are in an app store, the more valuable it becomes to consumers. More consumers attract more app developers, which, in turn, attracts more users. Therefore, due to the network effect, Disconnect cannot reach the same number of users using other Android app stores. Sideloading also has its own problems, one of which is increased search costs. This is because Google Play offers users search and promotional features such as 'App of the day', which make it easier for users to find the apps they are interested in. According to some estimates, the majority of app installations happen this way.[102] Without promotional and search features, the search costs for finding apps increases. Moreover, sideloading deprives apps of certain benefits such as trust and credibility that come with being in the app store. Thus, the existing alternatives are less advantageous compared to Google Play.

This notwithstanding, alternatives are not to be discounted merely because they are 'less advantageous'. In its complaint to the national authorities, Mr Bronner argued that the available alternatives, such as kiosk sales, are not 'sufficiently interchangeable' with the home-delivery scheme because one cannot reach consumers in the early mornings.[103] The CJEU rejected this argument and held that

[99] ibid para 34.
[100] ibid para 44.
[101] *Disconnect Complaint* (n 19) para 40 (indicating that Disconnect distributes 'its products to EEA consumers through the Google Play Store, the Apple Store, the Google Chrome Store, and its own site').
[102] ibid para 301 (references omitted).
[103] *Bronner* (n 51) para 8.

postal delivery and kiosk sales were viable alternatives, 'even though they may be less advantageous for the distribution of certain newspapers'.[104] Thus, the above-mentioned alternatives (ie the use of other Android-based app stores, sideloading, and web browsers) can be viable substitutes to Google Play, even if they are less optimal channels for reaching consumers. In light of these discussions, one could plausibly argue that access to Google Play is not indispensable for apps such as Disconnect to carry out their business. However, a closer look at the whole ecosystem might be necessary to understand the complexity of the issue.

Apart from the dominant app store, Google also owns the dominant MOS, Android. With more than 80 per cent of the market share (and 95 per cent of the market for licensable smart MOS), the Android MOS sits between the hardware, applications, and users. Google also has a dominant position in the market for Internet search, with more than 90 per cent of market share in Europe and globally. Moreover, Google Chrome is the most used browser in Europe, with more than 50 per cent of market share. These are key gateways for PETs to reach consumers. This combined control over Android, Chrome, and Search puts Google in a close-to-unassailable position, with the power and ability to limit the extent to which app developers can rely on the above-mentioned alternatives as viable substitutes.

One of the alternative channels for apps such as Disconnect to reach consumers is through other Android-based app stores, such as Aptoide. In this regard, one needs to look at how Google uses its control and dominance of the Android MOS to make life difficult for these competing app stores. For example, Aptoide filed a complaint with the Commission against Google for obstructing its app store's functionality on certain devices.[105] Aptoide claims that Google used its Android security system, Google Play Protect, to encourage users to uninstall the Aptoide app store by warning of potential harm. When users disregarded the warning, the app store ceased functioning, preventing app installations. Aptoide contests the safety allegations and argues that Google's actions breach EU competition rules.[106] In fact, Aptoide won a case against Google for abuse of dominance in a national court.[107] Similarly, Google removed the Amazon app from its Play Store for providing users with links to the Amazon app store.[108]

Moreover, these competing Android app stores are not allowed to feature Google's most popular and 'must-have' apps, such as YouTube, Search, Chrome, and Maps, and this significantly reduces the attractiveness of these stores to

[104] ibid para 44.

[105] Natalia Drozdiak, 'Google Play Store Rival Files Antitrust Complaint to EU', *Bloomberg* (12 July 2018).

[106] Inge Graef, 'Aptoide versus Google and the Boundaries of Competition Law' (2018) 68 Wirtschaft und Wettbewerb 437.

[107] See Andrei Khalip, Catarina Demony, and Foo Yun Chee, 'Aptoide Wins Court Battle against Google in Landmark Case', *Reuters* (22 October 2018).

[108] Michael Rougeau and Matt Hanson, 'Amazon Explains Why Its App Was Kicked from Google Play' *Techradar* (12 December 2014).

consumers. Thus, to the extent that Google uses its ownership of the MOS and other proprietary apps to disadvantage other Android-based app stores, the viability of the other Android app stores as effective substitutes is limited. This may, in turn, strengthen the argument regarding the indispensability of Google Play for apps such as Disconnect to carry out business.

Google can also leverage its control of the dominant search engine and leading browser to undermine the viability of existing alternatives. Sideloading, the second alternative discussed above, involves downloading an app directly from the app developer's website. However, unless consumers know the exact website address (which is unlikely in many cases), they will probably rely on search engines to reach the website.[109] This poses a problem as Google owns the dominant search engine, which it can use to restrict the visibility of such websites by demoting their rankings or even removing them from search results. For example, in 2012, Google stopped showing the website of Adblock Plus, an anti-tracking and ad-blocking software, in its search results.[110] With Google receiving more than 90 per cent of search queries, not appearing or being demoted to the second page of the search results can be catastrophic.[111]

In principle, if consumers cannot find the developer's website using Google Search, they can still use other search engines. However, this possibility is significantly reduced because Google Search comes pre-installed on many Android devices and is set by default. Google uses its dominance in Android to force device manufacturers to set Google Search as the default 'for all Web search access points', including 'voice search', and to 'be activated when a user presses and holds a device's physical "Home" button or "swipes up" from a digital home button'.[112] Google also offers financial payments to large device manufacturers and mobile operators on the condition that they exclusively pre-install Google Search on their devices. As such, users are more likely to stick with Google, which, in turn, reduces the possibility that users will download the app from the developer's website, especially if it has been removed or demoted from Google Search results.

Even if consumers overcome all these challenges and reach the developer's website, Google uses its control over Android to make this process more cumbersome. For example, when users attempt to download apps from 'unknown sources', Google warns them that they are solely responsible for any damage to their phone or loss of data. If users are using Chrome, which is likely given it is installed by default on Android devices, they will see an additional warning message when they

[109] See *Google Search (Shopping)* (n 39) para 454 (finding that most of the traffic for shopping websites comes from search engines, particularly Google).

[110] Natasha Lomas, 'AdBlock Plus Responds to Play Store Ban: "Unilateral Move by Google Threatens Consumer Choice"', *TechCrunch* (14 March 2013).

[111] Almost 99 per cent of users do not click on websites listed on the second page or beyond. See *Google Search (Shopping)* (n 39).

[112] See Damien Geradin and Benjamin Edelman, 'Android and Competition Law: Exploring and Assessing Google's Practices in Mobile' (2016) 12 European Competition Journal 159, 165–66.

click 'download', which is absent if users are using Firefox.[113] Even if users manage to bypass these messages and download the app, there is no guarantee that it will work on their device. Google can easily make such apps incompatible or unworkable on the users' device, as it did by forcing Android users to manually configure a proxy server to run Adblock Plus.[114] These practices significantly limit the extent to which 'sideloading' can be considered a 'sufficiently interchangeable' alternative to Google Play for apps such as Disconnect to reach consumers.

The third alternative, which involves using web browsers to reach consumers, presents similar challenges. This is because the leading browser, Chrome, is owned by Google. This means that Google can also ban anti-tracking and ad-blocking apps from its Chrome store. Again, this is not hypothetical, as Google has banned AdNauseam and Adblock Plus from its Chrome store.[115] Since Chrome has a significant market share on Android devices, this restricts the reach of apps to a majority of Android users. Although consumers could resort to other web browsers to access these apps, the pre-installation of Chrome on many Android devices reduces the likelihood of users switching to other browsers. As a result, the use of web browsers as a viable alternative to Google Play is limited, which further restricts the ability of apps such as Disconnect to reach a wider audience.

In light of the above practices, it is questionable whether the three alternatives can be considered comparable substitutes for Google Play. Thus, one could argue that access to the Google Play Store is not, in and of itself, indispensable for anti-tracking and ad-blocking apps to carry out their business as other, *albeit* poor, alternatives exist. However, the key question is what happens if the owner of the requested input, as demonstrated by Google's actions, can prevent customers from accessing these alternatives. The line taken here is that competition policy should be open to the possibility that several alternative facilities, when owned by the owner of the requested input, could, in combination be considered indispensable. This is particularly relevant when there is evidence that the dominant undertaking uses its control over these facilities to impede customers from using these alternatives. This would make it possible to consider emergent competitive harms from multiple bans across different markets, which, when viewed in isolation, might not meet the standards required for refusal to deal under existing case law, particularly due to the indispensability test, but when considered together, could cause lasting harm to competition. Section IV.D delves further into this issue.

2. Emergent Harms from Systematic Practices Targeting Several Actors

The above section shows some of the emergent competitive harms from multiple cross-market practices. But the source of emergent competitive harms is not

[113] See *Complaint of Disconnect, Inc.* (n 19) para 317.
[114] Lomas (n 110).
[115] ibid.

limited to cross-market practices as it can also arise from systematic practices targeting several players in the same market, over time, and at critical moments. This consideration is important in assessing the anticompetitive impact of conduct. The systematic nature of the practices raises the question of whether competition law is equipped to deal with a pattern of conduct targeting several actors over time, which, taken as a whole, may eliminate effective competition in a relevant market without any particular practice, in and of itself, causing such harm. As shown in Section IV, these potential harms could be mitigated by adopting a holistic approach in defining the relevant market, in assessing market power, and establishing abuse of dominance.

Again, the case of PETs serves as a good example of how leading digital players may engage in systematic and subtle practices targeting several actors in the same market, which may lead to emergent competitive harms. Given that Google identifies such players as threats to its business model, its offensive is not limited to a single player. As previously mentioned, Google has removed several anti-tracking and ad-blocking apps from Google Play, including Adblock Plus, AdBlocker, AdAway, and AdFree.[116] Further, Google also bans the same players from other gateways such as its Chrome web store and search results. Thus, it is crucial to consider the pattern and consistency in Google's specific targeting of several players competing on privacy when analysing whether the conduct eliminates effective competition in a market. Although this consideration is important in assessing whether alleged conduct is capable of eliminating effective competition more generally (the standard test in many cases),[117] to continue the above discussions on the ban on PETs, the focus here is on its relevance to the application of the essential facilities doctrine.

In applying the essential facilities doctrine, an important consideration is whether the refusal is 'capable of' or 'likely to eliminate competition' in the secondary market.[118] The CJEU seems to employ different standards in relation to tangible assets and IP rights. In the case of IP rights, the CJEU has indicated that for a refusal to license to be abusive, the conduct must exclude 'all competition in the secondary market'.[119] This imposes a very strict test that is based on total foreclosure of the market.[120] However, in *Microsoft*, the GC adopted a lower standard based on the elimination of 'effective' competition, rather than 'all competition'.[121]

For tangible assets, the CJEU employs a standard based on the requirement that the refusal is 'likely to eliminate all competition in the daily newspaper market on

[116] See Velazco (n 18).
[117] See *Slovak Telekom* (n 69) para 50.
[118] ibid para 47; also *Microsoft Corp v Commission* (n 53) paras 561–63.
[119] *IMS Health* (n 50) paras 38–39.
[120] Robert O'Donoghue and Jorge Padilla, *The Law and Economics of Article 102 TFEU* (2nd edn, Hart Publishing 2013) 551.
[121] *Microsoft Corp v Commission* (n 53) para 563.

the part of the person requesting the service'.[122] According to this test, the second condition is fulfilled if the refusal is likely to foreclose the access seeker. It is true that if there are other players operating in the market using other inputs, the likelihood that the requested input will be considered indispensable is reduced because of the possibility that the access seeker may use other alternatives to carry out its business. However, the *Bronner* test can make a difference if those other market players are also using the input of the dominant undertaking or/and if the alternatives are controlled by the dominant undertaking and access is refused to one or several of these inputs. This notwithstanding, here, the standard based on 'elimination of effective competition', rather than the test based on the 'elimination of competition on the part of the customer seeking access', is employed.

When assessing the impact of alleged conduct by a dominant undertaking, a relevant consideration is the extent to which such conduct forecloses competition in the relevant secondary market.[123] This means that competition is not foreclosed if there are a sufficient number of players operating in the market even after the refusal by the dominant undertaking. However, the mere existence of other players in the market does not preclude the fact that the refusal can exclude competition in the secondary market. In *Microsoft*, the access seekers were active in the market, despite Microsoft's refusal to provide interoperable information. The GC emphasized that the requirement regarding the 'likely elimination of competition' does not mean that 'there is no more, or practically no more, competition on the market'.[124] More importantly, the Court noted that 'the fact that the competitors of the dominant undertaking retain a marginal presence in certain niches on the market cannot suffice to substantiate the existence of such competition'.[125]

Applying this test to the ban on PETs, even though several players, including Disconnect, continue to operate in the market for privacy-enhancing services, the requirement regarding the elimination of effective competition may still be met if these players have only retained 'a marginal presence in certain niches on the market'. An important consideration in this regard is whether the conduct targets not just one firm but also other players in the market. This is because the potential for leading digital players to engage in systematic practices targeting several players may, over time and taken as whole, effectively eliminate competition in a market. This is particularly important because of the role that momentum plays

[122] *Bronner* (n 51) para 41.

[123] In the example at hand, the secondary market can include all 'privacy and security' or 'privacy-enhancing' apps/services. This is consistent with recent Commission practice to define markets based on the functionality of apps/services including markets for 'consumer communications services', 'social networks', 'professional social networks', and 'productivity software'. See *Facebook/WhatsApp* (n 73); Case M.8124 *Microsoft/LinkedIn* decision of 6 December 2016.

[124] *Microsoft Corp v Commission* (n 53) para 461.

[125] ibid para 563.

in the adoption of technology in general but also in relation to privacy-enhancing services.[126]

Historians of technology talk about the importance of momentum in the successful adoption of technological systems, which can be accumulated through forms of capital including favourable social and political networks, economic resources, and acquired skills and knowledge.[127] Technological momentum 'provides the durability and the propensity for growth'.[128] The importance of technological momentum is consistent with economic theories of technology adoption, which suggest low level of deployment at the beginning that increases as technologies mature or information about the technologies spreads among potential users.[129] The role of technological momentum is especially important in the adoption and durability of technologies that impact privacy.[130] This implies that Google's conduct targeting several players across different platforms could be used to prevent privacy-enhancing technologies from gaining momentum, resulting in the relegation of all, or at least the key, players to a marginal presence in the market.

Momentum is also time-dependent, and this aspect is particularly important for privacy-enhancing services.[131] Studies indicate that the adoption of PETs is influenced by specific moments, such as publicized data breaches like Cambridge Analytica and revelations regarding government surveillance, such as those by Snowden. For example, after the Snowden revelations, there was a growing interest in the use and adoption of instant messaging apps that offer encrypted communication, such as Telegram and Signal.[132] Similarly, the use of Tor, a tool that allows users to conceal their location and browsing habits, increased significantly following these revelations.[133] Data from DuckDuckGo, a privacy-friendly search engine, also shows that its traffic increased after Google's 2012 privacy policy changes and the Snowden revelations. Moreover, the Commission's investigation into the *Facebook/WhatsApp* merger reveals that the announcement of the acquisition led many German WhatsApp users to download more privacy-friendly texting apps, such as Signal and Threema.[134]

[126] Thomas Hughes, 'Technological Momentum' in Deborah Johnson and Jameson Wetmore (eds), *Technology and Society: Building Our Societal Future* (MIT Press 2009); Ashlin Lee, 'A Question of Momentum–Critical Reflections on Individual Options for Surveillance Resistance' (2014) 11 Teknokultura 425.

[127] Hughes (n 126) 146; also Lee (n 126) 146.

[128] Hughes (n 126) 147.

[129] London Economics, *Study on the Economic Benefits of Privacy-Enhancing Technologies* (2010) xii <https://londoneconomics.co.uk/wp-content/uploads/2011/09/17-Study-on-the-economic-benefits-of-privacy-enhancing-technologies-PETs.pdf>.

[130] See Shoshana Zuboff, *The Age of Surveillance Capitalism: The Fight for a Human Future at the New Frontier of Power* (PublicAffairs 2019) 225; Lee (n 126).

[131] Hughes (n 126) 142.

[132] See Sören Preibusch, 'Privacy Behaviors after Snowden' (2015) 58 Communications of the ACM 48.

[133] ibid.

[134] *Facebook/WhatsApp* (n 73) para 174.

The examples presented above show the crucial role that moments play in the adoption of privacy-friendly services. However, this also highlights the potential for dominant undertakings to exploit these key moments to suppress competition on privacy. Specifically, companies like Google, who control multiple and key gateways, can use patterns of conduct to undermine the momentum of emerging privacy-friendly services following a triggering event. For this to happen, it is not necessary for the dominant platform to completely ban/remove one or several such services. If employed systematically, even short-lived bans targeting a specific service while it is gaining momentum can do the job. Ultimately, these practices can limit thc growth of the market and relegate competitors to a marginal presence.

In fact, dominant platforms do not even need to engage in the drastic conduct of banning or blocking such apps from key gateways. Subtle practices, such as depriving the apps of promotional and search features of an app store, can be used systematically to suppress competition. For example, despite the long list of app categories that makes it easy to find apps in the Play Store, Google does not provide a category for privacy and security. This increases search costs, as users need to find these apps within other categories. Google could also use its promotional and search features across its platforms to make it difficult for consumers to find and download such apps at critical moments. Thus, competition policy should consider such systematic and subtle ways of eliminating competition in a market (see more in Section IV.C and IV.D.

IV. Beyond an Atomistic Approach and Towards a Holistic Analysis

Just as in life, where death can result from a single bullet or a thousand cuts, competition can be harmed by disparate forms of misconduct taken as a whole. This is relevant in the context of platform-to-business relationships, where a handful of firms control multiple and key digital gateways that provide access to consumers and data, which gives these firms the power to engage in multiple and systematic practices across several markets. This can lead to emergent competitive harms where individual practices, considered in isolation, may not meet the necessary standards for competition law intervention, but their cumulative impact may have a lasting negative effect on competition. Further, discussions above have also shown the limitations of an atomized approach to competition law enforcement, which may hinder competition authorities from recognizing and addressing emergent competitive harms resulting from multiple practices that span across different relevant markets.

Thus, this section advances the argument that competition analysis involving ecosystems needs to extend beyond isolated, individual relevant markets (ie an atomistic approach) and involve a holistic and system-level analysis, taking into account the possibility that leading digital players may hinder effective competition by multiple actions across different markets and by targeting several players simultaneously. The holistic approach can be applied in defining the relevant market (Section A), in assessing market power (Section B), and abuse of dominance (Section C). Section D shows how the holistic approach and emergent thinking can be incorporated into the essential facilities doctrine to help reinvigorate the doctrine's importance for digital platforms.

A. Holistic Approach to Market Definition

It has been noted that the main challenges faced by competition law in the wake of the commercialization of personal data and the rise of ecosystems stem from the atomized approach taken in applying the rules, which tends to focus on identifying and assessing the impact of conduct on well-defined and delineated relevant product or service markets. This is because multi-market ecosystems, together with the central role that personal data plays in linking the different markets, blur the boundaries between what were previously separate relevant markets and complicate the attribution of a competitive harm to a specific relevant market. Further, the atomized approach to defining relevant market may potentially overlook emergent competitive harms from multiple and systematic practices in seemingly different relevant markets within the comprehensive ecosystem. Addressing these challenges and emergent competitive harms requires changes and adaptations in the mechanics of market definition. This section outlines some potential solutions.

The nature of ecosystems dictates that competition authorities define markets that go beyond a specific product or service. In 2019, the Commission initiated a review of the 1997 market definition notice to assess its ongoing relevance given the developments since its adoption. The evaluation involved public consultations and feedback. Many scholars and commentators have indicated the challenges in using the current market definition tools to effectively address multi-product companies or ecosystems.[135] The Commission's findings show that while the core principles remain relevant, their application to digital markets can raise challenges, particularly in defining markets for multi-sided platforms where services are offered at no monetary cost, defining markets for '*ecosystems*' and data.[136] Some have suggested defining 'cluster' or 'ecosystem' markets that go beyond a single

[135] See European Commission, Directorate-General for Competition, Jacques Crémer, Yves-Alexandre de Montjoye, and Heike Schweitzer, *Competition Policy for the Digital Era* (EU Publications Office, 2019) 4; Inge Graef, 'Feedback on the Evaluation of the Market Definition Notice' <http://file:///C:/Users/A1910484/Downloads/090166e5cf4d1601.pdf> 7.

[136] Commission Staff Working Document, 'Evaluation of the Commission Notice on the Definition of Relevant Market for the Purposes of Community Competition Law of 9 December 1997' (SWD(2021) 199 final, 12 July 2021) 52 (emphasis added).

product or service.[137] This suggestion is partially motivated by the desire to address harms stemming from 'corporate strategies that are no longer geared towards single product or services markets'.[138] The ecosystem-level analytical lens allows competition authorities to account for the emergent effects (harms) from discrete practices across multiple markets within the ecosystem. If the revised market definition notice incorporates these suggestions, it may help competition authorities overcome some of the challenges associated with the atomized approach. However, there are concerns that ecosystem markets have not received sufficient attention in the revision, with much focus given to multi-sided and zero-priced markets.[139]

Some initiatives at national level are particularly informative in this regard. For example, one of the proposals put forward by the Greek Law-Making Commission for the Modernization of Competition Law included adding a new provision specifically targeting 'ecosystems' into the Competition Act.[140] The proposed provision prohibits undertakings holding a dominant position in an ecosystem of paramount importance with regards to competition in Greece from abusing their dominance.[141] This new provision does not deviate from the established concepts of dominance and abuse as used in the context of Article 102 of the TFEU. What is different about this provision is that both dominance and abuse can be established in '*an ecosystem rather than a relevant market*'.[142]

In this regard, the Competition Commission has first to identify ecosystems that are of 'paramount importance' for competition in Greece.[143] Second, the authority must establish that the undertaking holds a dominant position in the particular ecosystem. Given that ecosystem competition involves vertical and conglomerate relationships (ie not just competition for market share but also for more of the surplus value of the ecosystem), the factors used to assess dominance are tailored to

[137] See European Commission, Crémer, Montjoye, and Schweitzer (n 135) 4. For a US perspective, see Herbert Hovenkamp, 'Digital Cluster Markets' (2021) <https://ssrn.com/abstract=3820062>.

[138] Schallbruch, Schweitzer, and Wambach (n 15) 27.

[139] See Jacobides and Lianos (n 8) 1212.

[140] This specific proposal did not get to the final text, but there are similar initiatives in other member states, including the 10th amendment of the German Competition Law. See ibid 1217.

[141] However, the new proposed addition 'becomes applicable if the provisions in Articles 1 and 2 of Greek Law 3959/2011 and/or the equivalent provisions in Articles 101 and 102 TFEU cannot sort out the specific competition problem': ibid 1220.

[142] ibid (emphasis added). However, this approach may 'challenge the important role of competitive markets as the main social institution to reward productivity': Ioannis Lianos, 'Competition Law for the Digital Era: A Complex Systems' Perspective' (Centre for Law, Economics and Society (CLES) Research Paper Series 6/2019, CLES 2019) 161–62.

[143] The proposed law defines an ecosystem as

> a web of interconnected and largely interdependent economic activities carried out by different undertakings with the intention of supplying products, services or a nexus of products and/or services that impact the same set of users, or a platform of economic activities carried out by different undertakings with the intention of supplying products, services or nexuses of products and/or services that impact the same users or different categories of users. Jacobides and Lianos (n 8: 1220–21)

reflect this relationship.[144] Thus, apart from turnover, important factors in such assessments are whether the undertaking is an orchestrator (ie manages a multi-product or multi-actor system and decides the rules of engagement), whether the undertaking controls gateways that are difficult for other firms in the ecosystem to acquire, and the general technological and financial advantages of the company.[145] As Section IV.B shows, these factors extend beyond the conventional metrics for assessing market power, which is based on a firm's specific characteristics and exceptional attributes, and capture power dynamics stemming from managing interactions.[146] Next, the competition authority should examine whether conduct by the dominant undertaking restricts competition and so constitutes abuse.

Clearly, the above proposal caters to the challenges discussed in relation to the atomized approach and emergent competitive harms. As noted above, one of the challenges with the atomized approach is the difficulty in drawing boundaries between individual relevant markets that form an ecosystem and in attributing a competitive harm to a specific relevant market. In this sense, the ability to define a market at ecosystem level and condemn a practice within that market mitigates this difficulty. Additionally, the atomized approach limits the ability of competition authorities to assess the impact of conduct in relation to markets other than the target market. However, the proposed approach allows for assessing the impact of conduct across markets, even if they are not necessarily linked with each other in the traditional sense, as long as they are part of the ecosystem. In other words, the ability to define markets and establish dominance at the ecosystem level allows competition authorities to consider multiple practices and the cross-market effects of such practices, which is often difficult to do under the atomized approach.[147] Section IV.B will illustrate how this approach empowers competition agencies to address emergent competitive harms.

B. Holistic Approach to Market Power Assessment

The previous discussions have shown how multi-product ecosystems and the web of interactions they foster increase the level of complexity. This complexity challenges the atomistic approach to the application of competition law. Ecosystems pose a similar challenge for market power assessment, since the latter depends

[144] ibid 1221.

[145] ibid.

[146] Ioannis Lianos and Bruno Carballa-Smichowski, 'A Coat of Many Colours—New Concepts and Metrics of Economic Power in Competition Law and Economics' (2022) 18 Journal of Competition Law & Economics 795.

[147] See Khan (n 27) 747 (arguing that accurately assessing Amazon's true structural power necessitates viewing it as a unified, multi-product entity. Isolating a single business line of Amazon and analysing solely on a specific behaviour—eg its competitive pricing—in that sector does not adequately reveal the company's overarching dominance.)

on defining a relevant market as the competitive field. This challenge to the contemporary understanding of market power, which denotes the ability to profitably increase prices and decrease output, stems from two interconnected assumptions related to the fields of competition and power dimensions.

The first assumption is that firms only compete within a specific market: their profitability is contingent upon their performance in comparison to other firms within that market.[148] This notion of market power is predicated on an economic model that assumes equal access to technology, capital, and information by firms. Firms compete for superiority and larger market shares through product and cost efficiencies.[149] EU competition law embodies this approach by using market share as an important indicator of dominance, a form of market power.[150] While other competitive constraints (such as entry barriers and economies of scope and scale) are considered, the focus is primarily on product and cost efficiencies. Therefore, the prevailing understanding of market power centres on the relevant market as the principal competitive arena, where a company's unique characteristics, such as dominance over critical inputs, are deemed to be the source of its competitive edge. The second and related assumption is that this market power is exerted at the immediate vertical (eg suppliers or customers) or horizontal (eg competitors operating in the same market) level.[151]

The nature of ecosystems alters these dynamics, in terms of the field of competition, the sources of market power, and the modalities of expression of market power. First, in addition to competition within the relevant market, firms compete by redefining and shaping the boundaries of markets. Research on mergers and acquisitions in the technology sector suggests that these actions are driven not solely by 'the desire to integrate capabilities' into existing products but also by the desire to shape the trajectories of markets and industries by eliminating alternative technologies that might limit or threaten their business models.[152]

Second, the current notion of market power neglects the various dimensions of economic power related to value chains and ecosystems, which generate value by creating and exploiting economic interactions.[153] As noted in Chapter 1, ecosystems generate value by fostering interactions among unique complements. This is typically achieved using application programming interfaces (APIs) or software development kits but can also involve establishing the rules of interaction. These interfaces can give rise to positional power.[154] Unlike traditional market power,

[148] Lianos, 'Competition Law for the Digital Era' (n 142) 141; Petit and Schrepel (n 83) 543.

[149] Petit and Schrepel (n 83) 546.

[150] See Case 85/76 *Hoffmann-La Roche v Commission* ECLI:EU:C:1979:36, para 44 (noting that very large market shares 'are in themselves, and save in exceptional circumstances, evidence of the existence of a dominant position').

[151] Lianos and Carballa-Smichowski (n 146) 818.

[152] Facebook's acquisition of WhatsApp and Instagram are examples. See Jacobides and Lianos (n 8) 1203.

[153] Lianos and Carballa-Smichowski (n 146) 799.

[154] ibid 812.

which is based on a firm's specific characteristics, positional power is determined by the network structure and the actor's pivotal position within it.[155] This form of power can be exerted over other members of the ecosystem/value chain even when they are not located immediately upstream or downstream and they are not direct competitors within a market. Positional power allows an actor to obtain a higher share of the value created within the value chain or ecosystem.[156]

The current conception of market power overlooks the ability of firms to leverage their positional advantage within an ecosystem to capture a large share of the surplus derived from the interconnections therein. Firms with a central position within an ecosystem may harness this position to collect valuable information on end-users and their competitors. Facebook and Google are prominent examples. Both companies offer technologies that enable customers to interact with a diverse range of actors while also using these connections to gather valuable information on real-time customer preferences and activities. The collected data can be utilized to refine targeted advertising, enhance matchmaking, or facilitate entry into adjacent markets. The increased level of personalization and diversification may result in customer lock-in, which the (positionally) dominant companies can exploit by imposing unfair terms on end-users and businesses seeking to reach these end-users.[157]

Furthermore, the current model of market power and its associated metrics undermine the 'monopoly rents of the knowledge-economy'. In the knowledge economy, firms compete for advantage through financialization, and factors such as increasing returns on adoption, lock-in, and path dependency can determine market outcomes.[158] Financialization refers to a phenomenon where companies are valued by financial markets based on their anticipated future profits, which often surpass their present cash flows.[159] This tendency is particularly evident in the digital economy, where companies are often willing to incur significant losses and prioritize expansion by acquiring innovative companies, entering adjacent markets, and gaining access to data. Financial markets reward this behaviour; they expect future profits to surge as a result of a firm's control of key gateways and data access. This contradicts the conventional notion of market power, which emphasizes firms within a particular market competing for a greater share of revenue through cost and product efficiencies.[160] Similarly, the classic economic model employed in competition law assumes that the interactions between economic agents are linear and additive in nature.[161] However, this assumption neglects the

[155] See ibid.
[156] ibid 818–20.
[157] Jacobides and Lianos (n 8) 1209.
[158] See Petit and Schrepel (n 83) 546; Ioannis Lianos, 'Competition Law for a Complex Economy' (2019) 50 IIC-International Review of Intellectual Property and Competition Law 643.
[159] Lianos, 'Competition Law for a Complex Economy' (n 158) 645.
[160] ibid.
[161] Petit and Schrepel (n 83) 543.

phenomenon of emergence and the non-linear dynamics inherent in complex digital markets, where new firms can quickly ascend to become industry leaders through network effects, learning effects, and market tipping.[162]

Essentially, the current methods for measuring market power and dominance inadequately capture the value stemming from financialization and the monopolization of a substantial portion of the surplus generated by managing relationships, whether competitive or cooperative, horizontal, vertical, or conglomerate. To accurately reflect these different competitive fields and interactions, economic power must encompass both direct vertical and/or horizontal power relations, as well as power at the ecosystem/value-chain level.[163] Therefore, just as the rise of ecosystems is pushing competition policy to adopt a multi-level analysis in defining the relevant market, the assessment of market power should consider how the network structure and features of the ecosystem/value chain influence the distribution of power among participants. A growing body of literature conceptualizes the dimensions of power at the ecosystem/value-chain level. This literature can, and should, inform competition law.

Lianos and Carballa-Smichowski draw upon multidisciplinary perspectives to identify various dimensions of power that are pertinent to the ecosystem level.[164] Of particular significance to the discussions in this chapter is positional power, which encompasses panopticon power and architectural power.[165] Panopticon power, derived from the works of Jeremy Bentham and Michel Foucault, describes an actor's capacity to leverage their position within a network, such as a value chain or an ecosystem, to acquire valuable information about consumers and competitors.[166] Many key digital platforms, such as Amazon, are able to gather diverse data types, including information on customer purchasing habits, searches, and product returns, as well as on retailers' responses to inquiries and product ratings. This positional advantage may also enable these companies to gather information from actors with whom they have no direct relationship, such as the end-users of business customers. Such access may enable these companies to leverage and strategically use the data to obtain a higher share of value.

In addition to describing panopticon power, Lianos and Carballa-Smichowski propose a metric for measuring this type of power, based on the volume, quality, and scope of data.[167] As illustrated in Section V, recent competition cases involving companies such as Facebook and Amazon have focused on data collected in one market and then repurposed to gain a competitive advantage in another market.

[162] Jacobides and Lianos (n 8) 1211.

[163] See Petit and Schrepel (n 83) 549 (suggesting the need for competition law to establish a macro-level lens that takes into account the competition dynamics at ecosystem and industry level.)

[164] Lianos and Carballa-Smichowski (n 146).

[165] ibid.

[166] ibid 815; Orla Lynskey, 'Grappling with "Data Power": Normative Nudges from Data Protection and Privacy' (2019) 20 Theoretical Inquiries in Law 189.

[167] Lianos and Carballa-Smichowski (n 146) 828.

Similarly, Chapter 4 highlights the increasing recognition of data and data-driven network effects as sources of market power by competition authorities. These developments signify a growing acknowledgement of the significance of panopticon power in competition law. However, as Chapters 4 and 7 will note, there are still gaps in competition authorities' understanding of the implications of panopticon power and their ability to address such power.

Competition law should also consider architectural power, another form of positional power. Architectural power refers to a firm's capacity to exert influence over the configuration and governance of an industry as well as the distribution of value among its participants.[168] The term 'industry architecture' defines the conditions in which firms operate in a particular industry. It encompasses aspects such as the division of labour, interactions among firms, and business models.[169] While firms operate within existing conditions, they also vie to reshape these conditions to their advantage. For example, a firm may gain a competitive edge if it holds a central position in the industry architecture or ecosystem, enabling it to reshape technological, institutional, or social interfaces in its favour.[170] One factor that contributes to a firm's ability to influence industry architecture is technological path dependence, which arises from a self-reinforcing process initiated by a first-mover advantage, potentially culminating in a 'dominant design' within the industry and subsequent customer lock-in.[171] Firms can leverage these advantages to extract disproportionate amounts of the surplus value created by the industry through complex strategies, such as manipulating the setting of technology standards or denying interoperability with competing technologies. Companies such as Apple and Google have used their central positions within their respective ecosystems to influence industry architecture in ways that benefit them, often at the expense of smaller competitors and final consumers.

For instance, a firm's control over MOS, which are essential for the functionality of smartphones, can give rise to architectural power. The design of the MOS, its availability as an open or closed system, and the conditions governing its access can shape the smartphone industry.[172] Google's use of Android is a good example. The company made the MOS available as open source, enabling it to capture a significant market share and establish itself as a dominant design in the industry. This strategy has since been used to promote Google's other services. Equipment manufacturers installing Android must agree to pre-install Google apps, allowing

[168] ibid 816.

[169] See Michael Jacobides, Thorbjørn Knudsen, and Mie Augier, 'Benefiting from Innovation: Value Creation, Value Appropriation and the Role of Industry Architectures' (2006) 35 Research Policy 1200, 1203–204.

[170] Lianos and Carballa-Smichowski (n 146) 816.

[171] For a discussion on the notion of dominant design, see Lisanne Hummel, 'Dominant Positions or Dominant Designs? Market Power and Innovation in European Competition Law' in Václav Šmejkal (ed), *EU Antitrust: Hot Topics & Next Steps* (2022).

[172] Lianos and Carballa-Smichowski (n 146) 816.

Google to collect more data and further entrench its dominance in these services. This strategic positioning has allowed Google to earn extraordinary profits from its targeted advertising.

The revenue, in conjunction with control over other key gateways, is subsequently used to shape the entire Google ecosystem towards a data-intensive industry, with significant implications for users' privacy. Google has succeeded in creating an ecosystem that rewards entities who collect data and track users while punishing those who attempt to prevent or mitigate such practices. For example, Google's AdSense and AdMob allow websites and apps to earn extra revenue through advertising. These reward mechanisms foster competition for more clicks on the ad, further incentivizing websites and apps to collect personal data to better target their advertising. This alignment in commercial interest can lead the platform (and the websites or apps) to disregard users' privacy concerns.[173] However, Google's influence reaches beyond its own ecosystem. The company uses its financial strength to impact Apple's ecosystem by paying substantial amounts to have Google Search set as the default in Safari, for example. This demonstrates the capacity of firms possessing architectural power to influence multiple segments within a single industry or ecosystem in their favour.

Thus, competition law must consider the role of architectural power in extracting value and its effect on the distribution of value across various segments. While metrics have been developed to measure panopticon power, measuring architectural power is more complex and depends on contextual factors. As such, the appraisal of architectural power requires an understanding of ecosystem architecture and governance.[174] Ecosystem architecture refers to the norms of engagement, encompassing 'the roles and relationships of all parties that engage in an ecosystem, the conditions for monetizing, and payments used'.[175] In contrast, ecosystem governance determines 'who is allowed to compete in a (multi-actor) ecosystem and under what terms; and how disputes are resolved'.[176] These conditions can be scrutinized under competition law by establishing well-defined criteria for evaluating how the rules of engagement produce anticompetitive outcomes.[177]

The discussions in Section III.B on Google's use of its control over vital gateways to obstruct and demote anti-tracking and ad-blocking services, while rewarding entities engaged in user tracking and data collection, exemplifies the company's exercise of architectural power. It is evident that Google employs its rules of engagement and governance to configure the ecosystem and industry to be data-intensive,

[173] Esayas, 'Competition in (Data) Privacy' (n 17).
[174] Jacobides and Lianos (n 8) 1218.
[175] ibid.
[176] ibid 1210.
[177] ibid 1218. However, addressing architectural power requires interfering with the businesses' monetization strategies and product design, areas where competition law has played a marginal role. See Pablo Ibáñez Colomo, 'Product Design and Business Models in EU Antitrust Law' (2021) <https://ssrncom/abstract=3925396> accessed 7 February 2024.

while redistributing the surplus among actors in a manner that primarily benefits Google. To address this issue, it may be beneficial to integrate systems thinking and emergence into competition law, as in the application of the essential facilities doctrine. These reward-and-punishment mechanisms also raise the costs for entities endeavouring to compete by reducing data collection and enhancing user privacy. This, coupled with users' inability to fully understand privacy policies, may potentially lead to a dysfunctional equilibrium,[178] a relevant consideration when addressing privacy in the context of mergers, as will be shown in Chapters 4 and 5. Additionally, Chapter 6 demonstrates how powerful players endeavour to influence industry architecture by reducing information competition in the context of standard setting. This tactic underscores the need for competition law to recognize and address the exertion of architectural power.

Moreover, an architectural approach to market power emphasizes the need for a more dynamic approach to competition restrictions.[179] In addition to using the rules of engagement and governance to shape opportunities available to customers, firms possessing architectural advantage may also leverage their resources to influence the trajectories of innovation in a manner that benefits them. For instance, Facebook's acquisition of WhatsApp highlights how firms with an architectural advantage may undermine alternative business models that could limit their power, underscoring the importance of a dynamic perspective in competition law.[180] Chapter 5 discusses how Facebook's acquisition of WhatsApp could have provided insights into the competitive constraints imposed by WhatsApp on Facebook's privacy practices and how adopting a dynamic perspective that examines the merger through a maverick firm theory might have been beneficial. The discussion reveals that the merger deprived users of an alternative business model that was built on prioritizing users' privacy for a small fee.

Developments in some member states also suggest a desire to consider architectural power. For example, the proposed amendments to the Greek Competition Act, which include the ability to define an ecosystem-level relevant market, incorporate several factors that might help establish market power at this level. The proposed law employs the concept of 'central position' in an ecosystem as a trigger for competition law intervention.[181] This centrality is to be assessed, among other aspects, by considering 'the control by that undertaking of resources and infrastructures necessary for the economic activity of other undertakings' and 'the undertaking's ability to set out rules governing the operation of the ecosystem and

[178] Joseph Farrell, 'Can Privacy Be Just Another Good?' (2012) 10 Journal on Telecommunications & High Technology Law 251.

[179] Jacobides and Lianos (n 8) 1210.

[180] See Samson Esayas, 'Data Privacy in European Merger Control: Critical Analysis of Commission Decisions Regarding Privacy as a Non-Price Competition' (2019) 40 European Competition Law Review 166.

[181] Jacobides and Lianos (n 8) 1221.

the access of third parties to it'.[182] This is a clear instance of architectural power and a power that extends beyond a specific relevant market.[183]

An approach that establishes dominance at the ecosystem level is also better able to deal with emergent competitive harms. According to the proposed amendments to the Greek Competition Act, an undertaking that does not possess a dominant position in a single product or service market—because of a lower market share than those traditionally required for a finding of dominance—can, nevertheless, be found to have dominance in the ecosystem. The ability to establish dominance at the ecosystem level reflects emergent property thinking in that the sum (the ecosystem-level market) displays a property (dominance), which is non-existent in the constituent parts, that is the individual markets within the ecosystem. Moreover, the approach would help address some of the emergent harms.

As the discussion on PETs demonstrated, divergent incentives have led key digital players to ban or demote several anti-tracking and ad-blocking apps/services from key gateways—such as the Play Store, the Chrome web store, and Google Search. Although the sum of these practices across the different markets may hinder effective competition, the focus on a specific relevant market meant that these practices, seen in isolation, may not necessarily meet the required standard for violation of Article 102 of the TFEU. One such standard for applying Article 102 is that the undertaking must occupy a dominant position in each of the relevant markets concerned. This means, under the current approach, that unless conduct occurs in a market where the undertaking has a dominant position, its impact is largely ignored for the purposes of Article 102.[184] In contrast, practices that could have gone unpunished under existing competition law, because the undertaking lacks dominance in a specific market, could be caught under the proposed provision, which allows the authorities to establish dominance at the ecosystem level.

Taking the PET example, Google would be found to have a dominant position in the ecosystem consisting of Internet search, browser, app store, and MOS, despite it lacking dominance in each of these markets separately. By establishing dominance at the ecosystem level, competition authorities would be able to capture practices that might have gone unchecked under Article 102 for want of dominance in each individual market. Furthermore, once dominance is established in an ecosystem, as shown in Sections IV.C and IV.D, competition authorities can easily account for the harms arising from multiple cross-market practices within the ecosystem.

[182] ibid.

[183] ibid 1219–21. The UK code of conduct for firms with 'Significant Market Status' also addresses architectural power. The code sets out three key objectives: fair trading (exploitation), open choices (exclusion), and trust and transparency (consumer protection), which are expected to be adapted to the specific 'activity, conduct, and harms' being targeted. This approach considers both the nature of business models and industry architecture as a basis for the application of the code.

[184] Although to a limited extent, rules on abuse of the state of economic dependency can play a gap-filling role in relation to the atomized approach and emergent competitive harms. See Section IV.D.1.

The above discussion shows how ecosystems engender various forms of power that extend beyond a specific market. Although panopticon and architectural power are addressed in detail, other types of power may also give rise to concerns.[185] Given that the application of competition law requires proof of market power, it is crucial to incorporate notions of power that transcend a specific relevant market and arise at the industry and ecosystem levels. This approach would recognize the complexities of the digital economy, where the field of competition has become multidimensional and the dimensions of power have evolved.

C. Holistic Approach to Assessing Anticompetitive Effects and Abuse

The rise of ecosystems as new organizational forms also presents undertakings in control of such ecosystems with the possibility to engage in multiple practices across the different markets. The question arises whether the sum of these practices may violate competition rules, particularly Article 102, even if the actions considered separately are not detrimental to competition. For example, the German Expert Commission report acknowledged that the benefits from data-driven network effects for advertisement-driven business models could 'trigger corporate strategies that are no longer geared towards single product or services markets'.[186] The report emphasized the need for new competition law concepts to assess companies' ability 'to foreclose competition through the use of cross-market strategies'.[187] In this regard, establishing dominance at ecosystem level, despite a lack thereof at the level of single product/service markets, and sanctioning its abuse are crucial. This can capture competitive harms from multi-market practices within an ecosystem that would have otherwise escaped scrutiny under the traditional rules of abuse of dominance owing to the lack of a dominant position in the individual relevant markets.

This development is not sufficient, however, to arrest emergent competitive harms. Although the approach allows competition authorities to consider conduct across the entire ecosystem, it does not necessarily ensure that authorities are able to combine disparate practices to meet the required threshold for abuse, where the practices fall short of the legal standard individually. The ability of competition authorities to do this depends on deliberate consideration and recognition of emergent properties. Thus, the question is whether the current case law and practice can accommodate emergent property thinking in assessing abuse of dominance.

[185] See European Commission, Crémer, Montjoye, and Schweitzer (n 135) 6. See Communication from European Commission, 'Shaping Europe's Digital Future' (19 February 2020) 5.
[186] Schallbruch, Schweitzer, and Wambach (n 15) 27.
[187] ibid.

The US legal framework appears to be receptive to addressing emerging competitive harms.[188] For example, Newman indicates that although 'no single illegal act necessarily implies an antitrust violation, courts have found that a series of illegal or improper actions can add up to section 2 liability'.[189] Newman cites a ruling from the US Court of Appeals, which held that 'no one of the instances of improper conduct, standing alone, would lead to section 2 liability. Taken together, however, they show a pattern of exclusionary behaviour sufficient to support the jury's verdict.'[190] Similarly, Crane discusses the potential that a series of behaviours, which are not harmful on their own, can collectively lead to exclusionary conduct.[191] Additionally, Stucke and Grunes argue that a hypothetical boycott of anti-tracking and ad-blocking applications by Google Chrome, Apple Safari, and Internet Explorer cannot be defended on the basis that it only impacts a small-scale company, whose elimination would make no significant difference.[192] According to their viewpoint, the US Supreme Court has held that 'monopoly can as surely thrive by the elimination of such small businessmen, one at a time, as it can by driving them out in large groups'.[193] Therefore, US law seems open to recognize and incorporate the idea of emergent properties into competition analysis.

As to the EU, the Commission *Android* decision signals the possibility that several practices spanning different markets may 'constitute a single and continuous infringement of Article 102 TFEU'.[194] However, as noted in Section II, while the Commission viewed the different practices as having the same objective and forming a single strategy, it also noted that each practice infringed Article 102 on its own.[195] Thus, although the Commission's approach addressed the issue of multi-market strategies, it did not directly address emergence, that is whether the behaviour of the dominant undertaking in different markets gave rise to a property (abuse of dominance), which did not exist in the component parts separately.

This notwithstanding, the case law from the CJEU has addressed the possible impact of multiple practices with emergence effects. While establishing the applicability of EU competition law, the CJEU underlined the need to look at Intel's 'overall strategy', rather than at its discrete practices, in assessing whether these practices have an effect on the European Economic Area (EEA).[196] Intel argued that

[188] See Nathan Newman, 'Search, Antitrust, and the Economics of the Control of User Data' (2014) 31 Yale Journal on Regulation 401, 440; Maurice Stucke and Allen Grunes, *Big Data and Competition Policy* (OUP 2016) 264; Daniel Crane, 'Does Monopoly Broth Make Bad Soup?' (2009) 76 Antitrust Law Journal 663.

[189] Newman (n 188) 440.

[190] See ibid.

[191] Crane, 'Does Monopoly Broth Make Bad Soup?' (n 188) 665.

[192] Stucke and Grunes (n 188) 264.

[193] See *Klor's Inc v Broadway-Hale Stores* 395 Supreme Court (1959) 705, 710. Cited in Stucke and Grunes (n 188) 264.

[194] *Google Android* (n 30) para 1340.

[195] ibid para 1339.

[196] Case C-413/14 P *Intel v Commission* EU:C:2017:632, paras 54–58.

some of the agreements it had concluded with its customers, which were found by the Commission and the GC to be abusive, only affected a limited number of products, were related to China, and were thus unlikely to have 'immediate and substantial effects in the EEA'.[197] In reaffirming the GC's position, the CJEU stated that 'it was appropriate to take into consideration the conduct of the undertaking viewed *as a whole* in order to assess the substantial nature of its effects on the market of the EU and of the EEA'.[198] To do otherwise, the Court held, 'would lead to an artificial fragmentation of comprehensive anticompetitive conduct, capable of affecting the market structure within the EEA, into a collection of separate forms of conduct which might escape the European Union's jurisdiction'.[199] In this sense, what matters is whether the synergistic impact of the practices has effects on the EEA and is likely to harm competition. This approach represents emergent property thinking since the Court attempted to avoid the well-known error in emergent property discussions (ie the fallacy of composition)[200] and emphasized the need for a holistic approach in analysing the impact of a pattern of conduct on competition.

Moreover, the EU courts have accepted the possibility for claimants to provide evidence under 'the totality-of-the-circumstances' standard, which reflects an emergent property thinking. In *British Airways*, the GC ruled that a dominant undertaking's conduct, considered as a whole, might harm the competitive process, even in the absence of measurable harm to the market position of individual firms in the relevant market. The Court emphasized that it was an abuse of dominance for a dominant undertaking to discriminate 'between business partners who are in a relationship of competition' and such discrimination could lead to a distortion of competition between those partners when viewed in the context of the case as a whole.[201] In such a situation, the Court further noted, claimants cannot be required to prove 'an actual quantifiable deterioration in the competitive position of the business partners taken individually'.[202] The CJEU has endorsed this standard and reiterated the need to have 'regard to the whole of the circumstances of the case'.[203]

Applying this standard to the discussion of the ban on PETs, it is possible that the full range of Google's conduct targeting privacy-enhancing apps/services could be considered to harm competition in the market without necessarily harming or foreclosing a single market player. Similarly, the totality of Google's conduct targeting these services across different platforms, such as Google Play, Search,

[197] ibid para 48.

[198] ibid para 56 (emphasis added).

[199] ibid para 57.

[200] This occurs when the property of a component part (eg compliance) is assumed to apply to the whole.

[201] Case C-95/04 P *British Airways v Commission* EU:C:2007:166, para 145.

[202] ibid.

[203] Case C-525/16 *MEO—Serviços de Comunicações e Multimédia SA v Autoridade da Concorrência* ECLI:EU:C:2018:270, paras 27–28.

Chrome, and Android, might be considered harmful to competition in the market for privacy-enhancing apps/services without any particular conduct, on a specific platform, causing harm in and of itself. Thus, arguably, the existing case law and practice could easily accommodate the holistic analysis. Even if the approach does not fit with existing case law and practice, however, with key platforms now controlled by a handful of firms and increasingly becoming enablers of B2C transactions, it is imperative that competition authorities be open to experimenting with different tools to address the new challenges. The holistic approach discussed above is one such tool.

Recent developments in some members states seem to suggest that such an approach would be viewed favourably. For example, in November 2018, the Bundeskartellamt opened an investigation into Amazon's operation of Marketplace.[204] The authority investigated whether several terms and conditions contained in the 'Amazon Services Business Solutions Agreement' with merchants constituted an abuse of dominant position. Some of the terms investigated included (1) the lack of transparency of the terms of business, (2) the unexpected termination and blocking of sellers' accounts, (3) the lack of possibilities for sellers to enforce a contractual obligation on Amazon and clarify matters of dispute, (4) the disadvantage of sellers in customer reviews, (5) the obligation for sellers to transfer the rights to use product information (especially images) to Amazon, (6) the obligation for sellers to bear the costs of obviously unjustified customer returns, and various other rules and practices on the marketplace.[205] The investigation was based on the rules on abuse of dominance and abuse of 'economic dependency' under the German Act against Restraints on Competition. But what is interesting, for the purposes of this section, is that the authority did not consider these terms and conditions individually, but rather analysed whether these terms, when assessed as a whole, unduly restricted the merchants' competitive activity and therefore constituted abuse.[206] According to the authority,

> not every clause of the terms and conditions that is potentially to the disadvantage of the sellers, or possibly even very burdensome for them, is objectionable under antitrust law. Rather, it was decisive whether, on the basis of an overall assessment, the application of the terms and conditions in question extremely restricted the sellers in their competitive activity on the marketplace or even made it impossible, particularly due to a lack of opportunities to enforce compliance by Amazon with its main contractual obligations.[207]

[204] Case Summary, 'Amazon Amends Its Terms of Business Worldwide for Sellers on Its Marketplaces—Bundeskartellamt Closes Abuse Proceedings' (B2-88/18, 17 July 2019) (Bundeskartellamt Case Summary, 'Amazon Amends Its Terms').

[205] ibid 1–2.

[206] ibid 7–8.

[207] ibid 8.

Although not explicit, the analysis reflects emergent thinking in its recognition that although the individual clause that Amazon imposed on traders might not constitute an abuse of dominance, several such clauses, taken as a whole, could do so. The Commission is looking into these practices by Amazon.[208] Ongoing investigations into Google and Apple involve multiple practices.[209] These cases will provide the Commission with the opportunity to experiment with the idea that although individual practices, considered in isolation, may not constitute abuse, taken as a whole, they may meet the required threshold for intervention under Article 102. At the very least, the Commission should put forward such an argument as an alternative to the analysis of each conduct as an abusive behaviour. This would leave room for the gradual incorporation of emergent properties thinking into competition law analysis.

The discussion on a holistic approach should not be restricted to scrutinizing the harmful effects on competition but also include the potential gains arising from the entirety of practices within the ecosystem. Some scholars have referred to such gains as systemic efficiencies, which arise 'in large complex systems through the interaction of multiple distributed components', overseen by an entity capable of exercising extensive control over the components and their interactions.[210]

Systemic efficiencies are distinct in their nature and scope. In terms of their nature, systemic efficiencies are extensive and can facilitate dramatic innovations that are unattainable in smaller, more insular settings, such as the individual markets within the ecosystem.[211] In terms of their scope, systemic efficiencies generate value that benefits not just the introducing firm but the entire industry.[212] Consequently, the suggestion is that they should be recognized as a distinct type of efficiency in competition analysis. Nevertheless, competition law must also consider systemic efficiencies because obtaining them may require engaging in conduct that may seem anticompetitive at first glance, such as denying interoperability to certain actors, tying, and excluding the use of certain technologies.[213]

Stylianou analyses the *Google Android* case and postulates that the various practices condemned by the Commission, and subsequently affirmed by the GC, may have been intended to achieve systemic efficiencies. Given that obtaining systemic efficiency necessitates the pervasive control of the production process or value chain, Google's bundling of Play Store with Android MOS and other Google services, the anti-fragmentation agreement, and payments to pre-install Google apps might be essential to ensure the 'well-being and evolution' of the Android

[208] See European Commission, 'Statement of Objections to Amazon' (n 22).

[209] See European Commission, 'Investigation into Google's Online Advertising' (n 22); European Commission, 'Commission Opens Investigations into Apple's App Store Rules' (16 June 2020).

[210] Konstantinos Stylianou, 'Systemic Efficiencies in Competition Law: Evidence from the ICT Industry' (2016) 12 Journal of Competition Law & Economics 557.

[211] ibid 558–59.

[212] ibid 558–59.

[213] ibid 560.

ecosystem.[214] In this respect, Stylianou explains how the various practices can benefit both consumers and app developers by providing enhanced security, speedy and streamlined processes for testing and disseminating new features, and a greater homogenization through the wider adoption of an 'official' or highly compatible versions of Android.[215] Whether Google's practices truly generate systemic efficiencies that outweigh the potential harms is a matter of empirical investigation. The key point is that a systemic view of the practices may reveal a different story than examining these practices in isolation, and competition authorities should adopt a holistic approach when dealing with such large and complex systems.

In general, the discussion regarding systemic efficiencies underscores some important points. It underlines the importance of emergence phenomena, whereby minor changes at the component level of a system can result in major and qualitatively different changes at the system level. Furthermore, it reflects previous discussions on actors that wield architectural power and the need to recognize such dimension of power in competition law. As mentioned earlier, the discussions of systemic efficiencies recognize the inevitability of 'pervasive control' over the production process or value chain, which can subsequently impact 'the position of competitors in the market or the structure of the industry'.[216] To the extent that firms are capable of influencing industry architecture in their favour, it is only reasonable to consider the positive externalities that are generated for the whole industry. This approach can easily be incorporated into the 'totality-of-the-circumstances' standard in the CJEU case law.

D. Holistic Analysis in the Application of the Essential Facilities Doctrine

As mentioned earlier, due to the high threshold for intervention and prevailing practices of digital platforms, it is imperative to consider the essential facilities doctrine as a prime example for analysing emerging competitive harms. Thus, in the same fashion as the above suggestions, the assessment of whether a refusal to deal by dominant digital platforms constitutes abuse needs to follow a holistic approach, considering the possibility that a dominant undertaking may hinder effective competition using multiple actions across different platforms (upstream markets) and targeting several players in the secondary (downstream) market. Although this holistic approach can be useful in other contexts, emphasis is given here to its importance in assessing what constitutes indispensable input and in analysing the elimination of effective competition in the secondary market. Incorporating

214 ibid.
215 ibid 581.
216 ibid 563.

emergent thinking could help address the key hurdles that the essential facilities doctrine faces in tackling harms pertaining to access to digital platforms and data.

1. Holistic Approach to the Indispensability Requirement

Section III.A highlights the obstacle that the indispensability test poses to applying the essential facilities doctrine to platform and data-access issues. Therefore, a holistic approach may be beneficial in assessing indispensability, particularly regarding the existence of actual substitutes. As platforms increasingly become key enablers of B2C relations and are controlled by a handful of firms, the assessment of whether an input is indispensable needs to go beyond a single input. The earlier discussion of PETs showed that anti-tracking and ad-blocking services could reach users through various alternative routes, such as app stores, sideloading, and browser extensions. The availability of these alternative routes suggests that each gateway, considered separately, may not constitute an indispensable input pursuant to the case law. However, the discussion also showed how Google, for example, could leverage its control over several of these gateways to prevent customers from accessing these alternatives. Apart from banning them from the dominant app store, Google could block such apps/services from its Chrome web store and demote or remove their websites from its dominant search engine. Additionally, Google could reduce the ability of apps such as Disconnect to use other Android app stores (eg Aptoide) by making such app stores incompatible with the dominant MOS. This is not a hypothetical claim, as Google has, in fact, engaged in a string of such actions across these platforms (Android MOS, Chrome, Google Search, and Google Play) targeting the anti-tracking and ad-blocking software Adblock Plus.[217]

In light of the above examples and the tendency of leading digital players to expand their control over multiple consumer gateways, competition policy should be open to the possibility that several alternative facilities, although not indispensable separately, may become so in combination. In this regard, two points are worth emphasizing.

The first is the possibility that an input owned by a dominant supplier becomes indispensable despite the existence of other alternatives, because the same undertaking controls these alternatives and deters the access seeker from dealing with these alternatives. In other words, because of the control over the alternatives and the related actions of the dominant undertaking, these alternatives are discounted from being considered 'sufficiently interchangeable' with the input for which access is sought. This claim presupposes that the undertaking is dominant in relation to the input for which access is sought. Using the Disconnect example, access to Google Play, dominant in the app store market, might not be deemed indispensable

[217] Lomas (n 110).

on its own due to the availability of alternatives like reaching users via browsers and sideloading. However, if Google leverages its control over the largest browser and search engine to hinder PETs such as Disconnect from reaching consumers, these alternatives should not be regarded as sufficiently interchangeable, rendering Google Play indispensable.

The second, but more difficult issue arises in cases where the undertaking does not have a dominant position regarding any of the inputs but, instead, has high market shares in each that fall short of dominance. Can access to these inputs be considered indispensable in combination? Answering this question raises several difficult sub-questions about defining the relevant market and the possibility of establishing dominance from scope (control over different access points). However, the proposed addition to the Greece Competition Act discussed in Section IV.A and IV.B above, which makes it possible to define markets and establish dominance at the ecosystem level, is a step in this direction. As noted there, key considerations in determining ecosystem-level dominance involve controlling 're-sources and infrastructures necessary for the economic activity of other undertakings' and the 'ability to set out rules governing the operation of the ecosystem and the access of third parties to it'.[218] These factors shift the assessment of dominance from a focus on scale, involving high market shares in relation to a single input, to a focus on scope and importance over the inputs. This approach allows competition authorities to scrutinize ecosystems comprising several markets under Article 102, despite the lack of a dominant position in any specific market forming the ecosystem, representing an emergent outcome. Once dominance is established at the ecosystem level, competition authorities would be better placed to have a holistic look at the practices in the different markets and assess whether the different inputs within the ecosystem, *albeit* not indispensable separately, could nonetheless qualify as indispensable in combination. As discussions in Section IV.C demonstrate, there is nothing that prevents competition authorities from adopting such an emergent thinking. Overall, the point is that competition authorities should be open to the possibility that denying access to several important, *albeit* not independently indispensable, inputs may produce the same degree of harm to competition.

Rules on abuse of the state of economic dependency could also help address the potential emergent harms from multiple bans across markets where the undertaking lacks a dominant position. Several member states have such rules, which allow competition authorities to address cases of refusal to deal in relation to undertakings not possessing a dominant position and impose obligations to deal under the traditional rules of abuse.[219] For example, Article 20(1) of the German

[218] Jacobides and Lianos (n 8) 1221.

[219] For a discussion of such rules in different member states, see Despoina Mantzari, 'Power Imbalances in Online Marketplaces: At the Crossroads of Competition Law and Regulation' (CLES Research Paper Series 4/2021, CLES 2021).

Act against Restraints on Competition extends the prohibition on abuse of dominance to situations of economic dependency, where small or medium-sized suppliers or purchasers are dependent on an undertaking in such a way that switching to other undertakings is not possible.[220] The recent amendment further extends the applicability of this provision to online relations, specifying that 'dependence may also arise from the fact that an undertaking is dependent on access to data controlled by another undertaking for its own activities (Art. 20, 1a) or on access to markets provided by intermediary services when reasonable alternatives do not exist'.[221] Given the strict interpretation of the indispensability test, pursuing abuse of economic dependence could represent a viable alternative in situations of platform dependence. This is because the provisions can capture abusive refusals to provide access to data or platforms by non-dominant undertakings. At the EU level, the DMA, which regulates actors that act as gatekeepers, may help address some of these concerns.

2. Holistic Approach to the Elimination of Effective Competition

The analysis of whether a refusal to deal eliminates effective competition in the secondary market needs to follow a holistic approach, considering the possibility that dominant undertakings may use systematic and subtle strategies targeting multiple players to weaken the competitiveness of the market over time. Such strategies may be systematic in that they are implemented at critical moments and over time. As discussed in Section III.B, certain critical moments, such as widely publicized data breaches can play a significant role in the adoption of PET, which dominant firms may exploit to suppress competition and the development of the market. Similarly, if done over time, even subtle practices, such as depriving the apps of the discovery and promotional features of an app store at critical moments, can be used to suppress competition. This suggests that while a particular strategy alone may not eliminate competition, a combination of various actions targeting similar actors across the same or different platforms may ultimately eliminate competition.

Thus, competition policy should consider condemning the systematic elimination of competition from the market. This includes considering how various subtle practices may be used strategically over time to kill the momentum for such services and hinder the emergence of effective competition. In this regard, whether the ban/removal is triggered by momentum (eg increase in adoption/popularity) and how such conduct affects adoption are factors that need to be weighed carefully. A related consideration is whether the ban is systematic in that previous similar practices are aimed to slow down the momentum following a trigger event. If the ban was triggered by momentum and was systematic, this could signal that the platform intended to slow down adoption of privacy-enhancing services and

[220] ibid 18.
[221] ibid 22.

thereby eliminate effective competition in the market. Such systematic practices can also be relevant to cases where an intention to eliminate is required.[222] This approach acknowledges the realities of life, where death can be provoked as much by a single bullet as by a thousand cuts.

V. Mapping Enforcement Trends Involving Digital Platforms

A common denominator in cases involving digital platforms that are attracting scrutiny from competition authorities is the multiplicity of practices, transcending different but interconnected relevant markets. There are some trends that seem to emerge when competition authorities tackle these practices. The aim of this section is to track these enforcement trends and discuss whether these trends fill some of the gaps identified in this chapter.

The first enforcement trend, which embodies the very essence of emergence or 'more is different', focuses on addressing emergent effects from a bundle of behaviours that, independently, may not meet the required threshold for intervention. This approach emphasizes the scale, multiplicity, and synergic effects of these behaviours. Going back to the Bundeskartellamt case involving Amazon, the agency evaluated numerous clauses imposed on traders, recognizing that examining individual terms separately could overlook potential harm from their collective impact. As a result, the agency assessed the synergistic effect of these clauses as a whole and deemed them abusive, even though each clause might not individually meet the threshold for abuse.[223] This point was made clearer in a recent remark by the head of the Bundeskartellamt, Andreas Mundt, underlying the importance of a holistic approach to abuse-of-dominance cases involving digital platforms. According to him, 'What is most interesting in these cases is you do not look so much at dominance on a certain market; the point is how it *all works* together.'[224] Accordingly, the desire to account for the totality ('allness') or emergent effects seems to be driven by the multiplicity of the practices and their interconnectedness. This is consistent with how emergence is conceptualized in this chapter. As noted above, the main source of emergent competitive risks is the change in scale, namely control over multi-product markets and the possibility to engage in multiple cross-market practices.

[222] There are arguments that the application of the essential facilities doctrine requires showing that the dominant undertaking 'intends to reserve the downstream markets to itself', which can be difficult to prove. In such cases, engaging in systematic practices, targeting several actors at critical moments, could be indicative of such intention.

[223] See Bundeskartellamt Case Summary, 'Amazon Amends Its Terms' (n 204) 8.

[224] Simon Van Dorpe, 'German Competition Chief Sees Vanguard Digital Role at Risk', *Politico* (20 December 2021).

Although, to a lesser extent, the Commission's decision in *Android* involved the combination of four practices into a single abusive strategy. However, unlike the Bundeskartellamt's approach, the Commission held that each practice infringed Article 102 on its own. Although the emergent effect is less pronounced, the Commission combined the four practices into a single overall abusive strategy to account for the synergic effect of these practices. The presence of a common objective is a crucial factor in establishing that multiple practices constitute a single and continuous infringement.[225] In *Android*, the Commission held that the four practices pursued 'an identical objective, namely to protect and strengthen Google's dominant position in general search services and thus its revenues via search advertisements'.[226] However, a common objective alone is not sufficient. The practices must also be complementary and contribute, through their interaction, 'to the realisation of the objectives intended within the framework of that overall plan'.[227] This principle allows for the possibility that multiple practices, which, taken separately, may not achieve the harmful outcome, could do so when considered together.

The fact that each behaviour was deemed abusive suggests that each behaviour was able to achieve the harmful outcome on its own. Nevertheless, there is no reason to believe that the Commission cannot conclude that the totality of the behaviours and their interactions could generate a harmful outcome even though each behaviour on its own may not.[228] Furthermore, even if each behaviour produces a harmful outcome, one could argue that the harm caused by each behaviour considered separately is qualitatively different from the harm caused by the four practices considered together. This is likely to be the case when these practices are implemented simultaneously and systematically.

This approach of tallying multiple practices into a single and continuous infringement can prove beneficial in the ongoing cases targeting Google, Apple, and Amazon, which involve multiple and interconnected practices. The Commission's investigation into Google, for instance, has uncovered six potentially harmful practices implemented across different channels, including the obligation to use Google services, like Video 360, for purchasing online ads on YouTube; restrictions on third parties, such as advertisers and publishers, accessing user data; and plans to replace third-party cookies with Privacy Sandbox.[229] These practices not only share a common goal of safeguarding and consolidating Google's position in the online advertising market but also reinforce one another. The application of the single and continuous infringement principle would enable the Commission to account for the synergistic effects of these practices. Nevertheless, the cases, notably

[225] *Google Android* (n 30) para 1338.
[226] ibid para 1341.
[227] ibid para 1338.
[228] See discussions in Section IV.B regarding the case law on totality of the circumstances.
[229] See European Commission, 'Investigation into Google's Online Advertising' (n 22).

the one involving Google, provide an opportunity to explore the idea of emergence and contend that while individual practices considered in isolation may not constitute abuse, taken together, they may meet the necessary threshold for intervention under Article 102.

At a minimum, the Commission should propose such an argument as an alternative to analysing each conduct as an abusive behaviour. In fact, in the same case against Google, the UK Competition and Markets Authority (CMA) has shown interest in considering this approach. Although Google's offer of commitment and the CMA's subsequent acceptance prevented the agency from taking infringement decisions, the CMA held that Google's plans relating to the Privacy Sandbox 'are likely to, *individually and/or collectively*, amount to an abuse of its likely dominant position in the market for the supply of web browsers in the UK'.[230] Here, the phrase '*individually and/or collectively*', particularly the use of the conjunction 'or', implies that Google's practices may be considered abusive collectively, even though each behaviour may not be abusive independently. This is a clear reflection of emergent thinking.

The second enforcement trend relates to the willingness to consider new practices and competitive harms. These practices, owing to their novelty and lack of precedent, may have previously escaped scrutiny but are now considered unlawful due to their broader impact across markets or connection with other illegal practices. One manifestation of this trend is the growing focus on data and privacy-related abusive practices. In the past, the Commission and the CJEU excluded privacy concerns from the scope of EU competition law.[231] However, this has changed considerably in recent years. For instance, the Bundeskartellamt held that Facebook abused its dominance in the market for social networks by imposing unfair privacy terms, which were found to be in breach of EU data privacy rules.[232] Similarly, the Italian Competition and Consumer Protection Authority (AGCM) accused Google of abusing its dominant position by preventing users from exercising their data portability right under the General Data Protection Regulation (GDPR).[233]

At the EU level, there several ongoing investigations into the practices of Google, Amazon, and Facebook focus on user data and privacy-related issues. For example, investigations into practices of Facebook and Amazon explore how repurposing of

[230] Case 50972 *Decision to Accept Commitments Offered by Google in Relation to Its Privacy Sandbox Proposals*, Competition and Markets Authority 11 February 2022 (CMA, *Decision to Accept Google's Commitments*) para 5.84.

[231] See *Facebook/WhatsApp* (n 73). Case C-238/05 *Asnef-Equifax v Asociacion de Usuarios* ECLI:EU:C:2006:734, para 63.

[232] Bundeskartellamt, *Case Summary: Facebook, Exploitative Business Terms Pursuant to Section 19(1) GWB for Inadequate Data Processing* (2019) 4.

[233] Regulation (EU) 2016/679 of the European Parliament and of the Council of 27 April 2016 on the Protection of Natural Persons with Regard to the Processing of Personal Data and on the Free Movement of Such Data, and repealing Directive 95/46/EC OJ L119/1 (GDPR); AGCM, 'Investigation Opened against Google for Abuse of Dominant Position in Data Portability' (14 July 2022).

data collected in one market may lead to an unfair advantage in another market, potentially violating EU competition law.[234] Moreover, in the ongoing investigation regarding Google's practices, including the Privacy Sandbox, the Commission has emphasized the need to consider users' privacy and respect to EU data privacy law when addressing competition concerns in the advertising market.[235] This has been confirmed by the CJEU in *Meta v Bundeskartellamt*, which underscores the vital role of data privacy rules in competition assessment, especially examining whether dominant undertaking's conduct constitutes abuse.[236] These developments mark a significant departure from previous decisional practice of the Commission and the CJEU.

The prominence of data and privacy-related harms is also evident in the United States despite the prevalent criticism that the US system is more price-centric than the EU.[237] For example, the US Federal Trade Commission's (FTC's) case against Facebook centres on the harm caused to consumers through reduction in privacy and increased exposure to advertisement.[238] Similarly, the US Department of Justice (DoJ) complaint accuses Google of restricting competition in Search and harming consumers 'by reducing the quality of search (including on dimensions such as *privacy, data protection, and use of consumer data*)'.[239] In a recent antitrust lawsuit, Texas accused Google of 'privacy fixing', an accusation equivalent to price fixing or forming a cartel but in the field of privacy.[240]

These examples show a major shift where data and privacy-related harms are now prominently featured in antitrust investigations. This is primarily due to the role that users' personal data plays in digital ecosystems. As noted in Section I, personal data plays a central role in linking activities across the different markets in the ecosystems. Given this wider importance, its misuse and disregard to users' privacy can have wider implications and strengthen market power across different markets. Therefore, condemning such practices may be seen as a way of controlling wider harms that can arise. These moves also demonstrate attempts from competition agencies to address some aspects of panopticon power.[241]

234 European Commission, 'Statement of Objections to Amazon' (n 22) <https://ec.europa.eu/commission/presscorner/detail/en/ip_20_2077>; European Commission, 'Investigation into Google's Online Advertising' (n 22) <https://ec.europa.eu/commission/presscorner/detail/en/ip_21_3143>; European Commission, 'Commission Opens Investigation into Possible Anticompetitive Conduct of Facebook' (4 June 2021) <https://ec.europa.eu/commission/presscorner/detail/en/ip_21_2848>.

235 European Commission, 'Investigation into Google's Online Advertising' (n 22).

236 Case C-252/21 *Meta Platforms Inc v Bundeskartellamt* ECLI:EU:C:2023:537, para 50.

237 Organisation for Economic Co-operation and Development (OECD), *Policy Roundtables: The Role and Measurement of Quality in Competition Analysis* (OECD Publishing 2013).

238 Case 1:20-cv-03590-JEB *Federal Trade Commission v Facebook Inc* in the United States District Court of Columbia filed 19 August 2021 (*FTC v Facebook*).

239 Case 1:20-cv-03010: *US Department of Justice v Google LLC* in the United States District Court Columbia filed 20 October 2020 (emphasis added).

240 Civil Action 1:21-md-03010-PKC *State of Texas v Google LLC* in United States District Court of Southern New York filed 14 January 2022.

241 This trend is reflected in the legislative front where many of the new forms of abuse or anticompetitive practices are data- and privacy-related. A good example is Section 19a(2(4)) of the German

The third trend in enforcement, which is closely linked to the second, concerns the increasing consideration of the nature of dominance and its wider impact across markets. As previously discussed in Section III.A, one of the critiques of the Commission's rulings in the *Google Shopping* and *Android* cases pertains to the evasion of the strict criteria of the essential facilities doctrine by devising new types of abuses, such as self-preferencing.[242] This evasion, however, may not be an isolated occurrence but rather an indication of an emerging trend, whereby competition authorities are willing to lower the standard for abuse or devise new theories of harms concerning some actors due to their position within the ecosystem. There are two notable manifestations of this trend.

One manifestation is the emergence of self-preferencing as a dominant theory of harm in relation to digital platforms, even in situations where the essential facilities doctrine could have been used. Several of the Commission's ongoing investigations into Amazon, Apple, and Google appear to rely on self-preferencing. For example, one of the main concerns in relation to Amazon's 'Buy Box' is 'the possible preferential treatment of Amazon's own retail offers and those of marketplace sellers that use Amazon's logistics and delivery services'.[243] Similarly, in the *Apple Pay* case, the Commission is concerned about Apple's refusal to make available 'key technology necessary to develop rival mobile wallet solutions on Apple's devices', which may have 'restricted competition, to the benefit of its own solution Apple Pay'.[244] The Commission's latest case against Google concerns Google's preferential treatment of 'its own online display advertising technology services ... to the detriment of competing providers'.[245]

This trend is not limited to the EU as national competition authorities have also followed suit. For example, the AGCM fined Amazon €1.128 billion for abusing its dominant position in the Italian market for intermediation services by favouring its 'own logistic services—Fulfilment by Amazon (FBA)—to the detriment of the logistics services offered by competing operators'.[246] Similarly, the agency fined Google €100 million for abusing its dominant position in the markets for the Android operating system and the Google Play app store by refusing to

Competition Act (GWB), which forbids undertakings with paramount significance for competition across markets from processing 'competitively sensitive data received from other companies' for certain purposes.

242 Graef, 'Rethinking Essential Facilities' (n 61) 12.

243 See European Commission, 'Statement of Objections to Amazon' (n 22).

244 European Commission, 'Commission Sends Statement of Objections to Apple over Practices Regarding Apple Pay (2 May 2022) (European Commission, 'Statement of Objections Regarding Apple Pay') <https://ec.europa.eu/commission/presscorner/detail/es/ip_22_2764>.

245 European Commission, 'Investigation into Google's Online Advertising' (n 22).

246 AGCM, 'Amazon Fined over €1,128 Billion for Abusing Its Dominant Position' (9 December 2021) <https://en.agcm.it/en/media/press-releases/2021/12/A528#:~:text=A528%20%2D%20Italian%20Competition%20Authority%3A%20Amazon,for%20abusing%20its%20dominant%20position&text=The%20Authority%20found%20that%20Amazon,review%20by%20a%20monitoring%20trustee>.

supply interoperability information, which is important to develop an app compatible with Android Auto.[247] The app Enel X, developed by Enel Italia, allows users of electric cars to find and book recharging stations. According to the agency, by refusing to supply the interoperability information, 'Google has unfairly limited the possibilities for end-users' to use the Enel X app to find and book recharging stations when driving and consequently 'favored its own Google Maps app'.[248] Outside of the EU, the UK CMA accused Google of distorting competition 'by the self-preferencing of Google's own advertising products and services'.[249]

A common feature in many of these cases is that they could be farmed as refusal to provide access to an essential facility. The case involving Apple serves as a clear example of a refusal to give access to a technology ('NFC input'), which would allow app developers to offer mobile payment services on Apple devices.[250] Similarly, the Italian case against Google involves Google's denial of interoperability information necessary for the development of an app that is compatible with Android Auto. Google's proposal to limit access to data through the Privacy Sandbox may also be framed as a refusal to deal or disruption of supply. Google has contested the approach taken by the Commission and the AGCM, arguing that they have failed to demonstrate the indispensability of the infrastructure for establishing abuse.[251] Nevertheless, both the Commission and the national competition authorities persist in pursing self-preferencing over the stricter test of essential facilities doctrine. Importantly, this trend has been endorsed by the GC in its *Google Shopping* decision. While the Court acknowledged that the case partly concerns a refusal by Google to give access to 'general results pages for competing comparison-shopping services',[252] it held that the facts of the case also have characteristics that allow the Commission to pursue a different theory of abuse. According to the Court, not every issue of access necessities the application of the conditions set out in *Bronner*.[253] The Court took this stance despite acknowledging that 'Google's general results page has characteristics akin to those of an essential facility'.[254] Thus, the confirmation from the GC that self-preferencing constitutes an abusive practice independent of refusal to supply would only reinforce the trend.

Another manifestation of the emerging trend to lower the standard for abuse or devise new theories of harms is the tendency to define markets narrowly whereby only a single actor is included in the relevant product or service market. This has been the case with Android, Apple Appstore, Apply Pay, and Amazon. For

[247] AGCM, 'Google Fined over 100 Million for Abuse of Dominant Position' (13 May 2021) <https://en.agcm.it/en/media/press-releases/2021/5/A52>.
[248] ibid.
[249] CMA, *Decision to Accept Google's Commitments* (n 230).
[250] European Commission, 'Statement of Objections Regarding Apple Pay' (n 244).
[251] *Google LLC v European Commission* (n 79) para 201.
[252] ibid para 219.
[253] ibid para 230.
[254] ibid para 224.

instance, the Commission defined a market for licensable operating systems for smartphones in Android and excluded China from the relevant market, which left Android MOS as the only product in the market. A similar trend was observed in the *Apple App Store* case, where the Commission defined the market for iOS mobile devices, which left Apple with a monopoly power. National competition authorities, such as AGCM and the Dutch competition authority, have also reached similar conclusions.[255] Across the Atlantic, the FTC defined a relevant market for personal social networking services in the United States and identified Facebook as holding 'monopoly power' in this market.[256] The examples indicate the willingness on the part of competition authorities to resort to the flexibility that market definition offers to condemn certain practices that could have escaped scrutiny.

Several driving forces underlie the aforementioned trend, including the reduction in threshold for abuse, the resort to new theories of harm, and the adoption of narrower market definitions. The gatekeeping function of dominant entities and the extensive influence their dominance can exert appear to be central elements in numerous decisions that employ less stringent tests. For example, the European Commission, in its statement of objections regarding Apple's alleged abuse of dominance in the App Store, emphasized the pivotal role app stores play in the digital economy for activities such as shopping, gaming, and accessing news, music, or movies.[257] The Commission contends that many of these actors rely on the Apple App Store as a gatekeeper for reaching users of Apple's iPhones and iPads, and that this 'significant market power cannot go unchecked as the conditions of access to the Apple App Store are key for the success of app developers'.[258]

Similarly, in its Google decision, the AGCM underscored the gatekeeping role of Google with respect to end-users and its significance in determining not only 'the competitive confrontation between Google and its competitors but also the very functioning of the market and its evolution as well as the introduction of innovative applications.'[259] The UK CMA has also indicated that the changes envisaged by Google through its Privacy Sandbox would transfer some of the functions currently executed by ad tech providers to Chrome, positioning the browser as a gatekeeper for the ad tech ecosystem and as 'the source of truth for marketers'.[260] The references to how control over gateways, such as MOS and app stores, can be utilized to shape not only the market and ecosystem where gatekeepers operate but also the trajectories of innovation invoke discussions surrounding the concept of 'architectural power'.

[255] OECD, *The Evolving Concept of Market Power in the Digital Economy* (OECD Publishing 2022) 8.
[256] *FTC v Facebook* (n 238) para 2.
[257] European Commission, 'Statement by Executive Vice-President Margrethe Vestager on the Statement of Objections Sent to Apple on App Store Rules for Music Streaming Providers (30 April 2021) (European Commission, 'Statement by Vestager Regarding Apple's App Store Rules').
[258] ibid.
[259] Case A529, *Enel X Italia v Google* Bollettino 20/2021, para 317.
[260] CMA, *Decision to Accept Google's Commitments* (n 230) para 5.71.

Another driver of the aforementioned trend pertains to the dual capacity of numerous entities as proprietors of crucial infrastructure (gateways to consumers) and competitors with third parties reliant on the infrastructure. As owners of the infrastructure, these actors set rules of the game but also arbiter the competition in the field where they participate. The Commission's statement of objection against Apple highlights this aspect, emphasizing that Apple not only manages the sole entry point for apps on its devices but also competes with other music-streaming services in the Apple App Store, such as Spotify or Deezer.[261] Similarly, in the Amazon case, the Commission underscored the company's dual role as both a marketplace for independent sellers, and as a retailer, selling its products in competition with those sellers.[262]

As indicated in Chapter 1, both the above drivers—the gatekeeping function and vertical integration—are fundamental characteristics of ecosystem markets. Indeed, control over the entire ecosystem is accentuated in many of the aforementioned cases. In the *Apple Pay* case, the Commission noted that 'Apple's iPhones, iPads and software form a closed ecosystem' and 'Apple controls every aspect of the user experience in this ecosystem'.[263] In the Italian *Google* case, the AGCM highlighted how control over the entire Android ecosystem—Android, Google Play, and Auto—bestows a regulatory role upon Google, granting the authority to independently determine the types of apps that can reach consumers, as well as the timing and specific configurations of these apps. The interconnection between various products within the ecosystem, either through complementarity or cross-sharing of data, is another aspect that has garnered significant attention. In the *Android* case, the Commission noted how Google leverages its control over the Android ecosystem to preserve and fortify its dominance in search and online advertising markets. In the Italian *Google* case, the AGCM indicated that Google's refusal to allow interoperability was partly intended to compel Enel X to integrate its features into Google Maps, consequently providing Google with access to a considerable volume of valuable data from Enel X's users.[264]

In summary, to the extent that these trends denote shifts in enforcement, either by diminishing the standard for abuse or defining a narrower relevant market, they are influenced by the gatekeeping function of the actors, their control over an ecosystem, and the far-reaching consequences that dominance within such ecosystems can engender. This shift seems to obscure the distinction between the existing rules on abuse of dominance and the emerging rules targeting gatekeepers (eg the DMA), entities possessing 'strategic market status' or 'paramount significance for competition across markets'. The new set of rules require a lower threshold in terms

[261] European Commission, 'Statement by Vestager Regarding Apple's App Store Rules' (n 257).
[262] European Commission, 'Statement of Objections to Amazon' (n 22).
[263] European Commission, 'Statement of Objections Regarding Apple Pay' (n 244).
[264] *Enel X Italia v Google* (n 259) para 170.

of market power and standard test for intervention while encompassing a broader range of conduct. The development of new theories of harm centring on self-referencing and data utilization may indicate a transition from penalizing abuse of dominance to 'behavior that, due to market characteristics, is likely to result in a dominant position, and once such a position is obtained, to lead to exclusion and tipping'.[265]

Many of above the trends embody attempts by competition authorities to tame new dimensions of power, such as panopticon power and architectural power, which, as mentioned in Section IV.B, are not sufficiently addressed under existing competition law. For instance, the OECD asserts that endeavours to narrowly define markets may represent efforts to counterbalance the inability of market shares to capture market power concerning ecosystems of interconnected digital products.[266] Although these initiatives to restrain these dimensions of power through more narrow market definitions or the development of new theories of harm may provide temporary respite, they could also result in undesirable outcomes.[267] For example, if the Commission's perspective in the *Android* case were adopted, in which Google and Apple are not deemed competitors, would a merger involving the two firms be considered presumptively lawful, consistent with the conventional methodology applied to mergers among non-competitors?[268] Instead, competition policy ought to fully integrate the emerging domains of competition and dimensions of power facilitated by ecosystems.

VI. The DMA and Its Impact

The above discussion on the holistic approach and the suggestion to incorporate emergent properties focus on measures in competition law to address enforcement gaps arising from ecosystems. However, there are ongoing initiatives that aim to tackle some of these concerns directly through regulation. A prime example is the DMA, which aims to ensure contestability and fairness of digital markets by establishing 'do's and don'ts' for large online platforms. It is beyond the scope of this book to examine the pros and cons of competition law vis-a-vis regulation; others have already done so.[269] The aim in this section is simply to highlight how the DMA could potentially help address some of the concerns raised in this chapter.

[265] OECD, *The Evolving Concept of Market Power* (n 255) 32.
[266] ibid 8.
[267] Jacobides and Lianos (n 8) 1211 (noting that such an approach to focus on a single and narrow market 'would miss the nature of competitive dominance that a powerful ecosystem orchestrator/gatekeeper enjoys').
[268] Petit and Schrepel (n 83) 544.
[269] Nicolas Petit, *Big Tech and the Digital Economy: The Moligopoly Scenario* (OUP 2020).

At its core, the DMA focuses on reducing entry barriers to digital markets and tackling harmful commercial practices by gatekeepers. A gatekeeper is defined as 'an undertaking providing core platform services' and includes providers of online intermediation services, such as Amazon Market Place and app stores, online search engines, social networking services, and operating systems.[270] In order for a gatekeeper to be subject to the regulation, it must meet certain thresholds, both in terms of turnover and number of business and end-users.[271] Once a provider meets these thresholds, it is designated by the Commission as a gatekeeper and must comply with the provisions of the DMA, particularly those set out in Articles 5 and 6.

An important departure point in the DMA, as compared to competition law, is that it moves away from the emphasis on relevant markets. This is because the designation of gatekeepers focuses the economic significance, scope, or size of an entity without limiting this assessment to a particular relevant market.[272] This aspect of the DMA addresses the challenges discussed in Sections I and II associated with the atomized approach in relation to gatekeepers. Additionally, some of the factors indicate recognition of new power dimensions discussed in Section IV.B. The inclusion of market capitalization and the fixed number of users as a threshold for intervention is a positive step in recognizing how leading platforms generate value through financialization and extracting surplus from connections and positional advantage.[273] These dimensions of power are not fully considered under existing competition law and the conventional understanding of market power. The DMA also incorporates provisions that capture the essence of panopticon power and architectural power.[274]

[270] Regulation (EU) 2022/2065 of the European Parliament and of the Council of 19 October 2022 on a Single Market for Digital Services and amending Directive 2000/31/EC OJ L277/1 (Digital Services Act, DSA), Article 2.

[271] Specifically, there are three cumulative criteria that bring a company under the scope of the DMA: (1) strong economic presence in the internal market: this is presumed to be the case if the company achieves an annual turnover in the EU equal to or above €7.5 billion in the last three financial years, or where its average market capitalization amounted to at least €75 billion in the last financial year, and it provides a core platform service in at least three member states; (2) strong intermediation position: this is presumed to be the case if the company operates a core platform service with more than 45 million monthly active end-users established or located in the EU and more than 10,000 yearly active business users established in the EU in the last financial year; (3) entrenched and durable position: this is presumed to be the case if the company met the other two criteria in each of the last three financial years. See DMA, Article 3(1 and 2).

[272] Lianos and Bruno Carballa-Smichowski (n 146) 803.

[273] ibid.

[274] Examples of provisions within the DMA that aim to mitigate the negative impact of panopticon power include Article 6(2), which prohibits the use of non-public data provided by business users or generated by end-users of these business users, and Article 5(2(a)), which places restrictions on the use of data of end-users of third parties using the core platform for advertising purposes. Similarly, the obligation pertaining to fair and non-discriminatory access to app stores under Article 6(12), and the requirement to allow business users to utilize third-party payment systems under Article 5(7), appear to target architectural power.

Furthermore, as the DMA applies to gatekeepers that do not necessarily have a dominant position under traditional metrics, it could help tackle some of the potential emergent harms from cross-market practices where the undertaking does not have dominance. Here, it bears mentioning that the provisions address some of the concerns raised in this chapter as regards the harms associated with digital platforms, particularly those pertaining to platform bans and problems of data access. For example, Article 6(10) requires gatekeepers to provide business users with access to aggregated or non-aggregated data generated by their end-users while using the business' services. This will address some of the prevalent practices adopted by leading platforms, who have, in the past, denied third parties' access to data generated by their users.

Similarly, although the DMA does not explicitly forbid gatekeepers from blocking or removing apps from app stores, it imposes certain obligations that could impact such practices. For example, app stores are required to employ fair and non-discriminatory terms,[275] which might capture some of the bans on PETs. The DMA specifies that unfairness can be assessed considering the conditions imposed on the same or similar services by other app stores or conditions imposed by the provider of the app store for different or related services. Thus, if Google's removal of PETs deviates significantly from the practices of other app stores or if Google fails to apply comparable conditions to related services, the ban would likely be deemed unfair. As such, the DMA can tackle harmful trading practices by gatekeepers, which, owing to lack of dominance in a specific relevant market, could have escaped scrutiny under Article 102. This, in turn, could curb the tendency to engage in multiple such practices and the resultant emergent competitive harms discussed in Section III.B.

Despite this, in its current form, the DMA provides only half-answers to the concerns raised in this chapter. First, although the DMA paves the way for recognizing a new form of market power through the concept of gatekeeper, the definition based on a list of providers of core platform services remains formalistic. This, in turn, reduces the flexibility need to apply the DMA to complex, and decentralized business models that are currently not well understood.[276] As noted by Jacobides and Lianos,

> The challenge here is that, as we have seen, there is as yet no underlying regulatory theory for digital ecosystems—particularly when we consider more decentralized blockchain-based platforms. The DMA takes this into account by allowing the presumed gatekeeper to rebut their status through dialogue (Art. 3(4) DMA). The

[275] DMA, Article 6(12). However, this provision seems to be dictated by exploitation concerns (fairness) rather than the leveraging concerns. See Pablo Ibáñez Colomo, 'The Draft Digital Markets Act: A Legal and Institutional Analysis (2021) 12 <https://ssrn.com/abstract=3790276> accessed 7 February 2024.

[276] Jacobides and Lianos (n 8) 1215.

> flip side of this approach is that the gatekeeper criteria remain formalistic, and it is not clear what the orchestrator will be gatekeeper to. Also, the DMA neglects the business models used. Although the Commission and the preparatory experts' reports often mention "ecosystems" nowhere in the DMA proposals is the concept given any operational function.[277]

Second, the DMA does not cover digital platforms that do not meet the thresholds or are not included in the list, as well as minor global or regional gatekeepers. Third, the DMA's emphasis on practices that have a market-wide impact may not be effective in addressing systematic practices that target specific actor or actors. This is because one of the gaps that the DMA seeks to fill in is the fact-specific and case-by-case analysis under competition law, which allegedly leaves too many instances of bad behaviour unpunished. Therefore, the DMA focuses on general categories of business conduct, leaving individualized behaviour unaffected.[278] For example, Article 6(12) refers to 'general' conditions of access to app stores, which leaves the possibility of individualized terms and conditions of access for a specific actor or set of actors. Consequently, competition law remains the primary avenue for case-by-case analyses of conduct based on individualized terms and conditions of access. This approach is consistent with the DMA's aim of supplementing, not replacing, the application of competition law.

Finally, the DMA does not address the core problem, namely the atomized approach adopted when applying competition rules and its inadequacy in tackling emergent competitive harms due to multiple and systematic practices across markets. Although, as noted above, the DMA can curb some of the sources of emergent harms in relation to specific gatekeepers, the need to consider such harms in competition law is equally relevant in relation to gatekeepers that are not listed under the DMA, platforms that do not meet the threshold under the DMA, digital players that are not gatekeepers, and non-digital markets where an undertaking has the possibility to engage in multi-market and systematic practices.[279]

VII. Conclusion

This chapter explores the challenges to competition law enforcement amid the rise of ecosystems. Drawing on emergent properties, the chapter portrays the current application of competition law as fundamentally atomistic, focusing on the

[277] ibid.

[278] See Nicolas Petit, 'The Proposed Digital Markets Act (DMA): A Legal and Policy Review' (2021) 17–21 <https://ssrn.com/abstract=3843497> accessed 7 February 2024.

[279] Ioannis Lianos, 'Reorienting Competition Law' (2022) 10 Journal of Antitrust Enforcement 1, 18 (noting that the concept of gatekeeper does not cover 'platforms that may emerge in more traditional sectors, such as banking, automobile industry, retail').

identification of relevant product/service markets as a target of regulation and assessing the impact of conduct within these domains. It demonstrates that this atomized approach presents considerable enforcement challenges in competition law due to the shifts induced by the commercialization of personal data and big data. These shifts pertain to the transition from offering single products/services to providing ecosystems that encompass multiple integrated products/services, with personal data assuming a central role in coordinating activities across various markets. The amalgamation of multi-market ecosystems and the pivotal function of personal data in linking various markets obscure the boundaries between previously distinct relevant markets and render the attribution of competitive harm to a specific relevant market more complex. Additionally, the atomized approach to defining relevant markets may potentially overlook emergent competitive harms stemming from multiple and systematic practices in seemingly separate relevant markets within the overarching ecosystem. The chapter further highlights how the market power assessment and existing metrics, due to their reliance on market definition and emphasis on a firm's unique attributes, fail to capture new dimensions of power originating from a firm's position within the network and its ability to facilitate connections between complementary entities.

Thus, the discussion emphasizes that competition analysis involving ecosystems must move beyond focusing on individual relevant markets (ie an atomistic approach) and adopt a holistic analysis, accounting for the possibility that dominant digital players could obstruct effective competition through multiple actions across various markets and targeting numerous players. This holistic approach can be applicable in different contexts. First, since the main challenges are associated with the mechanics of market definition, the holistic approach can be applied in defining the relevant market and assessing market power. In this regard, the discussion showed that initiatives to define markets and establish dominance at ecosystem level can go a long way in addressing some of the challenges associated with the atomized approach and emergent competitive harms. This would allow competition authorities to consider multiple practices and the cross-market effects of such practices, which is often difficult to do under the atomized approach. Relatedly, competition policy and enforcement ought to incorporate notions of power that transcend a specific relevant market and acknowledge power dimensions that arise at the industry and ecosystem levels. This may entail considering novel dimensions of market power, such as panopticon power or architectural power, and devising metrics to quantify these powers.

Further, the holistic approach needs to be implemented in assessing anticompetitive effects and abuse of dominance. This dictates that competition law be receptive of the prospect that multiple disparate practices, which individually do not meet the legal standard, could generate anticompetitive outcomes that warrant intervention when considered in their entirety. To exemplify this notion, Section IV.D explored how the holistic approach and emergent thinking can be incorporated into the essential facilities doctrine, thereby revitalizing the doctrine's importance for digital platforms. Concurrently, the discourse on a holistic approach to assessing anticompetitive effects and abuse should encompass the potential benefits stemming from the entirety of practices across the ecosystem—systematic efficiencies. In this regard, the discussion shows that the existing case law and practice, particularly the CJEU's 'totality-of-the-circumstances' standard, lay the groundwork for increasing adoption of the holistic approach in assessing anticompetitive effects.

Using the lens of emergent properties, the discussion aims to show the substantial similarity in the mechanics of application of EU data privacy and competition laws, leading to a systemic problem common to both legal regimes. It shows how the concept of emergent properties might offer a unifying framework for understanding the challenges posed by big data when enforcing both data privacy and competition laws. There are two particularly important takeaways from the discussion via the lens of emergent properties. First, although the idea of 'one thing at a time' is a useful guiding principle in life, it may prove inadequate in a world where the line between one thing and another is unclear. Importantly, data privacy and competition law must recognize the prospect that the sum of fully compliant behaviours may still engender non-compliant conduct or actions deviating from the intended spirit of the law.

Next, the chapter highlighted three enforcement trends in relation to digital platforms. The first trend involves the desire to account for emergent effects originating from a combination of behaviours that, when assessed individually, may not attain the necessary threshold for intervention. This inclination, exemplified in the actions of the Bundeskartellamt and UK CMA, encapsulates the quintessence of emergence or the notion that 'more is different' and necessitates reinforcement. Ongoing investigations into Google and Apple, which involve multiple practices, afford the Commission the prospect to explore analogous concepts. At a minimum, the Commission should propose such an argument as an alternative to scrutinizing each conduct as abusive behaviour. The second enforcement trend pertains to the readiness to contemplate novel practices and competitive harms. A noteworthy manifestation of this inclination is the burgeoning emphasis on data and privacy-related abusive practices, which were not prominently featured in competition law cases until recently.

The third trend signifies the willingness of competition authorities to lower the standard for abuse or devise new theories of harms concerning some actors and their behaviours because of the wider impact such practices may have. One manifestation is the emergence of self-preferencing as a dominant theory of harm concerning digital platforms, even in scenarios where the essential facilities doctrine could have been employed. Another manifestation of this trend is the propensity to define markets narrowly such that only a single actor is included in the relevant product or service market. To the extent that these trends denote shifts in enforcement, they are influenced by the gatekeeping function of the actors, their control over an ecosystem, and the far-reaching consequences that dominance within such ecosystems can engender. Many of these trends represent attempts by competition authorities to address new dimensions of power, including panopticon power and architectural power. However, instead of stretching existing tools to address new dimensions of power, which may lead to inconsistent outcomes, competition law should directly address these aspects of power.

Finally, the chapter discusses the impact of the DMA in addressing some of the shortcomings in competition law enforcement concerning ecosystems. The DMA's approach to deviate from a relevant market, coupled with its reliance on the economic significance, scope, or size of an entity as a criterion for intervention, may alleviate some challenges associated with the atomized approach in relation to gatekeepers. Some of the factors used to designate gatekeepers, such as market capitalization and fixed number of users as a threshold for intervention, also suggest an acknowledgment of novel sources of competition and power dimensions. Furthermore, by tackling harmful trading practices by gatekeepers, which, owing to lack of dominance in specific relevant market, may have escaped scrutiny under Article 102 TFEU, the DMA could curb the tendency to engage in multiple such practices and the resultant emergent competitive harms.

Despite this, the DMA does not fully address the problems discussed in this chapter. Owing to its formalistic nature, it does not cover all digital gatekeepers and systematic practices that target specific actors. Additionally, the problems with the atomized approach and potential emergent competitive harms, though especially pertinent to digital platforms covered by the DMA, are equally applicable to gatekeeper practices not covered by the DMA, non-gatekeeper practices that nonetheless concern digital markets and ecosystems in traditional markets wherein an undertaking possesses the capability to engage in multi-market and systematic practices.

PART III

HARNESSING COMPLEXITY TO UNDERSTAND THE INTERFACE

Part III of the book delves into the interface between data privacy law and competition law, exploring both the areas of convergence and conflict resulting from the commercialization of personal data. Chapter 4 explores the broad manifestations of this interface from both empirical and normative perspectives. Empirically, the commercialization of personal data has prompted two developments that increase the intersection of the two legal fields. One development relates to the increased attention paid to personal data in competition assessments, especially in defining the relevant market, assessing market power, and imposing remedies. The other development involves increased attention to data privacy in competition analysis, particularly as a form of non-price parameter. Subsequently, the chapter examines the normative implications of these developments, highlighting the convergence—where the two sets of rules work together to promote a particular objective or complement each other—and the tensions—exemplified by increased recourse to data privacy obligations to justify potentially anticompetitive practices. The chapter argues that despite these tensions, there are ways to settle them amicably through joint efforts and dialogue between both legal regimes.

The chapter further contextualizes these discussions within the macro level by drawing on insights from complexity science. Specifically, it illustrates how the shifts brought about by the commercialization of personal data—notably the tendency to process data for a plethora of purposes and the emergence of multiproduct ecosystems—give rise to a complex economic landscape. This landscape is characterized by a multitude of actors, a network of interactions, and non-linear, emergent outcomes. In light of these developments, the book underscores the importance of three insights from complexity science: (1) its use of a system-level unit of analysis, (2) its emphasis on interconnections that lead to non-linear and emergent outcomes, and (3) its adoption of a polycentric approach to navigate such complexity. These insights inspire and are woven throughout the discussions in the book. In essence, the emergence of multiproduct, complex systems underpins all discussions in the book.

Chapters 2 and 3 underscore the need for a systems-level analysis that takes account of emergent harms. Chapters 4–7 then highlight that these complex systems are populated by heterogeneous agents with dynamic roles. In this sense, the recognition of data privacy as a non-price parameter and the increasing attention paid to privacy-related conduct in competition law is a positive step to embracing complexity thinking. Specifically, this step recognizes the potential harms faced by consumers as data producers and the adverse effects that may result from new forms of power (eg panopticon power) stemming from managing interconnections. These chapters further explore the growing intersection between data privacy law and competition law, advocating for a polycentric regulatory approach.

Chapter 5 explores how data privacy fits into competition analysis as a non-price competition parameter in the context of merger control. The chapter critically analyses three theories of harm for incorporating privacy as a non-price competition parameter: privacy-as-a-quality, consumer choice, and maverick-firm theories. In outlining the theories, the chapter draws on EU data privacy rules to determine what constitutes a reduction in privacy as a non-price parameter. Chapter 6 probes new ground, investigating possible privacy-related anticompetitive cooperation. Using recent examples involving big technology companies, the chapter explores the concept of privacy fixing and its place in competition law, including why digital companies may find it worthwhile to fix the level of privacy, how this may harm consumers, and the extent to which competition law can tackle such harms. Chapter 7 examines the issue of whether the data collection practices of dominant undertakings, including excessive data collection and unfair conditions related to the use of data, may amount to exploitative abuses under Article 102 of the Treaty on the Functioning of the European Union. Next, the chapter explores the question of whether, and to what degree, breaches of data privacy rules can contribute to breaches of competition rules or may represent a deviation from competition on the merits.

The book concludes with a call to reorient data privacy law and competition law to a complex economy, emphasizing the need for a holistic, systems-level perspective that takes account of emergent harms and a polycentric regulatory approach that harnesses insights from both data privacy law and competition law.

4

The Interface between Data Privacy and Competition Law

Insights from Complexity Science

I. The Commercialization of Personal Data and the Need to Harness Complexity Thinking

The digital economy is characterized by increased complexity.[1] Multi-product ecosystems represent a central aspect of this increased complexity, bringing together multiple actors and markets under a single umbrella and facilitating a web of economic links and interactions. Importantly, the collection of personal data contributes to complexity in several significant ways.[2] First, and as noted in Chapter 1, personal data plays a crucial role in linking different markets. Data collected in the context of a specific commercial activity can be instrumental in other markets by, for example, enabling targeted advertising, enhancing the quality of various digital services, or fostering the creation of new products/services.

Second, the commercialization of personal data displaces the role of price in the economy. There is a shift from 'markets to cybernetics': algorithm-generated preferences replace price as the information tool used to communicate consumer preferences.[3] Firms use vast quantities of personal data to forecast consumer preferences and to differentiate among various groups of consumers. They adopt a pricing structure that subsidizes some groups while imposing higher prices on others. As a result, there is less reliance on decentralized markets as sources of knowledge about consumer preferences.[4] Moreover, the commercialization of personal data increases complexity by creating actors with multifaceted roles.[5] End-users are not just consumers of products and services but contribute to the production of value by providing their data, a key resource for many digital services. Individual users can be consumers, providers of data, workers, and products,

[1] Gregory Gundlach, 'Complexity Science and Antitrust?' (2006) 51 Antitrust Bulletin 17; Ioannis Lianos, 'Competition Law for a Complex Economy' (2019) 50 IIC-International Review of Intellectual Property and Competition Law 643, 645.

[2] Lianos, 'Competition Law for a Complex Economy' (n 1) 645.

[3] ibid.

[4] ibid 646.

[5] Ioannis Lianos, 'Competition Law for the Digital Era: A Complex Systems' Perspective' (Centre for Law, Economics and Society (CLES) Research Paper Series 6/2019, CLES 2019) 11.

Data Privacy and Competition Law in the Age of Big Data. Samson Y. Esayas, Oxford University Press.
 DOI: 10.1093/oso/9780198891420.003.0005

all at the same time.[6] To a certain degree, the growing focus on personal data and data privacy within competition law, as demonstrated in this chapter, represents a positive stride towards acknowledging this emerging complexity. At the same time, these developments increase the convergence and tensions between data privacy law and competition law; both will require careful consideration.

The increased complexity, driven by the commercialization of personal data, has created an institutional gap in both data privacy and competition law. As noted in Chapters 2 and 3, this complexity creates systemic challenges to the atomized application of data privacy law and competition law. There are also concerns that the lack of an appropriate framework to understand this complexity has led to underenforcement of both sets of rules.[7] Given that the challenges to both sets of laws are rooted in the increased complexity of the digital economy, numerous scholars (including the author) have turned to complexity science for new insights and new tools to help address these challenges.[8] Indeed, as demonstrated in Chapters 2 and 3, the adoption of systems thinking and the concept of emergence can help overcome some of the challenges. This section expands on these discussions and seeks to frame the debates presented in this and subsequent chapters considering insights derived from complexity science.

As a conceptual framework, complexity science offers unique insights that arise from the incorporation of three components: (1) the use of a system-level unit of analysis, (2) an emphasis on interconnections and coevolutionary explanations to understand behaviour, and (3) the adoption of associated methodologies for analysing such complexity.[9] These three insights have widespread applicability across numerous fields, including law. However, in this section, the focus is on their relevance to tackling the challenges related to the commercialization of personal data in data privacy law and competition law.

The initial insight from complexity science relevant to data privacy and competition law is the need for a system-level analytical framework. This approach recognizes that different sectors of the digital economy operate as an interconnected web of organizations, technologies, consumers, and products.[10] Products or companies should not be perceived as belonging to a single market, sector, or industry but rather as belonging to a more extensive business environment spanning multiple industries, sectors, and markets.[11] This portrayal of the economy

[6] ibid 23.

[7] See Ioannis Lianos, 'Mind the (Institutional) Gap: Digital Economy, Competition Law and the Toolkit Approach' (Fall 2022) Network Law Review <https://www.networklawreview.org/lianos-institutional-gap/>; Bert-Jaap Koops, 'The Trouble with European Data Protection Law' (2014) 4 International Data Privacy Law 250, 250.

[8] See articles published in the special issue of Antitrust Bulletin 2006, which highlight the significance of complexity science in the realm of antitrust.

[9] Gundlach (n 1) 19; Nicolas Petit and Thibault Schrepel, 'Complexity-Minded Antitrust' (2023) 33 Journal of Evolutionary Economics 541.

[10] Gundlach (n 1) 19.

[11] ibid.

generates challenges where the analytical framework used to apply the law demands that the components of such systems be viewed as isolated parts, potentially overlooking the effects of interconnections and of coevolution of the system as a whole. As emphasized in Chapters 2 and 3, a systemic issue arises in competition law and data privacy law due to their atomized approach to complex systems comprising numerous interrelated components. Thus, proposals for a holistic, system-level analytical framework, including the ability to define markets at the ecosystem level, have been put forth.[12] In a similar vein, some authors have suggested that we develop frameworks that establish market power at the ecosystem or value-chain level, as well as methods for assessing systemic efficiencies. All of these proposals are driven by the need for a multi-level analytical framework.

The second insight from complexity science concerns the description of the essential features of a system: its components; the connections, interactions, and dynamic processes between components; and their evolution over time.[13] This approach emphasizes the significance of features such as feedback loops, non-linearity, and emergence. In this regard, both Chapters 2 and 3 underscore the need to address emergent risks in the application of data privacy law and competition law. Moreover, the discussion in Chapter 3, Section IV.B, illustrates how interconnections within the system, together with feedback loops, give rise to new types of power—such as panopticon and architectural power—that are not adequately addressed in competition law. Indeed, this and the ensuing chapters demonstrate that the increased attention to data, data-driven network effects, and data-related anti-competitive practices positively contributes to recognizing aspects of panopticon power and the feedback loops arising from interconnections. However, as shown in this chapter, there are still gaps in our capacity to address these novel forms of power, including, for example, the question of how to incorporate data privacy law when evaluating market power (Section IV.A.1). Moreover, the increased attention to personal data in competition law gives rise to increased tension with data privacy interests, as competition authorities may resort to data-related remedies. These developments raise several questions on the impact of such measures on users' privacy, the limits imposed by data privacy law, and how to balance privacy and competition interests. Section IV.B explores these issues.

Another crucial insight from complexity theory pertains to its description of agents. Complex systems are made up of a heterogeneous set of agents whose states both influence and are influenced by others. This insight is particularly relevant to competition law. Specifically, it has been argued that the current methods for evaluating market power and associated metrics fail to capture the impact of behaviour on agents other than producers or consumers. This includes agents acting

[12] See Petit and Schrepel (n 9) (suggesting other multi-level frameworks of analysis under competition law).

[13] Gundlach (n 1) 19.

as data producers and workers, who contribute to the socio-economic value of the ecosystem.[14] This has led to suggestions to broaden the objectives of competition law to incorporate impacts on privacy and labour conditions.[15] While discussions on the need to broaden the goals of competition law are beyond the scope of this book, recognizing data privacy as a non-price parameter and increasing the attention paid to practices that harm privacy are steps in the right direction. These efforts acknowledge the potential harms faced by consumers as data producers and mitigate some of the adverse effects resulting from panopticon power.

Despite this, as demonstrated in the current and subsequent chapters, the integration of privacy considerations into competition law is still in its infancy. Numerous questions remain about how to effectively implement this incorporation. How does privacy competition manifest? What does a reduction in privacy entail? What is the role of data privacy law? These questions are addressed here and in subsequent chapters, offering a systematic analysis of privacy as a non-price competition parameter under European Union (EU) merger control and Articles 101 and 102 of the Treaty on the Functioning of the European Union (TFEU).

The third insight from complexity science relates to the methodologies used to analyse and model complex systems, such as simulation models and network analysis. An emerging body of literature explores the application of agent-based models and scenario analysis in competition law to investigate the impacts of economic behaviour within ecosystems.[16] These tools facilitate the modelling of agent heterogeneity and foster a deeper understanding of the uncertainty, emergent properties, and non-linearity that may arise in complex systems. It has even been suggested that such models can be used to consider and measure reductions in non-price parameters of competition, such as data privacy.[17] Furthermore, complexity science provides valuable insights on the design of regulatory systems able to effectively navigate complex economic landscapes.

In essence, the complexity of the ecosystem economy must be met by a regulatory system that is polycentric in nature. This means establishing a network of legal regimes that interact with and complement each other, along with a system for collaboration among different centres of legal authority.[18] It is a 'mix-and-match' approach, combining diverse institutional mechanisms that transcend the boundaries of different legal regimes.[19] For example, as part of such an approach, one might

[14] Petit and Schrepel (n 9) 545.

[15] See Ioannis Lianos, 'Reorienting Competition Law' (2022) 10 Journal of Antitrust Enforcement 1; Julie Cohen, 'Law for the Platform Economy' (2017) 51 University of California, Davis Law Review 133.

[16] Gundlach (n 1) 20; Petit and Schrepel (n 9) 566.

[17] Lianos, 'Reorienting Competition Law' (n 15). While these topics are important, they fall beyond the scope of this book.

[18] Ioannis Lianos, 'Polycentric Competition Law' (2018) 71 Current Legal Problems 161.

[19] ibid 200.

consider establishing a system for the joint review of mergers—particularly those involving data combinations—by data protection and competition authorities.[20]

The call for a polycentric approach aligns well with the central argument of this book, which emphasizes the need to move beyond the either/or mentality and embrace a coordinated approach to address the challenges associated with the commercialization of personal data. However, this requires an understanding of the points of intersection between data privacy law and competition law both from an empirical (Sections II and III) and a normative perspective (Section IV). Once these points of intersection have been located, it becomes easier to see the areas in which the two sets of rules could (and perhaps should) collaborate.

In this chapter and those that follow, the aim is to flesh out a path for a polycentric approach in the enforcement of data privacy law and competition law. This involves uncovering the points of convergence and conflict between the two fields of law, identifying the appropriate set of legal rules to deploy, depending on the context, and highlighting areas for cooperation. These chapters argue that the interface, when complemented by a coordinated approach, presents a unique opportunity to enhance the efficacy of both data privacy and competition rules.

II. Increased Attention to Personal Data in Competition Analysis

In the digital age, the volume and the quality of the personal data controlled by a company have a major impact on its competitive performance. They determine the company's ability to deliver relevant and high-quality services as well as its capacity to monetize services (which directly impacts its revenues). The increased importance of personal data for competitive performance has led to increased attention to personal data in competition assessment, both in defining the relevant market and in assessing market power. The following subsections highlight these two developments in competition law, which contribute to the increased interface between data privacy and competition rules.

A. Increasing Importance of Data in Defining the Relevant Market

As discussed in Chapter 3, defining the relevant market is an important step in applying competition law, both in its *ex ante* and *ex post* forms. The objective is to identify the competitive constraints affecting a firm's ability to raise prices or

[20] Nicholas Economides and Ioannis Lianos, 'Restrictions on Privacy and Exploitation in the Digital Economy: A Market Failure Perspective' (2021) 17 Journal of Competition Law & Economics 765, 799.

decrease output. To achieve this, competition law authorities employ different tools and techniques, including the substitutability test. This test considers both demand- and supply-side substitutability, which means that a relevant market is typically defined when there is both demand and supply for the product/service.[21] In the case of data-driven business models (DDBMs), the existing tools are well suited to analysing markets where data is traded as a standalone product, for example when data brokers sell aggregated consumer data. The European Commission has defined different data markets in its past decisions. For example, in its *Apple/Shazam* merger decision, the Commission defined a market for the 'licensing of music data', in which both parties were active.[22]

The problem arises when the data is not traded as a standalone product but is a key input in the provision of other services, for example advertising or improving the quality of the underlying services. This is typically the case with platforms like Google and Facebook. These platforms generate data as part of a service provided 'free' of charge for the user. This data is then used as a key input to provide targeted advertising. In such cases, the data serves as intermediary product and, thus, no demand or supply exists for the data per se. Consequently, competition authorities have been reluctant to define a data market unless such data is directly offered in the market.[23] Thus, in past decisions involving data mergers, the focus has been on the service market, with little or no regard for the data that powers the service.

The *Google/DoubleClick* merger was the first case to raise novel questions about the importance of data and the challenges associated with zero-price markets. Loyal to the conventional competition law trade, both the European Commission and the US Federal Trade Commission (FTC) analysed only the paying side of the market (ie the advertising market) and cleared the merger without conditions.[24] However, this approach overlooks the possible competitive constraints that the 'free' side exerts over the paying side and the potential consumer harms—in the form of compromised privacy—on the free side. Importantly, it fails to consider the central role of data in the merger.

In a dissenting opinion to the FTC decision, then Commissioner Harbour criticized the majority for focusing only on the service market for advertising and analysing the merger solely as vertical integration.[25] In such markets, the size and scope of the data are vital, and horizontal concentration can arise from the repurposing of data under the control of the merged entity. The Commissioner

[21] European Commisson, 'Commission Notice on the Definition of Relevant Market for the Purposes of Community Competition Law' [1997] OJ C372/5, para 13; Inge Graef, 'Market Definition and Market Power in Data: The Case of Online Platforms' (2015) 38 World Competition 473, 489.

[22] Case M.8788 *Apple/Shazam* decision of 6 September 2018, para 119ff.

[23] Case M.7217 *Facebook/WhatsApp* decision of 3 October 2014, para 72.

[24] Case M.4731 *Google/DoubleClick* decision of 11 March 2008. See also Statement of US Federal Trade Commission Concerning Google/DoubleClick FTC File No 071-0170.

[25] Dissenting Statement of Commissioner Pamela Jones Harbour in the Matter of Google/DoubleClick FTC File No 071-070 (Dissenting Statement of Commissioner Harbour).

suggested that the merger should also be viewed as horizontal overlap over 'input data' for advertising.[26] Considering the existing network effects and additional network effects from the merger, Harbour argued that the merger could lead to dominance in the 'database of intentions', which may not be replicated by competitors.[27] More data about users' preferences and intentions means more successfully targeted ads, resulting in a higher conversion rate, which, in turn, attracts more advertisers. Therefore, by combining Google's and DoubleClick's data, the merged entity gains 'access to [an] unparalleled data resource' that enables 'highly targeted advertising', thereby tipping the market in its favour.[28] Harbour argued that had the FTC taken a more dynamic approach and defined an 'input data' market, separate from the market for services provided using such data, the outcome may have been different.[29]

In light of Harbour's argument, defining a market for 'input data' separate from the service market opens up the possibility of assessing whether the combination of data by the merged entity could lead to market power in the service market. This argument gained some traction in subsequent decisions of the European Commission. While the Commission did not explicitly define a market for 'input data' when approving the same merger, it examined whether the combination of user data from Google and DoubleClick would enable the merged entity to achieve a position that could not be replicated by competitors, an aspect missing from the FTC's assessment.[30] Likewise, without specifically defining a separate market for 'input data' in the *Facebook/WhatsApp* case, the Commission delved deeper into the issue of potential data concentration, investigating whether the merger was 'likely to strengthen Facebook's position in the online advertising market or any of its sub-segments'.[31]

While the Commission's approach in *Facebook/WhatsApp* represents a step in the right direction by recognizing the significance of data, it adopts an unnecessarily narrow perspective by focusing on data's importance for a single market, specifically online targeted advertising. This approach fails to consider the non-exhaustive nature of data and its potential to enhance multiple services beyond advertising, including fostering the development of new services. It is true that the current tools at the Commission's disposal allow for the definition of intermediate product markets, such as 'specialized assets', which competitors need to access to compete effectively in a market.[32] However, these tools were designed with

[26] ibid.
[27] ibid 4.
[28] ibid 7–8.
[29] Pamela Harbour and Tara Koslov, 'Section 2 in a Web 2.0 World: An Expanded Vision of Relevant Product Markets' (2010) 76 Antitrust Law Journal 769, 784.
[30] *Google/DoubleClick* (n 24) paras 359ff.
[31] *Facebook/WhatsApp* (n 23) para 164.
[32] European Union, 'Guidelines on the Applicability of Article 101 of the Treaty on the Functioning of the European Union to Horizontal Co-operation Agreements' (2011) OJ C11/1 (EU Guidelines on Horizontal Cooperation) para 120.

exhaustive assets (eg capital) in mind, and unless adapted, they may not be ideally suited to data, which is non-exhaustive in nature. This shortcoming has prompted suggestions that competition authorities should consider defining separate 'input-data' markets.[33]

As shown in the subsequent paragraphs, defining hypothetical markets for input data, separate from the service markets, can help address concerns related to the narrowly defined importance of data. Furthermore, Section IV.A.1 underscores the need to consider data privacy law in assessing the effectiveness of the competitive constraints stemming from comparable data sets held by competitors. This consideration is crucial because the availability of a comparable data set accessible to other entities does not mean that such data may be used or licensed without difficulty, as there may be different legal frameworks applicable to the different actors, limiting their ability to reuse data across markets or sectors.

In more recent decisions, the Commission seems to have recognized the multipurpose characteristic of data and has experimented with defining hypothetical markets for input data. In the *Microsoft/LinkedIn* decision, despite acknowledging that LinkedIn does not sell data directly to third parties, the Commission analysed data-related concerns arising from the merger by defining a 'hypothetical market for the supply of data'.[34] Specifically, the Commission evaluated two markets, namely a 'hypothetical market or segment for the provision of data for the purposes of ML [machine learning] in CRM [customer relationship management] software solutions' and 'a hypothetical market or segment for provision of data for the purposes of ML in productivity software solutions'.[35] This approach allowed the Commission to examine the extent to which the combination of data might enhance the ML capabilities of the merged entity in CRM and productivity software and the extent to which competitors in these markets could access comparable data sets. Although the Commission did not identify any competition concerns, its use of 'hypothetical markets' in analysing the impact of merged data sets represents a positive development. This approach recognizes the significance of data for multiple markets and purposes, which, as noted above, is the source of complexity. These 'input-data' markets can serve as a foundation for analysing the importance of data across various markets, including addressing data-related concerns for end-users.

At the same time, the growing importance of data in defining the relevant market results in an increased interface between data privacy law and competition law. As demonstrated in Section IV.A.1, while competition authorities are considering the competitive constraints that data privacy rules impose on the merged firm's ability

[33] See Graef, 'Market Definition' (n 21); Autorité de la Concurrence and Bundeskartellamt, *Competition Law and Data* (2016).

[34] Case M.8124 *Microsoft/LinkedIn* decision of 6 December 2016, para 179.

[35] ibid paras 254 and 347.

to reuse or combine data, they overlook the analogous constraints on competitors' abilities to repurpose data they already possess or to procure data from third parties to compete with the merged entity. In essence, the current approach appears to overestimate the constraints imposed by data privacy rules on intra-firm data sharing and underestimate the same constraints on inter-firm data sharing.

B. Data as a Source of Market Power and a Barrier to Entry

As personal data becomes increasingly crucial for providing various digital products and services, competition authorities have also started to examine the extent to which the accumulation of personal data can give rise to, or perpetuate, market power by creating barriers to entry. Indeed, discussions of data as a source of market power and a barrier to entry are not new under EU competition law. The Court of Justice of the European Union (CJEU) has addressed this question in several decisions, including *Magill* and *IMS Health*.[36] These decisions acknowledge that control over data, which is subject to intellectual property (IP) protection, can be used to foreclose competition.

While these cases focus on data protected by exclusivity rights due to IP protection, they clarify the circumstances under which data may create an entry barrier. For example, in *Magill*, the CJEU stated that the broadcasting companies were the only sources of information on programme listings, which served as the indispensable raw material for compiling a comprehensive weekly television guide.[37] Thus, one instance in which data may create an entry barrier is if the data is subject to IP protection and this right is exercised to prevent competitors from entering the market or offering a new product.

Importantly, the assessment of data as a source of market power rests on demonstrating that the data is indispensable to the provision of a service/product. This requires showing that there are no alternative sources of data that could be used to provide the service and that there are technical, legal, or economic obstacles that make it impossible or unreasonably difficult to replicate the data.[38]

Applying this test to personal data poses challenges, not least because personal data is considered ubiquitous.[39] In addition, personal data is non-rivalrous: consumers provide their data to many entities, and multiple entities can use identical information concurrently without it losing its value.[40] Data that is ubiquitous and

[36] Joined Cases C-241/91 P and C-242/91 P *Radio Telefis Eireann (RTE) and Independent Television Publications Ltd (ITP) v Commission (Magill)* ECLI:EU:C:1995:98; Case C-418/01 *IMS Health v NDC Health* ECLI:EU:C:2004:257.

[37] *Magill* (n 36) paras 53–54.

[38] See Case C-7/97 *Oscar Bronner GmbH & Co v Mediaprint Zeitungs-und Zeitschriftenverlag GmbH* ECLI:EU:C:1998:569, para 44.

[39] See Darren Tucker and Hill Wellford, 'Big Mistakes Regarding Big Data' (December 2014) Antitrust Source 7.

[40] See ibid 3–4.

non-rivalrous are unlikely to create entry barriers, as there are no technical, legal, or economic obstacles that make it impossible or unreasonably difficult to replicate the data.

Some of the Commission's earlier decisions seem to echo this view of personal data. In its *Facebook/WhatsApp* decision, the Commission noted that even if Facebook were to combine its data with WhatsApp's, the merger would not impede competition, because other market players—such as Google, Apple, Microsoft, AOL, Twitter, LinkedIn, Adobe, and Yelp—have access to 'Internet user data' that are valuable for advertising.[41] This approach treats all kinds of online data as 'fungible' or interchangeable. The Commission's view of consumer data belonging to different entities as being equally valuable for advertising purposes reflects the adage outlined above: consumer data is widely available (ubiquitous) and can be collected and used by various actors at the same time (non-rivalrous).

However, the above claims underestimate the value of data-driven network effects, that is network effects due to the scale (volume), scope (variety), and speed (velocity) of data.[42] For example, many of the arguments that downplay the value of data for market power often confuse the cost of acquiring a piece of information and the value of that information to a firm. Acquiring a piece of information may, indeed, be cheap. However, this does not necessarily mean that this information is equally valuable. One important factor that affects the value is the scale of the data set within which such information is put to use. The benefits from data increase with the scale of the data set. The essence of big data is that the increase in scale creates opportunities to generate new forms of value that are unattainable at smaller scales.

Scale is not the only factor affecting the value of data. The gains from scale can be further augmented with variety. The combination of data from various sources can create synergies and enable the contextualization of data, that is the ability to obtain insights from data that would not have meaning on its own. Thus, variety in data can generate 'superadditive insights'.[43] Another dimension relevant to competition is data velocity: the ability to access data in real time. The argument that new entrants can procure data from brokers and compete with incumbents overlooks the importance of speed.[44] Competing effectively involves not only learning but also learning and reacting in real time. A company with real-time data access is better positioned to generate value than one without. Temporality—or knowing something at a crucial moment—also plays a role. Search engines have an advantage, as

[41] See *Facebook/WhatsApp* (n 23) paras 188–89.

[42] While the arguments on data-driven network effects are framed to encompass non-personal data, the implications for personal data are equally significant. See Maurice Stucke and Allen Grunes, *Big Data and Competition Policy* (OUP 2016); Dissenting Statement of Commissioner Harbour (n 25) 4.

[43] Organisation for Economic Co-operation and Development (OECD), *Data-Driven Innovation: Big Data for Growth and Well-Being* (OECD Publishing 2015) 184.

[44] See arguments in Daniel Sokol and Roisin Comerford, 'Antitrust and Regulating Big Data' (2016) 23 George Mason Law Review 1129, 1137.

they know when consumers search for specific products in real time. While having access to past search queries, as proposed by the Digital Markets Act (DMA), may address some network effects due to scale, it does not tackle the temporality advantage. The dominant search engine would still have an edge in learning about unfolding events and responding to relevant queries. This partly explains why first-party data, collected directly from users, is considered more valuable than third-party data, initially gathered by another entity.[45]

Therefore, the quality of data and its importance for competition depend not only on volume and variety but also on data velocity (the three Vs of data discussed in Chapter 1). Entering a market where a company has all three advantages is more challenging than entering a market where the company benefits solely from scale. This suggests that any assessment of whether control over personal data creates barriers to entry should consider all three dimensions of data. Moreover, with respect to personal data, data privacy rules—particularly purpose limitation and data minimization principles—introduce further barriers, preventing firms from collecting vast and diverse data sets (Section IV.A.1).

Despite initial scepticism, in the past few years competition authorities have come to recognize the importance of data and related network effects for competition. For example, the importance of data for competition has led the OECD to suggest that in markets in which zero-priced services are exchanged for data, 'market power is better measured by shares of control over data than shares of sales or any other traditional measures'.[46] Indeed, numerous initiatives are underway to encapsulate the role of data as a source of market power, with some countries even updating their competition rules to reflect its importance. A notable example is the amendment to the German Act against Restraints on Competition, which underscores the need to consider access to data when assessing the competitive impact of mergers related to new business models and when assessing the market power of multi-sided platforms.[47]

Similarly, ongoing reforms to merger notification thresholds aim to reflect the competitive significance of data for competition. This is because current turnover-based notifications might not be well suited to industries that rely heavily on the monetization of personal data, potentially allowing many data-driven mergers to escape review.[48] This issue is partly related to the different phases in developing ad-supported business models. Given the importance of network effects for such businesses (ie the more users, the more attractive they become to advertisers), the

[45] Monica Bulger, Greg Taylor, and Ralph Schroeder, *Data-Driven Business Models: Challenges and Opportunities of Big Data* (Oxford Internet Institute 2014) 33.

[46] Ania Thiemann and Pedro Gonzaga, *Big Data: Bringing Competition Policy to the Digital Era* (OECD 2016) 17.

[47] See Act against Restraints of Competition (German Competition Act, GWB) as last amended by Article 4 of the Act of 9 July 2021.

[48] See European Commission, 'Consultation on Evaluation of Procedural and Jurisdictional Aspects of EU Merger Control' (28 August 2017).

initial phase focuses on attracting audiences and strategically positioning oneself in terms of data access. Thus, most ad-supported business models start out ad-free until they gather a certain mass of users. This is followed by the monetization of their audience and data.

It is true that when companies mature and begin to monetize their audience and data, the value generated from personal data can be reflected in their turnover. Thus, the acquisition of firms at this stage can be caught by current notification thresholds. The problem arises when firms that have succeeded in the initial phase are acquired by dominant players before they start monetizing their data and audience.

There are initiatives to update current merger control rules to better reflect the importance of data for competition. For example, both German and Austrian competition laws have been amended to include notification based on transaction value.[49] The EU is considering introducing a similar rule under the Merger Regulation.[50] One rationale for this proposal is that it would acknowledge the value of data in such mergers. As Commissioner Vestager has indicated, the current rules fail to capture 'a merger that does not meet our thresholds because turnover has not showed yet, but you still have a very valuable company because of the potential of data'.[51] The Commissioner believes that 'the value of a merger could be a good guide to its importance'.[52] Introducing a transaction value-based notification threshold is a step in the right direction, as it might help capture mergers that would otherwise escape review.[53] This paves the way for a substantive analysis of the competitive significance of data for market power. Not surprisingly, there are encouraging developments on this front, with competition authorities recognizing the importance of data and data-driven network effects as sources of market power and barriers to entry.

In its *Google Shopping* decision, the Commission acknowledged that the volume and scale of search query data are significant barriers to entry and expansion.[54] It also pointed out the positive feedback and monetization effects: the more users a search engine has, the more appealing it becomes to advertisers, because ads are more likely to match a given search and be converted into a sale.[55] This cycle

[49] Michael Ristaniemi and T Alexander Puutio, 'The Power of Data: Is It Worth All the Hype?' (*Kluwer Competition Law Blog*, 21 July 2016) <https://competitionlawblog.kluwercompetitionlaw.com/2016/07/21/the-power-of-data-is-it-worth-all-the-hype/>; Franz Urlesberger, Volker Weiss, Hanno Wollman, and Christoph Haid, 'Significant Amendments to Austrian Competition Law—Part II (Merger Control)', *Schoenherr* (11 April 2017) <https://www.schoenherr.eu/content/significant-amendments-to-austrian-competition-law-part-ii-merger-control/>.

[50] European Commission, 'Refining the EU Merger Control System', speech by Commissioner Vestager (10 March 2016).

[51] Rochelle Toplensky, 'EU Considers Tougher Competition Powers', *Financial Times* (2 July 2017).

[52] European Commission, 'Refining the EU Merger Control System' (n 50).

[53] However, this could lead to underreporting of the transaction value to avoid notification.

[54] Case AT.39740 *Google Search (Shopping)* decision of 27 June 2017, para 287.

[55] ibid para 293.

allows Google to charge higher prices for advertising, boosting its revenue, which can then be reinvested in attracting more users, thereby drawing more advertisers. Accordingly, the Commission views the data-driven network effects, together with the monetization feedback loop, as forces protecting Google from competition. They have allowed Google to favour its own comparison-shopping product and thereby harm consumer welfare. The Commission's analysis was confirmed by the General Court (GC).[56] This approach, which considers the importance of data, along with the associated network effects and feedback loops, is a positive step towards embracing a complexity-orientated mindset in competition analysis.

The Commission has taken further steps to acknowledge the importance of data-driven network effects. A notable example is the Commission's decision in *Apple/Shazam*, which assessed the importance of data, in line with the discussions above, by focusing on four dimensions: volume, variety, velocity, and value.[57] Moreover, in its *Google/Fitbit* merger decision, the Commission held that the potential combination of data belonging to the merging parties could create barriers to entry and foreclose competition in the market for online advertising and submarkets/segments thereof.[58] In so doing, the Commission examined 'the *volume, value, variety and velocity* of the databases maintained by Fitbit, its competitors and also Google'.[59] According to the Commission, none of Google's competitors in online advertising has access to a database or data collection capabilities equivalent to those of Fitbit, and the acquisition could strengthen Google's dominance in the online search advertising market and further marginalize the limited competitors in this market.[60] Thus, the Commission expressed concerns about the merger's compatibility with the internal market.

To allay these concerns, Google offered various commitments; it would maintain data separation, refrain from using Fitbit data for advertising, and assent to monitoring by a third-party trustee.[61] Similar concerns over control and access to data have led the UK Competition and Markets Authority (CMA) to order Meta to sell Giphy.[62] Overall, the growing recognition of data and data-driven network effects as sources of market power by competition authorities, along with measures to address such power, represent important steps in curbing the new dimensions of power (eg panopticon power), which, as noted in Chapter 3, are not adequately addressed by current tools. Despite this progress, current practice seems to underestimate the barriers to entry arising from data privacy rules (see Section IV.A.1). Moreover, measures taken by competition authorities to curb panopticon

[56] Case T-612/17 *Google LLC v European Commission* ECLI:EU:T:2021:763, para 226.
[57] *Apple/Shazam* (n 22) para 317.
[58] Case M.9660 *Google/Fitbit* decision of 17 December 2020, para 434.
[59] ibid para 418 (emphasis added).
[60] ibid para 454.
[61] ibid section A.1 Commitments.
[62] Competition and Markets Authority (CMA), 'CMA Orders Meta to Sell Giphy' (18 October 2022) <https://www.gov.uk/government/news/cma-orders-meta-to-sell-giphy>.

power, or efforts by incumbents to maintain such power, bring about tensions between data privacy law and competition law, requiring careful consideration (see Section IV.B).

III. Increased Attention to Data Privacy as a Non-Price Competition Parameter

Another implication resulting from the commercialization of personal data is the increased attention to data privacy in competition analysis, particularly as a form of non-price parameter. EU competition law is concerned with market power that may harm consumer welfare, which, according to the CJEU, must be assessed by considering the negative effects on the price, quantity, or quality of goods and services.[63] Thus, at least in principle, agreements, mergers, and unilateral conduct that negatively affect non-price parameters are as harmful to consumer welfare as price increases. Despite this, accounting for non-price parameters in competition analysis faces major challenges.

For example, despite wide recognition of the importance of the quality of goods and services for consumer welfare, establishing harm to quality is not straightforward. One of the challenges is due to the multidimensional nature of quality: quality can be measured in many ways, and an increase in one attribute may negatively affect another attribute.[64] Additionally, quality is subjective: different consumers value different aspects of a good or service differently. As a result, competition analysis based on quality often involves balancing several imprecise and subjective attributes. This has led the OECD to describe quality as an 'important but somewhat elusive topic'.[65] Moreover, microeconomic theory does not offer a clear relationship between the intensity of competition and its impact on quality (including choice and innovation).[66] This suggests that, unlike price competition, no general conclusions can be drawn as to the effect of competition on quality; understanding the impact of competition on quality would require empirical studies tailored to individual markets.[67] As a result, non-price parameters are often 'relegated to the footnotes of the analysis, where they are too often forgotten'.[68]

[63] Case C-67/13 P *Groupement des cartes bancaires* ECLI:EU:C:2014:2204, para 51.

[64] See Ariel Ezrachi and Maurice Stucke, 'The Curious Case of Competition and Quality' (2015) 3 Journal of Antitrust Enforcement 227, 227–29.

[65] OECD, *Policy Roundtables: The Role and Measurement of Quality in Competition Analysis* (OECD Publishing 2013) 5.

[66] ibid 1.

[67] However, one argument is that this is less of a concern in relation to services offered at zero price as firms' price-making decisions are not unconstrained in these markets. See Samson Esayas, 'Competition in (Data) Privacy: 'Zero'-Price Markets, Market Power, and the Role of Competition Law' (2018) 8 International Data Privacy Law 181.

[68] Robert Lande, 'Consumer Choice as the Best Way to Describe the Goals of Competition Law' (University of Baltimore School of Law Legal Studies Research Paper, University of Baltimore 2012) 4.

Despite this, non-price considerations have featured in key areas of EU competition law, in light of both their procompetitive and anticompetitive effects. For example, in the proposed takeover of Aer Lingus by Ryanair, the Commission's decision to prohibit the merger was based on quality considerations, such as flight times and frequencies.[69] Additionally, while enforcement actions regarding anticompetitive coordination typically focus on prices, there are instances where agreements affecting non-price parameters have been found in breach of Article 101.[70] For example, the Commission has found that agreements between automobile manufacturers regarding the implementation and timing of emission reduction technologies were likely to restrict competition with regard to cars' product characteristics and thereby limit technical development and customer choice.[71]

The CJEU has, on a few occasions, confirmed the applicability of Article 101(1) to agreements that restrict non-price parameters.[72] The Court has also held that a finding that a concerted practice is anticompetitive by object does not require establishing a direct connection between the practice and consumer prices.[73] Some decisions under Article 102 have also emphasized the role of consumer choice.[74]

Similarly, there are many instances where EU courts and the Commission have accepted quality improvements as justifying restrictions on competition.[75] In *Coty*, the CJEU accepted a restriction imposed by a supplier of luxury cosmetics on authorized retailers not to sell the goods via third-party online marketplaces for quality reasons.[76] The Court found that such a restriction did not infringe Article 101(1) as it aimed to preserve the 'quality of those goods'.[77] According to the Court, the absence of a contractual link between the brand owner and the third-party platform makes it difficult to ensure that the third party observes the same quality standards as are imposed on authorized retailers.[78]

Overall, these decisions demonstrate that despite the challenges, competition authorities do factor in non-price considerations in their analyses, even without recourse to sophisticated quantitative evidence as to the effects of competition on these parameters. However, until recently, the treatment of personal data and privacy protection has not been part of competition assessment. For example, the terms 'personal data' and 'privacy' do not feature in the Commission Guidelines on abuse of dominant position or in the Guidelines on horizontal mergers. The

[69] See Commission input in OECD, *Policy Roundtables* (n 65) 83.
[70] See Chapter 6 for more detail.
[71] See Case AT.40178 *Car Emissions* decision of 8 July 2021, paras 7 and 125.
[72] Case C-8/08 *T-Mobile Netherlands* ECLI:EU:C:2009:343, paras 36–39.
[73] ibid.
[74] For more, see Chapter 5, Section III.C.
[75] See Case M.5727 *Microsoft/Yahoo! Search Business* decision of 18 February 2010, para 163 (where the Commission accepted post-merger quality improvements in search and search advertising resulting from data combination).
[76] Case C-230/16 *Coty Germany GmbH v Parfümerie Akzente GmbH* ECLI:EU:C:2017:941.
[77] ibid para 46.
[78] ibid para 48.

question is whether the ubiquity of services offered at zero price and in exchange for personal data necessitates a change in approach. Price is customarily viewed as the chief competition parameter, partly because quality can be factored into the price (quality-adjusted price). However, the reliance on price to factor in quality or other parameters starts to break down when the product is offered for 'free', as is the case with the most popular digital services. In the *Microsoft/Yahoo!* merger, the Commission indicated that when a product is 'free', quality becomes an essential competition parameter.[79]

Thus, as consumers are increasingly exchanging their personal data to access such services, privacy is attracting considerable attention as a non-price parameter. For example, in the *Facebook/WhatsApp* and *Microsoft/LinkedIn* merger decisions, the European Commission held that data privacy constitutes a key parameter of non-price competition in the market for consumer communications and for professional social networks (PSNs). In the former, the Commission indicated that in markets for consumer communication services, data privacy and data security constitute key parameters of non-price competition.[80] The Commission further affirmed this stance in its *Microsoft/LinkedIn* decision, claiming that data privacy is 'a significant factor of quality' in the market for PSNs.[81]

Outside the EU, privacy was included as an element of quality in the 2021 revision of the UK Merger Guidelines.[82] Additionally, in its investigation of Google's proposed implementation of the 'Privacy Sandbox', the UK CMA noted the importance of privacy as a parameter of competition in the market for web browsers.[83] There are similar developments across the Atlantic. For example, recent antitrust lawsuits against Google and Facebook have recognized privacy as an important dimension of quality.[84]

Overall, there is a growing consensus among regulatory authorities and academics that privacy can be subject to competition—whether we consider it an element of quality, choice, or innovation—and that mergers, coordinated conduct, or unilateral conduct may reduce incentives to compete on these parameters. The recognition that companies can exercise market power by reducing the level of privacy protection brings competition policy closer to a complex digital reality in which users are not merely consumers but also contribute to value creation through their data. Acknowledging data as a source of market power and

[79] *Microsoft/Yahoo!* (n 75) para 101.

[80] *Facebook/WhatsApp* (n 23) para 87.

[81] European Commission, 'Commission Approves Acquisition of LinkedIn by Microsoft, Subject to Conditions' (6 December 2016).

[82] CMA, 'Merger Assessment Guidelines' (18 March 2021) para 2.5.

[83] Case 50972 *Decision to Accept Commitments Offered by Google in Relation to Its Privacy Sandbox Proposals*, Competition and Markets Authority 11 February 2022 (CMA, *Decision to Accept Google's Commitments*) para 5.81.

[84] Civil Action 1:21-md-03010-PKC *State of Texas v Google LLC* United States Southern District of New York, filed 14 January 2022, para 501.

data privacy as a non-price competition parameter are both positive steps towards embracing the complexity of the digital economy, largely driven by the commercialization of personal data. Simultaneously, these developments carry significant normative implications, as they increase the intersection between data privacy law and competition law, a subject for Section IV.

IV. Implications for the Intersection between Data Privacy Law and Competition Law

The previous sections highlighted the growing focus on personal data and data privacy in competition assessments, stemming from the commercialization of personal data. This section explores the normative implications of this development, emphasizing the increased intersection between data privacy and competition rules. One example of this intersection is convergence, where the two sets of rules complement each other to achieve a specific objective (Section IV.A). This may occur when data privacy law informs competition assessment, such as when determining the reduction in data privacy as a quality parameter or when competition law addresses macro-level harms to data privacy. The intersection can also manifest as tension between the two fields of law (Section IV.B). This could arise, for example, when digital incumbents rely on users' privacy and obligations under data privacy laws to justify potentially anticompetitive conduct or when competition authorities employ data-related remedies that may negatively impact user privacy. These discussions underscore the need for increased dialogue between the relevant enforcement agencies. By discussing the intersection between data privacy law and competition law and highlighting potential areas for cooperation between the two legal regimes, this section, along with the ensuing chapters, underscores the importance of a polycentric regulatory approach, essential for navigating complex economic landscapes.

A. Intersection through Convergence

As noted above, the convergence of the two sets of laws is one outcome resulting from the increased attention to personal data and data privacy in competition assessments. This convergence manifests in three ways. First, as personal data become a key resource in the provision of digital services, data privacy rules move centre stage in competition assessments, both as a competitive constraint and as a barrier to market entry. Second, the recognition of data privacy as a non-price parameter helps address broader macro-level harms to data privacy in the form of privacy fixing or reductions in choice due to mergers or exclusionary practices. This helps enhance the efficacy of data privacy law. Third, as competition law begins to incorporate data privacy as a non-price parameter, data privacy rules can offer normative guidance on the dimensions of privacy that are relevant for competition and help determine what constitutes a reduction in the level of data privacy.

1. Increased Normative Influence of Data Privacy Law in Competition Assessment

As shown in Section II.B, combining data may increase market power significantly. In this context, data privacy rules—particularly the lawfulness and purpose limitation principles—may be seen as imposing constraints on a firm's ability to combine data and increase their market power. This is something competition analysis should take into account. Indeed, competition authorities have started to incorporate this perspective in their assessments, especially in mergers.

This is evidenced in the *Microsoft/LinkedIn*, *Google/Sanofi*, and *Apple/Shazam* decisions, where the Commission held that data privacy rules impose competitive constraints on the ability of the merged entity to combine data or lock in users, consequently increasing market power. For example, in its *Apple/Shazam* decision, the Commission noted that the lawfulness and purpose limitation principles under the General Data Protection Regulation (GDPR) and the confidentiality requirements under the ePrivacy Directive impose restrictions on the post-merger combination of data and its subsequent use by the merging parties.[85] The Commission reiterated this stance in *Google/Fitbit*.[86] In this sense, data privacy rules seem well aligned with competition law's objective of protecting the competitive process by preventing companies from gaining market power through data concentration or increased switching costs. While this is commendable, current Commission practice has some limitations.

First, while the Commission considers the competitive constraints that data privacy rules impose on the ability of the merged entity to combine data, it ignores the same constraints on the competitors' ability to use data in their possession or license data from third parties. This problem stems from the Commission's focus on the availability of similar data sets to other entities as a competitive constraint, regardless of whether these entities operate in different markets or even separate sectors. In its appraisal of a joint venture involving UK mobile operators, the Commission stated that the information generated by the joint venture through its mobile wallet platform and its advertising intermediation services would also be available to other market players 'such as Google, Apple, Facebook, card issuers, reference agencies or retailers'.[87]

[85] *Apple/Shazam* (n 22) para 314.
[86] *Google/Fitbit* (n 58) para 408.
[87] Case M.6314 *Telefónica UK/Vodafone UK/Everything Everywhere/JV* decision of 4 September 2012, para 543.

Similarly, in *Facebook/WhatsApp*, the Commission noted that, even if Facebook were to combine the data from WhatsApp with its services, the merger would not impede competition because other market players like Google, Apple, Microsoft, AOL, Twitter, LinkedIn, Adobe, and Yelp have access to 'Internet user data' that are valuable for advertising.[88] Thus, the availability of such data to other entities is seen as imposing competitive constraints on the merged entity, preventing it from gaining market power through data concentration. However, these decisions overlook the constraints imposed by the same rules on the ability of the competitors to reuse the data, which could potentially tip the balance in favour of the merged entity.

The focus on availability presupposes that the competitors can use or reuse the data from the different markets or across sectors to impose competitive constraints on the merged entity. However, the presence of a comparable data set accessible to other entities does not mean that such data may be used or licensed for advertising purposes without difficulty, as there may be different legal frameworks applicable to the different actors, limiting their ability to reuse the data. This is because data privacy rules, especially the purpose limitation principle, may limit data collected in one market (sector) from being used in another market (sector). For example, when it comes to reusing data for purposes other than those for which they were originally collected, the rules in the telecom sector are stricter than those applicable to other digital services, such as search engines.[89]

In this context, the Commission's assessment, which includes both telecom and non-telecom providers as entities possessing data sets of comparable competitive significance for advertising, overlooks the reality that privacy-related legal barriers are more substantial in the telecoms sector. In other words, the competitive constraint stemming from data sets held by telecom companies may be weaker than the competitive constraints imposed by data sets held by internet companies. This suggests that the ability of various entities to repurpose data in their possession for advertising and the subsequent level of competitive constraints they can impose may vary, depending on the applicable data privacy rules. This warrants consideration, especially since the level of constraints on combining data may differ depending on the organizational structure of firms. Although data privacy rules apply equally to inter- and intra-firm sharing of data, there are indications that firms find it easier to share or combine data from entities within the same corporate structure.[90] Thus, to the extent that the Commission considers constraints from data privacy on the merged entity, it should also factor in restrictions on the

[88] *Facebook/WhatsApp* (n 23) para 188.

[89] Marc Bourreau, Alexandre de Streel, and Inge Graef, *Big Data and Competition Policy: Market Power, Personalized Pricing and Advertising* (Centre on Regulation in Europe (CERRE) 2017) 30.

[90] For example, respondents to the Commission investigation in *Google/Fitbit* indicated that 'Google would manage to obtain user consent to data usage more easily than absent the Transaction': *Google/Fitbit* (n 58) para 452.

competitor's ability to reuse/license similar data and challenge the merged entity in the relevant markets.

The right to data portability is another aspect of data privacy law that has received attention in competition assessments. In the joint venture (JV) involving Sanofi and Google, the Commission examined the extent to which the JV could lock in customers (in this case, medical patients) by limiting the portability of their data to other platforms.[91] However, the Commission indicated that data privacy rules (particularly the right to data portability under the GDPR) would limit the JV's ability to lock patients in.[92] The decision recognizes the role of data portability rights as a means of controlling market power and preventing user lock-in, with positive effects on competition. The implication is that a breach of the right to data portability (eg by a dominant undertaking) can disrupt the competitive process by raising the barrier to entry or obstructing access to consumers. Thus, as competition authorities assess the positive competitive effects of data portability rights, they should also account for firms' disregard for such rights, and dominant firms in particular. In other words, if the data portability right can limit market power based on user lock-in, disregarding the right could lead to illegal acquisition of dominance or further consolidation of existing dominance.[93]

Furthermore, competition authorities ought to factor in some of the legal and practical obstacles associated with the data portability right. First, data portability is essentially applicable to the data provided by users (volunteered data), although there are suggestions that the right should extend to 'observed data'.[94] This means that users cannot port 'inferred data', which include personal data created by a service provider. Second, the right is only available when the legal basis for processing is consent or contractual necessity, excluding processing based on legitimate interest or other legal grounds. Third, the scale and scope of data are associated with practical difficulties in exercising the right to data portability—that is, the more, and more diverse, the data a controller possesses about a user, the more challenging it becomes to transfer that data. These potential inconveniences may deter users from exercising their right to data portability against big players.

The competitive significance of data privacy rules extends beyond their use as competitive constraints; they can also represent formidable barriers to entry, which need to be considered in competition analysis. In this context, there are broad arguments suggesting that the compliance costs associated with EU data privacy rules, possibly due to their fixed nature, put smaller firms at a competitive

[91] Case M.7813 *Sanofi/Google/DMI JV* decision of 23 February 2016, para 67.
[92] ibid para 69.
[93] See Chapter 7, Section IV.
[94] Article 29 Data Protection Working Party (WP242), 'Guidelines on the Right to Data Portability' (2017) 9–10.

disadvantage.[95] The discussion in this section suggests that the barriers to entry extend beyond the cost disadvantages experienced by smaller entities; the rules may also prevent newcomers from overcoming barriers related to data-driven network effects by purchasing access to voluminous and diverse data on consumers.

Needless to say, data privacy rules impose compliance costs on data-driven businesses. This is because, as laid down in the GDPR, any processing of personal data must be based on a legitimate legal basis (eg the consent of the individual) and must adhere to the core data privacy principles.[96] Furthermore, individuals are given certain rights, including the right to access their data; to rectify inaccurate data; and to be informed about the type of information being processed, the purpose of the processing, potential recipients, and the retention period for the data. All these requirements impose costs on the collection, storage, and use of data. For example, the requirements for legitimizing the processing through consent (or other grounds) and providing information on the processing entail costs on collection. The rules on data security and the restriction on the transfer of data to countries that do not ensure adequate levels of protection entail storage costs. The fact that India does not ensure an adequate level of protection, for example, means that smaller players cannot make use of cheap IT resources by outsourcing their operations to India. Furthermore, the core principles, particularly the purpose limitation principle, entail data usage costs. To the extent that control of data affects the balance of economic power, such rules also affect the competition analysis.

A common rebuttal to the possibility of market power emerging from data-driven network effects is the assertion that newcomers and small businesses may acquire data from third parties.[97] For example, in the *Google/DoubleClick* merger, the Commission held that the combination of data from the merging parties did not amount to an insurmountable challenge, because competitors could purchase data from third parties, including internet service providers (ISPs).[98] However, in light of the above requirements, the ability of newcomers to enter the market by purchasing consumer data from other entities is curtailed by the requirements for legal basis under EU rules. It is true that even incumbents have to incur similar costs of compliance during collection, but given the importance of scale and scope in offering better-quality services and advertising, data privacy rules—particularly the data minimization and purpose limitation principles—limit the ability of newcomers to overcome data-driven network effects by purchasing data of equivalent scale and scope from established players. Compliance with the purpose limitation

[95] See Damien Geradin, Theano Karanikioti, and Dimitrios Katsifis, 'GDPR Myopia: How a Well-Intended Regulation Ended Up Favoring Google in Ad Tech' (Tilburg Law and Economics Center (TILEC) Discussion Paper DP 2020-012, TILEC 2020).

[96] See Regulation (EU) 2016/679 of the European Parliament and of the Council of 27 April 2016 on the Protection of Natural Persons with Regard to the Processing of Personal Data and on the Free Movement of Such Data, and repealing Directive 95/46/EC OJ L119/1, Articles 5(1) and 6.

[97] See Sokol and Comerford (n 44) 1137.

[98] *Google/DoubleClick* (n 24) paras 364–66.

and data minimization principles limits the volume and variety of data companies can collect or purchase from others at once.

It is possible that one could rely on consent to overcome some of these challenges (eg by soliciting consent for several different purposes), whether collecting data from users or licensing similar data from other players. However, as shown in Chapter 2, the cost of compliance with data privacy rules—particularly the consent requirement—disproportionately affects companies that lack scope and scale. Some studies show that firms possessing greater economies of scope and scale find it easier to obtain consent from users compared to small and medium enterprises (SMEs).[99] This is partly because of the lack of scalability in the EU legal framework. The idea underlying this argument is that when similar standards of consent are applied across the board, the entities engaged in smaller-scale processing suffer disproportionately.

Importantly, the atomized approach to the application of data privacy rules results in a reduced likelihood of detecting non-compliance as companies with economies of scope and scale start combining data across various operations. As noted in Chapter 2, the enforcement of the rules depends heavily on the ability to differentiate between distinct processing activities, to associate each item of personal data with a specific processing activity, and to evaluate the compliance of each processing activity in light of the data privacy principles. In other words, the compliance assessment, including the rules for ensuring transparency and accountability, focuses on the individual processing based on a specific purpose and distinct legal basis, regardless of the number of processing activities and data-aggregation practices across the different processing operations. However, such accountability and transparency mechanisms, based on the purpose limitation, start to break down when the entities accumulate and aggregate data across different services based on separate purposes.[100]

This suggests that as the number of channels (products/services) through which an entity collects and aggregates data about individuals increases, it becomes more challenging to hold entities accountable for non-compliance with data privacy rules. This diminished accountability and reduced likelihood of detection gives large firms the flexibility to experiment, use, and reuse data across different markets without falling foul of the rules. Thus, data privacy rules can, to a certain extent, give rise to or exacerbate market power. Scaling data privacy responsibilities, as suggested in Chapter 2, would partially alleviate the disproportionate disadvantage that such rules impose on smaller players.

[99] See also Avi Goldfarb and Catherine Tucker, 'Privacy and Innovation' in Josh Lerner and Scott Stern (ed), *Innovation Policy and the Economy, Volume 12* (University of Chicago Press 2012) 83.

[100] See Samson Esayas, 'The Idea of 'Emergent Properties' in Data Privacy: Towards a Holistic Approach' (2017) 25 International Journal of Law and Information Technology 139.

Another barrier resulting from data privacy law, which may have a disproportionate impact on smaller players, comes from the ePrivacy Directive: more specifically, the requirement commonly referred to as the 'cookie rule'.[101] This rule requires website operators to obtain affirmative consent when they place 'cookies' on users' browsers or devices. The use of cookies allows smaller players (eg advertising networks) to track users through third-party websites (publishers) and compete with the incumbents (eg Google) in the advertising market. However, the 'cookie rule' imposes extra costs on companies that rely on third parties to collect data and gives a comparable advantage to companies, such as Google, that have existing gateways (eg Search, Maps, Gmail, and YouTube) for collecting data without using cookies.

Moreover, the proposed ePrivacy Regulation introduces an amendment to this provision, differentiating between first-party and third-party cookies and requiring web browsers to give users the option to block third-party cookies.[102] This amendment places companies that do not directly collect data from consumers at a disadvantage compared to those with a wide array of services enabling data collection. For example, Google can track users using cookies across its services because such cookies qualify as first-party cookies. However, potential rivals, who do not have consumer-facing services to collect comparable data from third-party websites, would be at a disadvantage. Amendments such as these exacerbate the impact of the rules on the ability of new entrants to collaborate with publishers and collect data. This can further entrench the power of big platforms. Overall, although the rules apply to all players, the 'cookie rule' in the ePrivacy Directive (and proposed Regulation) and the atomized approach of the GDPR may disproportionately disadvantage smaller players. This imbalance could potentially increase market concentration in digital markets.

2. Competition Law to Address Macroeconomic Harms to Data Privacy

A frequently raised question regarding the recognition of data privacy as a non-price parameter, particularly in the EU, where a comprehensive data privacy framework exists, pertains to the (added) value of incorporating privacy into competition analysis as opposed to addressing the issue under data privacy law. The question is relevant in terms of competence and the effective use of regulatory resources: what justifies the expenditure of additional resources in competition enforcement? The simple answer is that, to the extent that consumers value data privacy in services,

[101] Directive 2002/58/EC of the European Parliament and of the Council of 12 July 2002 Concerning the Processing of Personal Data and the Protection of Privacy in the Electronic Communications Sector OJ L201/37, Article 5.

[102] First-party cookies are installed by the website the user is currently visiting, while third-party cookies are installed by entities other than the website being visited by the user; Proposal for a Regulation of the European Parliament and of the Council Concerning the Respect for Private Life and the Protection of Personal Data in Electronic Communications and repealing Directive 2002/58/EC COM/2017/010 final, Article 10(1).

competition law has to consider these demands, regardless of the existence of a regulation.[103] In the *Facebook/WhatsApp* merger, the Commission justified the need to recognize data privacy as a competition parameter because privacy and security are 'becoming increasingly valued' by consumers.[104] Thus, as long as consumers value data privacy, the question for competition law is whether the market fulfils these needs and whether the failure to satisfy these needs can be attributed to market power (failure).

It is worth noting that while data privacy law aims to remedy market failures, it focuses primarily on those that are internal to the individual, resulting from information and power asymmetries that hinder individuals from effectively controlling their personal data.[105] The individual-centric nature of data privacy law suggests that broader, macro-level harms to data privacy may not be captured. For example, agreements among companies to restrict innovation that could enhance users' data privacy are not captured by data privacy rules. The same goes for competitive harms arising from the exclusion and foreclosure of firms that try to use data privacy as a value proposition, such as the removal of anti-tracking and ad-blocking applications from dominant platforms. In contrast, competition law addresses market failures that are external to the individual, such as reductions in consumer choice from mergers (Chapter 5), firms colluding to suppress a privacy-enhancing technology (PET) or restrictions on information competition (Chapter 6) or exploitative practices (Chapter 7). Additionally, while data privacy law protects users from exploitative economic power, it fails to address all the possible long-term harms to a platform's users, due to its reliance on consent and the limited remedies it offers. Nor does data privacy law pay sufficient attention to the unique position of certain actors who can exploit users.[106] In this sense, competition law can complement and enhance the efficacy of data privacy rules by ensuring that companies do not conspire or use their market power to limit choices, exploit consumers, or stifle innovation that enhances users' data privacy. This, in turn, can incentivize competition and innovation in data privacy.

One macro-level harm to data privacy may arise from reduced consumer choice due to mergers as discussed in Chapter 5. In discussions on the interface between data privacy law and competition law, prompting consumer choice is often viewed as an objective connecting these two legal fields. While competition rules aim to guarantee that consumers have access to a wide range of choices, data privacy law—especially the rules on transparency—strives to ensure that consumers make

[103] This is consistent with the CJEU's jurisprudence, which stipulates that the existence of a regulation does not prevent the application of competition rules. See Case C-280/08 P *Deutsche Telekom v Commission* ECLI:EU:C:2010:603.

[104] *Facebook/WhatsApp* (n 23) para 87.

[105] Francisco Costa-Cabral and Orla Lynskey, 'Family Ties: The Intersection between Data Protection and Competition in EU Law' (2017) 54 Common Market Law Review 11, 18–19.

[106] Economides and Lianos (n 20) 772.

informed choices based on accurate information. This implies that the effectiveness of data privacy rules partly relies on the effectiveness of competition rules. If individuals do not have choices or are dealing with monopolies, 'free' consent and information control become illusionary. Thus, competition law can render data privacy more effective by ensuring that the market remains competitive and users have choices in relation to data privacy. However, until recently, there was little evidence that competition law intervened to address users' privacy choices directly. This has now started to change with the recognition of data privacy as a non-price competition parameter. As shown in Chapter 5, the *Microsoft/LinkedIn* merger is one instance where competition rules were used to ensure that a merger did not reduce users' privacy choices and thereby enhance the effectiveness of data privacy.

Similarly, competition law plays a vital role in condemning behaviour that perpetuates what Farrell refers to as 'dysfunctional equilibrium'.[107] Dysfunctional equilibrium occurs when users encounter credibility issues regarding the privacy practices of firms and when they fail to read privacy policies.[108] Even when privacy policies are read, users often expect firms to act differently from what they have promised. Newcomers are discouraged from adopting more protective policies and clearer disclosures to attract users, since users do not reward such behaviour. This leads to a 'dysfunctional equilibrium'.[109] Farrell explains it as follows:

> If firms perceive that few consumers shift their demand in response to actual privacy policies, then the firm's incentives are to make its policy noncommittal and/or non-protective, and to go for the biggest available [revenue from data monetization] ... It would then be tempting to design disclosures so as not to really communicate the choice of policy, if it is possible to obfuscate for the minority of consumers while retaining the ability to claim that the policy was disclosed. Meanwhile, if consumers perceive that firms behave in this kind of way, they will not expect attentive reading of privacy policies to be a rewarding activity. These patterns of conduct and expectations would reinforce each other, which is what makes them a game-theoretic or economic equilibrium.[110]

The 'dysfunctional equilibrium' can be very hard to break because (1) consumers are unlikely to start reading privacy policies once they have learned that it is not a rewarding activity and (2) even if they do, they are likely to learn little or, worse perhaps, their cynical suspicions may simply be confirmed, as firms expect few consumers to read policies and opt for vague policies.[111] Similarly, a smaller

[107] Joseph Farrell, 'Can Privacy Be Just Another Good?' (2012) 10 Journal on Telecommunications & High Technology Law 251, 257 (describing the dysfunctional equilibrium as 'cynical market failure' as it makes 'mutually beneficial trades impossible').
[108] ibid 257.
[109] ibid 259.
[110] ibid 258–59.
[111] ibid 259.

firm's ability to break this equilibrium is limited: users do not reward such behaviour, and the firm's demand is not likely to shift significantly as a result of such efforts. The firm ends up sacrificing revenue from data monetization.[112] Thus, more often, Farrell argues, escaping this equilibrium requires action by 'large and powerful players'.[113] However, in the current state of competition, the 'large and powerful' digital players lack the incentive to shake this equilibrium. Their interests align better with the status quo, and they may even have incentives to perpetuate the equilibrium by creating hurdles for smaller players attempting to disrupt it by blocking or demoting such players from their platforms. Furthermore, in the rare instances in which a small player manages to break the equilibrium and attract users, the 'large and powerful' digital players may use their financial muscle to acquire such players and thereby suppress emerging competition. A case in point is the acquisition of WhatsApp by Facebook and the subsequent changes to WhatsApp's privacy policy, contributing to the perpetuation of the 'dysfunctional equilibrium'.

The acquisition is important because WhatsApp was trying to disrupt the market conditions that were based on harvesting personal information and offering behavioural advertising by adopting a business model that was built on respect for user privacy for a small fee. Contrary to Facebook, WhatsApp stored only limited information about its users and did not offer targeted advertising. Thus, WhatsApp was seeking to disrupt the most commonly used business model, one that benefited Facebook and resulted, in part, from the 'dysfunctional equilibrium' and the 'free effect'.[114] Using its popularity, WhatsApp was succeeding in disrupting the equilibrium and overcoming the challenges of the 'free effect'. This seems to have been halted by the merger, however.[115]

Following the merger, WhatsApp changed its privacy policy to enable it to share data with Facebook and abandoned the subscription-based model by adopting a monetization strategy that allows users to communicate with businesses via WhatsApp. These changes could be sources of new information, as WhatsApp could gain insights from user communications, and WhatsApp has indicated that it will not exclude the possibility of introducing ads.[116] The merger seems to deprive users of choices that the market had previously provided.

[112] ibid.

[113] ibid.

[114] The free effect relates to the tendency of free goods to generate externalities by creating expectation among consumers for similar services to be offered free in comparable markets. This reduces consumers' willingness to pay for a similar but much better alternative. See Esayas, 'Competition in (Data) Privacy' (n 67).

[115] WhatsApp had managed to acquire 600 million users in a shorter time than Facebook itself and had twice as many users as Facebook Messenger. See *Facebook/WhatsApp* (n 23) para 84.

[116] Deepa Seetharaman, 'Facebook Tees Up WhatsApp to Make Money', *Wall Street Journal* (5 Sep 2017).

Before the merger, users had the option to choose from among the leading messaging apps: one that was based on a subscription fee, minimal collection of personal data, and an ad-free experience and another that relied heavily on the collection and monetization of user data. This choice seems to have disappeared post-merger. Following the merger, the two leading messaging apps rely on the monetization of personal data, nullifying the initial steps that WhatsApp had taken to disrupt the 'dysfunctional equilibrium' and overcome the 'free effect'. Thus, in the rare case in which a small player breaks this equilibrium and manages to attract users, competition policy seems to be the appropriate regulatory tool for protecting consumers' interests and preventing the nascent competition from being cut short.[117] Absent this, acquisitions of the WhatsApp kind will perpetuate the 'dysfunctional equilibrium', and competition efforts in the field of privacy and PETs are unlikely to reach maturity.

Similarly, as demonstrated in Chapter 6, collaborative efforts, such as Google's attempt to restrict Microsoft's promotional activities related to data privacy, can deprive users of a valuable source of information on privacy practices, thus contributing to a dysfunctional equilibrium. These examples show that certain privacy-related harms fall squarely within the purview of antitrust; these are cases in which data privacy legislation alone cannot provide an adequate solution. In this sense, considering privacy issues under competition law could help foster incentives to compete on privacy and prevent certain behaviours from perpetuating the dysfunctional equilibrium.

From a data privacy perspective, considering privacy in competition analysis may have added value. Not only do data privacy rules provide users with minimal protection, but they also impose an upper ceiling because of the goal of facilitating the free flow of data. In the *Car Emissions* cartel decision, the Commission noted that the collusion between the car manufacturers removed the uncertainties and competitive risks arising from choosing cleaning solutions that exceeded regulatory requirements.[118] Similarly, recognizing privacy as a competition parameter could incentivize firms to aspire to provide even higher levels of privacy than those guaranteed under the rules.

3. Data Privacy as Normative Guidance

Another implication of the recognition of data privacy as a competition parameter is that it opens up competition law to greater normative influence from data privacy law. The incorporation of data privacy into competition analysis is relatively recent, and competition law authorities are encountering challenges in their endeavour to incorporate data privacy considerations. One such challenge involves determining the relevant dimensions of data privacy as a non-price competition parameter

[117] For more on this, see Chapter 5, Section II.

[118] *Car Emissions* (n 71) para 128.

and deciding when two firms should be considered competitors based on these dimensions. The question is important because, absent a clear understanding of the relevant dimensions, the manifestations of competition on privacy could easily be overlooked. The Commission's decision in *Facebook/WhatsApp* exemplifies this issue. Although the Commission recognized data 'privacy and security' as key competition parameters, it considered the differences in privacy policies to be evidence that WhatsApp and Facebook Messenger were complementary services rather than competitors. In reaching this conclusion, the Commission specifically mentioned the differences relating to 'the privacy policy (contrary to WhatsApp, Facebook Messenger enables Facebook to collect data regarding its users that it uses for its advertising activities)'.[119]

The Commission's approach is based on the understanding that firms with identical privacy policies compete more fiercely than firms with dissimilar privacy policies. However, this approach has flaws.[120] To begin with, if privacy and data security are competition parameters, one way this competition can manifest is by deploying PETs (eg end-to-end encryption) and designing privacy-friendly policies (offering better conditions of data collection and use). In such cases, competition in privacy and privacy policies is more sequential than simultaneous. Indeed, there is research showing such sequential change in privacy policies among competitors.[121] Thus, when it comes to privacy and privacy policies, dissimilarity in either the technology or policy can be just the beginning of competition that exerts competitive pressure on others, rather than making firms complementary. In the context of the merger, this implies that the Commission may have underestimated the competitive constraints that WhatsApp—by opting for a different privacy policy and luring users from Facebook—imposed on Facebook to compete on privacy conditions and PETs.

Part of the problem with the Commission's analysis can be attributed to the lack of a framework for identifying the relevant dimensions of competition on data privacy and PETs. For example, it might have facilitated understanding of how competition is manifested to consider the data minimization principle, a key principle under the GDPR. In refraining from collecting data, or collecting only the minimum necessary, WhatsApp may be seen as attempting to appeal to Facebook Messenger users, who value their privacy. This suggests that the differences in their privacy policies on data collection are a manifestation of competition on data privacy. Indeed, the Commission seems to have changed its stance in the *Microsoft/LinkedIn* decision where the differences in XING and LinkedIn's privacy policies were taken as a sign of competition on privacy.[122] This is a step in the right

[119] *Facebook/WhatsApp* (n 23) paras 102–105.

[120] See Samson Esayas, 'Competition in Dissimilarity: Lessons in Privacy from the Facebook/WhatsApp Merger' (2017) 1 Antitrust Chronicle 57.

[121] See ibid.

[122] *Microsoft/LinkedIn* (n 34) paras 437–38.

direction. Yet, a clear framework for identifying the relevant dimensions of privacy competition remains essential if competition authorities are to easily detect manifestations of this competition. The following paragraphs discuss one such framework based on data privacy rules.[123]

Given that the EU data privacy rules specify the different dimensions of data privacy, they can be used to highlight the attributes of data privacy as a non-price parameter. This is because, at least in the EU, data privacy is a normative concept, and seeking normative guidance is not only justified but may also be necessary.[124] This is consistent with the calls to develop frameworks for cooperation among competition, consumer, and data protection authorities that reflect data protection principles.[125]

Thus, in light of the core principles and rights enshrined under the GDPR, data privacy as a non-price parameter could include the following attributes:

(1) the nature of data collected, both in terms of its sensitivity and volume;[126]
(2) the purposes for which data is used, the duration of its storage, and the parties it is shared with;[127]
(3) the clarity of information provided to users regarding data collection and usage, as well as the means of conveying this information;[128]
(4) the ease with which users can access, modify, delete, and port their data;[129]
(5) the range of choices available to users—for instance, whether they can use the service without providing personal information;[130]
(6) the security measures implemented to safeguard data from unauthorized access, accidental loss, destruction, or damage;[131]
(7) the incorporation of PETs like end-to-end encryption, pseudonymization, and anonymization;[132] and
(8) whether privacy enhancing features are enabled by default.[133]

[123] Another alternative could be to conduct surveys on what aspects of data privacy users find desirable when using a product/service (eg social media or search service).

[124] Costa-Cabral and Lynskey (n 105) 29 (arguing that treating privacy as 'normatively neutral: [ie] the quality of privacy is no different from the quality of any other good or service' undercuts its normative foundation under EU law and is open to criticism).

[125] European Data Protection Supervisor (EDPS), *Opinion 8/2016 on Coherent Enforcement of Fundamental Rights in the Age of Big Data* (2016).

[126] Derived from the data minimization and sensitivity principles. See GDPR, Articles 5(1(c)) and 9.

[127] Derived from the purpose limitation and storage limitation principles. See ibid Articles 5(1(b)) and 5(1(e)).

[128] Derived from the transparency principle. See ibid Articles 5(1(a)) and 12–14.

[129] Derived from the right of access, rectification, erasure, and portability of data. See ibid Articles 15–20.

[130] Partly informed by the lawfulness, fairness, and transparency principles, particularly the requirements on consent. See ibid Articles 5(1(a)) and 6(1(a)).

[131] Derived from the data security principle. See ibid Article 5(1(f)).

[132] Derived from the data security principle and the privacy by design. See ibid Articles 5(1(e)) and 25(1).

[133] Derived from the provision on privacy by default. See ibid Article 25(2).

These attributes can be placed in two broader categories: first, attributes concerned with data collection and the conditions of its use (attributes 1–5) and, second, data security and PETs (attributes 6–8). Thus, a reference to competition on data privacy and PETs covers these two broad categories.

The objective here is not to provide an exhaustive list of attributes but rather to provide a basic analytical framework for discussing data privacy as a non-price parameter. A look at the privacy policy of the Internet search engine DuckDuckGo can illustrate how the suggested dimensions can help identify the manifestation of this competition. For example, DuckDuckGo's privacy policy states that it 'does not collect or share personal data'. In making this choice, DuckDuckGo is trying to compete based on the principles of data minimization and purpose limitation. DuckDuckGo's privacy policy also states that it 'does not store personal data', where the relevant dimension of competition is the storage limitation principle. The search engine also undertakes to highlight policy changes in 'red text', which manifests competition on the transparency principle and in terms of informed consent. Moreover, when conducting a search, users' location is turned off by default, which manifests the privacy-by-default dimension as a competition parameter. In this sense, the differences in privacy policies between DuckDuckGo and Google are a sign that DuckDuckGo is trying to compete based on privacy and PETs, rather than suggesting that these two services are complementary.

Moreover, the above attributes could serve as a basis for assessing what constitutes a reduction in data privacy, for example, when defining the market or when assessing the anticompetitive impact of conduct (see Chapters 5 and 7). Accordingly, a reduction in data privacy could be broadly understood to involve the following: (1) an increase in the amount of personal data demanded or in the time personal data is stored, (2) a reduction in transparency in relation to the collection and use of data, (3) a reduction in the level of control (choice) users have over their data, and (4) abandoning the use of PETs. The Commission's assessment in *Facebook/WhatsApp* lends support to this claim. Investigating the impact of the *Facebook/WhatsApp* merger on the advertising market, the Commission indicated that a reduction in privacy as a quality parameter could happen if—post-merger—WhatsApp abandoned its end-to-end encryption and began collecting more data about its users to offer targeted advertising.[134] These two aspects exemplify the two dimensions of data privacy competition identified above, one based on the conditions of data collection and use and the other on data security and PETs.

Furthermore, in its investigation of Google's proposed implementation of the 'Privacy Sandbox', the UK CMA identified two parameters of privacy competition that are in line with the above suggestions. According to the agency, effective competition ensures that users of web browsers are given 'significant control over

[134] *Facebook/WhatsApp* (n 23) para 174.

whether and how their personal data is used, subject to suitable defaults and an adequate choice architecture'.[135] These features recognize the two main components of competition in data privacy discussed above. The first aspect (ie whether users have control over how their personal data is used) reflects privacy competition on the conditions of data collection and use, whereas the implementation of 'suitable defaults and an adequate choice architecture' reflects the other dimension of privacy competition based on data security and PETs.

In light of the above discussion, the interface between data privacy law and competition law resulting from the recognition of privacy as a non-privacy parameter proves to be mutually beneficial. Competition law can complement data privacy rules by tackling macro-level harms, while data privacy law can enhance competition law by providing useful tools and normative guidance needed to tackle new forms of commercial conduct based on harms to data privacy.

B. Intersection Giving Rise to Tensions

The increased attention to personal data and data privacy in competition analysis may also give rise to tensions between data privacy law and competition law. In such instances, there is a need to engage in some form of balancing exercise. To the extent that the accumulation of data creates barriers to entry, competition authorities are likely to resort to data-related remedies to address the competition concerns. For example, facilitating access to data is seen as a remedy for some of the competition concerns in digital markets in which there are data-driven network effects.[136] Similarly, there is an emerging trend for certain digital incumbents to resort to user privacy and obligations under data privacy laws to justify potentially anticompetitive conduct. A case in point is Google's Privacy Sandbox initiative, which aimed to remove third-party trackers from Chrome and replace them with its own set of privacy-enhancing tools. This and related developments have led to a rising 'tug-of-war between privacy and competition', which presents a significant 'legal policy dilemma'.[137] This section delves into the implications of these developments, in terms of their impact on users' privacy, and discusses the limits imposed by data privacy law and the mechanisms called upon to balance privacy and competition interests.

[135] CMA, *Decision to Accept Google's Commitments* (n 83) para 5.81.
[136] See Autorité de la Concurrence and Bundeskartellamt (n 33).
[137] Maureen Ohlhausen and Ben Rossen, 'Privacy and Competition: Discord or Harmony?' (2022) 67 Antitrust Bulletin 552, 559.

1. Data Privacy Implications from Competition Remedies

To address the concentration concerns stemming from data accumulation, competition authorities are envisaging different measures that might impact users' privacy, such as forced sharing of data, divestiture of data, and prohibitions on combining data. These measures can affect users' privacy both positively and negatively. On a positive note, if the combination of data is considered to confer market power, mergers leading to data concentration may be blocked or merging entities may be prohibited from combining data. In its study on digital platforms and online advertising, the CMA proposed a variety of strategies aimed at addressing the sources of market power in this sector including mandating data silos and implementing operational or ownership separation.[138] In its *Google/Fitbit* merger decision, the European Commission accepted similar commitments in order to approve the merger. As noted in Section II.B above, the Commission held that the potential combination of data from the merging parties could create barriers to entry and foreclose competition in the market for online advertising.[139]

To allay these concerns, Google offered different commitments, which could be seen as positive for users' privacy. First, Google agreed not to use health and wellness data collected from wrist-worn wearable devices and other Fitbit devices for advertisement.[140] The commitment covers a broad array of data including 'Processed and derived data, manually inputted data, as well as Data generated through the use of Fitbit Coach service'.[141] This entails that Google must maintain a 'data silo', which will ensure a technical separation of the relevant Fitbit data from any other Google data that is used for advertising. Second, Google must implement strict audit and documentation requirements in relation to individuals and services that will have access to Fitbit data. Further, Google agreed to be monitored and audited by a third-party trustee, who will then share the reports with the Commission and the Irish Data Protection Commission.[142]

These measures may be positive for data privacy. Such interventions can prevent the data privacy risks resulting from the accumulation of personal data and aggregation practices. As noted in Chapter 2, when entities process personal data for a wide array of purposes and combine data across these processing activities, there are emergent data privacy risks, such as overexposure of the individual and loss of transparency, accountability, and practical obscurity. These risks are less likely to exist when entities process personal data for a handful of purposes or in silos. For example, blocking a merger or prohibiting data combination prevents the concentration of several data-processing operations in the hands of a single entity and the potential for the aggregation of data across services. This, in turn, mitigates the

[138] CMA, 'Online Platforms and Digital Advertising: Market Study Final Report' (2020) 24.
[139] *Google/Fitbit* (n 58) para 434.
[140] ibid section A.1 Commitments.
[141] ibid para 966.
[142] ibid section B Commitments.

emergent risks discussed in Chapter 2, specifically those stemming from the 'summative complex' (multiplicity of processing activities) and the 'interrelation complex' (the combination of data across these different processing activities).

This notwithstanding, where there are data concentration concerns, divestiture of the data set or a copy thereof is the most common remedy to which competition authorities resort. Although not specifically related to personal data, in the *Thomson/Reuters* merger, the Commission allowed the consummation of the merger on the condition that the parties divest 'a copy of the database'.[143] In *Bazaarvoice/PowerReviews*, the US Department of Justice (DoJ) successfully sought a similar commitment concerning consumer data.[144] The question, then, is whether transferring data into the hands of a new entity is desirable from a data privacy perspective.

Providing a definitive answer to the above question is difficult, as the data privacy risks may differ, depending on the type and amount of data held by the merging entities, the potential risks stemming from the aggregation of such data, and the data privacy practices of the entity acquiring the divested data. Generally, divestiture can have both positive and negative implications for data privacy. It can be positive for data privacy because, like blocking a merger, it can reduce the data privacy risks resulting from the accumulation and aggregation of data in the hands of a single entity. As discussed in Chapter 2, Google's collection of data from nearly 100 services and subsequent combination of data across these services allows for the creation of detailed individual profiles, leading to overexposure and a loss of practical obscurity. These risks consequently threaten users' free choice, personal autonomy, and integrity. Thus, measures requiring the divestiture of a data set or a service generating such data, such as CMA's order in Meta/Giphy, could greatly reduce these privacy concerns, leaving the merged entity with a less detailed profile of the individual. However, this might not happen if the remedy is the divestiture of a *copy* of the data set.

Thus, an argument can be made that divesting a copy of a data set could negatively affect data privacy rights because the data may be transferred to an entity that the data subject has not envisaged when providing the data. Privacy and trust are closely intertwined.[145] Decisions on whether to provide one's data, the type of data one is willing to provide, how much data to provide, and how one will protect oneself from data misuse are all influenced by the level of trust placed in the company. In other words, trust can lead to increased disclosure and vulnerability, as people are willing to expose their most vulnerable side—compromising their privacy—to

143 Case M.4726 *Thomson Corporation/Reuters Group* decision of 19 February 2008, para 480.

144 The US Department of Justice, 'Justice Department and Bazaarvoice Inc. Agree on Remedy to Address Bazaarvoice's Illegal Acquisition of PowerReviews' (14-435, 24 April 2014).

145 Neil Richards and Woodrow Hartzog, 'Taking Trust Seriously in Privacy Law' (2015) 19 Stanford Technology Law Review 431, 431 (defining trust as the willingness to make oneself vulnerable to others).

those they trust most.[146] In this sense, transferring data from a party in which individuals have had such trust to a third party could be seen as a betrayal of trust and may expose individuals to increased data privacy risks, such as unauthorized disclosure. According to Solove, if trust plays a role in the provision of information, disclosing data to another party constitutes a breach of confidentiality.[147] However, this is only the case if the data transfer is carried out without involving the affected individuals.

Data privacy rules, which aim (among other things) to foster trust between data subjects and data controllers, can mitigate some concerns surrounding divestiture. This is especially true if both the entity divesting the data and the entity receiving the divested data are subject to the same rules. Thus, if divestiture can be complemented with measures to protect individuals' privacy, such as obtaining consent before transferring the data to a third party, this may mitigate the risks associated with such transfers. Similarly, competition remedies may include restrictions on changes to the privacy policy and on the use of data for purposes other than those initially intended. The Commission's decision in *Google/Fitbit* clearly shows that this is achievable, as the accepted commitments included restrictions on using Fitbit health data for advertising. Thus, some of the negative effects of divestiture can be mitigated by complementing the competition law measures with data privacy remedies (such as requiring consent prior to divestiture or restricting reuse for purposes other than those initially intended). These measures are particularly relevant if privacy is considered a competition parameter.

One problem with this approach remains: competition authorities may not have the authority, or see it to be within their competence, to order such measures. This may be particularly problematic at the EU level, where data protection authorities (DPAs) and competition authorities tend to work in silos. However, the situation seems to be changing. In the *Microsoft/LinkedIn* decision, the Commission noted the need for Microsoft to obtain consent from users in accordance with EU data privacy law if it wanted to integrate LinkedIn into Microsoft Outlook.[148] It is not clear whether competition authorities would actually follow up were merging parties to fail to comply with such measures, but it is nevertheless a step in the right direction regarding the consistent application of competition and data privacy rules. Such measures allow data subjects to reconsider whether they want to entrust their data to the new entity.

Importantly, in its recent Facebook ruling, the CJEU established that competition authorities can incorporate GDPR compliance (or its absence) into their assessments of abusive behaviour, particularly in determining whether a dominant

[146] See Adam Joinson and others, 'Privacy, Trust, and Self-Disclosure Online' (2010) 25 Human–Computer Interaction 1, 15.

[147] Daniel Solove, *Understanding Privacy* (Harvard UP 2008) 142.

[148] *Microsoft/LinkedIn* (n 34) para 328.

entity's actions deviate from competition based on merits.[149] The Court also insisted that these authorities, in assessing whether certain behaviour amounts to abuse, can find that the conduct violates the GDPR and prescribe measures to halt such abuses.[150] This could include ordering the dominant undertaking to cease the GDPR-infringing behaviour.[151] Therefore, as long as data privacy issues are relevant to competition assessments, competition authorities have the power to impose data privacy-related measures, for example preventing companies from merging data in violation of the GDPR.

In this context, the CJEU acknowledges the potential for divergence that may arise if competition authorities adjudicate GDPR-related issues. The Court highlighted that both competition and data protection authorities have a duty of sincere cooperation as per Article 4(3) of the Treaty on European Union (TEU).[152] This entails that agencies 'must assist each other, in full mutual respect, in carrying out tasks which flow from the Treaties … and refrain from any measure which could jeopardise the attainment of the European Union's objectives'.[153] In his opinion, Advocate General (AG) Rantos hinted at the need for EU legislators to consider adopting clear rules to facilitate cooperation between competition and data protection authorities.[154] Indeed, these clarifications from the CJEU regarding the duty to cooperate are crucial in ensuring consistent application of data privacy and competition rules.

The need to ensure consistency also entails that competition authorities must consider data privacy concerns when imposing remedies. Indeed, effectively addressing competition concerns may sometimes require measures that could negatively impact user privacy. Therefore, consistency is more about balancing rather than avoiding negative impacts entirely. However, competition authorities can leverage the flexibility offered by commitments to ensure that competition measures do not adversely affect users' privacy. The Commission decision in *Google/Fitbit* exemplifies this flexibility. In that decision, Google agreed not only not to use Fitbit data for advertising but also that reports by the monitoring trustee could be shared with DPAs to better enforce the rules.[155] Similarly, the commitments offered by Google to address the CMA's concerns regarding the Privacy Sandbox proposal leave space for the involvement of the Information Commissioner's Office (ICO) in assessing the impact of such proposals on users' privacy.[156] These measures are

[149] Case C-252/21 *Meta Platforms Inc v Bundeskartellamt* ECLI:EU:C:2023:537, paras 47 and 48.
[150] ibid.
[151] ibid para 49.
[152] ibid para 53.
[153] ibid.
[154] Case C-252/21 *Meta Platforms Inc v Bundeskartellamt* ECLI:EU:C:2022:704, Opinion of AG Rantos, para 29.
[155] *Google/Fitbit* (n 58), section B Commitments.
[156] CMA, *Decision to Accept Google's Commitments* (n 83) paras 6.44ff.

important in ensuring that competition remedies take data privacy interests into account.

Another competition remedy that could potentially have negative consequences for data privacy is data sharing. If control over personal data is deemed to create a barrier to entry, competition measures might resort to enforcing data sharing as a remedy.[157] This prompts the question of how such measures could impact users' privacy and the limitations imposed by data privacy laws.

Although not in the context of digital markets, the French Competition Authority ordered energy and gas supplier GDF Suez to grant its competitors access to parts of its database related to consumers, arguing that the database gave GDF Suez an incomparable advantage over its competitors.[158] The agency held that the cross-usage of data collected in one market as an input in another market resulted in a restriction of competition because the database was not the 'product of a specific innovation' but rather was inherited from its past monopoly.[159] Similar suggestions for mandated data sharing have been made for certain digital markets to prevent market tipping.[160] For example, one amendment to Section 19 of the German Competition Act (GWB), which addresses abuse of dominance, involves the introduction of a new prohibition on refusals to grant another undertaking access to data.[161] Accordingly, a dominant undertaking may be forced to provide data access if such access is deemed 'objectively necessary in order to operate on an upstream or downstream market and the refusal threatens to eliminate effective competition on that market'. This amendment removes the requirement for indispensability, which is often the main obstacle to the application of the doctrine to data and platforms. The DMA also includes provisions that impose obligations on search engines to share data with competitors.[162]

Such measures are likely to raise data privacy concerns. One argument posits that data-related competition law remedies—such as forced access or divestiture of a copy—may generate new privacy concerns because sharing with third parties introduces the possibility of additional risks and misuse.[163] However, most arguments suggesting that potential competition remedies increase data privacy risks are predicated on the assumption that absent these interventions (divestiture or forced access), the privacy risks remain unchanged. As shown in Chapter 2, this is not the case. The privacy risks faced by individuals increase in the event of a

[157] See *IMS Health* (n 36) para 30; Inge Graef, *EU Competition Law, Data Protection and Online Platforms: Data as Essential Facility* (Kluwer Law International 2016).

[158] Autorité de la Concurrence and Bundeskartellamt (n 33) 20.

[159] ibid.

[160] See Graef, *EU Competition Law* (n 157).

[161] See GWB (n 47).

[162] Regulation (EU) 2022/1925 of the European Parliament and of the Council of 14 September 2022 on Contestable and Fair Markets in the Digital Sector and amending Directives (EU) 2019/1937 and (EU) 2020/1828 OJ L265/1 (Digital Markets Act, DMA).

[163] Sokol and Comerford (n 44) 1159.

merger, with the subsequent possibility of combining data. Thus, the question is often whether the privacy risks posed to individuals from independent data processing by two firms surpass the risks associated with the consolidated processing of such data under the control of a single firm.

Moreover, to the extent that competition authorities are aware of the data privacy interests at stake and collaborate closely with DPAs, the risks of divestiture or forced access can be mitigated. In fact, this occurred in the *GDF Suez* case: the Competition agency and the DPA collaborated and required opt-out consent from users before their data could be shared with competitors.[164] Interestingly, many consumers chose not to share their data with competitors,[165] demonstrating that it is possible to protect data privacy interests when enforcing competition measures. Overall, if complemented by relevant data privacy measures, the data-related competition law remedies could have a positive effect on the data privacy of individuals. This is particularly the case if, as shown in the *Google/Fitbit* merger, competition remedies also include measures limiting data combination and restrictions on privacy policy changes.

2. Data Privacy Concerns as Justifications

Another implication arising from the increased importance of personal data in competition is the degree to which privacy considerations can justify potentially anticompetitive practices. This can be the case where companies refuse to provide (or discontinue) access to users' data, citing the enhancement of users' privacy or compliance with data privacy laws as justification. The *GDF Suez* case above and Google's Privacy Sandbox plans both fall under this category.

The first scenario arises in instances in which access to personal data is considered a barrier to entry or essential to competition, and competition authorities order access to such data as a remedy. In these cases, the question is whether the firm can object based on its obligations to users under data privacy law. This issue has already surfaced in the *GDF Suez* case. When ordered to grant competitors access to parts of its consumer database, the company argued that complying with the order would prevent it from fulfilling its data privacy obligations, as it could not ensure that the competitors would provide an adequate level of data protection for users' personal data.[166] This raises a number of questions: What limits do data privacy rules impose on competition law? How can data privacy and competition law interests be balanced?

The first point that needs to be addressed is the extent to which firms can resort to data privacy rules to resist the implementation of competition law remedies.

[164] Autorité de la Concurrence and Bundeskartellamt (n 33) 20.

[165] ibid. One could ask whether the opt-out mechanism complies with the EU rules. At the same time, an order from competition authorities could legitimize the sharing of data based on GDPR, Article 6(1(c)), which pertains to legal obligations, eliminating the need for consent.

[166] Autorité de la Concurrence and Bundeskartellamt (n 33).

It is a well-recognized principle under competition law that firms can justify anticompetitive conduct if it is mandated by legislation. This is known as the state compulsion doctrine. However, this justification is accepted only if the applicable regulation leaves no room for autonomous conduct.[167] Thus, the question is whether the applicable data privacy rules leave room for a firm to comply with the competition remedy. The answer seems to be yes. Under the EU data privacy rules, personal data can be processed if there is a legitimate basis for doing so. Among other grounds, Article 6(1)(c) of the GDPR allows personal data to be processed (eg shared) if this is 'necessary for compliance with a legal obligation to which the controller is subject'. Thus, the mere fact that a firm is subject to data privacy rules does not prevent the firm from sharing data with third parties to comply with its obligations under competition law. This is particularly the case if the third party with whom the data is shared is also subject to the GDPR.

The second point relates to the question of whether competition authorities must factor in—based on their own initiative or by request—data privacy interests in imposing competition remedies. In this regard, there are arguments (following the changes in the EU constitutional framework introduced by the 2009 Lisbon Treaty and the recognition of data privacy as a fundamental right) that EU institutions are under an obligation to take data privacy considerations into account in all their activities. This flows in particular from Article 7 of the TFEU, which mandates consistency between the EU's policies and activities.[168] Similarly, Graef refers to Article 51(1) of the EU Charter, which requires that EU institutions respect and promote the application of the rights contained in the Charter.[169] This obligation encompasses both 'a negative duty to avoid violations' and 'a positive obligation' to take measures that uphold the fundamental right.[170] Thus, Graef argues, the Commission is bound to respect the fundamental rights under the Charter, including the right to data protection stipulated in Article 8, when enforcing EU competition law.[171] This means that the Commission and EU courts must consider data privacy considerations in enforcing competition rules and ensure consistency between the two sets of rules. Is it possible though, in practice, to ensure consistency among all conflicting interests? And what would such consistency entail?[172] Similarly, although it is theoretically possible for consumers to challenge

[167] See *Deutsche Telekom v Commission* (n 103).
[168] See Costa-Cabral and Lynskey (n 105); Graef, *EU Competition Law* (n 157).
[169] Graef, *EU Competition Law* (n 157) 339.
[170] ibid.
[171] ibid.
[172] See Louise O'Callaghan, 'The Intersection between Data Protection and Competition Law: How to Incorporate Data Protection, as a Non-Economic Objective, into EU Competition Analysis' (2018) 21 Trinity College Law Review 118, 118–20 (discussing the multifaceted nature of consistency, which could mean 'absence of contradiction', 'positive connections', or 'absence of contradiction unless justified' and noting the difficulty of achieving consistency based on the requirement of 'absence of contradiction').

competition decisions that interfere with their privacy rights, there are 'onerous' procedural difficulties that need to be overcome.[173]

This notwithstanding, in limited cases, the Commission and the EU courts have taken into account non-competition-related considerations in the areas of employment, environment, and proper administration of a profession in enforcing Article 101 and the merger rules.[174] This means that there may be instances, albeit limited, in which the Commission and the CJEU might weigh in the balance non-competition considerations, including objectives pursued by data privacy rules, and conclude that these outweigh the competition considerations.[175]

In the German *Facebook* case, the Federal Supreme Court underlined the need for competition authorities to consider constitutional and fundamental rights to communications and information self-determination.[176] In an earlier decision suspending the Bundeskartellamt's prohibition on Facebook's data combination, the Higher Regional Court of Duesseldorf questioned whether Facebook's conduct could qualify as exploitative abuse. Users are not dependent on Facebook and can freely decide whether or not to use it.[177] However, the Federal Supreme Court refuted this assessment, noting the critical function Facebook plays in public debate as an essential medium for communication. Due to this vital role, Facebook is, to some extent, bound to respect the fundamental rights enshrined under the German Constitution.[178] Furthermore, the constitutional right to self-determination entitles users to options with regard to how their data is used by Facebook. Thus, quitting Facebook cannot be considered a means of protection from exploitative practices as this would undermine users' constitutional rights. Similarly, the constitutional right to self-determination and the GDPR dictate that users must be protected from overly far-reaching commercial exploitation of their personal data, and this needs to be considered in the competition assessment.[179]

The decision by the German Federal Supreme Court underscores the need for competition authorities to actively consider data protection and other fundamental rights in the enforcement of competition rules. This is particularly relevant in cases involving super-dominant platforms that play public-like functions in political,

[173] ibid 123 (noting that this would require the user to 'to demonstrate individual concern' and show that the 'decision affects an individual by reason of certain attributes which are peculiar to him or her').

[174] See Chapter 1; Case C-309/99 *Wouters v Algemene Raad van de Nederlandse Orde van Advocaten* ECLI:EU:C:2002:98, para 105.

[175] See Graef, *EU Competition Law* (n 157) 339; Costa-Cabral and Lynskey (n 105) 38ff.

[176] See BGH (German Federal Court of Justice), decision of 23 June 2020—KVR 69/19; Rupprecht Podszun, 'FACEBOOK @ BGH', *D'Kart* (23 June 2020).

[177] Klaus Wiedemann, 'A Matter of Choice: The German Federal Supreme Court's Interim Decision in the Abuse-of-Dominance Proceedings Bundeskartellamt v. Facebook (Case KVR 69/19)' (2020) 51 IIC-International Review of Intellectual Property and Competition Law 1168, 1173.

[178] The Court refers to case law from the German Constitutional Court on 'third-party effects of fundamental rights (*mittelbare Drittwirkung*)', which attributes responsibilities to certain private entities stemming from the German constitution: ibid.

[179] ibid 1173–74.

societal, and economic terms. The level of dominance and the public-like function of these platforms are important considerations in determining how closely competition authorities should investigate data protection and fundamental rights. While the CJEU does not clearly address this issue in its ruling, it indicated that users are entitled to refuse to consent to the processing of data that is not 'necessary for the performance of a contract' and yet continue to use the service.[180] If this is the case, the social network operator should provide these users with an equivalent alternative that does not involve such data processing—if necessary, for a reasonable fee.[181]

At first glance, it might appear that the CJEU supports a 'pay-or-consent' approach, but this interpretation is overly simplistic. On the contrary, it is plausible to suggest that the CJEU's perspective aligns with the German Federal Supreme Court's recognition of the pivotal role social media occupies in modern society and the lack of viable alternatives due to Facebook's dominance in the market. Given these factors, entities offering these services should not resort to a 'take-it-or-leave-it' strategy, especially when the data being requested comes from outside the main service itself. Therefore, for services that are indispensable in today's world, providers must ensure that choices are available for users, even if this means some users are charged for access to the service.

Furthermore, the recognition of data privacy as a non-price parameter and the increasing role that data privacy rules play in the competitive process make it easier to account for data privacy considerations as matters affecting competition. For example, can potential competition concerns about a merger be ameliorated by possible improvements to data privacy, such as increased effectiveness in PET? Under Article 101, one example might be agreements not to collect sensitive personal data or not to use such data for advertising. In the case of Article 102, this issue might arise when a dominant firm tries to justify potentially abusive conduct on the ground that it enhances users' privacy.

In relation to mergers, the Commission decision in *Microsoft/LinkedIn* shows that data privacy interests can justify intervention where the merger leads to market power and a consequent reduction in the level of data privacy as a quality parameter.[182] However, the discussion so far has been focused on how a merger might negatively affect data privacy as a non-price parameter. The extent to which a merger's positive impact on data privacy may trump potential competition concerns arising from the merger remains an unexplored issue. This issue is particularly important because the conventional understanding is that firms with similar privacy policies compete more fiercely than firms with dissimilar privacy policies. This implies that when entities exhibit significant differences in terms of how much

180 *Meta Platforms Inc v Bundeskartellamt* (n 149) para 150.
181 ibid.
182 See Chapter 5.

they value privacy and how they handle personal data, they are not considered to be competitors. This seems to be the approach adopted by the Commission in the *Facebook/WhatsApp* merger.[183]

Following this line of reasoning, it is not the acquisition of WhatsApp by Facebook or DuckDuckGo by Google that results in reduced privacy; instead, it is the merger between two privacy-friendly social networks or search engines. While a merger of firms that attract customers due to their superior privacy policies could, indeed, lead to reduced competition, especially if the market for such services is already concentrated, it could also have a positive effect on privacy in the current market landscape. Given the significance of network effects and the dominance of a few players whose business models rely heavily on personal data monetization, such a merger could improve the data privacy of users by offering bigger networks that satisfy their privacy preferences and reduce the need to multi-home with established networks.[184] This, in turn, could force the leading platforms to rethink their privacy practices. In this context, the maverick theory of harm, discussed in Chapter 5, could serve as a shield when a merger increases the effectiveness of the maverick's business strategies. Thus, it could be used to defend a merger between two privacy-friendly social networks or search engines.

It is also possible to take into account privacy considerations in applying Article 101. The Commission guidelines indicate that goals pursued by other treaty provisions can be taken into account under Article 101(3) 'to the extent that they can be subsumed under the four conditions'.[185] The four conditions under Article 101(3) stipulate that the conduct brings efficiency benefits (improving the production or distribution of goods or promoting technical or economic progress), provides a fair share for consumers, does not impose conditions that are not indispensable, and does not eliminate competition. As noted above, the CJEU has held that quality considerations can justify restrictions on competition under Article 101(1).[186] Thus, in light of the recognition of data privacy as a non-price (quality) competition parameter, there is a possibility that improvements in data privacy might ameliorate the potentially adverse effects of agreements. Conduct that improves data privacy could lead to an increase in consumer welfare by enhancing the quality of the service, perhaps justifying otherwise anticompetitive conduct (provided the other conditions are fulfilled).

Although the wording of Article 102 of the TFEU does not contain an efficiency defence, the CJEU has recognized that dominant companies are entitled to raise efficiency arguments to justify conduct that may otherwise be regarded as abusive.[187] In its submission to the OECD roundtable, the Commission indicated

[183] See Esayas, 'Competition in Dissimilarity' (n 120).
[184] See ibid.
[185] European Commission, 'Communication from the Commission—Notice—Guidelines on the Application of Article 81(3) of the Treaty' [2004] OJ C101/97, para 42.
[186] *Coty Germany v Parfümerie Akzente* (n 76) paras 46–48.
[187] See Case C-209/10 *Post Danmark AS v Konkurrencerådet* EU:C:2013:172, para 42.

that dominant undertakings can refer to efficiency gains resulting from quality improvements under Article 102.[188] To the extent that data privacy forms a non-price competition parameter, improvements thereof could justify a potential abuse of dominant position. The *Google Privacy Sandbox* case serves as a prime example of how data privacy considerations are a central part of competition assessments.

As noted above, Google has taken various initiatives purportedly aimed at improving users' privacy, which have attracted scrutiny from competition authorities. First, Google imposes restrictions on advertisers, publishers, or competing online display advertising intermediaries, preventing them from accessing data about user identity or user behaviour when providing display advertising services, while this same information is available to Google.[189] Second, Google has announced plans to stop making the advertising identifier available to third parties on Android. Third, Google plans to ban the placement of third-party 'cookies' on Chrome and replace them with the 'Privacy Sandbox' set of tools. Both the advertising ID and third-party cookies are important sources of user data for publishers and competing online display advertising intermediaries. The Commission is investigating the effect of these data access restrictions on online display advertising and online display advertising intermediation markets.[190]

In its assessment of the Privacy Sandbox, the CMA indicated that the removal of third-party cookies and related restrictions on user tracking would deprive rival publishers and ad tech providers of the ability to offer granular and personalized ad inventory, while having little to no impact on the quality of Google's services.[191] This, in turn, could give Google a significant competitive advantage over rival publishers and ad tech providers operating in the open display market.[192] According to the CMA, if implemented without regulatory scrutiny and oversight, these practices could foreclose competition in the markets for digital advertising, likely amounting to an abuse of dominance.[193]

These investigations lie at the crux of the intersection between data privacy and competition. While Google's moves may improve users' privacy, they are likely to harm competition in the market for digital advertising. How should public agencies balance these interests?

One way of looking at these practices is to suggest that the restrictions on data distort competition, and competition measures ought to ensure continued access to users' data. As noted above, data privacy rules do not necessarily prevent competition authorities from imposing such measures as this can be justified based on

[188] OECD, *Policy Roundtables* (n 65) 77.
[189] CMA, *Decision to Accept Google's Commitments* (n 83).
[190] European Commission, 'Commission Opens Investigation into Possible Anticompetitive Conduct by Google in the Online Advertising Technology Sector' (22 June 2021) (European Commission, 'Investigation into Google's Online Advertising').
[191] CMA, *Decision to Accept Google's Commitments* (n 83) para 5.40.
[192] ibid para 5.66.
[193] ibid para 5.28.

legal obligations under competition law. However, such measures would deprive users of the potential privacy improvements included in the proposal. One of the measures in the Privacy Sandbox is to limit cross-site tracking of users by websites via cookies, which is a major privacy-intrusive practice. A Belgian Court described cross-site tracking as looking 'over the shoulders of persons while browsing from one site to the next', without proper disclosure or consent, enabling the collection of sensitive data such as health, sexual, and political preferences.[194] Thus, Google's measures to prevent cross-site tracking could potentially bring significant improvements to users' data privacy and reinforce the GDPR principles of data minimization, storage limitation, consent, privacy by design, and privacy by default. Any measure that deters the implementation of the Privacy Sandbox proposals, though it may address the competition concerns, could negatively affect potential privacy improvements.

Another angle to consider is the importance of enforcing similar restrictions on companies that rely on privacy justifications to potentially excuse or mask anticompetitive behaviour. If anything, the manner in which the CMA has addressed the issues is instructive. First, the CMA's framing of the restrictions on data access as self-preferencing—as opposed to a refusal to supply (disruption of supply)—shifts the focus of the competition remedies in a way that has positive effects on user privacy. Framing the issue as one of disruption of access to data might have led to measures that ensured continued access to users' data. As noted above, this would have had a negative impact on potential improvements to privacy.

In contrast, framing the restrictions as self-preferencing has led the CMA to demand equal treatment, namely that Google refrain from using the data for its own purposes. Among other things, the commitments accepted by the CMA require that Google not use any of the individual-level user data from its 'current and future user-facing services, including Android', 'Chrome browsing history, including synced Chrome history', 'a publisher's Google Analytics account', and 'data uploaded by an advertiser to Customer Match'.[195] This means that, after the implementation of the Privacy Sandbox proposals, Google must abstain from using user data from these sources in offering its advertising products and services.

This is a significant win for users' privacy, demonstrating that competition authorities can address the competition concerns without undermining the privacy improvements contained in Google's plans. Despite the initial tensions, the competition measures have actually enhanced users' data privacy. The competition measures not only maintained Google's plan to restrict user tracking by third parties but also imposed additional constraints on Google's use of specific data for advertising.

[194] *Willem Debeuckelaere v Facebook* Brussels Court of First Instance Roll Number 2016/153/A 9 and 69.

[195] CMA, *Decision to Accept Google's Commitments* (n 83) para 6.55.

Second, the way in which the CMA has addressed the issues shows that competition authorities see the importance of privacy in relation to digital advertising and are willing to consider it in their assessments. Both the CMA and the Commission have emphasized the need to account for users' privacy and compliance with data privacy rules in their assessments.[196] The Commission stresses that competition and data protection laws 'must work hand in hand' to ensure a level playing field in the display advertising market where 'all market participants protect user privacy in the same manner'.[197]

In this context, the outcomes of CMA investigations into Google's Privacy Sandbox are exemplary in relation to the closer collaboration needed between competition and data privacy authorities to address issues at the intersection of the two legal fields. The CMA collaborated closely with the ICO during the investigation and in assessing the impact of Google's proposals 'on privacy outcomes and compliance with data protection principles'.[198] This collaboration also extended to examining 'the design of default options and choice architectures related to user controls'.[199] The CMA has insisted that this collaboration reflects the pivotal role of data protection and privacy in the Privacy Sandbox proposals, as well as the strong connection between data protection and competition factors in digital markets.[200]

The effective manner in which the CMA resolved the tension between data privacy and competition interests was contingent on its willingness to incorporate expertise from various legal domains and collaborate with relevant agencies. A contrasting case from the United States, which involved disruption of access to data, clearly illustrates the differences in potential outcomes. LinkedIn was accused of unfair competition practices for terminating a firm's access to publicly accessible information about LinkedIn users.[201] In its defence, LinkedIn contended that its actions were motivated solely by a concern for its users' privacy. In its summary judgment, the Court rejected LinkedIn's argument, citing, inter alia, LinkedIn's own disregard for its users' privacy. Specifically, the Court noted that LinkedIn makes users' data available to third parties, sometimes without users' consent.[202] This was evidenced by how LinkedIn advertised its service to potential recruiters, promising to offer updates about users' job changes without their knowledge.[203] The Court further indicated that LinkedIn had 'wrongfully harvested users' contacts' email addresses' and 'repeatedly sent emails soliciting them to join LinkedIn without the members' consent'.[204] Thus, LinkedIn's own disregard for privacy

[196] European Commission, 'Investigation into Google's Online Advertising'(n 190).
[197] ibid.
[198] CMA, *Decision to Accept Google's Commitments* (n 83) para 6.45.
[199] ibid.
[200] ibid para 6.44.
[201] *hiQ Labs, Inc v LinkedIn Corp* Dist Court, ND California 3d vol 273 (2017).
[202] ibid 22.
[203] ibid 7.
[204] ibid 22.

seemingly justified a third party's continued access to user data, despite the potential privacy implications. The case represents a glaring example of how privacy interests can suffer two distinct losses. The first loss occurred when LinkedIn disregarded users' privacy for its own commercial gain. The second loss occurred when this disregard was used to justify further interference with user privacy.

The key takeaway from both the CMA and US cases is that, with data privacy and its regulations becoming increasingly significant in competition assessments, there is a pressing need for platforms that foster collaboration between data privacy and competition agencies. The ICO and the CMA have established the Digital Regulation Cooperation Forum with the aim of 'supporting a coordinated and coherent ongoing approach to digital regulation'.[205] Similarly, at the EU level, the EDPS has established a digital clearing house that facilitates cooperation between competition, consumer, and data protection authorities.[206] Initiatives such as these that facilitate cross-institutional dialogue and collaboration should be strengthened, given their crucial role in effectively addressing issues that go beyond specific legal domains, a frequent occurrence in today's complex digital landscape.

V. Conclusion

This chapter presents a comprehensive analysis of the intersection between data privacy law and competition law resulting from the commercialization of personal data. It starts by highlighting how the shifts brought about by the commercialization of personal data, notably the tendency to process data for a plethora of purposes, and the emergence of multi-product ecosystems give rise to a complex economic landscape. This increased complexity suggests the need for a more complexity-orientated mindset. Accordingly, the chapter highlights three key insights from complexity science that can be instrumental for addressing some of the challenges to data privacy and competition law. These include the need for a systems-level unit of analysis, the importance of emphasizing interconnections, and the need to account for emergence and adopting a polycentric approach.

While Chapter 2 and 3 addressed the need for a systems-level analysis in data privacy law and competition law, this chapter, and the subsequent ones, show that the increasing attention to personal data and data privacy in competition assessment reflects a step towards acknowledging the new forms of power derived from managing interconnections and the dynamic roles of economic agents within ecosystems. Importantly, the understanding that companies can exercise market

[205] CMA and Information Commissioner's Office (ICO), 'Competition and Data Protection in Digital Markets: A Joint Statement between the CMA and the ICO' (19 May 2021) 27 <https://ico.org.uk/media/about-the-ico/documents/2619797/cma-ico-public-statement-20210518.pdf>.

[206] EDPS, 'Big Data & Digital Clearinghouse' <https://edps.europa.eu/data-protection/our-work/subjects/big-data-digital-clearinghouse_en> accessed 8 February 2024.

power by reducing the level of privacy protection brings competition policy closer to the complex digital reality in which users are not merely consumers but also contribute to value creation by making their data available. Similarly, recognizing data as a source of market power and data privacy as a non-price competition parameter are positive steps towards curbing panopticon power.

The complexity of the digital economy requires that we move beyond the either/or approach and embrace a polycentric regulatory system. This involves establishing a network of legal regimes that can interact and complement each other, along with a system for coordination and collaboration among different centres of legal authority. However, the successful implementation of a polycentric approach requires an understanding of the points of intersection between the various legal domains and the areas in which these systems could (and should) collaborate. This chapter has delved into this issue, highlighting both the points of convergence and the tensions that arise between data privacy law and competition law as a result of the commercialization of personal data.

This increased interface can manifest as convergence, as when the two sets of rules complement each other to promote a specific objective. By adopting a polycentric approach, this convergence can be leveraged to enhance both data privacy law and competition law. Competition law can enhance the efficacy of data privacy rules by tackling macro-level harms to data privacy in the form of privacy fixing, a reduction in choice due to mergers, or exclusionary and exploitative practices related to data and data privacy. Similarly, data privacy law can provide competition law with the necessary tools and normative guidance needed to address new forms of anticompetitive conduct through harms to data privacy. However, the interface can also manifest as tension or conflict between the two legal fields when addressing a specific issue, as exemplified by the increased recourse to data privacy obligations to justify potentially anticompetitive practices. This chapter demonstrates that these tensions can be amicably resolved through joint efforts and ongoing dialogue between the two legal regimes.

5

Merger Control and Theories of Harm on Data Privacy as a Non-Price Parameter

I. Data Privacy in Merger Control

With the growing importance of data for commercial purposes, data privacy has attracted considerable attention in competition law, particularly in mergers involving data-rich companies. A notable example is the recognition by the European Commission that data privacy constitutes a key parameter of non-price competition. As noted in Chapter 4, the Commission decisions in *Facebook/WhatsApp* and *Microsoft/LinkedIn* underscore the importance of data privacy as a non-price competition parameter in markets for consumer communication services and professional social networks (PSNs).[1] There are similar developments in the United Kingdom and the United States.[2] These approaches treat data privacy as an element of quality, choice, or innovation of the product/service offered to consumers and underscore the importance for competition law to consider how mergers might reduce incentives to compete on these parameters. This development brings competition policy closer to digital reality by acknowledging that market power may be exerted by reducing the level of privacy.

As elaborated in Chapter 4, these efforts are attuned to the calls for complexity-minded antitrust. This arises from the role that acknowledging data privacy as a non-price factor has in addressing challenges associated with emerging power dynamics in complex systems and the diversity of participants within them. In this regard, the discussion in Chapter 3, Section IV.B, illustrates how managing interconnections in complex systems, together with feedback loops, gives rise to new types of power, such as panopticon power, which are not adequately addressed in competition law. Furthermore, as shown in Chapter 4, Section I, current methods for assessing market power and associated metrics often fail to capture the impact of behaviour on agents other than producers and consumers. This includes those acting as data producers and workers, who contribute to the socio-economic value

[1] Case M.7217 *Facebook/WhatsApp* decision of 3 October 2014, para 87; Case M.8124 *Microsoft/LinkedIn* decision of 6 December 2016.

[2] Case 50972 *Decision to Accept Commitments Offered by Google in Relation to Its Privacy Sandbox Proposals*, Competition and Markets Authority 11 February 2022 para 5.81; Case 1:20-cv-03590-JEB *Federal Trade Commission v Facebook, Inc* in the United States District Court of Columbia, filed 19 August 2021.

Data Privacy and Competition Law in the Age of Big Data. Samson Y. Esayas, Oxford University Press.
 DOI: 10.1093/oso/9780198891420.003.0006

of the ecosystem. Thus, the recognition of data privacy as a non-price parameter and the increasing attention paid to practices that harm privacy help protect consumers in their role as data producers and mitigate some adverse effects stemming from panopticon power.

Despite this, questions on how to operationalize such an approach through a concrete theory of harm remain largely uncharted. For example, little attention has been paid to laying out a concrete theory of harm that outlines what constitutes a reduction in privacy.[3] In addition, it is not clear whether—and if so, to what extent—framing privacy as a quality, a choice, or an innovation affects its application in practice. This chapter is an initial step in filling in this apparent gap in the literature by considering the theories of harm behind data privacy as a non-price parameter.

To this end, it offers an analysis of the prospects and challenges, in light of European Union (EU) competition law, of three theories—namely privacy-as-a-quality, consumer choice, and the maverick firm. In outlining the theories, the chapter draws from EU data privacy rules to determine what constitutes a reduction in privacy as a non-price parameter. The discussion on the various theories of harm, notably the consumer choice and maverick theories, aligns well with appeals for a complexity-orientated approach to antitrust law. These appeals emphasize the importance of diversity as a crucial factor in addressing competition concerns in a complex economy.[4] They also urge for more careful consideration of the concepts of uncertainty, dynamic competition, and increasing returns.[5]

It bears mentioning that drawing clear boundaries in terms of whether conduct harms product quality, choice, or innovation may be difficult. This is because the three are closely related. For example, the choice that a company (eg a retail store) offers can be an indication of the quality of service provided by the store.[6] Here, choice becomes an integral part of quality. Similarly, when one talks about choice, the underlying factor that differentiates the goods/services can be quality, and thus choice becomes the driver for availability of goods with qualities that fit the preferences of different consumers. The same holds true for the relationship between quality/choice and innovation. Although innovation can be viewed as an independent factor, it is often the need to improve quality or provide choice that drives innovation. This means that conduct that harms innovation or limits choice can easily involve a reduction in quality: users do not get high-quality products (due to the harm to innovation) or do not get products that are sufficiently differentiated in

[3] See Geoffrey Manne and Ben Sperry, 'The Problems and Perils of Bootstrapping Privacy and Data into an Antitrust Framework' (2015) 2 Antitrust Chronicle 3.

[4] Joseph Farrell, 'Complexity, Diversity, and Antitrust' (2006) 51 Antitrust Bulletin 165.

[5] Nicolas Petit and Thibault Schrepel, 'Complexity-Minded Antitrust' (2023) 33 Journal of Evolutionary Economics 541.

[6] Organisation for Economic Co-operation and Development (OECD), *Policy Roundtables: The Role and Measurement of Quality in Competition Analysis* (2013) 14.

quality (due to the restrictions of choice).[7] Thus, the precise classification is less important than addressing the competition issues. The following sections address the theories of harm for incorporating privacy as a dimension of quality, choice, and innovation, emphasizing the main differences between these theories.

II. Theory of Harm behind Privacy-as-a-Quality

Competition policy is as much concerned with quality as it is with price. This is partly justified because reduced quality can sometimes be more harmful to the safety of consumers than price increases, for example in the case of consumer goods.[8] Similarly, considering quality dimensions in competition analysis drives innovation and economic growth.[9] Thus, in principle, mergers that negatively affect quality are as harmful to consumer welfare as output reduction/price increases. To the extent that data privacy can be seen as an element of quality, a merger could, in theory, harm consumer welfare by degrading the level of privacy protection. However, what constitutes a reduction in privacy as a quality parameter remains largely uncharted territory.

The argument in this section is that, to the extent that consumers view data privacy as an element of quality, a reduction in data privacy could be approached in light of the attributes identified in Chapter 4, Section IV.A.3. These attributes are informed by and reflect the key principles under EU data privacy law. In the case of price competition, firms compete by lowering prices, and anticompetitive conduct is assessed considering its impact on price increase. In the case of data privacy, firms compete by increasing the level of privacy protection, which could include (1) reducing the amount of personal data collected or not collecting data at all (data minimization); (2) limiting data storage, either by not storing personal data at all or attaching brief timestamps (storage limitation); (3) providing clear, precise, and understandable privacy policies (transparency); (4) providing more and better choices (consent); (5) deploying privacy-enhancing technologies (PETs) such as end-to-end encryption (data security and privacy by design); (6) implementing privacy-protective features by default (privacy by default). This implies that an analysis of data privacy as a non-price component needs to focus on the incentives and the impact of conduct that reduces these attributes.[10]

7 ibid 80.

8 Ariel Ezrachi and Maurice Stucke, 'The Curious Case of Competition and Quality' (2015) 3 Journal of Antitrust Enforcement 227, 229.

9 OECD (n 6) 5.

10 Samson Esayas, 'Data Privacy in European Merger Control: Critical Analysis of Commission Decisions Regarding Privacy as a Non-Price Competition' (2019) 40 European Competition Law Review 166.

Accordingly, a merger might be viewed as entailing a reduction in data privacy if it leads to market power that could be used, inter alia, to (1) increase the amount of personal data demanded or prolong the time personal data is stored, (2) reduce the transparency in data collection and use, (3) reduce the level of control (choice) users have over their data, or (4) abandon the use of PETs or their implementation by default. These are just a few examples, and the concrete theory of harm will depend on the specific dimensions of privacy that are relevant to the merging parties.

For example, in testimony provided to the US Federal Trade Commission (FTC) in relation to the *Google/DoubleClick* merger, Swire outlined a theory of harm based on the amount of personal data.[11] Swire argues that a reduction in quality is a standard category of antitrust harm and that privacy harms could constitute reductions in the 'quality of a good or service'.[12] According to Swire, a merger that leads to an increase in the amount of personal data demanded to access a service reduces consumer welfare because consumers, particularly those with 'high privacy preferences', 'pay more' for such a service.[13] Swire further concretizes this argument by outlining the 'deep' and 'broad' information on consumers that is involved in the merger.

Google collects massive amounts of personal data through several services, including email, search, map, video sharing, and browser use—leading to 'deep' information about individuals. DoubleClick, on the other hand, offers websites a variety of tools to display graphic-based ads and monitor their performance. In so doing, it has amassed a 'broad' array of information about consumers by tracking their browsing behaviour across millions of websites. Thus, the merger, Swire argues, could lead to a search product that becomes conditional on Google being able to combine its own 'deep' and DoubleClick's 'broad' information about individuals.[14] As noted in Chapter 4, the combination of data from the merging entities can raise competition concerns, due to the potential for data concentration. However, beyond these data concentration concerns, the combination of data may also constitute 'a significant reduction in the quality of the search product' for individuals with 'high privacy preferences'.[15] Swire reasons as follows:

[11] See Peter Swire, 'Submitted Testimony to the Federal Trade Commission Behavioral Advertising Town Hall on Google/DoubleClick' (2007)<https://www.europarl.europa.eu/meetdocs/2004_2009/documents/dv/testimony_peterswire_/Testimony_peterswire_en.pdf>.

[12] ibid 5.

[13] ibid.

[14] ibid.

[15] ibid. It is important to note that while the data concentration concerns and privacy degradation resulting from the combination of data largely overlap, they are distinct issues. In certain circumstances, the combination of data could, in fact, increase competition in some markets, such as advertising, while simultaneously reducing the level of privacy on offer. For more on this, see Samson Esayas, 'Privacy-as-a-Quality Competition Parameter' in Björn Lundqvist and Michal Gal (eds), *Competition Law for the Digital Economy* (Edward Elgar 2019).

> Before a merger, a consumer may be able to surf subject to one level of tracking, kept in a database of one magnitude. After the merger, doing a search or doing other surfing may carry with it a significantly higher level of tracking, in a larger database. To the extent that is true, then antitrust regulators should expect to assess this sort of quality reduction as part of their overall analysis of a merger or dominant firm behavior.[16]

Accordingly, a degradation in the level of privacy occurs if, following a merger, users are required to share more data to use a specific service than they were prior to the merger. Thus, the amount of data collected and used in providing the service becomes a relevant consideration in assessing the level of privacy and the overall quality of the search product.[17] While the FTC acknowledged that privacy constitutes a non-price competition parameter in the merger, it offered little help regarding when and how a merger might reduce this dimension of competition.

Similar decisions from the European Commission also leave the question largely unanswered. In *Facebook/WhatsApp*, although the Commission identified data privacy as a key parameter of competition, it did not specifically assess how the merger might affect this parameter. However, the Commission did examine how a reduction in privacy might serve as a constraint on the merged entity's incentive to introduce targeted ads in WhatsApp. According to the Commission, for WhatsApp to introduce targeted ads, it would need to change its privacy policy and start collecting more data (age, gender, country, and message content) from its users.[18] The Commission argued that such a scenario was improbable, as it would likely cause WhatsApp users to migrate to other messaging apps perceived as 'less intrusive' and ad free.[19] Although the Commission did not explicitly articulate the relationship between more data and a reduction in privacy-as-a-quality, it suggested that demanding more data to introduce targeted ads could constitute a reduction in privacy provided it followed from reduced competition.[20] Hence, a reduction in data privacy could be understood to involve an increase in the amount of personal data demanded or an expansion in the usage of existing data for purposes other than those initially envisaged.[21]

16 Swire (n 11) 5.

17 See also Competition and Markets Authority, 'Completed Acquisition by Facebook, Inc (now Meta Platforms, Inc) of Giphy, Inc' (Final Report, 22 October 2022) para 8153(b) <https://assets.publishing.service.gov.uk/media/635017428fa8f53463dcb9f2/Final_Report_Meta.GIPHY.pdf> (noting that 'the quality of rival social media platforms' services may also immediately suffer from the perspective of users that value privacy' if, following the merger, they must agree for sharing of their data with a third party).

18 *Facebook/WhatsApp* (n 1) paras 174–86.

19 ibid.

20 However, the Commission also noted that privacy concerns arising from the mere combination of data fall outside competition law: ibid para 164.

21 See also Eleonora Ocello, Cristina Sjödin, and Anatoly Subočs, 'What's Up with Merger Control in the Digital Sector? Lessons from the Facebook/WhatsApp EU Merger Case' (2015) 1 European Commission-Competition Merger Brief 1, 6.

Moreover, the Commission stated that the introduction of ads in WhatsApp might lead to abandoning end-to-end encryption, creating dissatisfaction among users who value their privacy.[22] In this sense, the Commission seemed to address, *albeit* indirectly, two possible reductions in data privacy, one based on an increase in data collection and the other based on abandoning end-to-end encryption. These considerations fit well within the two broader categories of competition on data privacy identified in Chapter 4, namely competition on the conditions of data collection and use, and competition on data security and PETs.

In light of the above espoused theory of harm, the post-merger changes to WhatsApp's privacy policy (to share WhatsApp users' data with Facebook with a view to improving advertising) represent a reduction in the quality of privacy resulting from an increase in the use of personal data (for purposes other than those initially promised) by WhatsApp. With post-merger hindsight, one could also argue that this reduction stems from market power or reduced competition: the merger lifted the competitive constraint that Facebook, as an established network, imposed on WhatsApp.[23]

As a latecomer, WhatsApp was trying to attract Facebook users by offering better data privacy based on a small annual fee. The fact that 80–90 per cent of WhatsApp users were users of Facebook's social network demonstrates that WhatsApp was largely successful.[24] Thus, the existence of Facebook as the more established and leading communication service provider imposed competitive constraints on WhatsApp's privacy policy. In other words, to keep Facebook's social network users using WhatsApp's messaging service, WhatsApp had to offer something that Facebook did not—better privacy protection and an ad-free experience. If WhatsApp had started collecting personal data or sharing its existing data with Facebook, its unique feature that attracted Facebook users would have disappeared, and its customers might have spent less time on WhatsApp and more time on other services, including Facebook Messenger. This is even more true when one considers that Facebook Messenger offered far richer functionality than WhatsApp and 'free' of charge. Thus, the fear of losing Facebook social network users to Facebook Messenger served as a competitive constraint on WhatsApp's privacy policy. The merger removed this competitive threat because, post-merger, any loss of WhatsApp users following the policy change could be recaptured through an increase in Facebook Messenger use or an increase in revenue from more targeted advertising on Facebook using WhatsApp's data.[25]

In this sense, the merger seems to have removed the competitive constraint on WhatsApp, leading to the privacy policy change. The policy change, in turn, leaves

22 *Facebook/WhatsApp* (n 1) para 174.

23 See Esayas, 'Data Privacy in European Merger Control' (n 10).

24 *Facebook/WhatsApp* (n 1) paras 70–80 and 105.

25 See Samson Esayas, 'Competition in Dissimilarity: Lessons in Privacy from the Facebook/WhatsApp Merger' (2017) 1 Antitrust Chronicle 57.

WhatsApp users with a messaging service whose quality is inferior to that available before the merger. A report by the Catalan Competition Authority highlights the reduced quality of the application as follows:

> The merger, therefore, has entailed a loss of options by the user. That is, where prior to the said merger two different models coexisted (WhatsApp—with greater data protection but with the requirement of an annual cash payment) and Facebook Messenger (less privacy protection but free) there is now just one (free service but with little privacy). Consequently, for those users who valued their privacy at a monetary amount higher than requested by WhatsApp, with the merger they have seen their welfare decrease (*decreased quality in terms of privacy*).[26]

Similarly, the FTC complaint against Facebook alleges that Facebook's acquisition of WhatsApp and Instagram has allowed it to monopolize the market for 'personal social media services' and led to the degradation of consumer privacy without competitive consequences.[27] Specifically, the complaint emphasizes that WhatsApp's growth was largely driven by its 'top grade privacy', which was neutralized by the acquisition and the subsequent changes to WhatsApp' privacy policy.[28] According to the complaint, the acquisition deprived users of an alternative messing app that was built on 'privacy-focused offerings and design, including the principle "of knowing as little about you as possible" and an ads-free subscription model'.[29] Thus, the Facebook/WhatsApp merger and the subsequent change in WhatsApp's privacy policy is an instance where a merger may lead to market power that is subsequently used to reduce the quality of data privacy by increasing the amount of personal data demanded and/or expanding the use of the data for purposes other than those for which it was originally collected.

The *Microsoft/LinkedIn* decision brings more clarity and improvement to the competition analysis on how a merger might lead to market power and a consequent reduction in privacy as a quality. In this decision, the Commission examined the extent to which the pre-installation of LinkedIn with Windows PCs operating system (OS) and its integration with Office products, such as Outlook and Word, could harm consumers. Having already identified data privacy as 'a significant quality' parameter of competition between PSNs, the Commission held that if Microsoft were to pre-install LinkedIn in Windows and integrate it with Office products, it would reduce consumer choice in relation to privacy.[30] Specifically,

[26] Autoritat Catalana de la Competència, *The Data-Driven Economy Challenges for Competition* (2016) 26 (emphasis added).
[27] *Federal Trade Commission v Facebook* (n 2) paras 105, 127.
[28] ibid paras 113, 127.
[29] ibid.
[30] *Microsoft/LinkedIn* (n 1) para 350.

the Commission noted that, given the large market share of Windows OS in the PCs market and its importance for user engagement and acquisition, pre-installing LinkedIn could raise entry or expansion barriers by making it difficult for other PSNs to acquire consumers or by making switching more difficult.[31]

Moreover, the Commission noted the lack of effective strategies for competing PSNs to counter the effect of LinkedIn's pre-installation on Windows PCs. This is because original equipment manufacturers (OEMs) 'may lack incentives to pre-install a second PSN application' and users are 'unlikely to decide spontaneously to download an application that is not already pre-installed'.[32] Thus, the increase in the number of users resulting from this pre-installation, the network effects of the increased number of users, and the inertia resulting from the pre-installation would all combine to deny competing PSNs equivalent access to customers and ultimately lead to their foreclosure from the market.[33] The integration of LinkedIn into Office products, particularly Outlook, was considered to have similar effects, increasing LinkedIn's user base and usage, and leaving competing PSNs with no effective counter-strategy to respond to the merged entity's actions, ultimately leading to their foreclosure.[34]

In light of these considerations, the Commission noted that the market could tip in favour of LinkedIn. According to the Commission, this would harm consumers in two ways. First, the conduct would lead to 'a substantial reduction of consumer choice' as LinkedIn would remain the only PSN service provider accessible to users in the European Economic Area (EEA), with scant prospects of entry by new PSN service providers.[35] Second, and more importantly, the conduct would reduce consumer choice in relation to privacy. This is because the conduct would lead to marginalization and eventual foreclosure of PSN providers such as XING that 'offer a greater degree of privacy protection than LinkedIn'.[36] Highlighting why XING was considered to offer better (quality of) privacy than LinkedIn, the Commission refers to the differences in privacy policies as follows:

> during the registration process, *XING asks users to actively accept XING's privacy policy and Terms & Conditions by ticking a box*, whereas LinkedIn users accept LinkedIn's privacy policy automatically when they press the button 'join now'. Moreover, *when XING introduces new services which have an implication on how it collects and/or uses its members' data, it explicitly seeks active consent from the members*. In addition, *regardless of whether members give their consent in such*

[31] For example, Windows PC accounted 'for more than half of total LinkedIn sign-ups' and 'for more than 30% of LinkedIn usage': see ibid paras 309–19.
[32] ibid.
[33] ibid.
[34] ibid paras 329–30.
[35] ibid para 349.
[36] ibid para 350.

specific cases or not, they will be able to continue to use XING as such without losing any of the functions to which they previously had access. In contrast, when LinkedIn makes changes to its collection, storing, processing or usage of personal data, LinkedIn only informs the members of those changes and considers that LinkedIn members agree with those changes, if they continue to use LinkedIn's services after they have been notified of the changes.[37]

Three points require particular mention in the above paragraph. First, the theory of harm clearly recognizes that the choices users have when providing their data and their ability to control its use are key attributes of competition on data privacy. In other words, users' valuation of privacy as a quality parameter is not limited to how much personal data is collected but also includes other dimensions, such as their ability to control their data and make informed decisions. As highlighted in the above paragraph, companies can compete on the quality of consent by actively seeking users' consent via a tick-box, not only during registration but also when making policy changes. Moreover, even when users decline to consent to changes, companies can still compete by allowing users to continue to use functionalities to which they previously had access.

Second, although the decision makes no reference to EU data privacy rules, the theory of harm reflects the different qualities of consent under these rules. The fact that 'XING asks users to actively accept XING's privacy policy and Terms & Conditions by ticking a box' and 'explicitly seeks active consent from the members' when introducing new features shows the existence of competition based on the notion (dimension) of 'unambiguous' consent. The notion of unambiguous consent requires that consent must be given before the processing activity starts and should be manifested through a positive and definite act (such as ticking a box) as opposed to continuous usage of a service.[38] In this regard, the Commission views XING's approach as *more unambiguous* and thus as providing users with a higher level of privacy protection than LinkedIn.

Additionally, XING's approach separates the act of giving consent from the user's activity, such as joining the network or continuing to use the service. This separation shows that competition also exists on the requirement (dimension) that consent be 'freely given' and 'informed'. As indicated by Advocate General Szpunar, the duo entails that consent must be 'separate', meaning that an individual's online activities, such as watching a video, and the act of granting consent 'cannot form part

[37] ibid (emphasis added).

[38] See Article 29 Data Protection Working Party (WP187), 'Opinion 15/2011 on the Definition of Consent' adopted on 13 July 2011, 12 (WP187); also Regulation (EU) 2016/679 of the European Parliament and of the Council of 27 April 2016 on the Protection of Natural Persons with Regard to the Processing of Personal Data and on the Free Movement of Such Data, and repealing Directive 95/46/EC OJ L119/1 (GDPR), Recital 32.

of the same act'.[39] LinkedIn's approach, which infers consent when users click the 'join button' or 'continue to use the service', bundles the act of giving consent with the activity the user is pursuing. In this sense, the consent users give to LinkedIn can be considered inferior in quality compared to the consent given to XING.

Moreover, the possibility that users may 'continue to use XING without losing any of the functions to which they previously had access', even when withholding consent to new features, is evidence of competition based on 'freely given' consent. This dimension requires that the user be given the opportunity to make a genuine choice, including the ability to withhold/withdraw consent without fearing negative consequences.[40] In this sense, by allowing users to continue to use existing functionality while withholding consent for new features, the consent obtained by XING qualifies as *more 'freely given'* than the consent obtained by LinkedIn, thus offering users better (quality) of privacy than LinkedIn. Thus, the potential foreclosure of XING was considered anticompetitive because it would deprive users of a better-quality PSN. Had the merger been allowed, users would have been left with just one PSN, namely LinkedIn, with an inferior quality of privacy. Thus, Microsoft offered solutions to allay the foreclosure concerns and to mitigate the adverse effects on privacy.[41]

Finally, the decision shows that reductions in the level of privacy may result from classical anticompetitive conduct, such as tying, provided competition authorities recognize data privacy as a form of non-price competition. The decision is particularly important because it shows that it is not always necessary to quantify the reduction in privacy. In this instance, the Commission reached its conclusion by looking at the foreclosing effect of the conduct (ie tying) without tackling the thorny issue of measuring the quality of privacy.

In summary, the above analysis of the *Facebook/WhatsApp* and *Microsoft/LinkedIn* decisions demonstrates that reductions in data privacy as a quality can result from (1) an increase in the amount of personal data demanded or expanded use of existing data, (2) abandoning end-to-end encryption, and (3) conduct that negatively affects users' ability to control their data and make informed decisions. The application of the theory in the *Microsoft/LinkedIn* merger further shows its maturity, with discussions no longer restricted to the academic realm.

[39] Case C-673/17 *Planet49 GmbH v Verbraucherzentrale Bundesverband eV* ECLI:EU:C:2019:246, Opinion of Advocate General Szpunar, para 66.

[40] WP187 (n 38) 12–13.

[41] These include the commitment to (1) ensuring that the availability of Microsoft's and its partners' application programming interface (API) to competing PSNs, (2) allowing users to disable LinkedIn from Office products and Windows PC OS, (3) 'not to offer the LinkedIn Windows PC Application or the LinkedIn Windows PC Tile to Users through Windows, prompt Users to install such application or tile, or include such application or tile in updates of Windows PC OS'. See *Microsoft/LinkedIn* (n 1) paras 437–38.

III. Consumer Choice Approach

The unclear boundaries between the different non-price parameters are also evident in the different theories of harm. As demonstrated by the previous analysis of the *Microsoft/LinkedIn* decision, drawing boundaries between the quality-based and choice-based theories might seem difficult. This is particularly true when choice results from quality differentiation. However, at times, the difference between the two appears to be more of a semantic issue than one of substance. For example, Graef argues that framing privacy as a quality could potentially reinforce the incorrect perception that any additional data collection and usage is inherently detrimental to consumers.[42] She suggests that such a viewpoint would not hold if the comparison was instead drawn with consumer choice or product variety. The reasoning is that since there might be users that view collection of more data and the subsequent personalization as an improvement, referring to such conduct as entailing quality reduction and thereby consumer harm is not (semantically) appropriate. Instead, a reduction of choice better encapsulates such harm.

However, first, given that quality can be subjective, the reduction in quality need not affect all users; one can talk about a reduction in quality in relation to a specific set of users. Second, Graef's argument is based on a narrow view of the quality-based theory of harm. As noted above and confirmed in the *Microsoft/LinkedIn* decision, the quality-based theory of harm includes broader dimensions of data privacy than just an increase in the amount of personal data collected. Moreover, for the purposes of this section, the choice-based theory of harm entails a significant substantive departure from the quality-based theory and treats variety as the ultimate competition policy goal.

A. Consumer Choice vs Consumer Welfare

The consumer choice theory has its main point of departure in the shortcomings of contemporary US (and to some extent EU) antitrust enforcement based on 'price and efficiency' (consumer welfare approach).[43] The main criticism raised is that, although the consumer welfare approach is open to non-price parameters, 'factors such as service, innovation, quality, privacy and variety are as a practical matter sometimes relegated to the footnotes of the analysis, where they are too often

[42] Inge Graef, *EU Competition Law, Data Protection and Online Platforms: Data as Essential Facility* (Kluwer Law International 2016) 313.

[43] Neil Averitt and Robert Lande, 'Using the "Consumer Choice" Approach to Antitrust Law' (2007) 74 Antitrust Law Journal 175; Neil Averitt and Robert Lande, 'Consumer Sovereignty: A Unified Theory of Antitrust and Consumer Protection Law' (1997) 65 Antitrust Law Journal 713; Robert Lande, 'Consumer Choice as the Best Way to Describe the Goals of Competition Law' (University of Baltimore School of Law Legal Studies Research Paper, 2012).

forgotten'.[44] This is primarily because a price- and efficiency-based approach deals with non-price parameters indirectly in the form of price-adjusted quality or by assuming that markets exhibiting price competition will also be competitive on non-price parameters.[45] In contrast, the consumer choice approach does not attempt to translate non-price parameters into price terms, nor does it try to explain how 'efficiency' really means 'choice'.[46]

Not only is this translation difficult, but it is also unworkable in markets where the price is zero. Thus, the consumer choice approach elevates the role of non-price parameters in competition analysis by factoring in choice both explicitly and directly. As a result, conduct amounts to an antitrust violation if it 'significantly limits the range of choices that the free market, absent the restraints being challenged, would have provided'.[47] The practical implication of this approach is that, in certain circumstances, competition policy needs to protect rivalry and variety per se.

Three areas are identified where the consumer choice approach might yield a superior result. These are (1) markets that exhibit little or no price competition; (2) scenarios where market-specific conduct increases consumers' search costs or impedes their decision making; or (3) markets where competition is driven by 'independent decision making and creativity', rather than price-based factors.[48] The third market will be sufficient for the purposes of illustration in this section. Some of the specific markets where 'independent decision making and creativity' play substantial roles include communications media (eg newspaper) and high-tech markets.[49] For example, editorial independence is crucial to the variety of ideas offered in the media. Similarly, in high-tech markets, different research approaches, designs, and philosophies may impact the kind of technological innovation brought to the market. However, consumers cannot know after the fact (eg merger) what independent firms might have offered in terms of variety of ideas and the different kinds of innovation.[50] In fact, even the firms themselves might not be fully aware that their decisions are pushing certain ideas or innovation more than others.[51]

[44] See Lande (n 43) 4.
[45] Averitt and Lande, 'Using the "Consumer Choice" Approach' (n 43) 176.
[46] ibid 186–89.
[47] ibid 182–84.
[48] ibid 196. A pertinent question arises about how rivalry in markets, devoid of price competition, can yield improved outcomes on non-price factors, including data privacy. This query has been tackled by the author in another publication: Samson Esayas, 'Competition in (Data) Privacy: 'Zero'-Price Markets, Market Power, and the Role of Competition Law' (2018) 8 International Data Privacy Law 181. The article explores how, when entities' abilities to set prices are constrained (as seen in zero-price markets due to the 'zero effect' and transaction costs), increased competition might lead to quality improvements including superior data privacy. The work draws from the literature on regulated markets, which shows that an increase in the intensity of competition can lead to better quality if firms' price-making decisions are constrained.
[49] Averitt and Lande, 'Using the "Consumer Choice" Approach' (n 43) 202.
[50] ibid 179.
[51] ibid.

The implication is that mergers leading to reduced variety (eg in media markets) need to be prevented even if they entail 'tremendous cost savings in reporting'.[52] This is because the concentration of companies in the hands of a single parent corporation may foster uniformity of views within the different divisions of the conglomerate and thereby inflict serious harm to consumer choice 'in terms of perspectives, editorial independence, and the quality and varieties of approaches to news coverage'.[53] Such harms have been overlooked by competition law focused on price and efficiency.[54] For these reasons, the competition analysis in such markets should consider the effects of conduct on innovation, ideas, quality, privacy, and variety directly. This is achieved by ensuring that there are divergent and independent centres of innovation in the market, which in turn requires ensuring that more suppliers are left in the market than is necessary for effective price competition.[55] Thus, the consumer choice approach encompasses and extends beyond the price and efficiency approach.[56]

The consumer choice approach, which considers variety as the paramount objective of competition policy, is a prevailing perspective within the EU. Discussions around this approach are frequently linked to the Ordoliberal school of thought, which recognizes the positive role of the state in protecting the economic freedom of market players and the competitive order.[57] Advocates of Ordoliberalism propose that competition law should primarily aim to foster a level playing field for economic actors to exercise their freedom to compete (*wettbewerbsfreiheit*) without restraints from state and private power.[58] In the Ordoliberal view, competition policy should be broadly conceived to safeguard competition as a system that facilitates individual freedom of choice within the marketplace. Ensuring consumer choice in turn presupposes the existence of a rivalry among a sufficient number of producers in the market.[59] In practical terms, this philosophy requires that competition policy should focus on protecting rivalry and market structure as its main goal.

This yields a distinction between the consumer choice approach and the price and efficiency approach, particularly in the evaluation of how certain behaviours might promote or impede efficiency. The price and efficiency approach assumes that a business strategy, such as a merger, yielding micro-level benefits like reduced

52 Lande (n 43) 1.

53 ibid; Averitt and Lande, 'Using the "Consumer Choice" Approach' (n 43) 206.

54 See Allen Grunes and Maurice Stucke, 'No Mistake about It: The Important Role of Antitrust in the Era of Big Data' (April 2015) Antitrust Source 1, 7.

55 Lande (n 43) 1; Averitt and Lande, 'Using the "Consumer Choice" Approach' (n 43) 185, 203–205.

56 Averitt and Lande, 'Using the "Consumer Choice" Approach' (n 43) 185.

57 Mathias Siems and Gerhard Schnyder, 'Ordoliberal Lessons for Economic Stability: Different Kinds of Regulation, Not More Regulation' (2014) 27 Governance 377, 379.

58 Eugène Buttigieg, *Competition Law: Safeguarding the Consumer Interest: A Comparative Analysis of US Antitrust Law and EC Competition Law* (Wolters Kluwer 2009) 5–6.

59 Peter Behrens, 'The "Consumer Choice" Paradigm in German Ordoliberalism and Its Impact upon EU Competition Law' (Discussion paper No 1/14, Europa-Kolleg Hamburg 2014) 23.

costs from economies of scale, will subsequently result in macro-level benefits in the form of innovation and more choice to consumers.[60] This implies that the price and efficiency approach might tolerate conduct that could potentially reduce choice if the expected benefits to innovation from economies of scale appear significant (without necessarily proving that the economies of scale will actually lead to more innovation). Thus, this approach infers macroeconomic benefits from micro-level gains. On the other hand, the consumer choice approach defers the determination on whether a business strategy generates macro-level gains to 'the competitive process that allows consumers to make choices'.[61] This implies that macro-level efficiencies are protected as outcomes of protecting the rivalry and the market structure.[62] In essence, the consumer choice approach requires that the micro-level benefits also muster at the macro-level in terms of consumer choice, that is whether the business strategy reduces consumer choice or variety.

The emphasis on variety or diversity as a goal of competition policy is viewed as a mechanism for dealing with, and accounting for, the complexity of the digital economy. For example, in 'Complexity, Diversity, and Antitrust', Farrell argues that diversity is 'most valuable in complex markets, because in simple markets everyone knows what to do'.[63] Conversely, complex markets are characterized by network effects, feedback loops, and non-linearity, which makes it difficult to predict their future trajectories and how the markets will evolve. These characteristics are particularly prominent in digital markets, which display the traits of complex systems and often lead to entrenched market positions.[64] In such cases, cultivating an open and diverse marketplace, characterized by numerous distinct firms employing varying strategies and business models, becomes essential to foster experimentation and innovation. The underlying argument seems to be that, given the complexity and significant uncertainty, it might be imprudent to 'put all your eggs in one basket and closely monitor that basket'.[65]

Similarly, in their article 'Complexity-Minded Antirust', Petit and Schrepel underscore the need to consider the role of increasing returns, an important attribute of complex systems.[66] According to them, the economic theory of increasing returns anticipates a potential risk of markets becoming irreversibly locked into inferior products, services, or technologies.[67] The implication for competition policy is that 'two birds in the bush is better than one in the hand'.[68] Thus,

[60] ibid 31.
[61] ibid 28.
[62] ibid 27.
[63] Farrell, 'Complexity, Diversity, and Antitrust' (n 4) 168.
[64] Ioannis Lianos, 'Competition Law for a Complex Economy' (2019) 50 IIC-International Review of Intellectual Property and Competition Law 643.
[65] Farrell, 'Complexity, Diversity, and Antitrust' (n 4) 167.
[66] Petit and Schrepel (n 5).
[67] ibid 24.
[68] ibid.

in situations characterized by increasing returns, competition policy 'must safeguard alternative products, services, and technology, even if this requires imposing a tax or granting a subsidy to maintain second best options'.[69]

Overall, the consumer choice approach brings several benefits relative to the price and efficiency model.[70] First, it is thought to result in 'better substantive outcomes', particularly in markets where there is little price competition. Second, it brings simplicity to the application of competition rules. This is because framing the issues in terms of consumer choice makes it easier to communicate policy objectives in simple and intuitive terms both to non-specialists and to the public.[71] Moreover, its focus on observed proxies brings more transparency because variety is easier to quantify and assess than quality or innovation.[72] This simplicity and quantifiability are especially important in markets characterized by complexity. Third, the consumer choice approach provides a unifying framework for the application of competition and consumer protection laws, highlighting their synergies and policy boundaries.[73] Finally, data privacy as a non-price competition parameter receives more prominence in the consumer choice approach than in the price and efficiency paradigm.

B. Application to Data Privacy

The next question is how the consumer choice approach applies to competition concerning privacy and how it differs from the quality-based approach. Data privacy, be it as an element of quality or choice, features prominently in the consumer choice approach. This is particularly true because some of the sectors where the consumer choice approach is considered to yield superior results are also areas where data privacy plays a crucial role. For example, the consumer choice approach is considered important in markets where price competition is minimal or non-existent. It is worth noting that most digital markets, especially those where privacy is a key concern, typically lack monetary price competition. The approach is also considered to yield better outcomes in markets 'where independent decision making and creativity, rather than price, are the main forms of competition'.[74]

69 ibid.

70 However, the approach does face certain criticisms. One critique concerns its limited applicability to complex non-price exclusionary strategies and its neglect of the trade-offs consumers often make between price and non-price factors. Additionally, some critics highlight the absence of empirical evidence supporting the assertion that heightened rivalry invariably leads to greater innovation and consumer welfare. See Nicolas Petit, 'Intel, Leveraging Rebates and the Goals of Article 102 TFEU' (2015) 11 European Competition Journal 26, 63.

71 Averitt and Lande, 'Using the "Consumer Choice" Approach' (n 43) 179.

72 Neil Averitt, Robert Lande, and Paul Nihoul, '"Consumer Choice" Is Where We Are All Going—So Let's Go Together' (2011) 2 Concurrences 1–2.

73 Neil Averitt and Robert Lande, 'Consumer Choice: The Practical Reason for Both Antitrust and Consumer Protection Law' (1997a) 10 Loy Consumer L Rev 44.

74 Averitt and Lande, 'Using the "Consumer Choice" Approach' (n 43) 196.

Specific markets in this category include media, health-care, and high-tech sectors, where privacy is important. This is because, first, given the lack of price and the dynamic nature of the digital economy, innovation is crucial for many digital markets.

Second, certain digital platforms, including Facebook and Google, are increasingly assuming the role of media companies by tailoring content for users through their algorithms. Related to this, there exist concerns regarding the consolidation of the digital sector and its potential repercussions on media plurality.[75] To the extent that this is valid, a variety of algorithms and organizational independence can be crucial for fostering innovation and providing choice in terms of perspectives. More importantly, with the rising concern over fake news and privacy issues, there is a growing discourse on the need for alternatives to ad-supported business models, which benefit from lower privacy protection.[76] Organizational independence seems to be an important component in ensuring a variety of business models (and algorithms) that accommodate different approaches to data privacy.

Third, it is argued that industries where diversity and choice hold paramount importance are also particularly prone to market failures related to information.[77] This is equally relevant for the discussion on data privacy in the digital context, where market failures stemming from information asymmetry, status quo bias, cognitive limitations, and 'dysfunctional equilibrium' are pervasive.[78] Thus, it is plausible that privacy will benefit from the consumer choice approach. The question is how.

Broadly speaking, the application of the consumer choice approach to data privacy resembles the quality-based theory of harm, particularly the approach adopted by the Commission in *Microsoft/LinkedIn*. However, a few notable differences merit attention.

The major difference between the consumer choice approach and the quality-based theory is that while the former departs from the contemporary 'consumer welfare' (price and efficiency) framework, the latter is formulated within this framework. While the quality-based approach, as demonstrated in the *Microsoft/LinkedIn* merger, can address a decrease in consumer choice regarding privacy, the consumer choice approach goes further. The quality-based approach treats a reduction in choice regarding data privacy as one mechanism through which efficiency and consumer welfare could be harmed, whereas the consumer choice approach presupposes a harm to efficiency and consumer welfare when choice is

75 See Autoritat Catalana de la Competència (n 26) 5–6.

76 See Shoshana Zuboff, *The Age of Surveillance Capitalism: The Fight for a Human Future at the New Frontier of Power* (PublicAffairs 2019).

77 Averitt and Lande, 'Using the "Consumer Choice" Approach' (n 43) 179.

78 See Alessandro Acquisti, 'Privacy and Market Failure: Three Reasons for Concern, and Three Reasons for Hope' (2012) 10 Journal on Telecommunications and High Technology Law 227. Joseph Farrell, 'Can Privacy Be Just Another Good?' (2012) 10 Journal on Telecommunications & High Technology Law 251.

reduced. This suggests that with the quality-based theory, one needs to demonstrate that the decrease in choice is detrimental to consumer welfare. This process typically requires analysis of the incentives of the parties to engage in such conduct and balancing the reduction in data privacy with other efficiency gains.

On the other hand, when using the consumer choice approach, the focus is on assessing whether the conduct 'significantly limits the range of choices' in relation to data privacy that the free market would have provided. Under the consumer choice approach, one need not prove how conduct actually reduces efficiency; it is presumed from the reduction in variety or harm to the competitive process.[79] This significantly impacts the burden of proof in competition cases, especially when the behaviour in question is linked with alleged efficiency gains.

Taking the *Microsoft/LinkedIn* merger as an example, in the quality-based approach, the Commission identified and analysed the incentives behind Microsoft's pre-installation of LinkedIn on Windows PCs and its integration with Office products and how such conduct could foreclose competing PSNs. This foreclosure was considered harmful to consumer choice in terms of data privacy because it would reduce PSNs such as XING to outliers. In reaching this conclusion, the Commission had to show that XING provided better-quality privacy than LinkedIn and that its foreclosure would leave privacy-sensitive users with lower quality alternatives. In this sense, the ultimate harm is not the reduction in choice per se, but the reduction in the quality of privacy that results from a reduction in choice due to the foreclosure of XING. Thus, for the quality-based argument, it is the level of privacy after the merger (after XING is foreclosed) that is decisive and that must be shown to be inferior to the pre-merger level of privacy (where XING is active), whereas if one adopts the consumer choice approach, it suffices to demonstrate that XING and LinkedIn are sufficiently differentiated alternatives without the need to show that one is better than the other. This implies that the new level of data privacy after the merger (ie after XING is foreclosed) is not important; what matters is the elimination of a significant alternative. The *Facebook/WhatsApp* decision may be helpful here to elaborate this point further.

As noted in Section II, the theory of harm relates to a reduction in the level of data privacy following a change in WhatsApp's privacy policy, which allowed Facebook to use WhatsApp user data for advertising. In following the quality-based theory, one must demonstrate that, first, the merger will lead to changes in WhatsApp's privacy policy and that these changes are the result of reduced competition or market power. This involves analysing the extent to which Facebook imposes competitive constraints on WhatsApp's privacy policy, the incentives of the merged entity to change that policy, and the possible loss by WhatsApp of customers following the change. It also includes assessing consumers' ability to limit

[79] See Behrens (n 59) 28.

WhatsApp's policy change and determining whether the resulting loss of consumers by WhatsApp would be unprofitable in light of the other benefits accruing from the change. More importantly, one must demonstrate how the change in privacy policy entails a reduction in the level of privacy for its users, which is the most challenging task. This analysis is necessary because the conduct that reduces WhatsApp users' privacy is the decision to change WhatsApp's privacy policy. Thus, the competition analysis focuses on the incentives and counter-incentives to do so. In this regard, it is the new level of data privacy following the change in WhatsApp's policy that is problematic from the perspective of the quality-based theory of harm.

Conversely, when using the consumer choice approach, this level is not as important, if at all. What is important for the consumer choice analysis is whether Facebook and WhatsApp offer sufficiently differentiated services in terms of privacy (which they seem to do) and whether the merger would leave users with less choice than before the merger. It is not necessary, in this case, to examine whether the merged entity will change its privacy policy, its incentives for doing so, and whether the change in privacy policy constitutes a reduction in the level of privacy offered pre-merger. Indeed, such an analysis would strengthen the argument and could be conducted in relation to the consumer choice approach, but it is not required. Even if one saw the need to evaluate the incentives to change the privacy policy or alternatively to demonstrate the need for organizational independence in order to ensure that WhatsApp maintains its privacy policy, it is not necessary to show that the change in privacy policy entails a reduction in the level of privacy offered pre-merger. It suffices to show that users have fewer options, which is easier to prove than how the change in privacy policy entails a reduction in privacy, and that this change results from reduced competition.[80]

Another difference between the quality-based and consumer choice approaches might arise if the reduction in privacy is accompanied by efficiency gains, for example in the form of better-targeted ads for advertisers. In contrast to the quality-based approach, which requires consideration of efficiency gains when analysing competitive effects, the consumer choice approach presumes from the outset that any reduction in choice inflicts harm on efficiency and thus constitutes anticompetitive behaviour.[81] This effectively shifts the burden of proof onto the defendant. Thus, under the consumer choice approach, defendants would have an additional hurdle of showing that sufficient competition is left to ensure optimal choice for consumers.

[80] Most of the controversy over incorporating privacy into competition analysis revolves around what a reduction in privacy means and whether such a reduction is linked to market power. See Esayas, 'Privacy-as-a-Quality Competition Parameter' (n 15).

[81] See Nicolas Petit, 'The Judgment of the EU Court of Justice in Intel and the Rule of Reason in Abuse of Dominance Cases' (2017) 9 <https://ssrncom/abstract=3086402> accessed 8 February 2024; Behrens (n 59) 28.

Overall, to the extent that competition policy is open to the consumer choice approach, incorporating privacy into competition analysis as a non-price parameter becomes relatively easy, both in terms of measuring the harm and the burden of proof on the plaintiffs.

C. The Prospects and Challenges of the Consumer Choice Approach under EU Law

Given that choice and other non-price parameters are important in the price and efficiency paradigm, the key difference in practice with the consumer choice approach boils down to the following aspects: the extent to which the Commission is required to demonstrate that alleged anticompetitive conduct can lead to adverse effects on final consumers in terms of higher price, lower quality, or reduced innovation. Alternatively, to what extent can harm to consumer welfare and anticompetitive effects be presumed from a mere foreclosure? A related, yet more procedural matter pertains to whether efficiency gains constitute part of the dispositive analysis of the anticompetitive conduct or are simply a justification.

More generally, to the extent that the consumer choice approach aims to protect rivalry and variety, EU competition law seems to be more open to this approach than the US system. There may be two reasons for this. First, there is broad consensus that the price and efficiency approach is predominant in the US system because of the significant influence of the Chicago School of economics.[82] Second, despite the increasing influence of the Chicago School on EU competition policy, the practice of the Commission and the EU courts paints a rather mixed picture—endorsing the Ordoliberal-based consumer choice approach and the Chicago-inspired 'consumer welfare' approach at different times, and sometimes in one and the same judgment.[83]

On the one hand, the proposal by the Commission to adopt a 'more economic approach' together with the 'effects-based' philosophy advocated in its Treaty on the Functioning of the European Union (TFEU) Article 102 Guidelines seem to focus competition policy enforcement on price and efficiency as the driving forces.[84] This approach is widely acknowledged to be inspired by the Chicago School and

[82] See William Kovacic, 'Intellectual DNA of Modern US Competition Law for Dominant Firm Conduct: The Chicago/Harvard Double Helix' (2007) 1 Columbia Business Law Review 1.

[83] See Petit, 'The Judgment of the EU Court of Justice' (n 81) 13.

[84] See European Commission, 'Guidance on the Commission's Enforcement Priorities in Applying Article 82 of the EC Treaty to Abusive Exclusionary Conduct by Dominant Undertakings' [2009] OJ C45/7. Although this approach is advocated in relation to Article 102, a few merger decisions also adopt it. For a detailed discussion of the 'economic approach', see Josef Drexl, Wolfgang Kerber, and Rupprecht Podszun, *Competition Policy and the Economic Approach: Foundations and Limitations* (Edward Elgar 2011).

limits the application of Article 102 to situations where concrete harms for consumers (welfare) and efficiency can be shown using specific economic tools.[85]

One such economic tool that the Commission envisaged using is the 'as efficient competitor' (AEC) test, which involves examining whether the alleged conduct leads to foreclosure of competitors that are 'as efficient' as the dominant undertaking. This would require the Commission to consider 'economic data relating to cost and sales prices, and in particular whether the dominant undertaking is engaging in below-cost pricing'.[86] This implies that the Commission will normally intervene when the conduct is capable of foreclosing competitors that are as efficient as the dominant undertaking, which, in turn, means that foreclosure of less efficient competitors is tolerated. The analysis of 'costs and prices' also carriers procedural implications regarding the burden of proof; that is, an assessment of the efficiency gains forms part of the dispositive analysis needed to determine the anticompetitive effects. Conversely, the consumer choice approach presumes harm to consumers and efficiency from foreclosure, with the burden of proof resting on the defendant to establish and substantiate any efficiency gains. These differences set the stage for the subsequent analysis of the practices employed by the Commission and EU courts.

The Commission has adopted the 'effect-based' approach in several decisions. The *Microsoft/LinkedIn* merger decision discussed above is one example where the Commission not only had to show the potential foreclosure of competitors but also why such foreclosure produces harmful effects on consumers through a reduction in quality. In this regard, the Commission used privacy as one quality attribute that the foreclosure of competitors might negatively affect. The effect-based approach has been endorsed by EU courts on several occasions. For example, in *Post Danmark I,* the Court of Justice of the European Union (CJEU) held that Article 102 does not 'seek to ensure that competitors less efficient than the undertaking with the dominant position should remain on the market'.[87] This judgment clearly shows that harm to consumers cannot be presumed from the foreclosure of competitors that are less efficient and 'less attractive to consumers from the point of view of, among other things, price, choice, quality or innovation'.[88]

Moreover, highlighting the importance of the AEC test, the CJEU noted that the analysis of the anticompetitive effect of price-related practices needs to be based on the costs and prices of the dominant undertaking, particularly on whether prices are below cost.[89] The judgment, including the initial analysis by the Danish

[85] Paul Nihoul, 'The Ruling of the General Court in Intel: Towards the End of an Effect-Based Approach in European Competition Law?' (2014) 5 Journal of European Competition Law & Practice 521, 522.

[86] European Commission, 'Guidance on Article 102 Enforcement Priorities' (n 84) para 25.

[87] Case C-209/10 *Post Danmark AS v Konkurrancerådet* EU:C:2013:172, para 21.

[88] ibid para 22.

[89] ibid para 28.

Competition Authority, also takes into account the efficiency gains (or lack thereof) resulting from the alleged conduct. Thus, the judgment captures both aspects of the 'effect-based' approach, that is the need for concrete negative effects on consumers and the need for the dispositive analysis to consider the efficiency gains.

On the other hand, some decisions under Article 102 seem to espouse the consumer choice approach. Examples include the Commission decisions in *Microsoft*[90] and *Intel*,[91] the CJEU decisions in *Continental Can*, *Hoffmann-La Roche*, *France Telecom*, and *British Airways*.[92] The *Intel* decision by the Commission and the General Court (GC) are viewed as the most detailed and 'useful' for the consumer choice approach,[93] although the CJEU decision dampened this enthusiasm. The case attracted particular attention as it was the first price-related conduct decided after the adoption of Commission's Article 102 Guidance paper, which advocated the 'economic' and 'effect-based' approach. Intel was accused of two exclusionary practices in the market for x86 central processing units (CPUs or chips).[94] The first relates to Intel's financial payment to computer manufacturers 'to delay, cancel or in some other way restrict the commercialization' of products containing chips made by its competitor, AMD.[95] The second relates to rebates offered to computer manufacturers upon purchasing all, or nearly all, of their x86 CPU demands from Intel.[96] The Commission found both practices unlawful under Article 102. This was later affirmed by the GC.

In a statement that seemed to endorse the Ordoliberal view and the consumer choice approach, the Commission found the first practice abusive because it prevented AMD-based products from reaching the market, and thus '*customers were deprived of a choice* which they would have otherwise had'.[97] On the rebates, the Commission indicated that Intel's conduct was 'capable of inducing loyalty and thereby *limiting consumer choice* and *foreclosing the access of competitors to the market*'.[98] 'Choice' and 'access to the market' are concepts associated with the Ordoliberal school. The question is whether the mere reduction in choice makes the conduct illegal. Although the Commission conducted 150 pages of economic analysis using the AEC test, it indicated that this was 'not indispensable' to its finding of infringement.[99]

[90] Case COMP/C-3/37.792 *Microsoft* decision of 24 March 2004.
[91] Case COMP/C3/37.990 *Intel* decision of 13 May 2009.
[92] See also Paul Nihoul, '"Freedom of Choice": The Emergence of a Powerful Concept in European Competition Law' in Paul Nihoul, Nicolas Charbit, and Elisa Ramundo (eds), *Freedom of Choice—The Emergence of a Powerful Concept in European Competition Law* (Concurrences Review 2016).
[93] ibid 16.
[94] Case COMP/C3/37.990 *Intel* (n 91) para 917.
[95] ibid para 1641.
[96] ibid para 926.
[97] ibid para 1678 (emphasis added).
[98] ibid para 1679 (emphasis added).
[99] ibid para 925.

The EU courts have endorsed such an approach in several instances. For example, in affirming the Commission's decision in *Intel*, the GC found the exclusivity rebates as per se illegal because 'they are by their very nature capable of foreclosing competitors'.[100] The Court underlined that the practices 'are designed to remove or restrict the purchaser's *freedom to choose* his sources of supply and to deny other producers *access to the market*'.[101] Moreover, in contradiction to what the 'effect-based' approach and the AEC test seem to require, the GC stated that there is no need to establish concrete harms to any of these practices by using specific quantitative tools.[102] Furthermore, the Court stated that the AEC is not necessary to show anticompetitive effect because 'a foreclosure effect occurs not only where *access to the market is made impossible for competitors*' but also when '*access ... [is] made more difficult*'.[103] This seems to suggest that a further weakening of competition, albeit insignificant, as a result of the conduct of a dominant undertaking can be illegal. On the procedural aspect, the Court clarified that once it is proven that the actions of a dominant entity can potentially exclude competitors or hinder market access, the onus is on the dominant entity to objectively justify its actions, for example through efficiency gains.[104]

The CJEU's jurisprudence in *Hoffmann-La Roche*[105] and *Post Danmark II*[106] reflects this stance. For example, in the latter, the Court found the loyalty rebates offered by the dominant undertaking illegal because they 'tend to make it more difficult for those customers to obtain supplies from competing undertakings'.[107] Regarding the AEC test, the Court held that the 'application of the AEC test does not constitute a necessary condition for a finding of abuse'.[108] The judgment also considers efficiency gains as a defence mechanism.[109] These judgments were viewed as fundamentally 'irreconcilable' with, and signalling the end of, an effect-based approach in European competition law.[110]

The crux of the preceding discussion is that both the Commission's practice and the rulings of the EU courts indicate that, for certain practices, the mere foreclosure of competitors or making competitors' access to the market more difficult may suffice for such conduct to be deemed illegal under Article 102. One practical implication of this stance is that the Commission does not need to show concrete negative effects on consumers, using specific quantitative tools such as the AEC

[100] Case T-286/09 *Intel v Commission* EU:T:2014:547, para 85.
[101] See ibid paras 77, 78, and 176 (emphasis added).
[102] See ibid para 104.
[103] ibid paras 146–49 (emphasis added).
[104] ibid para 81. Also Case C-23/14 *Post Danmark A/S v Konkurrenceradet (Post Danmark II)* EU:C:2015:651, paras 47–48.
[105] Case 85/76 *Hoffmann-La Roche v Commission* ECLI:EU:C:1979:36.
[106] *Post Danmark II* (n 104).
[107] ibid para 42.
[108] ibid para 50.
[109] ibid paras 47–48.
[110] See Petit, 'The Judgment of the EU Court of Justice' (n 81) 4; Nihoul (n 85).

test. A related procedural implication is that the burden of proof rests on the defendant to present evidence of efficiency gains that might offset the harm to competition. This implies that the analysis of efficiency is not part of the substantive analysis of the finding of infringement but rather serves as a defence mechanism.[111] Moreover, the above judgments, particularly the Commission's and GC's decision in *Intel*, are widely seen as endorsements of Ordoliberal thought and the consumer choice approach.[112]

This notwithstanding, whether the above approach is (or should be) the driving force of EU competition policy in general, and even in rebate cases, continues to be controversial.[113] For example, Petit rejects the idea that *Intel* endorses the consumer choice approach.[114] First, although consumer choice played an important role in the above judgments, including *Intel*, it was by no means the only factor in the analysis. In other words, most often, the reduction in consumer choice was accompanied by foreclosure of competitors, and thus consumer choice was not treated as 'an end in itself'.[115]

It was amid this controversy that the CJEU delivered its verdict in *Intel* and was expected to resolve the controversy.[116] However, the Court seems to have chosen a cautious approach, siding with neither the 'effect-based' nor the 'consumer choice' approach. The Court set aside the decision and returned the case to the GC to assess the impact of the practices considering the efficiency gains presented by Intel. Specifically, the CJEU clarified that, if the dominant entity refutes allegations that its conduct has the potential to stifle competition, the Commission can only reach a finding of abuse after weighing the anticompetitive effects against the efficiency gains that could also benefit consumers.[117] Moreover, the Court noted the 'important role' that the AEC test played in the Commission's assessment (despite being conducted for the sake of completeness) and faulted the GC for failing to consider Intel's argument regarding the test.[118] The Court also reiterated the approach in *Post Danmark I* and indicated that Article 102 does not protect competitors less efficient than the undertaking in a dominant position.[119] For some, the

[111] Nihoul (n 85) 527.

[112] See ibid; Petit, 'The Judgment of the EU Court of Justice' (n 81) 13.

[113] Following the Commission's decision in *Intel* (n 100), two Commission officials disagreed in academic journals over the line to be taken in relation to the appeal. See Wouter Wils, 'The Judgment of the EU General Court in Intel and the So-Called 'More Economic Approach' to Abuse of Dominance' (2014) 37 World Competition 405; Lucas Peeperkorn, 'Conditional Pricing: Why the General Court Is Wrong in Intel and What the Court of Justice Can Do to Rebalance the Assessment of Rebates' (2015) 1 Concurrences Journal 43.

[114] Petit, 'Intel, Leveraging Rebates' (n 70).

[115] ibid 61–62. However, this argument treats foreclosure of competitors as an outcome of the reduction in choice. Although this is true with some judgments, in others, such as *Wanadoo (France Telecom)*, it is the foreclosure that leads to reduced consumer choice—then essentially protecting choice. See Averitt, Lande, and Nihoul (n 72) 2.

[116] Case C-413/14 P *Intel v Commission* EU:C:2017:632.

[117] ibid.

[118] ibid para 144.

[119] ibid para 133.

CJEU's decision is a clear endorsement of the 'effect-based approach' and a rejection of the Ordoliberal-based consumer choice approach.[120]

Although the decision dampens some of the enthusiasm that followed the Commission's and the GC's *Intel* decisions on the Ordoliberal view and the consumer choice approach, it does not kill it off entirely. Contrary to claims that the decision adopts an 'efficiency test' and an 'effect-based' approach for exclusive and royalty rebates, the judgment does not affect the principle that exclusive dealing and loyalty rebates are capable of foreclosing competitors and are prima facie abusive under Article 102.[121] Although the decision requires the Commission to 'assess the possible existence of a strategy aiming to exclude competitors that *are at least as efficient as* the dominant undertaking', this arises only when the dominant undertaking challenges, 'on the basis of supporting evidence', the Commission's conclusion on abuse.[122] Hence, the decision provides only a 'procedural answer to a substantive question'.[123]

The judgment's main clarification is that if the Commission conducts the AEC test, and this analysis plays a role in a finding of abuse, the defendant has the right to challenge the manner in which the AEC test has been conducted. In this case, the GC must examine its correct application. The decision does not address whether the Commission is obliged to conduct the AEC test,[124] nor does it consider what would have happened if the Commission had not, in fact, conducted the AEC test. Moreover, it still leaves the burden of proof on the defendant to show efficiency gains and produce corroborating evidence.[125] In so doing, the decision seems to take the middle ground in the sense that the 'effect-based approach' becomes part of the dispositive analysis only when the defendant challenges, 'on the basis of supporting evidence', the Commission's conclusion that the conduct restricts competition. Once the defendant presents evidence of efficiency gains, the Commission needs to establish the anticompetitive effect, among other mechanisms, by showing that the conduct forecloses an equally efficient competitor.

In light of the above discussion, the door is not closed for the Commission and the EU courts to rely on the consumer choice approach in some instances, which may benefit privacy. This is particularly the case with Article 102-related practices, such as blocking a privacy-friendly app from platforms or restricting the data-portability rights of individuals. This is because such practices could be viewed as limiting 'market access' and consumer choice. Additionally, given that the *Intel* judgment and the effects-based approach concentrate on price-related practices

[120] Petit, 'The Judgment of the EU Court of Justice' (n 81) 14–15.

[121] See Case C-413/14 *Intel v Commission* (n 116) paras 136–38.

[122] ibid paras 138–39 (emphasis added).

[123] James Venit, 'The Judgment of the European Court of Justice in Intel v Commission: A Procedural Answer to a Substantive Question?' (2017) 13 European Competition Journal 172.

[124] However, the Court indicated that the AEC is one mechanism for showing the effect of conduct on competition. See Case C-413/14 *Intel v Commission* (n 116) para 136.

[125] ibid para 138.

under Article 102, the Commission may still maintain a broader margin to resort to the consumer choice approach, particularly in merger cases affecting non-price parameters such as data privacy.

Indeed, even in the context of Article 102, the Commission is revisiting its stance on the more economic approach. In March 2023, it released a communication outlining proposals for amending the 2008 Guidance on enforcement priorities.[126] This communication was accompanied by a call for evidence and a policy brief that provides the background for these initiatives.[127] While the policy brief reiterates the Commission's commitment to the 'effect-based approach', it emphasizes the need to make it 'workable' in light of the experiences gathered over the years and the substantial developments in the economy. The Commission highlights the significance of two key drivers behind the amendment. The first driver is the growing trend of 'market concentration' and increasing 'importance of digital markets and services, in both economic and societal terms'.[128] Specifically, the Commission underscores the importance of strong network effects and 'winner-takes-all' dynamics in digital markets, necessitating effective and swift enforcement of Article 102 of the TFEU before markets tip.[129]

The second driver pertains to the challenges associated with the effect-based approach. Given the threat of market tipping, the effect-based approach could establish an excessively high standard for intervention, rendering enforcement against practices that restrict competition unduly burdensome or even impossible.[130] This can have serious adverse consequences for consumers, the EU economy, and society. As a result, the Commission has suggested several amendments to the 2008 Guidance that move away from the effects-based approach. Of special significance is the Commission's note on the role of competition law in ensuring consumer choice, which ultimately contributes to the achievement of broader societal objectives, including maintaining plurality in a democratic society.[131]

In this regard, one proposal is to broaden the definition of anticompetitive foreclosure. The Commission, drawing on its enforcement experience and the clarifications provided by case law, suggests that anticompetitive foreclosure 'should be understood as not only referring to conduct that can result in the full exclusion or marginalisation of actual or potential competition, but also to ... conduct that weakens an effective competitive structure even without necessarily producing the full exclusion or marginalization of competitors'.[132] According to the Commission,

[126] Amendments to the Guidance on the Commission's Enforcement Priorities in Applying Article 82 of the EC Treaty to Abusive Exclusionary Conducts by Dominant Undertakings C (2023) 1923 final.

[127] Linsey McCallum and others, 'A Dynamic and Workable Effects-Based Approach to Abuse of Dominance' (2023) 1 Competition Policy Brief 1.

[128] ibid.

[129] ibid 2.

[130] ibid 4.

[131] ibid 1 (citing the GC's judgment in Case T-604/18 *Google and Alphabet v Commission* EU:T:2022:541, para 1028).

[132] McCallum and others (n 127) 4.

this stance aligns with recent judgments that determine abuse based on whether the conduct in question negatively affects an effective competitive structure.[133]

Another suggested amendment pertains to the notion of foreclosure of as-efficient competitors. While the Commission recognizes the general importance of this standard in relation to price-related abuses, it underscores the need to give serious consideration to the role that smaller competitors and product diversity can play in the competitive process in certain markets. Highlighting the significance of such an approach for digital markets, the Commission observes as follows:

> In particular, in markets where barriers to entry and expansion are significant, such as in the presence of economies of scale or network effects that lead to the emergence of dominant firms, market challengers may not be expected to be able to achieve the same or even a similar cost structure as the incumbent. However, such competitors could still be successful in satisfying specific consumer needs. For instance, in certain digital markets, competitors may offer features that are particularly attractive to a specific group of customers. This may allow them to gain a foothold in the market, with the prospect of scaling up volumes and potentially increasing their efficiency at a later stage.[134]

These proposed amendments appear to highlight the significance of consumer choice and market structure. Specifically, the Commission appears to acknowledge the importance of diversity and choice in digital markets marked by network effects, where smaller entities can satisfy the needs of niche consumer groups and still play a critical role in the competitive landscape. This emphasis on diversity and market structure aligns well with the consumer choice approach, which consequently could facilitate the integration of data privacy considerations into competition analysis. Therefore, while the quality-based theory of harm, exemplified by the Commission's decision on the *Microsoft/LinkedIn* case, allows for the inclusion of data privacy within existing 'effects-based' frameworks, the analysis provided in this section offers a broader alternative for incorporating data privacy into competition analysis. Its primary advantages stem from its reliance on observable proxies, which simplify the process of quantifying and assessing harms to privacy and other non-price factors. This, in turn, makes it attractive in markets characterized by complexity, entry barriers due to network effects, and involving products or services with broader societal significance.

[133] ibid 4 (citing recent CJEU's judgments including Case C-680/20 *Unilever Italia Mkt Operations Srl v Autorità Garante della Concorrenza e del Mercato* EU:C:2023:33, para 36).

[134] McCallum and others (n 127) 5.

IV. The Maverick-Firm Theory of Harm

Another variation for incorporating data privacy into competition analysis is via the lens of the maverick-firm theory of harm that focuses on the acquisition or elimination of a firm that plays a 'disruptive role'.[135] The main departure from the above two theories of harm is that the maverick-firm theory may be used to enjoin a merger without the need to demonstrate that the merger leads to a significant increase in market power.[136] Another advantage of the maverick-firm theory is its potential application to a merger involving companies that are not close competitors in a market.

Both the EU and the US Guidelines for horizontal mergers underline the importance of a maverick firm. According to the EU Guidelines, mergers that fall below the Herfindal–Hirschman Index (HHI) level of 1,000 are unlikely to generate anticompetitive effects unless 'one of the merging firms is a maverick firm'.[137] The Guidelines do not provide a clear definition of a maverick firm but emphasize the 'disruptive role' of the firm in preventing market coordination. This could be exhibited by refusing to follow competitors' price increases or by choosing strategic paths that diverge from those of its coordinating competitors.[138] Thus, the Commission envisages intervening, regardless of low market shares, if the merged entity is likely to abandon the maverick business strategy following the merger.

The US Guidelines provide more elaborate guidance, designating a firm as a maverick if it disrupts market conditions to the benefit of customers. Specifically, a firm is a maverick if (1) it 'threatens to disrupt market conditions with a new technology or business model', (2) it has an 'incentive to take the lead in price cutting', (3) it has 'the ability and incentive to expand production rapidly using available capacity', or (4) it 'has often resisted otherwise prevailing industry norms to cooperate on price setting or other terms of competition'.[139] Under the US Guidelines, the existence of a maverick is evidence that the merger may have potential anticompetitive effects, and such evidence is given as much weight as the merging parties' market share and head-to-head competition.[140]

135 Pamela Harbour and Tara Koslov, 'Section 2 in a Web 2.0 World: An Expanded Vision of Relevant Product Markets' (2010) 76 Antitrust Law Journal 769, 795. Maurice Stucke and Allen Grunes, *Big Data and Competition Policy* (OUP 2016) 262; Taylor Owings, 'Identifying a Maverick: When Antitrust Law Should Protect a Low-Cost Competitor' (2013) 66 Vanderbilt Law Review 323; Courtney Lang, 'The Maverick Theory: Creating Turbulence for Mergers' (2014) 59 Saint Louis University Law Journal 257.

136 Directorate-General for Competition, 'EU Merger Control and Innovation', *Competition Policy Brief* (2016) 3.

137 European Commission, 'Guidelines on the Assessment of Horizontal Mergers under the Council Regulation on the Control of Concentrations between Undertakings' (2004) OJ C31/5, para 20.

138 ibid para 42.

139 US Department of Justice & FTC, 'Horizontal Merger Guidelines' (2010) 3–4 <https://www.ftc.gov/system/files/documents/public_statements/804291/100819hmg.pdf>.

140 ibid.

Looking only at the Guidelines, the maverick-firm theory of harm seems to have a broader reach in the United States than the EU and has been applied to several mergers.[141] The common thread in all these mergers is that big players try to acquire a player with a small market share that plays a 'disruptive role', such as through aggressive price cutting.[142] Given the small market share of the acquired firms, some of the acquisitions were less likely to raise anticompetitive concerns under traditional merger control focused on market power. In fact, most of the acquisitions were undertaken by the second largest player, and thus efficiency gains were foreseeable, by strengthening the competitive capabilities of the second-placed firms against the market leaders.[143] Nonetheless, the Department of Justice (DoJ) relied on the maverick-firm theory of harm to challenge the mergers, claiming that the smaller firms played a 'disruptive role' in the market and that their independence was important for competition in their respective markets.[144]

Although the EU Guidelines seem to focus on the maverick firm's role in disrupting coordinated conduct, the practical application of the theory has been broader and more in line with the US approach. According to one survey, of the five cases where a maverick was established, only one focused on the removal of a maverick firm that increases the risk of tacit collusion.[145] In the majority of cases, the maverick concept was used to assess the unilateral effects of the merger, focusing on the post-merger repositioning of the maverick.[146] In these decisions, the Commission describes the maverick as a firm with a small market share, insider to the merger, and perceived to be an aggressive competitor. Among the terms used to describe the maverick firm are 'aggressive competitor', 'aggressive maverick', 'low-price competitor', and 'pricing maverick'.[147] However, neither the (EU or US) Guidelines nor the decisions clarify how the maverick is to be distinguished from any other aggressive competitor.[148]

In this regard, there are efforts to elaborate the 'disruptive role' of the maverick firm by drawing insight from the literature on disruptive innovation.[149] According to this literature, disruption occurs in two ways: low-end and new-market footholds.[150] Low-end disruption arises when 'a smaller company with fewer resources'

141 See Owings (n 135) 332.

142 ibid 324. See also Lang (n 135).

143 Owings (n 135) 324.

144 See ibid 324–25.

145 Joseph Bromfield and Matthew Olczak, 'The Role of the Maverick Firm Concept in European Commission Merger Decisions' (2018) 14 Journal of Competition Law & Economics 179, 189.

146 ibid 189–90.

147 ibid 185–86.

148 See *US v H & R Block, Inc* (2011) 2d, 79 (Dist of Col) (criticizing the DoJ for failing to 'set out a clear standard, based on functional or economic considerations, to distinguish a maverick from any other aggressive competitor'). For critics of the European Commission's use of the theory, see Bromfield and Olczak (n 145).

149 See Owings (n 135); Lang (n 135).

150 Clayton Christensen, Michael Raynor, and Rory McDonald, 'What Is Disruptive Innovation?' (December 2015) Harvard Business Review <https://hbr.org/2015/12/what-is-disruptive-innovation>.

is able to challenge incumbents 'by successfully targeting those overlooked segments, gaining a foothold by delivering more-suitable functionality—frequently at a lower price'.[151] This occurs because incumbents focus on products and services that sustain growth and higher profitability, leading them to neglect some customer segments. The maverick then caters to the neglected segment and builds its way up to mainstream.[152] New-market disruption arises when a previously non-existent market is created, typically when the maverick finds ways to transform non-users into active consumers.[153] While both disruption models could be useful for incorporating privacy, the low-end foothold seems more attuned to current business practices. Thus, the focus here is on low-end disruption.

Using the above literature, the following three-criteria test could be used to identify a low-end maverick.[154] These are

> (1) the firm offers a product or service that is worse in some way than the traditional offerings, (2) the poor quality is accompanied by a lower price (or some other innovative benefit), and (3) the product or service only works well for a niche segment of consumers who substitute away from the traditional competitors.[155]

This test not only provides a clearer guideline but also imposes more specific and stricter conditions than the ones applied by the EU and the US guidelines. However, establishing that the target firm is a maverick does not necessarily mean that the merger will lead to anticompetitive effects.[156] Two additional conditions need to be fulfilled. The first is to show that the merger will lead to the elimination of the maverick's business strategy. The second condition demonstrates the existence of barriers preventing potential competitors from replicating the maverick's business strategy. This makes for a total of five conditions required to apply the maverick-firm theory.

In light of the above discussion, the question is to what extent this theory can be relied on to incorporate data privacy into mergers. For example, under the US Guidelines, one instance where the maverick-firm theory might be relevant is 'if one of the merging firms has a strong incumbency position and the other merging firm threatens to disrupt market conditions with a new technology or business model'.[157] The Facebook/WhatsApp merger could be viewed from this perspective. At the time WhatsApp was founded, in 2009, Facebook had already overtaken Myspace as the leading social network and had more than 360 million users.

[151] ibid.
[152] However, lack of success does not undermine a firm's disruptive role: see ibid.
[153] ibid. The iPhone is a good example, which disrupted the PC market by the creating 'a new market for internet access'.
[154] See Owings (n 135).
[155] ibid 349.
[156] However, this could create a rebuttable presumption of anticompetitive effects: see ibid 350.
[157] US Department of Justice & FTC (n 139) 2–3.

Moreover, at the global level, innovation is anchored in 'free' business models that rely heavily on collecting and analysing massive amounts of personal data and financing services through targeted advertising. Facebook was one of the success stories behind such business models and had established itself in the market. In contrast, WhatsApp, as noted in Section II, presented itself as a clear alternative to Facebook in terms of how it handled user privacy by offering users an ad-free experience and superior privacy protection for a nominal yearly subscription fee.

In this regard, it can be argued that the Facebook/WhatsApp merger would eliminate a maverick that threatened to disrupt market conditions by harvesting personal information under a new business model based on a small subscription fee, minimal data collection, and no targeted advertising. For example, in the *New York Times* article, entitled 'Founders of an Anti-Facebook Are Won Over', Chen and Goel describe the contrast in ideologies behind the two firms and how the establishment won over the maverick.[158] Similarly, Stucke and Grunes have argued that the acquisition of WhatsApp by Facebook could qualify as the elimination of a maverick that improved the quality of texting apps by offering enhanced privacy protection.[159] However, the authors offer little help on the concrete application of the maverick-firm theory in this particular case. One question that is not adequately answered is why WhatsApp's business model should be considered disruptive and what incentives exist for the merged firm to abandon the maverick's business model. Another question concerns the existence of barriers that might prevent new entrants from replicating WhatsApp's success.

Indeed, as partially discussed in Chapter 4, several behavioural and structural factors affect competition in the field of data privacy. These include information asymmetry, status quo bias, and businesses' deliberate shrouding strategies, which make understanding privacy policies daunting.[160] These challenges are compounded when companies leverage user inertia (through default settings) to complicate privacy-enhancing decisions, with WhatsApp's policy change serving as a prime example.[161] The outcome is a sense of resignation among users.[162] This, in turn, affects the supply of privacy-friendly services. Newcomers struggle to attract users by offering clearer and more privacy-friendly services. Often users do not reward such behaviour as they do not typically invest time in understanding privacy policies, or they have learned from past experiences that their investment is not

[158] Brian Chen and Vindu Goel, 'Founders of an Anti-Facebook Are Won Over', *New York Times* (20 February 2014).

[159] See Stucke and Grunes (n 135) 262.

[160] Farrell, 'Can Privacy Be Just Another Good?' (n 78) 259.

[161] See Esayas, 'Competition in (Data) Privacy' (n 48).

[162] See Joseph Turow, Michael Hennessy, and Nora Draper, 'The Tradeoff Fallacy: How Marketers are Misrepresenting American Consumers and Opening Them Up to Exploitation' (2015) 3 <https://ssrn com/abstract=2820060> accessed 8 February 2024.

rewarding—due to difficulties understanding the policy.[163] This alignment between users (demand) and the firm (supply) is what Farrell calls the 'dysfunctional equilibrium', a state that is very hard to disrupt.[164]

Another relevant consideration, especially significant for services offered for 'free', is referred to as the 'free effect'. This relates to the tendency of free goods to generate externalities by creating expectation among consumers for similar goods and services to be offered free in comparable markets.[165] In addition, the 'free effect' is considered to exert 'nudging' power as consumers gravitate towards free goods even if these goods do not advance their 'revealed preferences'.[166] There is a burgeoning literature on how consumers overvalue free products, with such valuation frequently surpassing cost–benefit disparities.[167] One implication of the 'free effect' is that consumers' willingness to pay for a similar but much better alternative (eg in terms of privacy protection) is significantly reduced.[168] This, in turn, can make entry into markets where services are provided for 'free' difficult.

In this sense, what WhatsApp achieved (building a customer base twice as big as that of Facebook Messenger), by charging small fees and offering an ad-free and more privacy-friendly messaging service, is an indication of a maverick. WhatsApp's success shows that it is possible, albeit difficult, to disrupt the dysfunctional equilibrium and overcome the challenges of the 'free effect'. For this reason, WhatsApp's business model could be considered as 'disruptive'. Similarly, the potential barriers to entry (from network effects, the 'free effect', etc) and the merged entity's incentives, as shown in Section II above, to change WhatsApp's privacy policy could be considered relevant to demonstrate why the elimination of the maverick might have anticompetitive effects. However, given that WhatsApp and Facebook were (and still are) the number one and number two texting apps, the merger could also be caught by the quality-based theory of harm. The added value of the maverick-firm theory comes into play when a dominant player tries to acquire a smaller firm that plays a 'disruptive role' in the market. Thus, here, I will focus on instances where the maverick-firm theory of harm could offer an alternative means of incorporating privacy. One such instance could be the hypothetical acquisition of the Internet search engine DuckDuckGo by the dominant search engine Google.

Google has more than 90 per cent market share in the market for Internet search, collects large amounts of personal data, and uses that data to personalize services

[163] In addition to this, there is significant research showing the limited willingness of users to pay for their privacy, although there is also significant research showing the opposite. See Alessandro Acquisti, Leslie John, and George Loewenstein, 'What Is Privacy Worth?' (2013) 42 Journal of Legal Studies 249.

[164] Farrell, 'Can Privacy Be Just Another Good?' (n 78) 259.

[165] See Michal Gal and Daniel Rubinfeld, 'The Hidden Costs of Free Goods: Implications for Antitrust Enforcement' (2016) 80 Antitrust Law Journal 521, 528–31 (Reference omitted).

[166] ibid 530.

[167] See ibid 528–31.

[168] ibid 531.

and provide targeted advertising. Bing and Yahoo! have a market share of less than 3.9 per cent each.[169] DuckDuckGo's market share in the United States is estimated to be less than 0.8 per cent, and in the EU, it is even smaller.[170] Thus, from a pure market-share perspective, DuckDuckGo's market presence is insignificant, and its acquisition is unlikely to affect market conditions. Despite its low market share, DuckDuckGo could be seen as playing a disruptive role through its data privacy practices, which are key to its growing user base.[171] Its business motto is 'the search engine that does not track you'. Its privacy policy states: 'DuckDuckGo does not collect or share personal information. That is our privacy policy in a nutshell.'[172] The company does not collect search terms or IP addresses and does not store users' search history. All communication between the user and the company servers is encrypted and users have the option to prevent sharing of their search data with sites they visit.

When changes to privacy policies are made, DuckDuckGo undertakes to provide users with a notice highlighting the new changes 'in red'. User location is turned off by default and users must turn it on to obtain localized search results. The advertising it offers is solely context-based, and users have the option to turn off ads. Moreover, the company is engaged in educating users on privacy issues. According to its Chief Executive Officer, one of the company's key strategies in attracting users involves publishing content on search privacy.[173] To this end, the company operates the DontTrack.us and Spreadprivacy.com websites that offer users privacy tips, including articles on how Google tracks user activity across the web, on 'How to Live without Google' and on 'How to Delete Google Search History'.

Due to these distinguishing features, some scholars have suggested that the potential acquisition of DuckDuckGo by Google ought to be caught by merger control as this may harm competition regarding data privacy. For example, a report from the OECD indicates that the acquisition of DuckDuckGo 'might substantially reduce the welfare of consumers with high privacy preferences'.[174] Similarly, Stucke and Grunes argue that '[i]f Google were to acquire DuckDuckGo, it is unlikely that prices for search would increase. Instead, a key issue would be the degradation in privacy protection post-merger..[175] However, none of these authors offers a concrete theory of harm to show how the acquisition might be captured. The following

[169] Case AT.39740 *Google Search (Shopping)* decision of 27 June 2017, para 278.
[170] ibid para 304.
[171] The number of search queries received by the search engine has increased from less than half a million in 2013 to almost six billion a year in 2017. See <https://duckduckgo.com/traffic.html> accessed 8 February 2024. Commissioner Vestager is one of DuckDuckGo's users, citing privacy for using it.
[172] DuckDuckGo Privacy Policy, <https://duckduckgo.com/privacy> accessed 8 February 2024.
[173] See Susan Adams, 'The Founder of DuckDuckGo Explains Why Challenging Google Isn't Insane', *Forbes* (19 February 2016).
[174] See Ania Thiemann and Pedro Gonzaga, *Big Data: Bringing Competition Policy to the Digital Era* (OECD 2016) 19.
[175] Stucke and Grunes (n 135) 266.

paragraphs examine whether this hypothetical acquisition satisfies the above tests for applying the maverick-firm theory of harm.

It is worth noting that the maverick-firm theory is a well-established standard in both the EU and US merger control regimes. Applying this theory involves identifying a maverick, assessing how a merger might curtail the maverick's distinctive business strategy, and highlighting barriers that preclude potential competitors from emulating that strategy. The key contribution of the discussion based on disruptive innovation is to provide a more refined framework for distinguishing mavericks from other aggressive competitors by differentiating between low-end and new-market footholds. Furthermore, as demonstrated in the subsequent paragraphs, this framework, with a focus on the low-end, proves valuable for incorporating privacy considerations into competition law.

The first step in the application of the theory is identifying the maverick. As noted earlier, this involves a three-criterion test. The first is to show that 'the firm offers a product or service that is worse in some way than the traditional offerings'. Taking the hypothetical example of a Google/DuckDuckGo merger, the relevant market would be 'Internet search' and the European Commission has identified quality, measured in terms of relevance and speed, as being a key competition parameter in this market. Given its data collection and aggregation practices (not only in Search but also via other services), Google benefits from data-driven network effects (of scale, scope, and speed in data). The advantages of these data-driven network effects mean that Google can offer the most relevant search results more quickly than DuckDuckGo.[176] From this angle, DuckDuckGo can be considered to offer worse service in terms of the relevance and speed of its search results.

The second test for identifying a maverick is that 'the poor quality is accompanied by a lower price (or some other innovative benefit)'. In our example, DuckDuckGo's relatively poor-quality search results (compared to Google) are compensated by its pro-privacy business strategy. It does not collect and store search queries, and it uses encrypted communication. It provides users with more control over whether and when they reveal their location data and options to limit the sharing of their data and to turn off ads. Moreover, it engages in vigorous privacy-awareness campaigns including educating users on how to protect their privacy while using Google. Thus, when using DuckDuckGo, users trade reduction in the relevance of search results for better data privacy protection.

[176] An interesting personal experiment as a Google search user is to do a search of similar words in Google and DuckDuckGo and compare the relevance of the results. Often, a user finds the most relevant result in Google more quickly (in the first few results) than with DuckDuckGo. At times, DuckDuckGo's users may find themselves resorting to Google due to the difficulty in finding pertinent results. In line with this, the Commission decision has indicated that users that have search engines other than Google as their primary search engine multi-home at a much higher rate, more than 70 per cent, than users that have Google as their primary search engine (less than 12 per cent). See *Google Search (Shopping)* (n 169) paras 304–10.

The third requirement for identifying a maverick is that 'the product or service only works well for a niche segment of consumers who substitute away from the traditional competitors'. This is true for DuckDuckGo because the product is not attractive for users who want to spend less time getting the most relevant results. DuckDuckGo lacks the scale and the data necessary to provide the most relevant results as quickly as Google. Thus, users of DuckDuckGo must spend more time trying to find the relevant result either by checking more page results than they would if they were using Google or by using a variety of search terms before getting the relevant results. Sometimes, none of these attempts will yield the relevant result, and users may have to resort to Google.[177] This implies that DuckDuckGo works only for users with high privacy preferences that are willing to spend more time obtaining the relevant results. On the basis of these three tests, DuckDuckGo could satisfy the maverick-firm status.

The next step in the application of the theory is to assess how the acquisition of the maverick produces anticompetitive effects. This assessment is twofold. The first is to demonstrate that a merger would lead to elimination of the maverick's business strategy. The reasoning behind this requirement is that, even if a firm is a maverick, if the merged entity has an incentive to use the 'disruptive' business strategy after the merger, there is no need for concern. This requirement can be fulfilled by showing that the merged entity has an incentive to eliminate the product/service offered by the maverick firm or that the organizational independence of the maverick is crucial for the firm to play its disruptive role. In the example at hand, one could possibly argue that DuckDuckGo's independence is necessary for it to continue to play its disruptive role.

Insights from the business literature show that the management culture in incumbents can prevent the success of disruptive strategies. For example, incumbents often foster a culture of stimulating growth via high profit margins, which makes the low profit margins required for a disruptive strategy less appealing.[178] Similarly, the culture at such firms 'tends to reward big investment opportunities, and the niche demand for disruptive innovation is not "large enough to be interesting"'.[179] Accordingly, such a culture can make incumbents 'inherently inhospitable to disruptive strategies'.[180] Given DuckDuckGo's focus on niche consumers, the absence of behaviourally targeted advertising and its low-profit margins,[181] Google's corporate culture could be seen as inhospitable to DuckDuckGo's business strategy. Moreover, DuckDuckGo needs its organizational independence to

[177] See Rebecca Sentence, 'Going Over to the Duck Side: A Week Using DuckDuckGo' *Search Engine Watch* (1 March 2016).
[178] Owings (n 135) 346.
[179] ibid.
[180] ibid.
[181] For example, in 2015, DuckDuckGo revenue from search advertising was estimated at around USD one million, whereas Google's revenue was USD 74.5 billion. See Adams (n 173).

continue with its vigorous anti-Google campaign on data privacy issues. Google welcoming in DuckDuckGo's business strategy would be akin to inviting an 'arsonist into one's home' and doing nothing about it.

The second test for assessing anticompetitive effects is to show the existence of barriers that hinder other players from replicating the maverick's business strategy. By now, it is trite to mention that the search market is characterized by high entry barriers resulting from economies of scope, as well as traditional and data-driven network effects. Providing Internet search services requires enormous financial investment in data servers, crawling, and the technology necessary to categorize and rank websites. In this regard, DuckDuckGo is one of the few companies to have a web index of its own with which to respond to searches.[182] The Commission's decision in *Google Shopping* also recognized such entry barriers, including the high financial investment needed to operate a search engine, the benefits of scale and scope in search data, and the existence of positive feedback effects from the user and advertising sides of the market.[183] Moreover, the existence of a 'dysfunctional equilibrium' means that new or existing players are unable to attract sufficient demand by offering more protective privacy policies and clearer disclosure.[184] Thus, the hypothetical acquisition could fulfil the two tests: first, the importance of independence for the maverick to continue to play its disruptive role, and second, the existence of entry barriers that might prevent others from replicating DuckDuckGo's business strategy.

In this sense, the maverick-firm theory of harm could provide an alternative for incorporating data privacy where a dominant firm tries to acquire a maverick that caters for users concerned about their privacy. The hypothetical acquisition of DuckDuckGo by Google offers a good example where this theory might be relevant and can be tested. However, the theory could also be used as shield where a merger increases the effectiveness of the maverick's business strategy. As a shield, the maverick-firm theory could be used to defend a merger between two privacy-friendly services. This is particularly important because, according to the conventional understanding, a merger is likely to reduce the level of data privacy if privacy is a key attribute for both the merging parties.[185]

If this is so, it is not the acquisition of WhatsApp by Facebook or DuckDuckGo by Google that is likely to reduce privacy competition but rather the merger between two privacy-friendly social networks or search engines.[186] Indeed, a merger of firms that attract customers due to superior privacy could, indeed, lead to

[182] Monopolkommission, 'Competition Policy: The Challenges of Digital Markets' (Special Report No 68, 2015) para 272.

[183] *Google Search (Shopping)* (n 169) paras 285–96.

[184] Farrell, 'Can Privacy Be Just Another Good?' (n 78) 251.

[185] See discussion in Esayas, 'Competition in Dissimilarity' (n 25).

[186] See Darren Tucker, 'The Proper Role of Privacy in Merger Review' (2015) 2 Antitrust Chronicle 1, 6.

reduced competition, especially if the market for such services is already concentrated. However, given the importance of network effects and the dominance of business models that rely heavily on the collection and monetization of personal data, mergers between privacy-friendly services could actually improve privacy by offering users bigger networks that satisfy their privacy preferences and reducing the need to multi-home with the established networks.

One could even advance the argument that such mergers should be permitted despite the risk of market concentration or monopolization. In their article on complexity-minded antitrust, Petit and Schrepel advocate for an antitrust approach that introduces uncertainty to stimulate competition.[187] To this end, they distinguish between the 'physicist' mentality of traditional antitrust institutions and the 'park-ranger' ethos of complexity-minded antitrust institutions.[188] Petit and Schrepel further explain the implications of these mindsets as follows:

> The difference in mental models is that physicists seek to reach static and predictable outcomes (moving a monopoly towards competition), while park rangers seek to maintain dynamic and unpredictable processes (moving a monopoly towards competition or *towards a new monopoly*).[189]

In light of this reasoning, competition policy should be open to the possibility of allowing a merger between two privacy friendly services, even in the face of potential monopoly, provided this is a new type of monopoly and increases uncertainty in the market. The maverick-firm theory could also cater to situations where dominant platforms such as Google and Facebook acquire start-ups trying to 'disrupt' the status quo by developing innovative data-protection and control systems, for example personal data management systems or anti-tracking and ad-blocking services. As highlighted in Chapter 4, this approach proves effective in addressing the architectural power of major digital platforms, which is demonstrated by their ability to steer innovation trajectories in ways that serve their interests. Overall, the new challenges posed by the digital economy require that we experiment with new tools and theories, and the maverick-firm theory could be useful in such experimentation.

V. Conclusion

This chapter has examined three theories of harm, each with their own unique insights for incorporating data privacy into merger assessments. The quality-based

[187] Petit and Schrepel (n 5).
[188] ibid 61.
[189] ibid 61 (emphasis added).

theory of harm fits within the conventional merger control criterion as it is anchored in the idea of a merger leading to a significant increase in market power that could be used to reduce the level of data privacy protection. The use of this theory of harm by the Commission in the *Microsoft/LinkedIn* decision is confirmation of the appeal of this theory and will further strengthen its utility going forward.

In comparison, the consumer choice theory treats variety as the ultimate policy goal for competition law. This focus on observable proxies simplifies the process of measuring and evaluating harms to data privacy and other non-price factors. While its current application seems to be limited to abuse-of-dominance cases, this approach presents a simplified means of incorporating data privacy into competition assessment. This is particularly attractive in markets characterized by complexity and entry barriers due to network effects, and involving products or services with broader societal significance. The Commission's emphasis on this approach in the proposed amendment to the 2008 Guidelines on Article 102, particularly in relation to digital markets, will further reinforce its importance going forward. This could also pave the way for addressing restrictions on market access in relation to Article 102, such as blocking a privacy-friendly app on certain platforms or restricting the data portability rights of individuals.

Furthermore, despite its limited use thus far in EU competition policy, the maverick-firm theory of harm may be useful for incorporating data privacy into merger assessments even when there are no concentration concerns. This theory is particularly relevant where leading digital players, such as Google or Facebook, attempt to acquire start-ups that try to 'disrupt' their business models by developing technologies and systems that offer greater privacy. This approach could also be useful to defend a merger between privacy-friendly services, which, under the conventional approach, might be considered to harm competition in data privacy more than a merger involving a privacy-friendly service and the established players. A competition policy that embraces complexity should be open to the possibility of moving a monopoly towards a new monopoly, thereby introducing an element of uncertainty.

Thus, while the quality-based and maverick theories allow for incorporating data privacy considerations within existing competition policy frameworks, each with a specific focus on mergers leading to market dominance and those involving mavericks, the practical impact of the consumer choice approach is contingent upon the ongoing policy changes. This is evident in the proposed amendment to the 2008 Guidelines on enforcement priorities under Article 102. However, the goal is not to advocate these theories of harm as the only ones available but to spur thinking about new ways to factor privacy considerations into competition analysis as markets and their relationships with consumers go through enormous changes.

Finally, the discussion in this chapter shows how the incorporation of data privacy in competition law opens for positive synergy between data privacy and competition laws. Data privacy law can offer competition law guidance in terms of what constitutes a reduction in privacy as a non-price parameter. Similarly, competition law can contribute to the effectiveness of data privacy law by ensuring that the market remains competitive and users have choices in relation to data privacy. The *Microsoft/LinkedIn* case serves as an example where such synergies have been observed. Data privacy rules seem to inform the competition analysis on privacy reductions, with competition rules playing a crucial role in ensuring that a merger does not reduce users' privacy choices, thereby enhancing the effectiveness of data protection.

6

Privacy Fixing and Other Forms of Anticompetitive Cooperation on Privacy

I. Anticompetitive Coordination on Data Privacy

Cartels are the most egregious violations of competition law and there is a relatively wide consensus on their harmful effects to competition. The availability of criminal penalties testifies to the severity with which cartels are treated. The reasoning behind prohibiting cartels or coordination among competitors is that companies should make independent decisions in achieving their economic goals, which in turn drives competition and innovation. In simpler terms, the uncertainty on a competitor's potential next move propels other companies to continually enhance their offering and meet the needs of their customers. Cartels remove this uncertainty and promote complacency.

As much as the idea of a cartel is deeply intertwined with fixing prices, as shown below, instances where companies conspire to fix non-price parameters such as quality, choice, and innovation are not uncommon. In principle, such cartels are as culpable as price fixing or market sharing.[1] In its guidance, the European Commission notes that horizontal agreements may restrict competition if they are likely to result in adverse effects with respect to 'prices, output, *product quality, product variety or innovation*'.[2] Moreover, the Court of Justice of the European Union (CJEU) has confirmed the applicability of Article 101 of the Treaty on the Functioning of the European Union (TFEU) to conduct that negatively impacts the quality of goods or services.[3] Thus, cartels are not just about prices or market sharing.

As users increasingly exchange their personal information for access to digital services (essentially 'paying' with information), questions arise on whether users' privacy can become a potential area for collusion. Indeed, to the extent that data privacy is recognized as a non-price competition parameter, certain collaborative

[1] Organisation for Economic Co-operation and Development (OECD), *Policy Roundtables: The Role and Measurement of Quality in Competition Analysis* (OECD Publishing 2013) 8.

[2] European Commission, 'Guidelines on the Applicability of Article 101 of the Treaty on the Functioning of the European Union to Horizontal Co-operation Agreements' (2011) OJ C11/1 (European Commission, 'Guidelines on Horizontal Cooperation') para 3 (emphasis added).

[3] See Case C-382/12 P *MasterCard Inc v Commission* ECLI:EU:C:2014:2201, para 93.

Data Privacy and Competition Law in the Age of Big Data. Samson Y. Esayas, Oxford University Press.
 DOI: 10.1093/oso/9780198891420.003.0007

arrangements may fall under the purview of Article 101.[4] Few scholars have explored the possibility of companies conspiring to harm users' privacy in breach of antitrust rules. In a 2016 article, Newman discusses a hypothetical agreement between Internet search providers to fix information costs by agreeing on the minimum retention period for search queries.[5] Similarly, Stucke and Grunes argue that agreements between web browsers or app stores to block anti-tracking and ad-blocking apps are potentially as harmful as agreements to fix prices.[6] Less controversially, agreements between companies not to deploy a certain privacy-enhancing technology (PET) (eg end-to-end encryption) or to delay its deployment are also likely to be liable. However, these types of agreements are rare in practice.

This is because, first, the recognition of data privacy as a competition parameter is a recent phenomenon with a scant literature and few decisions.[7] Second, data privacy harms can take different forms, and the difficulty in articulating the harms can frustrate the formation and monitoring of agreements to fix them.[8] Moreover, given that many users do not fully read or understand privacy policies, it might seem implausible that companies would collude with rivals to degrade user privacy when they can simply achieve this by tweaking their privacy policies. Thus, until recently, discussions on the existence of anticompetitive coordination to reduce users' privacy were primarily confined to academic circles. In fact, when the first version of this chapter was written in 2017, it could only conjecture about the potential for companies to coordinate in ways that would degrade users' privacy. This is now changing as the topic gains more attention from enforcement agencies. Two examples involving Google illustrate that privacy fixing may not be as unlikely as one might think.

The first example comes from the United States. In an antitrust lawsuit spearheaded by Texas's Attorney General (AG), Google is accused of 'privacy fixing', or coordinating with rivals to harm user privacy in violation of antitrust laws prohibiting cartels.[9] The complaint cites several instances where Google allegedly attempted to influence Microsoft's privacy-related promotional activities, sought alignment on 'privacy goals and strategies' with rivals, including Facebook and Microsoft, and coordinated efforts to thwart privacy legislation. The other example

[4] See Competition Committee and the Committee on Consumer Policy, 'Quality Considerations in the Zero-Price Economy—Note by the European Union' (2018) paras 28–30 (noting that when a reduction in non-price parameters, including the level of data privacy, 'stems from an agreement, ... there may be a case for competition enforcement').

[5] See John Newman, 'Antitrust in Zero-Price Markets: Applications' (2016) 94 Washington University Law Review 49, 95.

[6] See Maurice Stucke and Allen Grunes, *Big Data and Competition Policy* (OUP 2016) 263.

[7] See John Newman (n 5) 95 (noting the lack of case law addressing agreements to fix information/attention costs).

[8] ibid 96.

[9] Civil Action 1:21-md-03010-PKC *State of Texas v Google LLC* United States Southern District of New York, filed 14 January 2022.

comes from an investigation by the German and Austrian competition authorities into an agreement between Google and Eyeo, the company behind the anti-tracking and ad-blocking software, Adblock Plus.[10] After several efforts to squeeze Adblock Plus from the market, Google paid Eyeo millions in return for limiting Adblock Plus's ad-blocking and anti-tracking capabilities, in breach of antitrust rules prohibiting cartels.

Using these examples, this chapter examines the concept of privacy fixing and its relevance for antitrust law. The examples are intended to convey a picture of the range of issues associated with such collaborative efforts, highlighting the possible incentives for privacy fixing, the structural links that make such collaborations possible, and the potential harms to competition on data privacy and PETs, as well as the role that competition law can play in addressing these concerns. To this end, Section II lays the groundwork by surveying the decisional practice and case law on anticompetitive coordinated behaviour affecting non-price parameters of competition. Section III examines anticompetitive collaborations affecting data privacy and PETs. Finally, Section IV studies the role of standard setting and its potential impacts for competition in data privacy.

II. Anticompetitive Practices on Non-Price Parameters

At its core, Article 101 prohibits coordinated behaviour between undertakings resulting from 'agreements, decisions by associations of undertakings or concerted practices' that, by object or effect, restrict or distort competition. Although the legal precedents and enforcement actions regarding anticompetitive coordination typically focus on price fixing, instances where companies conspire to fix non-price parameters are not uncommon. As shown below, there are instances where cartels affecting non-price parameters are detected and punished by competition authorities and courts.

Some US examples are illustrative of such agreements. In one instance, the US Federal Trade Commission (FTC) found that an agreement among macaroni producers regarding the proportion of different flours in their products, following a shortage of the preferred flour, was anticompetitive, and this was upheld by a court.[11] Similarly, several US appeals courts have found that agreements among car dealers to remain closed on Saturdays and agreements among airlines on luggage allowances or the size of carry-on luggage were in breach of Section I of the Sherman Act, a provision equivalent to Article 101 of the TFEU.[12]

[10] Bundeskartellamt, 'Proceeding against Whitelisting Contract between Google and Eyeo Terminated after Amendments to the Contract' (21 January 2019).

[11] See Mark Patterson, *Antitrust Law in the New Economy* (Harvard UP 2017) 88.

[12] *In re Detroit Auto Dealers Ass'n, Inc* 955 F.2d Court of Appeals, 6th Circuit (1992) 457; Case C-82/01 P *Aéroports de Paris v Commission* ECLI:EU:C:2002:617; also Benjamin Dryden and Shankar Iyer,

In the European Union (EU), several Commission decisions address non-price aspects. In *Vimpoltu*, the Commission found that standard terms imposed by an association on its members regulating 'transfer of ownership and risk' and 'warranty, liability, advertising, after-sales service and settlement of disputes' were restrictive of competition.[13] According to the Commission, these standard terms aimed to regulate '*important secondary aspects of competition*' and 'may create greater uniformity in the terms on which business is transacted than would be the case in their absence'.[14] Similar standard terms agreed upon by several shipping companies were found to be in breach of Article 101(1) for restricting non-price competition, including aspects related to 'general transport conditions'.[15] The Commission reached a similar conclusion concerning an agreement among global freight forwarders on the conditions of airfreight,[16] which was upheld on appeal by the General Court (GC) and the CJEU.[17] The CJEU has, on a few occasions, confirmed the applicability of Article 101(1) to agreements that restrict non-price parameters.[18]

Of particular importance to privacy discussions is the Commission's decision to fine several truck manufacturers, including MAN, DAF, Daimler, Iveco, Volvo, Renault, and Scania for participating in a cartel that coordinated 'the timing for the introduction of emission technologies'.[19] This behaviour is considered to delay the roll-out of clean emissions technology, thereby 'passing the costs of new technologies to meet stricter emission rules' on to customers.[20] In a separate case, the Commission investigated a possible collusion between BMW, Daimler, and VW regarding the introduction of newer, better technologies to reduce emissions.[21] In this case, it was found that the companies regularly met to discuss the development and introduction of selective catalytic reduction ('SCR')-systems for diesel passenger cars.[22] The use of SCR-systems is one mechanism to reduce nitrogen oxides (NOx) concentration in exhaust gases of diesel vehicles and helps manufacturers to comply with European emissions standards Euro 5 and Euro 6.[23] These standards

'Privacy Fixing and Predatory Privacy: The Intersection of Big Data, Privacy Policies and Antitrust' (2017) 1 Competition Policy International Antitrust Chronicle 1.

13 Case IV/30.174 *Vimpoltu* decision of 13 July 1983, paras 30, 39.

14 ibid para 39 (emphasis added).

15 Case IV/35.134 *Trans-Atlantic Conference Agreement (TACA)* decision of 16 September 1998, para 380.

16 Case COMP/39.462 *Freight Forwarding* decision of 28 March 2012, paras 489ff.

17 See Case T-251/12 *EGL v Commission* ECLI:EU:T:2016:114; Case C-263/16 P *Schenker v Commission* ECLI:EU:C:2018:58.

18 See Case C-8/08 *T-Mobile Netherlands* ECLI:EU:C:2009:343, paras 36–39.

19 European Commission, 'Commission Fines Scania €880 Million for Participating in Trucks Cartel', (27 September 2017) <https://ec.europa.eu/commission/presscorner/detail/en/IP_17_3502>.

20 ibid.

21 Case AT.40178 *Car Emissions* decision of 8 July 2021.

22 ibid para 3.

23 The relevant legal framework is Directive 2007/46/EC of the European Parliament and of the Council: ibid paras 12, 41.

set the upper limits of emissions from gas exhaust in order to get approval for EU/European Economic Area (EEA) markets.

According to the Commission, the use of SCR systems can significantly reduce NOx emissions in exhaust gases by up to 90 per cent or more through the injection of a liquid urea solution known as AdBlue and a process called denoxification.[24] The effectiveness of this cleaning process is determined by various factors, such as the quantity of AdBlue injected and the size of the tank used to inject it. These factors also affect the 'AdBlue range'—how far a vehicle can be driven without needing to refill AdBlue.[25] This is important to consumers as refilling AdBlue can be perceived as inconvenient and incurs costs. Additionally, while larger AdBlue tank sizes may increase the AdBlue range, they also add weight to the vehicle, potentially increasing carbon dioxide emissions.

The Commission's investigation found that DAIMLER, VW, and BMW coordinated their market conduct with regard to SCR-systems, particularly 'the AdBlue tank sizes and ranges between two refills', and also 'exchanged information about assumed average AdBlue-consumption'.[26] In 2011, the companies discussed their strategies on SCR systems, including 'the medium-term goal of moving to smaller AdBlue tanks for Europe and therefore to shorter ranges between AdBlue refills'.[27] Specifically, they agreed on 'AdBlue tanks for the EEA with an effective range of 10 000 km'.[28] According to the Commission, these discussions on AdBlue tank seizes and refill ranges created a common understanding on average AdBlue consumption of 0.8–1.0 litres per 1,000 km.[29]

The Commission concluded that such behaviour inherently had the potential to restrict competition regarding 'product characteristics of new diesel passenger car models' and thereby limit technical development and consumer choice in the field of NOx-cleaning with SCR-systems for new diesel passenger cars in the EEA.[30] As a result of this behaviour, consumers would have to refill their tanks more frequently, which is perceived as a deterioration in the overall quality of the vehicles.[31] The Commission found that the car manufacturers' behaviour aimed to restrict competition on innovative emission cleaning systems and thereby 'denied consumers the opportunity to buy less polluting cars, despite the technology being available to the manufacturers'.[32] According to the Commission, while this conduct does not amount to 'price fixing or market sharing', it would violate EU competition laws

[24] ibid para 48.
[25] ibid para 49.
[26] ibid para 5.
[27] ibid para 77.
[28] ibid para 77.
[29] ibid para 79.
[30] ibid paras 7, 125.
[31] European Commission, 'Commission Sends Statement of Objections to BMW, Daimler and VW for Restricting Competition on Emission Cleaning Technology' (5 April 2019) <https://ec.europa.eu/commission/presscorner/detail/en/ip_19_2008>.
[32] ibid.

that prohibit cartels that limit production, markets, or technical development, as per Article 101(1)(b).[33]

The examples of emission-technology cartels are particularly informative when considering possible cartels involving privacy and PETs.[34] Just as agreements to delay the roll-out of clean-emissions technologies can degrade the quality of cars, so can agreements between companies not to deploy or to delay certain PETs reduce the quality of the product or service in question.

III. Privacy Fixing in Practice

Given that data privacy is recognized as a non-price parameter of competition, it is becoming clear that agreements that fix data privacy conditions or restrict deployment of PETs are likely to fall within the purview of Article 101. Two notable cases involving Google provide valuable insight into what privacy fixing may look like in practice, how this may harm consumers, and the extent to which antitrust law can tackle such harms.

A. Google–Eyeo Agreement

Google has been a subject of joint investigation by the German and Austrian antitrust authorities for sabotaging users' privacy using contractual arrangements. The investigation looked at contractual clauses that imposed restrictions on Eyeo's ad-blocking business. Among other services, Eyeo offers anti-tracking and ad-blocking technology, Adblock Plus. Adblock Plus is a free browser extension that allows users to 'block annoying ads, disable tracking and block domains known to spread malware'.[35] Additionally, with its 'Acceptable Ads program', Eyeo offers advertisers and advertising marketers the possibility to exclude certain ads from its ad-blocking process (whitelisting) upon meeting certain criteria. To be whitelisted, the ad must adhere to certain standards, set out by the Acceptable Ads Committee, in relation to its size, placement, and prominence. In return, Eyeo demands a fee, estimated to be 30 per cent of the ad revenue, from larger advertisers and advertising marketers.[36]

[33] ibid.

[34] To the extent that personal data is the fossil fuel that drives the digital economy, the collection and usage generate externalities that are comparable to environmental pollution.

[35] See <https://adblockplus.org/en/about> accessed 9 February 2024.

[36] Sally Hubbard, 'Google: Ad Blocking Chrome Extension Raises Antitrust Issues' (2017) 5 Capitol Forum <https://thecapitolforum.cmail20.com/t/ViewEmail/j/54522CFB200A367F/FBA63C641117D6654936C359EC0425C0>.

As the world's leading advertising company, Google entered into an agreement with Eyeo to have its ads whitelisted by Adblock Plus. The cost of this 'favour' was estimated to be in excess of USD 25 million in 2013, but it was also estimated to have saved Google roughly USD 1 billion.[37] In 2015, savings resulting from this 'favour' were estimated to be around USD 3 billion. Google's decision to pay (rather than fight) ad blockers illustrates the growing popularity of ad blockers. It suggests that even the 'juggernaut of surveillance capitalism'[38] can be made to listen to the terms of a firm that aims to enhance users' privacy and web experience. Simultaneously, the agreement illustrates Google's power. Not only did Google have its ads whitelisted for a fraction of what Eyeo charges other advertisers (2.8 per cent of Google's ad revenue instead of an estimated 30 per cent),[39] but it also forced Eyeo to compromise on its ad-blocking and anti-tracking business, which the joint investigation found to be restrictive of competition.

Although details of the agreement were not revealed in the press release, the joint investigation found the arrangement to be anticompetitive because it 'significantly restricted Eyeo's independent entrepreneurial ad-blocking activity'.[40] Importantly, the agreement 'restricted Eyeo's possibilities to further develop its products, expand, and invest in the market'.[41] In a paragraph that discusses the role of competition in addressing consumers' needs (including user privacy) and how the agreement harms this competition, Andreas Mundt, President of the Bundeskartellamt, commented,

> It is understandable that consumers are interested in controlling the type and amount of online advertising they see. The offer of ad blockers is an integral part of the competitive process in online advertising services. Regulations in contracts aimed at restricting the offer of ad blockers are therefore anticompetitive and hence unacceptable.[42]

It is clear from the investigation that Google not only managed to restrict Adblock Plus's ad-blocking functionality in dealing with ads served by Google but also imposed restrictions on future improvements to, and investment in, its services. Article 101(1)(b) prohibits agreements that 'limit or control production, markets, technical development, or investment', and the Google–Eyeo agreement is a clear example of a privacy cartel, restricting technical development and investment that could improve users' privacy and web experience. Just as the agreement

[37] ibid.

[38] Shoshana Zuboff, *The Age of Surveillance Capitalism: The Fight for a Human Future at the New Frontier of Power* (PublicAffairs 2019).

[39] Hubbard (n 36).

[40] Bundeskartellamt (n 10).

[41] ibid.

[42] ibid.

between car manufacturers denied buyers the opportunity to buy less polluting cars, the Google–Eyeo agreement denied users potential improvements to their privacy and web experience from increased investment in ad-blocking technology. Moreover, Adblock Plus users now see more of Google's ads than before the agreement, thus exposing users to more tracking and the spread of malware via Google's ads. This is because Adblock Plus, by blocking ads, also reduces the number of tracking cookies and malware associated with the ads.

Google's decision to enter into an agreement with Eyeo should be considered in light of its previous attempts to squeeze Adblock Plus out of the market. In 2012, Google banned Adblock Plus from its Play Store and removed Adblock Plus's browser extensions from the Chrome web store.[43] When users resorted to Search, Google stopped showing Adblock Plus's website in its search results. Users' attempts to sidestep the Play Store and download Adblock Plus directly to their Android phones were met with technical challenges. When Google's efforts to halt Adblock Plus's rise failed, Google paid Eyeo millions to get its ads out to users. This is a clear example of privacy fixing in practice.

Although the ad-blocking functionality seems to be emphasized in the investigation, it should not undermine the importance of the decision in relation to users' data privacy. First, given that most of Google's ads are behaviourally targeted (ie based on data collected across the web from Google's own services and its partners), the ad-blocking technology offered by Adblock Plus gives users the ability to control how their data is used. When blocking Google ads using Adblock Plus, users are preventing Google from using their data to serve them behaviourally targeted advertising. Thus, the restriction on 'Eyeo's independent entrepreneurial ad-blocking activity' undermines users' ability to control how their data is used (information self-determination). Additionally, by blocking ads, most ad blockers reduce the number of tracking cookies that get installed on users' devices. This means that the restrictions on Eyeo exposes users to more tracking from Google. The resulting overexposure from such tracking can lead to additional consumer harms.[44] Furthermore, given that Adblock Plus allows users to block tracking and the spread of malware, the anticompetitive impact on users' data privacy, particularly from restrictions on investment and the future development of the technology, is equally harmful.

[43] Natasha Lomas, 'AdBlock Plus Responds to Play Store Ban: "Unilateral Move by Google Threatens Consumer Choice"', *TechCrunch* (14 March 2013).

[44] See Ryan Calo, 'Digital Market Manipulation' (2013) 82 George Washington Law Review 1026–27. Overexposure can facilitate what Calo refers to as 'digital market manipulation', which either induces or exacerbates several economic harms. For example, companies, especially platforms, can use their knowledge of the user, together with behavioural biases, to extract consumer surplus through dynamic price discrimination and persuasion profiling. Moreover, the accumulation of data about consumers and related network effects can increase or exacerbate market power and generate consumer harms. See Nathan Newman, 'Search, Antitrust, and the Economics of the Control of User Data' (2014) 31 Yale Journal on Regulation 401, 441.

The agreement between these two companies—one of which has built its business empire on tracking and monetizing user data through targeted advertising and the other that has built its reputation on tools that seek to reduce tracking and advertisement—shows how apparently opposed company incentives can align to make privacy fixing possible. Adblock Plus started off as a simple ad-blocking and anti-tracking service. It gained enough consumer support and trust to get Google's attention, went on to introduce the Acceptable Ads model to whitelist ads, and ultimately faltered in the face of Google's significant financial offer. Where this is the case, competition law is the appropriate regulatory instrument to discipline such conduct. Thus, it is only appropriate that the German and Austrian competition authorities view ad blockers as the market's response to users' demand for privacy and any agreement to restrict this kind of technology as anticompetitive conduct. This is a step in the right direction because, to the extent that the market is responding to privacy needs, competition agencies need to be attentive to practices that can suppress competition on data privacy and PETs. Finally, the decision signifies the need for competition authorities to be open-minded about agreements that could potentially restrict privacy competition. The complaint from Texas AG accusing Google of 'privacy fixing' is a good instance of such open-mindedness and willingness to explore new terrains in antitrust.

B. Texas 'Privacy-Fixing' Complaint

As noted in Section I, the Texas AG, along with nine other US states, levelled accusations against Google for 'privacy fixing', an accusation equivalent to price fixing but in the field of privacy. This is just one of several antitrust lawsuits that Google has faced across the United States in the past few years. Both the Justice Department and a group of 38 states have filed lawsuits accusing Google of unlawfully maintaining its monopoly in the market for general search services and search advertising.[45]

Many of the allegations mirror practices that the EU has tried to address over the past few years. In three separate legal cases, Google was fined a total of EUR 8.25 billion (around USD 10.1 billion) for violating the EU's antitrust rules.[46] However, Texas's accusation of 'privacy fixing' stands out as novel and is, hence, the focus of this section. This complaint accuses Google of conspiring with rivals to fix the level of users' privacy:

[45] Case 1:20-cv-03010 *US Department of Justice v Google LLC* in the United States District Court Columbia, filed 20 October 2020; Case 3:21-cv-05227 *State of Utah v Google LLC* in United States District Court of California, filed 7 July 2021.

[46] Case AT.39740 *Google Search (Shopping)* decision of 27 June 2017; Case AT.40099 *Google Android* decision of 18 July 2018; Case AT.40411 *Google Search (AdSense)* decision of 20 March 2019.

> Google actively coordinates with its competitors when it comes to privacy.... Of course, effective competition is concerned about both price and quality, and the fact that Google coordinates with its competitors on the quality metric of privacy—***one might call it privacy fixing***—underscores Google's selective promotion of privacy concerns only when doing so facilitates its efforts to exclude competition.[47]

The complaint contains several efforts from Google to coordinate with rivals (including Facebook and Microsoft) regarding users' privacy. Although Google's efforts are interconnected, they can be classified into two broad categories.

The first relates to Google's efforts to impede privacy legislation in both the United States and the EU. Following proposals for regulation of child privacy in the United States, Google sought to coordinate efforts with other companies to 'forestall and diminish child privacy protections'.[48] The complaint cites a Google internal document from July 2019, where Google wanted to use upcoming meetings with other technology companies, including Facebook, Apple, and Microsoft, to 'find areas of alignment and narrow gaps in our positions and priorities on child privacy and safety'.[49] In the same document, Google admitted that it had been 'working behind the scenes hand in hand with the other companies' and had thus far 'been successful in slowing down and delaying the [EU ePrivacy Regulation] process'.[50]

Both the EU and US systems offer companies some immunity from antitrust liability when lobbying governments jointly and the resulting government-imposed restrictions on competition.[51] However, as the competition concerns associated with joint lobbying efforts are not unique to privacy matters, they are not specifically addressed in this chapter.[52] The focus in this chapter will be on the second category, which involves Google's request for Microsoft to stop privacy attacks and efforts to align privacy practices with Microsoft and Facebook.

1. Plea to Stop Privacy Attacks and Efforts to Find Alignment on Privacy

Of particular importance to this book are Google's efforts to have common approach on privacy with Facebook and Microsoft. In an internal document, Google

47 *State of Texas v Google* (n 9) para 501 (emphasis added).

48 ibid para 497.

49 ibid.

50 ibid para 496.

51 *Eastern R Conf v Noerr Motors* 365 US Supreme Court (1961) 127, 135–36. See Case C-204/00 *Aalborg Portland v Commission* ECLI:EU:C:2004:6; Case C-38/97 *Autotrasporti Librandi Snc di Librandi F & C* ECLI:EU:C:1998:454. For a good overview of these decisions, see Adrian Vossestein, 'Corporate Efforts to Influence Public Authorities, and the EC Rules on Competition' (2000) 37 Common Market Law Review 1383.

52 These issues are addressed in Samson Esayas, 'Privacy Fixing (Cartel): The Evolving Frontier of Antitrust Law in the Wake of *Texas v. Google LLC*', paper presented at the 2023 Privacy Law Scholars Conference in Colorado.

accused Microsoft of 'taking child privacy more seriously than Google' and sought to reinforce with Microsoft, 'at this meeting or at another forum', that 'this is an area of particular importance to have a coordinated approach'.[53] Google also attempted to persuade Microsoft 'to stop directing 'subtle privacy attacks' at Google and other Big Tech companies.[54] The internal document reveals that employees were given direction from Kent Walker, President of Global Affairs and Chief Legal Officer of Alphabet, 'to find alignment' with Microsoft wherever possible and to remain 'wary of their activity [in promoting privacy] and seek to gain as much intel as possible'.[55] Similarly, citing the document, the complaint notes Google's frustration over Facebook's actions regarding privacy, particularly the difficulty in getting Facebook to align on privacy goals and strategy and how Facebook 'have at time[s] prioritized winning on reputation over its business interest in legislative debates'.[56]

From the above statements, it is clear that Google's efforts are aimed at restricting existing and potential competition on privacy. Google's plea for Microsoft to stop directing 'subtle privacy attacks' and its implied request for Facebook to stop prioritizing reputation gains are indications that Google feels the competitive pressure on privacy. These pleas suggest Google's desire for the 'quiet life of a monopoly', free from the pressure and reputational risks that come from competition. Additionally, Google's effort to find alignment might restrict competition by creating uniformity in privacy conditions. Google's efforts to have the allegations dismissed summarily have been unsuccessful so far.[57] The following sections will evaluate the extent to which these efforts may violate Article 101.

Based on the information that is publicly available, it is difficult to determine whether an agreement or concerted practice has taken place, if at all. Google complains that Facebook and Microsoft have not come into common ground on different aspects of privacy. While there may be enough evidence to suggest that a concerted practice exists,[58] this remains a factual question. The discussions in this section primarily focus on how these efforts may restrict competition in data privacy and the extent to which they violate Article 101. However, before delving deeper into these issues, it is important to understand the dynamics of privacy as a factor in competition, particularly involving Google and Microsoft.

2. Some Context for Understanding Google's Efforts

The competition dynamics between Google and Microsoft can be traced back to 2012, when Microsoft launched the 'Scroogled' (a portmanteau of 'screwed' and

[53] *State of Texas v Google* (n 9) para 497.
[54] ibid para 499.
[55] ibid para 499.
[56] ibid para 498.
[57] Paresh Dave, 'Google Must Face Most of Texas Lawsuit over Ad Dominance, Judge Rules' *Reuters* (14 September 2022).
[58] See Esayas (n 52).

'Google') campaign, which targeted Google's privacy practices. As part of this campaign, Microsoft ran several advertisements, including on TV and in newspapers, criticizing Google's products and highlighting the advantages of Microsoft's products, such as Bing and Outlook, in terms of privacy.[59] This campaign began with Google's 2012 privacy policy change that allowed for the combination of data across Google's services. In response, Microsoft ran ads in major newspapers, including the *Wall Street Journal* and the *New York Times*, criticizing this policy change. The ad, entitled 'Putting People First', contained the following text:

> Google is in the process of making unpopular changes to some of their popular products. Those changes cloaked in language like "transparency", "simplicity", and "consistency" are really about one thing: making it easier for Google to connect the dots between everything you search, send, say or stream while using one their services. But the way they're doing it is making it harder for you to maintain control of your personal information. Why are they so interested in doing this that they would risk this kind of backlash? One logical reason: Every data point they collect and connect to you increases how valuable you are to an advertiser.[60]

The ad concludes by urging users concerned about these changes to switch to Microsoft's 'award-winning products' such as Bing, Hotmail, Internet Explorer, and Office 365.[61] Microsoft subsequently targeted Gmail through its 'Gmail Man' campaign, a video that depicts a mailman reading through letters (emails) to find keywords for ads and asks viewers if they 'would trust this guy to deliver their mail'. The campaign accuses Google of violating users' privacy by scanning the contents of emails to generate targeted advertising and recommends Outlook instead.[62] Next, Microsoft targeted Google's Android mobile operating systems (MoS) and Play Store for leaking users' information to app developers without users' explicit permission.[63] The ad attempted to convince Android users to switch to Windows phone and also suggests that this privacy problem is not limited to the app store. In the video, a narrator says, 'If you can't trust their app store, maybe you can't trust them for anything.' At some point, Microsoft even started selling 'Scroogled' mugs and T-shirts featuring designs attacking Google's privacy practices, with proceeds going to charity.[64]

[59] Sean Hollister, 'Scroogled: The Microsoft Attack Ads that Treat Google Like a Political Opponent' *The Verge* (6 Dec 2013).

[60] Tom Warren, 'Microsoft Exploits Google Privacy Concerns in Newspaper Ads', *The Verge* (1 February 2012).

[61] ibid.

[62] Tom Warren, 'Microsoft Makes Its "Gmail Man" Video Official in Privacy Fight against Google', *The Verge* (2 February 2012).

[63] Tom Warren, 'Microsoft's Latest "Scroogled" Ad Attacks Android with Privacy Fears', *The Verge* (9 April 2013).

[64] Brad Chacos, 'Microsoft Store Now Selling Snarky Anti-Google "Scroogled" Mugs and T-Shirts', *PC World* (21 November 2013).

It is clear that Microsoft's campaigns aimed to attract users to its products by highlighting their superior privacy features compared to Google's. While these campaigns may not have led to a significant shift in market share towards Microsoft, they did appear to have an impact on Google's reputation. According to statistics published by AdAge, based on data collected by Answers Research for Microsoft, following a visit to Scroogled.com, the favourability gap between Google and Bing among users narrowed from 45 points to 5 points.[65] Additionally, after watching a Scroogled ad, the likelihood of a viewer recommending Google to a friend fell by 10 per cent, while the likelihood of recommending Bing rose by 7 per cent.[66] These initiatives put pressure on Google to address these concerns or refute Microsoft's claims. As a result, Google filed a lawsuit against Microsoft for running misleading ads in the United Kingdom, specifically targeting Gmail, which Google ultimately lost.[67] Thus, Google opted for a different strategy and decided to coordinate with Microsoft, which raises concerns under Article 101.

3. Restrictions on Competition

Article 101(1) prohibits agreements and concerted practices that have as their object or effect to restrict competition. This provision provides a non-exhaustive list of such practices including price fixing and market sharing as well as arrangements that align any other trading condition. It also prohibits practices that 'limit or control production, markets, technical development, or investment'. Google's actions may be in violation of this provision as they have the potential to restrict competition by aligning trading conditions and limiting market development.

a) Plea to stop privacy attacks

Google's plea for Microsoft to stop subtle attacks on privacy is comparable to restrictions on advertising. Competition is about attracting consumers to own products or services, and advertising plays a vital role in providing customers with the information necessary to make informed decisions.[68] The importance of advertising as a source of information is especially significant in markets characterized by information asymmetry (overload), such as the privacy market.[69] Accordingly, there are many cases where restrictions on advertising are found to violate competition rules.

[65] Alex Wilhelm, 'Microsoft's Scroogled Ad Campaign Appears to Be Working', *TechCrunch* (15 Oct 2013).

[66] ibid.

[67] Mark Sweney, 'Microsoft Wins Battle over Ads Attacking Google Privacy Standards', *The Guardian* (26 March 2014).

[68] Case IV/36.147 *EPI Code of Conduct* decision of 7 April 1999, para 40.

[69] See Joseph Bonneau and Sören Preibusch, 'The Privacy Jungle: On the Market for Data Protection in Social Networks' in Tyler Moore, David Pym, and Christos Ioannidis (eds), *Economics of Information Security and Privacy* (Springer US 2010) 149.

In the United States, restrictions on advertising are treated as an indirect form of price fixing and, as such, are per se illegal.[70] Similarly, there have been several instances where such restrictions on advertising have been found to violate Article 101(1) of the TFEU. For example, in the *Austrian Banks Cartel*, the Commission held that agreements between banks to refrain from advertising interest rates and lending fees violated Article 101(1). The Commission held that these practices constitute restrictions by object, a finding later confirmed by the CJEU.[71] In *Consumer detergents*, the Commission found that an agreement between three producers of washing powder to restrict promotional activities and fix prices was in violation of Article 101(1).[72] Additionally, the Commission has found that terms of trade fairs that restrict participating companies from participating in other fairs violated Article 101(1).[73]

Of particular importance to the case at hand is the Commission's decision in *EPI Code of Conduct*. In this case, the Commission held that restrictions on comparative advertising by patent agents practicing at the European Patent Office are in violation of Article 101(1).[74] The Code of Conduct prohibited agents from engaging in the following practices: (1) 'comparison of the professional services of one member with those of another' (Article 2(b)(1) of the Code); (2) 'the mention of the name of another professional entity unless there is a written cooperation agreement between the member and that entity' (Article 2(b)(2)); and (3) 'any exchange of views about a specific case which he knows or suspects is being handled by another member with the client of the case, unless the client declares his wish to have an independent view or to change his representative' (Article 5(c)).[75] The first two prohibitions concern comparative advertising, whereas the third prohibition relates to sending unsolicited advice or advertising to former clients of another agent.

The Commission explained the importance of comparative advertising for competition as follows:

> Advertising covers not only accurate information for the user but also a promotion of the services on offer, including comparison with a competitor or with the services of competitors. In addition, the members of a profession should have the freedom to actively seek out clients without thereby directly jeopardising the quality of the personal relationship between service providers and their clients. Providing information on the services on offer, where it is accurate and precise,

[70] See *California Dental Assn v FTC* 526 US Supreme Court (1999) 756.

[71] Case COMP/36.571/D-1 *Austrian Banks* decision of 11 June 2002, para 429; Case C-125/07 P *Erste Group Bank v Commission* ECLI:EU:C:2009:576.

[72] Case COMP/39579 *Consumer Detergents* decision of 13 April 2011.

[73] See Case IV/31.593 *British Dental Trade Association—BDTA* decision of 11 July 1988.

[74] *EPI Code of Conduct* (n 68) paras 39–45.

[75] ibid para 14.

> and comparative advertising, where it compares representative and verifiable aspects and is not misleading, are means of increasing user information to the benefit of users and are important elements of the competitive process. They allow users to distinguish between the alternatives which exist at the time of obtaining a service and to make a rational choice of service provider, whether it be within their national frontiers or elsewhere in the Community. They also make it easier for new operators to establish themselves on the market and stimulate innovation in the means of providing services.[76]

The Commission held that these restrictions on advertising removed an important source of information for clients seeking services related to European patent applications and limited their ability to compare services.[77] Further, the restrictions, particularly the one under Article 5(c) of the Code, reduced the agents' ability to offer their services to potential clients who had already been clients of another representative in a specific case.[78] Thus, the Commission found that the provisions of the EPI Code of Conduct relating to comparative advertising and unsolicited exchange of views with former clients of another agent 'limit the freedom of members and have as their object or effect to restrict competition between members of the profession'.[79]

While the GC partially annulled the Commission's decision,[80] it largely upheld the assessment on the comparative advertisement. The Court acknowledged the importance of advertising for competitive process, as it provides customers with 'a better picture of the merits of each of the operators, the quality of their services and their fees' and relevant information to make informed choices.[81] The Court further noted that the ban on comparative advertising 'restricts the ability of more efficient professional representatives to develop their services, with the consequence, inter alia, that the clientele of each professional representative is crystallised within a national market'.[82]

In the same fashion, Google's request for Microsoft to stop the 'subtle privacy' attacks impose restrictions on Microsoft's promotion activities. This request should be viewed in the context of Microsoft's previous campaigns, such as the Scroogled campaign, which aimed to lure Google's customers to Microsoft by promising better privacy conditions. Although these campaigns have not produced mass

[76] ibid para 41.
[77] ibid para 43.
[78] ibid.
[79] ibid para 39.
[80] Case T-144/99 *Institute of Professional Representatives before the European Patent Office v Commission* ECLI:EU:T:2000:117, paras 70–71 and 94–100. The Court annulled the Commission's assessment as regards Article 2(b)(2) and 5(c) of the Code of Conduct, which respectively prohibit 'the mention of the name of another professional entity' and unsolicited exchange of views with former client of another agent.
[81] ibid paras 72–73.
[82] ibid para 74.

desertion of consumers from Google's services, they have created uncertainty and some competitive pressure on Google to either dispel these claims as false or correct the course in its privacy practices. Google's plea for Microsoft to stop the attacks and statements in the internal document indicate that Google feels the pressure (is 'wary') but prefers to take another route than compete on merits. If the attacks were to stop, it would remove the competitive pressure on Google but also the incentive for Microsoft to improve its privacy practices.

Relatedly, the campaigns launched by Microsoft provide valuable information for users to understand Google's privacy practices and make comparisons with Microsoft. Google's effort to stop these privacy attacks would remove a crucial source of information for users regarding Google's privacy. This is particularly important considering the current market conditions regarding competition on privacy. Scholars have discussed the 'lemons market for privacy', whereby users' inability to assess the quality of privacy on offer not only lessens the incentive of sites to compete on privacy but also leads to disregard of privacy promises, even by sites that use privacy as a promotional tool.[83] This inability to assess the privacy conditions often leads to cynicism, where users do not see any reward in investing time in reading privacy policies. As a result, firms often opt for vague or non-committal policies, expecting that few consumers will read them and demand will not change significantly, thereby creating dysfunctional equilibrium. This 'cynical market failure' makes it difficult for companies to attract users by offering a greater level of privacy than that offered by the dominant undertaking.[84]

In light of these realities, Microsoft's campaign on privacy is important for consumers' ability to compare privacy conditions and contribute to breaking the dysfunctional equilibrium that hinders effective competition on privacy. By seeking to stop Microsoft's privacy campaigns, Google's effort ultimately perpetuates the dysfunctional equilibrium and hinders effective competition on privacy conditions. This is achieved by removing the incentives for both Google and other companies to improve their privacy offerings as well as for Microsoft to maintain its promises and to further improve its own privacy conditions.

In light of the discussions and the Commission's view in *EPI Code of Conduct*, which considers restrictions on advertising as object restrictions, Google's efforts to restrict Microsoft's comparative advertisement on privacy matters is likely to be considered a restriction of competition by object. Further, the fact that these efforts concern privacy, as opposed to price, does not affect the assessment. This is because the CJEU has clarified that a practice does not need a direct connection to consumer prices to be considered anticompetitive by object.[85]

[83] See Bonneau and Preibusch (n 69) 149.

[84] Joseph Farrell, 'Can Privacy Be Just Another Good?' (2012) 10 Journal on Telecommunications & High Technology Law 251, 257.

[85] *T-Mobile Netherlands* (n 18) paras 36–39.

Indeed, the plea to stop promotional activities could be justified if the advertising is misleading or inaccurate. As the Commission noted in *EPI Code of Conduct*, advertising must be accurate to serve its competitive function. Google has previously claimed that some of Microsoft's attacks on its privacy practices, particularly the Mailman campaign, are misleading. However, Google has pursued this claim in court, which it lost to Microsoft. Moreover, according to the case law, a restriction of competition by object may also exist, where the conduct of the undertakings simultaneously serves a legitimate purpose. This is notably the case if the coordination of competitors goes beyond what is necessary to achieve the additional legitimate purpose.[86]

b) Efforts to find alignment on privacy matters

As previously mentioned, Google not only sought to limit promotional activities but also aimed to align its privacy goals and strategies with Microsoft and Facebook. Such practices, as shown by the decisions of the Commission and EU courts, have the potential to restrict competition by object. As discussed in Section II, the Commission decisions in *Vimpoltu* and *TACA* held that the agreed-upon standard terms relating to various aspects, including contract duration, liquidated damages, transfer of ownership and risk, warranty, liability, and advertising, were restrictive of competition.[87] The Commission stated that these standards regulate important secondary aspects of competition and could lead to greater uniformity in business terms than would exist without them.

The Commission's decision in the *Car Emission* cartels is another example of significant relevance. The Commission found that DAIMLER, VW, and BMW coordinated their market conduct relating to SCR-systems, specifically by agreeing on AdBlue tank sizes and refill intervals, as well as exchanging information about expected average AdBlue consumption. This conduct was found to have the potential to restrict competition in the product characteristics of new diesel passenger cars, thereby restricting consumer choice and technical advancement in the field of NOx cleaning with SCR systems.[88] The Commission stated that the exchange of information on average AdBlue consumption decreased uncertainty about future conduct and eliminated the risk that any of the parties would be disadvantaged for not going along with more effective NOx-cleaning.[89] In essence, the coordination helped the companies to avoid competition on how best to achieve their objectives and removed competitive risks arising from divergent solutions, such as choosing between 'small tank or large tank' and 'cleaning solution with the sole aim of meeting or exceeding regulatory requirements'.[90] The Commission found

[86] See *Car Emissions* (n 21) para 133; Case C-67/13 P *Groupement des cartes bancaires* ECLI:EU:C:2014:2204, para 70.
[87] *Vimpoltu* (n 13) paras 30–39; *TACA* (n 15) para 446.
[88] *Car Emissions* (n 21) paras 7, 125.
[89] ibid para 136.
[90] ibid para 128.

that the conduct constituted a restriction by object even though actual tank sizes remained well above the volumes discussed and the cleaning strategies used by the manufacturers were different.[91]

Google's efforts to find alignment with Facebook and Microsoft on 'privacy goals and strategies', including on child privacy, have the potential to restrict competition with regard to privacy conditions and limit consumer choice. This could be achieved directly either by reducing their terms of trade with relation to privacy or, otherwise, by jointly limiting competition that might offer consumers a differing level of privacy. The alignment on privacy goals and strategies is intended to remove the risks arising from Microsoft and Facebook talking a more pro-privacy approach. In fact, the internal document reveals as much where Google expresses its worry over Microsoft taking child privacy seriously and Facebook prioritizing privacy in legislative debates. Similarly, the desire to find alignment aims to eliminate the competitive risks arising from the divergent solutions on privacy matters including child privacy.

Although the specific path for a common conduct is not clearly outlined in the meetings, the exchange of information on alignment removes strategic uncertainty regarding the future course of conduct regarding privacy practices and thus facilitates collusion. For example, based on the meeting, Facebook and Microsoft could easily deduce a future course of conduct where they would, based on Google's suggestions, refrain from promoting privacy matters and putting Google's privacy practices in a negative spotlight. As noted above, this would harm competition in privacy and remove an important source of information for consumers. Thus, Google's efforts to find alignment have the effect of eliminating the competitive risks arising from the divergent solutions such as choosing between 'more or less' privacy approaches and how to best meet customers privacy expectations.

To render the discussion more concrete, let us look at the potential alignment paths—namely upward and downward alignment—and how they might restrict competition. A downward alignment occurs when the companies offering a higher level of privacy settle for the lower level. In the case of Google and Microsoft, the Scroogled campaign showed that, as opposed to Google, Microsoft offered better privacy terms regarding users' email privacy, as it does not scan users' email contents for the purpose of advertising. Similarly, Microsoft's attack on Google's privacy policy change shows that Microsoft does not combine data across all its services. Further, Microsoft advertised that, as opposed to Google, its Appstore on Windows Mobile does not leak information to app developers without consumers' consent. In this sense, a downward alignment would occur if Microsoft were to agree, explicitly or implicitly, to lower its privacy terms to Google's level. This includes, for example, Microsoft starting to use users' email communication

[91] ibid para 140.

for targeted advertising, adopting a 'one-account-one-policy' approach where data across services are shared and sharing data from its Appstore with app developers without users' consent. This is a clear instance of alignment that deprives users of a better privacy offering. This restricts competition by depriving Microsoft users of better privacy conditions as they would have to settle for lower privacy terms than prior to the coordination leading up to the alignment.

Similarly, such alignment could potentially limit Google's endeavours to enhance its privacy terms, to the detriment of its users. Knowledge about rivals' future conduct reduces market uncertainties that could have otherwise stimulated improved outcomes. In the case at hand, the knowledge that rivals such as Microsoft would refrain from promoting their privacy policies, instead adopting a comparable privacy approach, could reduce Google's incentive to strive for better privacy conditions. The impact of such alignment on non-price parameters is particularly pronounced in markets where price competition is absent, which is the case with many services offered by Google, Facebook, and Microsoft.

Even an upward alignment, which entails settling for the highest privacy standards on offer, does not necessarily mean that these companies can evade responsibility in competition law. Indeed, upward alignment could potentially deliver superior privacy options to certain users than those currently available. For example, in the above example, an upward alignment would lead Google to adopt Microsoft's privacy standards, which may involve restraining from using users' email content for targeted ads, discontinuing data sharing on the App Store with developers, and reversing its 2012 privacy policy change. In this sense, Google users may come out better off from the alignment. However, such an arrangement can also produce anticompetitive effects by limiting the companies' abilities to exceed what has been explicitly or tacitly agreed upon. According to the Commission Guidelines, accessible and non-binding standard terms and conditions for sale of goods and services will not infringe Article 101(1) unless their application in practice significantly limits consumer choice.[92] Therefore, while arrangements specifically endorsing upward alignment on privacy matters, such as refusing to use email content for advertising, might be compatible with Article 101(1), they can also be detrimental if they inhibit the parties' capabilities to transcend the stipulated agreement.

4. Some Anecdotal Evidence of Harmful Effects

Based on the above discussions, one could argue that the nature of the agreement, the market characteristics related to competition in privacy, and the market position of the involved parties collectively indicate that the practice restricts competition by object. As a result, there is no need to demonstrate concrete negative

[92] European Commission, 'Guidelines on Horizontal Agreements' (n 2) paras 302–305.

impacts on the market. Nevertheless, there appears to be anecdotal evidence suggesting the presence of detrimental effects. For example, Microsoft is not as aggressive on its promotional activities on privacy and has stopped its privacy attacks on Google. The website for the Scroogled campaign is no longer active and redirects to a new URL: WhyMicrosoft.com, which provides information to business customers.[93] In 2019, Microsoft even took the step of removing a blog post written by one of its senior product managers for Office 365, which referenced the old Scroogled campaign and criticized the privacy practices of Google apps.[94]

Some of the market behaviours of Google and Facebook also indicate a form of anticompetitive collusion. For example, Google's 2014 decision to shut down a rival social network, Orkut, has raised many questions among commentators. Importantly, there is evidence that, following Google's exit from the social network, Facebook changed its privacy policy and degraded its privacy offering. According to Srinivasan, Facebook revoked users' ability to vote on changes to its privacy policies following Google's departure.[95]

The Texas complaint contains even more evidence of this behaviour. In 2015, Google and Facebook entered into a secret agreement that granted Google an exclusive access to WhatsApp users' private messages.[96] After the agreement, WhatsApp users on Android were given the option to back up their messages and files, such as photos, video, and audio files, on Google Drive. Despite WhatsApp promoting its messaging service as end-to-end encrypted, with no third party, including WhatsApp itself, having access to such files, the agreement allowed Google to have access to such data unencrypted.[97] Both Google and Facebook failed to inform users about this access, leading to Google Drive gaining approximately 750 million new WhatsApp backup accounts and a billion new Google Drive customers involving more than 345 billion WhatsApp files.[98] This agreement raises the question of whether Facebook might be reciprocating Google's decision to shut down its Orkut social network.

Indeed, much of the evidence regarding the harmful competitive effects is circumstantial, as it is not clear whether these market outcomes are directly caused by contacts. However, this is less of a concern because, as the CJEU has noted, if the Commission finds explicit evidence of 'unlawful contact between traders, such as the minutes of a meeting, it will normally be only fragmentary and sparse, so that it is often necessary to reconstitute certain details by deduction'.[99] In this regard,

[93] Lara O'Reilly, 'Microsoft Has Finally Abandoned Its Google-Bashing "Scroogled" Ad Campaign', *Business Insider* (14 January 2015).

[94] ibid.

[95] Dina Srinivasan, 'The Antitrust Case against Facebook: A Monopolist's Journey towards Pervasive Surveillance in Spite of Consumers' Preference for Privacy' (2019) 16 Berkeley Business Law Journal 39.

[96] *State of Texas v Google* (n 9) para 485.

[97] ibid paras 485–90.

[98] ibid paras 491–95.

[99] *Aalborg Portland v Commission* (n 51) para 56.

it is essential to emphasize that Google admitted to having multiple contacts with competitors and achieving some success from these interactions. Importantly, the CJEU case law indicates that 'in most cases the evidence of anti-competitive practice or agreement must be inferred from coincidences and indica which, taken together, may, in the absence of another plausible explanation, constitute evidence of an infringement'.[100] Furthermore, the case law indicates that attending a meeting involving anticompetitive activities creates a presumption of illegality, which the undertaking must refute through evidence of public distancing.[101] This means that, at least within the EU, competition authorities can infer infringement of Article 101(1) of the TFEU based on the above-mentioned market outcomes and the contacts that occurred. Consequently, it is up to the involved parties to offer a plausible explanation proving that the outcomes are not a result of the illegal contacts.

IV. Privacy Protection and Standard Setting

Generally, standardization generates many procompetitive benefits, such as increasing and enhancing market information. This can take the form of standardized terms that enable consumers to compare conditions of supply or mechanisms demonstrating that a certain product or service adheres to specific quality standards. These benefits hold significant importance in markets characterized by information asymmetry or where consumers find it challenging to evaluate the quality or safety of products. The introduction of certification mechanisms, data protection seals, and marks under the General Data Protection Regulation (GDPR) serves a similar purpose. These tools aim to equip users with the means to assess the quality of a service's privacy protection considering compliance with the GDPR. Consequently, standards reduce transaction costs associated with imperfect product information for sellers and buyers.[102]

Despite these benefits, standard setting can, as shown below, raise competition concerns.[103] Four possible competition harms may arise from standardization. First, the standardization process might involve discussions and agreements among competitors, potentially reducing or eliminating competition based on price or quality.[104] In this sense, the standard-setting organization (SSO) essentially serves as a platform fostering collusive outcomes. Second, standards may limit technical development or innovation if the process does not allow alternative technologies to compete for inclusion in the standard.[105] This occurs where a

[100] ibid para 57.
[101] Case C-634/13 *Total Marketing Services SA v Commission* ECLI:EU:C:2015:614, para 21.
[102] FTC, *Standards and Certification* (FTC 1983) 50.
[103] See ibid; Ruben Schellingerhout, 'Standard-Setting from a Competition Law Perspective' (2011) *Competition Policy Newsletter* 3.
[104] European Commission, 'Guidelines on Horizontal Agreements' (n 2) para 265.
[105] ibid para 260.

certain technology is incorporated into a standard, thereby raising entry barriers for alternative technologies and eventually excluding such technologies from the market. Third, the refusal to grant access to standards that are essential for market entry could hamper competition by shutting out competitors from the market.[106] Foreclosure through standardization may also arise if there is 'capture' of the standard setting by a particular group, and this is used to advance the interests of the group to the detriment of others.[107]

The final, and perhaps less frequently discussed, harm arises when standard setting leads to the loss of information competition.[108] In many cases, particularly in Internet communication standards, standard setting involves collective agreement on information. While such agreements can bring procompetitive benefits (eg by reducing the costs of producing such information individually), they may occasionally produce anticompetitive effects by suppressing information competition. Standard setting can lead to such harm by advancing a 'unified position', which, absent the standard, might have been more diverse and varied.[109] This section discusses how standardization in privacy conditions and technical specification might affect competition in data privacy and the extent to which these practices may violate Article 101.

A. Collective Actions to Improve Data Privacy Conditions

Contrary to the examples presented in Section III, where companies conspire to diminish privacy levels, there could be scenarios where businesses collaborate to enhance the level of privacy. This could occur within the context of an umbrella organization or through multilateral arrangements. Such cooperation might encompass agreements to lower the data retention period or decisions not to collect or use certain sensitive data, such as health information, for behavioural advertising. Other examples include agreements to standardize privacy policies, perhaps by shortening them and enhancing their readability, thereby enabling users to easily compare different policies. The question is whether such agreements can restrict competition.

Collective efforts to enhance users' privacy are comparable to standardization agreements or standard terms as described in the Commission Guidelines for Horizontal Cooperation. The Guidelines recognize the benefits of such agreements as a way to 'share risk, save costs, increase investment, pool knowhow, enhance product quality and variety, and launch innovation faster'.[110] However, these

[106] ibid paras 365–66.
[107] ibid para 261.
[108] Patterson, *Antitrust Law* (n 11) 92.
[109] ibid 88.
[110] European Commission, 'Guidelines on Horizontal Agreements' (n 2) para 2.

agreements might harm competition in a way that outweighs the benefits by limiting product choice and innovation.[111] This happens if the 'terms define the scope of the end-product'.[112] The Commission decisions in *Vimpoltu* and *TACA* are relevant examples where standard terms affecting non-price parameters were found to violate Article 101(1).[113] Thus, in principle, collective efforts to enhance privacy or standardize privacy policies could violate Article 101 if they create greater uniformity in the level of data privacy conditions than would be the case in their absence. Agreements to standardize the data retention period, as well as the amount and type of data to be collected, could raise such concerns.[114]

Nonetheless, real-world examples of such practices are quite rare. One that comes close is something that happened between 2008 and 2010 regarding the retention period of users' search queries by major search engines. In April 2008, the Article 29 Working Party issued an opinion critiquing the retention of users' search queries for over a year and called on the search engine companies to delete or adopt strong anonymization after six months.[115] Following this suggestion, Microsoft announced that it was willing to reduce the retention period to six months and anonymize the data thereafter if competing search engines 'did the same'.[116] If Google and Yahoo! were to follow Microsoft's invitation and adopt a six-month data-retention policy, thus enabling Microsoft to keep its promises, would this constitute a breach of Article 101(1)?[117] Would it be different if the invitation were made without the Working Party's suggestion?

The first issue that needs addressing is the extent to which such conduct affects competition regarding data privacy. As noted in Chapter 4, the data-retention period is one relevant dimension of privacy competition, which is informed by the storage limitation principle of the GDPR. The principle dictates that data should not be stored for longer than is necessary to achieve the purpose. Competition on this aspect of privacy would lead firms to reduce the data-retention period to the minimum necessary or not storing data at all. The market behaviour of firms supports the existence of competition on this dimension. For example, Google, Yahoo!, and Microsoft responded to each other's changes to their privacy policies by shortening the data-retention period. In 2007, Google announced its policy to anonymize users' search queries after 18–24 months, as a 'step to further improve . . . [its] privacy practices'.[118] In September 2008, Google took '[a]nother step

[111] ibid para 263.
[112] ibid.
[113] *Vimpoltu* (n 13) para 39; *TACA* (n 15).
[114] See Dryden and Iyer (n 12).
[115] Article 29 Data Protection Working Party (WP148), 'Opinion 1/2008 on Data Protection Issues Related to Search Engines' (2008) 19.
[116] See Kim Dixon, 'Yahoo Cuts Data Retention to Three Months', *Reuters* (17 December 2008).
[117] See also John Newman (n 5) 95 (discussing a similar example).
[118] Google Blog, 'Taking Steps to Further Improve Our Privacy Practices' (14 March 2007) <https://googleblog.blogspot.com/2007/03/taking-steps-to-further-improve-our.html>.

to protect user privacy' by cutting its retention period from 18 to 9 months.[119] This further culminated in Yahoo! adopting a three-month policy in December 2008.[120] Microsoft followed suit, adopting a six-month policy in January 2010.[121] In light of this competition, the hypothetical scenario involving Microsoft might be viewed as an invitation to fix the level of data protection at the maximum level (six months) and a concerted practice, as evidenced by Yahoo! and Google's conduct, at this level of protection.[122] Indeed, if Yahoo! and Google were to officially accept the invitation, this might even be considered as an agreement, rather than a concerted practice.[123] The question is whether such conduct adversely affects competition on data retention.

Given that the hypothetical concerted practice reduces the data-retention period, leading to an improvement in data-retention practices at the time, it is comparable to agreements to fix maximum prices. Although such agreements generate benefits for users, they can also lead to restrictive effects on competition. The US Supreme Court has held that an agreement between a seller and a retailer that imposes maximum prices breaches Section 1 of the Sherman Act.[124] Similarly, an agreement among competing physicians imposing 'maximum fees that they may claim in full payment for health services' to certain policyholders was found to be per se illegal and in breach of Section 1.[125] According to the Court, schemes that fix maximum prices 'may severely intrude upon the ability of buyers to compete and survive in that market', limit dealers' incentives 'to furnish services and conveniences which consumers desire and for which they are willing to pay', and disproportionately favour 'a few large or specifically advantaged dealers'.[126] Moreover, where the maximum price is set near the actual cost, such restrictions may produce effects akin to those of fixing minimum prices.[127]

In the EU, the Commission guidance on vertical agreements indicates that imposing maximum resale prices is not generally problematic but can restrict competition, depending on the market share of the companies and on whether it facilitates alignment between suppliers or resellers.[128] In one instance, the Commission

[119] Google Blog, 'Another Step to Protect User Privacy' (8 September 2008) <https://googleblog.blogspot.com/2008/09/another-step-to-protect-user-privacy.html>.

[120] Dixon (n 116).

[121] See Bing Blogs, 'Updates to Bing Privacy' (19 January 2010) <https://blogs.bing.com/search/January-2010/Updates-to-Bing-Privacy>.

[122] John Newman (n 5) 95 (drawing comparisons of such conduct with fixing maximum prices and stating that 'If competitors were to engage in such behaviour vis-a-vis prices, their conduct would likely be a per se violation of Sherman Act S1').

[123] For more on the treatment of invitation to collude and some of the gaps in EU law, see Ioannis Lianos and Florian Wagner-von Papp, 'Tackling Invitations to Collude and Unilateral Disclosure: The Moving Frontiers of Competition Law?' (2022) 13 Journal of European Competition Law & Practice 249.

[124] *Albrecht v Herald Co* 390 US Supreme Court (1968) 145, 152.

[125] *Arizona v Maricopa County Medical Soc 457* US Supreme Court (1982) 332.

[126] *Albrecht v Herald* (n 124) 152–53.

[127] ibid.

[128] European Commission, 'Commission Notice Guidelines on Vertical Restraints' SEC(2010) 411, paras 48, 226–27.

found a vertical agreement imposing maximum prices compatible with Article 101. According to the Commission, such arrangements do not 'create significant alignment effects' and do not have an appreciable effect on competition, partly because the parties are not hindered from reducing 'the prices actually paid by the customer'.[129] Moreover, the CJEU has held that imposing a maximum resale price is equivalent to imposing a minimum price unless it is 'genuinely possible for the reseller to lower that sale price'.[130] Setting maximum prices by horizontal competitors, a fortiori, could be caught under Article 101. Thus, the door is open for agreements, whether horizontal or vertical, imposing maximum prices to fall foul of Article 101(1). The question is whether similar arrangements on data privacy, such as those imposing maximum data-retention periods as in the above hypothetical case involving search engines, could also fall under the purview of Article 101(1).

Interestingly, the Commission Guidelines on horizontal agreements address a scenario similar to the hypothetical example. In this example, major producers of processed food, who together hold over 70 per cent of the market share in a member state, agree to follow the recommended fat levels for their products as suggested by a government-funded think tank.[131] While acknowledging that such an agreement might reduce consumer choice, the Commission states that the agreement is unlikely to give rise to restrictive effects on competition within the meaning of Article 101(1). This is because the parties can still continue to compete across various other product features, such as price, size, quality, taste, and other nutritional content.[132] The Commission further indicated that the agreement did not prevent, and could even increase, competition on fat levels in such products 'where parties seek to offer products with the lowest levels'.[133] In light of this example and the above discussion, arrangements to fix maximum price or minimum quality are compatible with Article 101 unless they lead to alignment effects that restrict the ability of the parties to lower prices or increase quality beyond the agreed terms.

Applying this to the hypothetical scenario on data privacy, a concerted practice or an agreement to adopt a six-month policy would not breach Article 101(1) unless it prevented the parties from adopting a retention policy of less than six months. Punishing such conduct could be counterproductive, potentially depriving users of a higher level of protection than the market might offer. According to the Commission Guidelines and CJEU case law, the restrictive nature of an agreement should be assessed by taking into account the competition that could have occurred absent the agreement (counterfactual).[134] The above hypothetical arrangement to reduce the data-retention period to six months could be

129 Case COMP/B-1/38348 *Repsol CPP SA* decision of 12 April 2004, paras 18–20.
130 Case C-279 *CEPSA Estaciones de Servicio SA v LV Tobar e Hijos SL* ECLI:EU:C:2008:485, para 71.
131 European Commission, 'Guidelines on Horizontal Agreements' (n 2) para 320.
132 ibid.
133 ibid.
134 ibid para 29; Case C-56/65 *Société Technique Minière v Maschinenbau Ulm* ECLI:EU:C:1966:38.

seen as beneficial for consumers' data privacy as it reinforces the storage limitation principle vis-à-vis the situation before the arrangement, which was longer than six months.

This notwithstanding, competition authorities and courts should not readily accept that such agreements are always welfare enhancing. If the hypothetical arrangement were to include a provision limiting search engines' freedom to adopt a less-than-six-month policy, even for a period, this could prove problematic. This is because such a provision would align the search engines' data-retention period and create an effect akin to that of imposing a maximum level on the quality of data privacy. In fact, considering the above sequence of events and the reaction of the search engines to each other's policy changes, such an arrangement would have prevented Yahoo! from reducing (or at least reduced its incentive to reduce) its retention period to three months, which is a better level of protection than the agreed-upon six-month retention policy. This is in line with the Commission decision, as discussed in Section II above, regarding the collusion among truck manufacturers who coordinated the timing for the introduction of emission-reducing technologies. The Commission noted that by delaying when to roll out clean emissions technology, the parties have passed the costs of deploying the new technologies on to consumers. In a similar fashion, if search engines were to agree to fix the data-retention period at six months, they would be passing on to consumers the privacy risks (costs) that come with the retention of data for three additional months.

Relatedly, the fact that the six-month policy was recommended by the Article 29 Working Party does not necessarily preclude liability under Article 101(1).[135] This is because the recommendation does not preclude competitive activity below the six-month mark, while the hypothetical arrangement does. Overall, although many agreements to improve data privacy may generate benefits for consumers, especially considering the current situation, such agreements should not be used to restrict companies' ability to offer even better levels of data privacy protection. Similarly, arrangements to standardize privacy policies or facilitate data portability among service providers[136] should be approached with caution. Generally, competition authorities should remain alert to the limited, yet possible, scenarios where agreements, despite appearing to bolster data privacy, may inadvertently set a cap on the level of data privacy protection.

[135] European Commission, 'Guidelines on Horizontal Agreements' (n 2) paras 22, 319.

[136] See Russell Brandom, 'Google, Facebook, Microsoft, and Twitter Partner for Ambitious New Data Project', *The Verge* (20 July 2018).

B. Technical Standards and Harms to Competition

Design is of paramount importance to privacy protection. How technologies and services are designed has a considerable impact on the efforts and costs that users of these technologies expend in protecting their privacy. Design can affect privacy protection by communicating information about how the technology functions, the options users have, and by enabling (hindering) activities.[137] For example, design can increase the transaction costs involved in protecting privacy through defaults. Conversely, if deployed to benefit privacy, design can provide de facto privacy protection. Put simply, 'design picks data winners and privacy losers'.[138] To the extent that design is key for privacy, technical standards—which set out a defined (and efficient) engineering approach to accomplishing something—become of paramount importance for privacy protection.

Specifically, communication standards play a crucial role as they determine the ease with which privacy can be protected. For example, the use of domain names (eg <www.cancer.com>), instead of Internet protocol (IP) addresses (eg 129.240.178.47), serves mnemonic purposes but also reveals information about users' interests and concerns.[139] Similarly, the HTTP referrer header, a protocol enabling websites to interlink, is designed in such a way that when users engage with a hyperlink, their browser transmits information to the next website, including the content of the previous site, which also reveals the users' interests.[140] Hardware design could have similar implications. The decision by phone manufacturers, such as Apple, to assign unique IDs to their devices facilitates the continuous monitoring of users and their activities.

The implication is that, sometimes, design plays an influential role, at times even more so than data controllers, in deciding what data are collected and to whom they are communicated. Thus, as Hartzog compellingly argues, ignoring the role of design and standards for the protection of privacy in regulatory policy is potentially dangerous.[141] Although Hartzog's call focuses mainly on the need to give adequate attention to design in data privacy and consumer protection rules, standards can also be of interest to competition law.

As noted above, one way by which standardization might harm competition is by suppressing information competition. As Patterson puts it,

> The competition that is eliminated by standard-setting activities is not that within the standard-setting organization, but that which would have existed without it.

[137] Woodrow Hartzog, *Privacy's Blueprint: The Battle to Control the Design of New Technologies* (Harvard UP 2018) 26.

[138] ibid 50.

[139] ibid 77.

[140] ibid 22.

[141] ibid 23.

> In the absence of standard setting, individual sellers would provide their own information, and that information would compete for acceptance by buyers in the marketplace—the real marketplace of information, not the standard-setting organization.[142]

Thus, Patterson argues that, in some cases, competition policy needs to focus on the 'competitive conditions under which information and opinions are produced' and how the standard-setting process distorts this competition.[143] The following sections will delve into how standard setting can generate loss of information competition, followed by an illustration of such harm and its impact on data privacy using the World Wide Web Consortium (W3C) standard-setting process for Do Not Track (DNT).

1. Standard Setting and the Loss of Information Competition

One instance where standard setting can eliminate information competition is when it lacks clear procompetitive benefits and seems designed to make it more difficult to challenge the information produced.[144] In an article entitled 'Law-Fixing', Patterson discusses a case where major law firms agree on the interpretation of Section 402 of the US Sarbanes–Oxley Act 2002, which prohibits loans by publicly traded companies to their directors and officers.[145] The interpretation pertains as to what falls under the exception to this rule, which precluded pre-existing loans provided there was no 'material modification' to the terms. In a position paper, the law firms came to a common interpretation that total or partial forgiveness of pre-existing loans was permissible within the Act. This was because if a loan is forgiven, it no longer qualifies as a loan since it does not involve a modification of terms. Furthermore, the law firms agreed to adopt this interpretation of the statute in advising their clients.

Patterson views such an agreement as fixing the quality of an information product, which can have a 'significant effect on the market', namely the information market for lawyers.[146] To begin with, Patterson argues, there are no clear efficiencies in collectively taking a stand on this matter. Instead, these firms are seeking to offer interpretations that will appeal to their clients, but they prefer to do this with the reassurance that other companies are committed to providing similar counsel.[147] This approach not only shields these firms from potential competitive disadvantages against those that might offer more client-friendly advice but also

[142] Patterson, *Antitrust Law* (n 11) 93–94.
[143] ibid 91.
[144] ibid.
[145] Mark Patterson, 'Law-Fixing: Should Lawyers Agree How to Interpret Statutes?' (Fordham University School of Law Research Paper, Fordham University 2004) 50.
[146] ibid 5.
[147] ibid.

reduces their exposure to retrospective scrutiny if their guidance proves to be incorrect.[148] The adoption of the position paper has prompted some law firms to alter their advice, demonstrating the efficacy of such arrangements in forcing law firms to align with the interpretations presented in the document.[149]

The antitrust concern arises because, in the absence of the position paper, a lawyer and a law firm would provide their positions on Section 402, knowing that this interpretation may attract some clients and drive others to competitors. The agreement avoids this uncertainty in providing the advice. Similarly, when the relevant regulatory authority or courts provide an authoritative interpretation of Section 402, any lawyer that has given advice that goes against this interpretation could suffer in the market.[150] However, that danger is substantially lessened when lawyers and law firms agree to adopt a single position. Thus, to exclude such an agreement from the realm of antitrust, Patterson argues, would be to draw the boundaries of antitrust too narrowly.[151] As discussed below, a similar competitive concern arises in relation to W3C's standard-setting process for DNT.

2. The W3C's DNT Standard and the Potential Loss of Information Competition

The W3C is an international body that develops web standards. Its mission is 'to lead the World Wide Web to its full potential by developing protocols and guidelines that ensure the long-term growth of the Web'.[152] Work in the W3C is conducted by member organizations that pay an annual fee, full-time staff, and invited experts. The W3C has created many web standards and one that has significant implications for data privacy is the so-called DNT standard. The standard was inspired by the FTC's successful Do-Not-Call list, which enabled consumers to register their telephone number if they did not wish to receive unsolicited calls.[153] The W3C was tasked with providing technical specifications for the Tracking Preferences Expression (TPE), which would allow users to express their tracking preferences to each server and web application they interact with over HTTP. This, in turn, allows each service to modify its behaviour to align with the user's expectations or negotiate a new agreement.

One of the most controversial aspects of this process was whether web browsers should set DNT by default. The W3C's proposed specification mandated that users must manually signal their preferences and prohibited web browsers from turning on this option by default. The core idea is that an expression of tracking preference

[148] ibid 2.
[149] ibid 2.
[150] ibid.
[151] Patterson, *Antitrust Law* (n 11) 89.
[152] W3C, 'W3C Mission', <www.w3.org/Consortium/mission> accessed 9 February 2024.
[153] Joshua Fairfield, 'Do-Not-Track as Default' (2012) 11 Northwestern Journal of Technology and Intellectual Property 575, 581.

is transmitted to web applications only when it signifies a conscious, active decision by the user.[154] According to this specification, if a web browser sets the DNT standard by default, it is not considered a valid expression of the user's will. The TPE requires that web browsers set the default to 'unset', which would be interpreted by websites as no preference expressed, thus allowing websites to track consumers. If websites suspect that the default has been automatically activated by the web browser, they reserve the right to disregard the signal and continue tracking the user.[155]

What is even more interesting is that when Microsoft's Internet Explorer (IE) decided to prompt users to 'Express Choice' on the DNT during installation, Roy Fielding, the author of the TPE, responded by offering a patch for web servers that caused them to ignore all DNT flags set by IE.[156] The content of the standard, in light of the proposed specification and Fielding's reaction to Microsoft's prompt, opens up questions about how it limits competition among web browsers via data privacy. It also raises some procedural and sabotage concerns.

From a competition law perspective, the procedural aspects attract the most scrutiny. In this regard, some experts have claimed that the process of adopting the DNT standard was influenced by a few powerful firms. For example, Hartzog notes that the process for DNT adoption was 'co-opted solely to drive an industry's agenda'.[157] Similarly, Stucke and Grunes claim that the process was highly influenced by the key digital players, such as Google, Yahoo!, and Facebook.[158] Specifically, the authors assert that these players 'were deciding the rules of the game'.[159] The *New York Times* also featured an op-ed entitled 'The Slow Death of "Do Not Track"', which noted that the tracking protection working group, a group tasked with developing the DNT standard, was dominated by experts from Apple, Facebook, Google, and Yahoo!.[160] The article noted the 'murky process' behind the standard development 'that has devolved into an effort to protect the positions of Internet giants'.[161]

Whether the W3C process to adopt DNT was captured by certain interest groups in a sense that gives rise to liability under Article 101(1) is an empirical question and cannot be answered in the abstract. More generally, to the extent that the creation of the working group was unbalanced, and thus sabotaged to serve certain interests, it could potentially raise anticompetitive concerns. Participation in the W3C process is limited to paying members, and this opens it up for capture

154 W3C, 'Tracking Preference Expression (DNT): W3C Candidate Recommendation 19 October 2017' (2017) <https://www.w3.org/TR/2017/CR-tracking-dnt-20171019/>.
155 Fairfield (n 153) 587.
156 ibid 579.
157 See Hartzog (n 137) 164.
158 Stucke and Grunes (n 6) 47.
159 ibid 46.
160 Fred Campbell Jr, 'The Slow Death of "Do Not Track"', *New York Times* (26 December 2014).
161 ibid.

by certain groups. However, most of the claims seem to be based more on the outcome of the standard than on concrete evidence of the overbearing influence of specific groups.

This notwithstanding, as noted above, harms to competition from standard setting can result from a loss of information competition in the market. This occurs if the standard-setting process leads to a unified position, which, absent the standard, might be more diverse and varied. The harm to competition is even more acute if this unified position 'make[s] it more difficult to challenge the information produced' by the SSO.[162] As Patterson puts it,

> The fundamental point is that the recipients of information from standards providers should make their own decisions regarding what goods should be purchased, and they need information that is useful for making that decision. If standard providers deliver information in such a way as to cause a large proportion of downstream firms or consumers to act uniformly, and particularly if the standard-setters know that the information will cause the result, the standard-setting is causing a market failure, not remedying one.[163]

Patterson further asserts that standard setting that produces information agreements may bring procompetitive gains provided that the goal of such agreements is to ensure that the produced information was adequately considered and accorded its fair value.[164] However, if 'the effects of a powerful information provider went further, to be coercive or to drown out other speakers, those effects would be anticompetitive'.[165]

Arguably, there are some signs that the development of the DNT standard might have led to reduced competition on its implementation. In principle, the standard is voluntary, which means that web browsers can choose not to comply, opting instead to turn on DNT by default. However, the specifications of the standard subtly encourage websites to disregard such choice and continue their tracking activities. This suggests that if a web browser's request is largely ignored by websites, the potential for deviation from the norm is limited. As such, the standard becomes de facto binding as it encourages collective punishment for deviation.[166] Additionally, by publishing information on how to circumvent DNT requests that are activated by default, the W3C has reduced the costs of parties participating in the collective punishment of deviations from the standard. This, in turn, may cause websites to act uniformly in ignoring requests from web browsers that have turned DNT on by

[162] Patterson, *Antitrust Law* (n 11) 92.
[163] ibid 102.
[164] ibid 98.
[165] ibid.
[166] The Commission recognizes that even a purportedly voluntary standard could become de facto binding. See European Commission, 'Guidelines on Horizontal Agreements' (n 2) para 266.

default. In so doing, the practice makes it more difficult to challenge the information produced by W3C.

Furthermore, one could argue that the provision of information for ignoring default-activated DNT requests was strategically aimed at coercing or drowning out a potentially challenging source of alternative information, particularly Microsoft. This is because such information was only provided after IE, the then largest web browser, decided to turn DNT on by default. In fact, it was not clear that Microsoft's approach was a deviation from the recommended specification, given that IE merely prompted users to select from 'Express' and 'Custom' choices during the installation process.[167] Microsoft also informed users that selecting the 'Express' choice would enable DNT. Given that the user makes an active choice in selecting the 'Express', the deviation from the standard is debatable. What is even more interesting is that, even if one considers IE to have deviated from the standard, it was not the first browser to do so. The Tor browser had already turned on DNT by default, and this did not prompt W3C to offer information to websites on how to ignore requests from Tor.[168]

Thus, the publication by W3C of a patch to ignore requests from browsers that turn on DNT by default appears to be as much a response to Microsoft's market reach and the impact this might have on W3C's own power. Given IE's market reach and Microsoft's position at the time, websites could easily have respected Microsoft's DNT demands, thus overriding the information provided by W3C. By providing the patching information, Fielding seems to have used the authority of the W3C 'to cause a large proportion of downstream firms to act uniformly' and strengthen the coercive effect of the standard by penalizing actors that deviate from the TPE specification. Moreover, by targeting Microsoft, the information seems specifically aimed at drowning out a potentially powerful speaker or information provider.

In light of these facts, the standard-setting process and the provision of patching information might have caused a loss of information competition and led to a decrease in the diversity of responses among websites on how to handle Microsoft's approach. This could include determining whether Microsoft's approach constitutes a deviation from the standard, deciding on appropriate countermeasures, and outlining the process for implementation. Absent the information from the TPE's author, Fielding, websites would have had to determine whether Microsoft's approach was indeed compliant with the standard (and there were strong arguments in favour of such an interpretation). Even if websites were to reach the conclusion that Microsoft was deviating from the standard, they would still need to decide about whether to ignore requests and how to effectively do so. Absent the patching information, some might have chosen to respect all DNT requests from IE (thus

[167] Fairfield (n 153) 583–84.
[168] ibid 584.

improving the level of IE users' privacy), others might have gone for the middle ground and those choosing to ignore the request would have had to find a means to do so effectively. In developing such means, a variety of responses might have appeared, some effective and some less effective in ignoring IE's requests. Such a diverse and varied response would better serve users' privacy compared to the uniform position promoted by W3C that mandates and facilities ignoring all DNT requests activated by default.

In this sense, the publication of the patch has led to uniformity in website behaviour, and the standard setters could arguably foresee that the information would cause this result. In fact, one is hard pressed to argue that the provision of such information was aimed at anything but creating this uniformity by punishing a debatable deviation from the standard. Thus, the provision of the patch information has arguably led to the exclusion of information competition and possibly a subsequent market failure that led to the 'Slow Death of "Do Not Track" '.[169]

It is true that conventional competition analysis has often focused on elimination of competition within the SSO and may overlook practices that exclude information competition. However, one could argue that SSOs should be required to implement procedural safeguards.[170] Both the Commission Guidelines and the CJEU case law underline the need for SSOs to implement 'sufficient safeguards to prevent the standard-setting process from being biased towards one or several participants'.[171] These safeguards ought to apply to SSO practices that could lead to reduced information competition and trigger market failure. Such safeguards would serve to prevent SSOs' processes from being utilized to suppress information competition, for instance, by coercing powerful speakers into submission or coordinating punitive measures for deviations.

3. Restrictions on Automating Privacy Protection

The DNT standard is also interesting from a product design (substantive) perspective, where competition policy has a limited role, as it has significant implications for competition on data privacy. This is because, first, it requires consumers to set their privacy preferences manually. One of the justifications given for adopting this approach is that, if browsers activate DNT by default, it is not a genuine expression of the consumer's choice but rather the vendor's. This approach leaves end-users at a disadvantage. While software defaults provide no enforceable rights for consumers, they create perfectly enforceable rights for advertisers.[172] In so doing, the specification limits users from expressing their privacy preferences by choosing a web browser that systematically integrates and automates protection against

[169] See Campbell (n 160).
[170] Patterson, *Antitrust Law* (n 11) 101.
[171] European Commission, 'Guidelines on Horizontal Agreements' (n 2) para 301. Also Case C-96/82 *NV IAZ International Belgium v Commission* ECLI:EU:C:1983:310, paras 3384–86.
[172] Fairfield (n 153) 587.

third-party tracking. The only possibility for the user to signal such a preference is through the selection of a browser that ostensibly reflects a specific tracking preference. This is elaborated in the TPE specification, which states that the use of a general-purpose browser, like 'SuperFred', does not imply a tracking preference, but monikers like 'SuperDoNotTrack' or 'UltraPrivacyFred' could suggest a specific tracking preference.[173]

This suggests that, except for instances where the browser's name includes terms like 'Do Not Track' or 'privacy', users can only enhance their privacy protection manually and through a lengthy process of selecting a browser that does not inherently offer privacy protection, then tweaking and setting it up to do so.[174] This approach 'privileges feature choice over product choice' and has the effect of increasing the cost of making privacy-protective choices.[175] More importantly, the specification limits the ability of mainstream web browsers to attract consumers and build a reputation by turning on DNT by default and thereby automating privacy protection.[176] This is because the standard encourages websites to ignore requests from web browsers that activate DNT by default. Moreover, by publishing information on how to ignore DNT requests that are set by default, the W3C makes it easier to collectively punish non-conformity. Fairfield summarizes the effect as follows:

> Consumer choice is most often expressed at the product level, not at the feature level. Building a brand based on privacy requires that companies be free to add privacy features without retaliation from industry groups. Browser creators should not have to fork their products into separate, privacy-themed browsers. The bespoke standard, which requires feature-level choice rather than product-level choice, therefore *significantly inhibits competition in the privacy market*.[177]

It is evident that the above issues are related to product design, with competition law playing a limited role. Within the framework of Article 101, horizontal collaboration (especially in standard setting) to determine product specifications is often seen as procompetitive.[178] Meanwhile, product design considerations have traditionally been of peripheral significance under Article 102, warranting scrutiny only under 'exceptional circumstances'.[179] Such instances arise when

[173] W3C (n 154).
[174] Fairfield (n 153) 588.
[175] ibid.
[176] ibid 602.
[177] ibid 590 (emphasis added).
[178] European Commission, 'Guidelines on Horizontal Agreements' (n 2) paras 308–11.
[179] See Pablo Ibáñez Colomo, 'Product Design and Business Models in EU Antitrust Law' (2021) 4, 27, <https://ssrncom/abstract=3925396> accessed 9 February 2024. Product design changes are also considered part of the competitive process in US law. See Eleanor Fox, 'Monopolization, Abuse of Dominance, and the Indeterminacy of Economics: The U.S./E.U. Divide' (2006) 2006 Utah Law Review 725, 729.

modifying the product configuration becomes crucial to provide downstream players access to indispensable input. However, the landscape has shifted in recent years. Product design has come to the forefront in several antitrust cases involving digital entities.[180] Notable examples include the *Google Shopping* and *Apple Pay* cases. This emphasis seems to be driven by concerns related to the distribution of profits across value chains.[181] While addressing product design aligns with complexity-orientated antitrust and the calls to tackle architectural power, there is growing concern that the standard of intervention is inconsistent with the CJEU's case law.[182] Additionally, these cases appear to blur the boundaries between exploitative and exclusionary practices, diminishing the thresholds for intervention in exclusionary activities. In light of these nuances, addressing product design issues through *ex-ante* regulation is deemed a more suitable approach, mitigating inconsistencies.[183]

This notwithstanding, competition authorities can still make significant contributions in certain areas, particularly as data and privacy become central to numerous competition investigations. Indeed, some promising developments indicate that competition authorities are beginning to grasp the importance of standard setting for both competition and privacy protection. For instance, as part of Google's proposed implementation of the Privacy Sandbox, the United Kingdom's Competition and Markets Authority (CMA) identified potential concerns to competition within the advertising market and to privacy protection.[184] To allay these concerns, Google offered various measures, including a commitment to facilitate the CMA's participation in discussions on the Privacy Sandbox proposals within the W3C Consortium or any other requested forum.[185] Moreover, the CMA made a commitment to involve the UK Information Commissioner's Office (ICO) in assessing the impact on privacy from the design, development, and implementation of the Privacy Sandbox.[186]

Importantly, addressing the substantive competition concerns from standard setting would require a more proactive approach from data privacy and consumer protection authorities through active participation in standard setting that has implications for privacy. In this regard, the European Commission has published a communication which stipulates that it will consult relevant stakeholders (eg data protection authorities, DPAs) in order to incorporate PETs in its actions and the

[180] Colomo (n 179) 33ff.
[181] ibid 50.
[182] ibid.
[183] ibid. See also Thibault Schrepel, 'Predatory Innovation: The Definite Need for Legal Recognition' (2018) 21 Southern Methodist University (SMU) Science and Technology Law Review 19.
[184] See Chapter 4, Section IV.
[185] Case 50972 *Decision to Accept Commitments Offered by Google in Relation to Its Privacy Sandbox Proposals*, Competition and Markets Authority 11 February 2022, para 6.20.
[186] ibid para 6.45.

work of the European standardization bodies.[187] This will be paramount, in particular, where the debate identifies appropriate data protection standards requiring the incorporation and use of certain PETs.[188] This is a positive move but need not be limited to European standardization bodies.

Indeed, the Article 29 Working Party issued several letters following the call for comments on the TPE specification on DNT. In its comments, the Working Party raised several issues that the TPE specification needs to consider.[189] For example, the Working Party warned that the lack of active choice by users should not be interpreted by data controllers as consent to be tracked. In a follow-up letter, the Working Party suggested the addition of more nuanced options that would give users the possibility of specifying 'Do Not Collect', 'Do Not Use', and 'Do Not Share'.[190] These are encouraging moves that need to be strengthened. More particularly, DPAs, including the European Data Protection Board (EDPB), need to allocate adequate resources to actively engage in the Internet Engineering Task Force (IETF) and W3C standard-setting processes from the outset if they want to exert influence and ensure that the standards do not tip the scale against users' privacy. Moreover, the GDPR opens the possibility of certification and seal marks, which could be used to promote compliance with privacy-enhancing standards as one criterion for obtaining certification and seal marks.

V. Conclusion

This chapter examined the existence and potential of collaborative efforts among undertakings that could restrict competition in data privacy and PETs. Using the Google–Eyeo agreement and Texas's complaint against Google, the chapter illuminates the emerging concept of privacy fixing and its place in antitrust, including why digital companies may find it worthwhile to fix the level of privacy and how this may harm consumers. It also examines the extent to which antitrust law, specifically Article 101, can tackle such harms.

As consumer information becomes central to the value-creation process, companies may increasingly find it worthwhile to agree on low levels of user privacy. The Google—Eyeo agreement serves as a stark example of a practice that restricts competition in privacy, exposing users to increased tracking and advertisements while stifling technical development and investment that could improve users'

187 European Commission, 'Communication from the Commission to the European Parliament and the Council on Promoting Data Protection by Privacy Enhancing Technologies (PETs)' COM(2007) 228 final 7.

188 ibid.

189 Article 29 Data Protection Working Party, 'Comments in Response to W3C's Public Consultation on the W3C Last Call Working Draft, 24 April 2014, Tracking Preference Expression (DNT)' (2014).

190 Article 29 Data Protection Working Party, 'Comments in Response to W3C's Public Consultation on the W3C Last Call Working Draft, 14 July 2015, Tracking Compliance and Scope' (2015) 2.

privacy and web experience. Similarly, Google's plea for Microsoft to stop subtle privacy attacks on privacy is comparable to restrictions on advertising and could potentially fall under the prohibition in Article 101. Furthermore, Google's endeavour to align 'privacy goals and strategies' with Facebook and Microsoft could potentially limit competition by creating uniformity in privacy conditions.

These examples provide valuable insights into the interface between privacy and competition law. First, big technology companies have the incentive to coordinate privacy efforts both vertically and horizontally, even in the absence of direct competition. The Google–Eyeo agreement, for example, illustrates how companies with seemingly opposing business models (ie tracking and monetizing user data versus reducing tracking and advertising) can align to degrade user privacy. Second, these examples dispel the commonly held belief that these companies do not compete on privacy and lack incentive to degrade the privacy they offer their users. Even though these companies may not compete as intensely on privacy as they do on data collection and monetization, the potential for a change in policy by one company keeps the others from being complacent in how they treat users' privacy. Importantly, these examples demonstrate the crucial role that competition law plays in protecting user privacy by tackling macro-level harms to privacy arising from anti-competitive collaboration. Addressing privacy concerns within the realm of competition law does not signify an expansion of its scope to compensate for data privacy legislation shortcomings. Instead, the examples underscore that certain privacy-related harms fall squarely within the purview of competition law, for which data privacy legislation alone cannot provide an adequate solution.

Finally, the chapter has shown that harms to competition on data privacy and PETs could arise from standard setting. The discussions illustrate that while standard setting aiming to bolster privacy conditions can be beneficial to users, it may impose a ceiling on the level of data privacy protection offered. Additionally, the discourse surrounding the W3C DNT standard shows how standard-setting processes may supress information competition, thereby negatively impacting competition in data privacy and PETs. This occurs if the standard-setting process promotes a 'unified position' on how to proceed, making it difficult to challenge the information produced by the SSO. For instance, the discussion showed how the W3C standard-setting process on DNT led to the loss of information competition in the market for web browsers and succeeded in drowning Microsoft out as a powerful speaker, ultimately leading to the 'Slow Death of the DNT'. This chapter therefore stresses the need for safeguards, similar to those mandated by competition law, to prevent the standard-setting process from being skewed in favour of one or several participants. Such safeguards should also apply to practices that could potentially lead to loss of information competition and instigate market failure.

The W3C discussion also shows that the substance of a communication standard may affect competition on data privacy by making it difficult for companies to compete by integrating privacy enhancing features into their products. The W3C specification that forced users to set the DNT manually and prohibited browsers from setting the DNT by default increased the cost to users of expressing their privacy preferences and limited mainstream browsers' ability to build their reputation by implementing DNT by default, automating privacy protection. However, the substantive concerns fall largely outside the remit of competition law, underscoring the need for data privacy and consumer protection authorities to take a more proactive approach and engage in standard-setting activities.

Overall, the analysis in this chapter highlights how the market response to data privacy concerns may be hijacked by powerful players, to the detriment of users, and the need for competition authorities to widen their horizon of anticompetitive collaborations and take appropriate action when necessary.

7

Excessive Data Collection and Unfair Privacy Policies as Forms of Abuse of Dominance

I. Data Privacy-Related Exploitative Practices

A key attribute of many digital services is that consumers do not pay a monetary price—instead, they effectively hand over their personal information and attention in exchange for accessing a range of digital services. This is the case with the most popular digital services, such as Google and Facebook. However, this trend is gaining traction in other sectors, particularly insurance services, for which consumers are offered price discounts if they agree to the tracking of their activities. In this regard, Commissioner Vestager stated that users exchanging 'their data' to enable them to access digital services does not have to be a problem 'as long as people are happy that the data they share is a fair price to pay for the services they get in return'.[1] This might raise the question of whether there are instances in which the data exchanged could be seen as excessive or unfair and in breach of competition law, specifically Article 102 of the Treaty on the Functioning of the European Union (TFEU).

While Article 102 primarily aims to protect consumers indirectly by prohibiting practices that damage the competitive process (exclusionary), it also extends to practices that directly harm consumers (exploitative).[2] Similarly, although exclusionary practices are given priority in the Commission's actions, exploitative behaviours have gradually begun to garner attention. In May 2017, the Commission opened its first investigation into concerns about excessive pricing in the pharmaceutical industry.[3] Commissioner Vestager has also reiterated the need for competition authorities to step in 'where competition hasn't been enough to provide a real choice' and 'dominant businesses are exploiting their customers, by charging excessive prices or imposing unfair terms'.[4] With the lion's share of consumer-facing

[1] European Commission, 'Making Data Work for Us', speech by Commissioner Vestager at event on Data as Power in Copenhagen (9 September 2016).

[2] See Case 6-72 *Continental Can v Commission* ECLI:EU:C:1973:22, para 26.

[3] European Commission, 'Commission Opens Formal Investigation into Aspen Pharma's Pricing Practices for Cancer Medicines' (15 May 2017).

[4] European Commission, 'Protecting Consumers from Exploitation', speech by Commissioner Vestager at Chillin' Competition Conference (21 November 2016).

Data Privacy and Competition Law in the Age of Big Data. Samson Y. Esayas, Oxford University Press.
 DOI: 10.1093/oso/9780198891420.003.0008

digital services offered at zero price, the question is, what could form the basis for claims of exploitative abuse in these markets?

Clearly, the list under Article 102(a) addresses unfair conditions affecting prices, such as excessive pricing. However, the phrase 'other unfair trading conditions' suggests that the restriction also applies to conditions affecting other competition parameters, such as quality and choice.[5] Additionally, while most exploitative abuses tend to focus on conduct against industrial customers, the rules also apply to conditions imposed on final consumers.[6] Since data privacy is recognized as a non-price competition parameter, this chapter aims to examine whether excessive data collection or unfair conditions relating to data privacy by dominant firms constitute exploitive abuse in breach of Article 102. A related inquiry is the extent to which breaches of data privacy rules contribute to breaches of competition rules or represent deviation from competition on the merits, and the implications of this for the interface between data privacy and competition laws. But before proceeding, it is important to highlight how the Digital Markets Act (DMA),[7] which contains provisions regulating data usage by major digital platforms, might help address some of these privacy-related practices and clarify the role of competition law.

II. The DMA's Data-Centric Provisions and the Role of Competition Law

The DMA's data-centric provisions can be put into two broad categories: those that limit certain uses of data and those designed to facilitate data sharing and exchange. Each has distinct implications for users' privacy. In the first category, Article 5(2) prohibits gatekeepers from combining data across their own services or from third-party services unless the end-user 'has been presented with the specific choice and has given consent' in line with the General Data Protection Regulation (GDPR). Similarly, this category prohibits the gatekeeper's use of non-public data in competition with customers. The second category features provisions that aim to enhance data portability and sharing. For example, Article 6(9) expands upon the right to data portability outlined in Article 20 of the GDPR. It allows users to transfer data generated during their interactions with a gatekeeper; it even enables continuous and real-time access to their data. Additionally, Article 6(10) grants business users the right to access data: both data generated through

[5] Competition Committee and the Committee on Consumer Policy, 'Quality Considerations in the Zero-Price Economy—Note by the European Union' (2018) para 32.

[6] See Case IV/36.888-1998 *Football World Cup* decision of 20 July 1999 OJ L5/55, para 100.

[7] Regulation (EU) 2022/1925 of the European Parliament and of the Council of 14 September 2022 on Contestable and Fair Markets in the Digital Sector and amending Directives (EU) 2019/1937 and (EU) 2020/1828 OJ L265/1 (Digital Markets Act, DMA).

their interactions with a gatekeeper's platform and, subject to consent, data generated by end-users who interact with the business users' offerings on that platform.

These provisions address some of the privacy and data-related concerns discussed here and in earlier chapters. From a privacy perspective, these rules help mitigate some of the risks associated with data combination discussed in Chapter 2. For instance, Article 5(2) appears to demand that gatekeepers obtain explicit consent—in addition to any other legal grounds they may rely on—for data combination. This signifies that for those gatekeepers subject to the DMA, merely invoking a 'legitimate interest' or 'contractual necessity' is no longer adequate justification for combining data across services. Moreover, the DMA seems to impose even more stringent conditions for obtaining consent. Specifically, it mandates that designated gatekeepers provide a 'less personalized but equivalent alternative' to their service. Access to the core platform or specific functionalities cannot be made contingent upon user consent to data combination.[8] Additionally, the DMA stipulates that gatekeepers cannot seek renewed consent for data combination within one year of a user declining or withdrawing their prior consent.[9] These provisions raise the costs of combining data across services and offer users added layers of protection against potential misuse of their data, particularly through practices that exploit users' behavioural biases and choice architecture.

Importantly, these rules play a crucial role in mitigating some of the data-driven entry barriers discussed in Chapter 4. The prohibitions on data combination, along with the right of business users to access data, serve to limit the depth and breadth of data sets amassed by companies like Facebook and Google while simultaneously giving businesses access to some competition-relevant data. These provisions are especially noteworthy given the critique that the GDPR tends to favour intra-firm data exchanges over inter-firm data sharing, thereby giving multi-product platforms a competitive advantage.[10] Simultaneously, these rules raise questions about the relationship between the DMA and competition law, particularly with respect to how they address privacy and data-related practices.

Various provisions within the DMA, including those related to data, were inspired by specific cases under Article 102.[11] For example, the prohibition on cross-service data combination by gatekeepers has its roots in the *Facebook Germany* case, while the restriction on the use of non-public data in competition with customers echoes the Commission's case against Amazon. Moreover, there are ongoing investigations under Article 102 into Facebook and Google, focusing on

[8] ibid Recital 36.

[9] ibid Article 5(2(d)).

[10] See, eg responses to the Commission investigation in Case M.9660 *Google/Fitbit* decision of 17 December 2020, para 452.

[11] See the mapping of the various provisions to specific competition law cases in Fiona Scott Morton and Cristina Caffarra, 'The European Commission Digital Markets Act: A Translation', *VoxEU* (5 January 2021).

their data-usage practices, which are explicitly addressed by the DMA. These overlapping areas may generate confusion and prompt questions about the role of competition law, particularly Article 102, in governing such practices.

While this topic warrants further research, it is appropriate to briefly discuss the role of competition law concerning these practices. Section V of Chapter 3 discussed the prospects and limitations of the DMA in addressing the broader issues presented in this book. Those comments are also pertinent here. As emphasized in Chapter 3, the DMA focuses on digital gatekeepers and predefined anticompetitive practices. However, the digital ecosystem is vast; not all firms have gatekeeping power, nor can all their potential abuses be anticipated by the DMA. The release of ChatGPT highlights the legislators' inability to anticipate the trajectories of new technologies. While it is possible to update the list of practices, Article 102 remains a broad tool suited to tackling the privacy and data-related practices of non-gatekeepers and a variety of abusive behaviours not explicitly mentioned in the DMA.

Importantly, even for entities subject to the DMA, competition law will continue to play a critical role in addressing privacy and data-related issues. As noted in Chapter 3, the DMA is designed to complement, not supplant, competition law. One domain where competition law will be pivotal is in addressing excessive data collection. This is largely because the DMA's data-related provisions appear to focus more on ensuring market contestability than directly safeguarding user privacy. For example, while Article 5(2) of the DMA prohibits the combination of data across different services, it does not tackle privacy-related exploitative behaviours by dominant firms, including gatekeepers, in the form of excessive data collection or extensive consumer profiling related to a specific service.[12]

Moreover, competition law remains instrumental in securing a broader range of choices concerning user privacy. A key insight from the Bundeskartellamt's decision and its recent endorsement by the Court of Justice of the European Union (CJEU) is the critical role of competition law in ensuring a minimum standard of choice with respect to the collection and use of personal data.[13] For example, the CJEU insisted that dominant undertakings cannot provide their services on a 'take-it-or-leave-it' basis, compelling users to consent to the combination of their data as a precondition for accessing a specific service. The Court further noted that such dominant undertakings must provide users with a less personalized alternative service, even if that might mean users have to pay for the service.[14] Indeed, the DMA also requires gatekeepers to offer users a choice regarding the combination of data across services. However, choice in terms of data protection can extend

[12] Wolfgang Kerber and Louisa Specht, 'Synergies between Data Protection Law and Competition Law' (2021) 76 <https://ssrncom/abstract=3977039 accessed 9 February 2024.
[13] See ibid 58.
[14] Case C-252/21 *Meta Platforms Inc v Bundeskartellamt* ECLI:EU:C:2023:537, para 150.

beyond this specific issue, an area where competition law can offer valuable safeguards. This may include ensuring greater transparency regarding how user data is utilized, implementing shorter data storage durations, or even obliging companies to offer an option that allows consumers to access services without providing personal data.[15]

Even concerning the privacy and data-related practices that impact contestability, competition law will have an important role to play regarding business users' access to data. To begin with, the DMA does not impose a universal obligation for third-party data access, except in the case of search engines. And even then, any shared data must be anonymized. As a result, competition law remains the primary mechanism for ensuring that businesses have access to data relevant for competition. Discussions in Section IV.B.2 below about Google's and Apple's restrictions on business users' access to end-user data and the role of competition law in tackling such practices serve as illustrative examples.

Furthermore, while the DMA grants business users the right to access data generated during their interactions with gatekeepers (including the personal data of end-users), it requires user consent for such access. The consent requirement effectively excludes reliance on other legal bases like contractual necessity or legitimate interest. By contrast, competition law can facilitate access to such data, even in the absence of user consent, as data sharing can be justified based on legal obligation. As highlighted in Chapter 4, data sharing may be at odds with user privacy, but such tensions can be amicably resolved through coordinated efforts with data protection authorities. The discussions in Chapter 4 showed how coordinated efforts have led to more balanced outcomes where consumers are given the option to opt out of data sharing. This suggests that competition agencies can mandate data sharing under Article 102 under more lenient conditions, using opt-out rather than opt-in mechanisms—an option not currently present in the DMA.

Overall, competition law has a significant role to play in regulating privacy and data-related practices, particularly for non-gatekeeper entities and gatekeeper behaviour not covered by the DMA. Competition law remains crucial in ensuring that dominant entities, including those categorized as gatekeepers, offer users sufficient choice in terms of data collection and usage. Competition law also tackles restrictions on users' ability to share data with third parties. This is the background against which the following discussion on the application of competition law to privacy-related exploitative practices must be examined and understood.

[15] Kerber and Specht (n 12) 76. However, there are concerns about the use of competition law to dictate product design decisions and monetization strategies. See Pablo Ibáñez Colomo, 'Product Design and Business Models in EU Antitrust Law' (2021) <https://ssrncom/abstract=3925396> accessed 9 February 2024.

III. Excessive Data Collection as Exploitative Abuse

As users increasingly exchange their data to access digital services, there is an emerging argument that excessive data collection by dominant undertakings could be challenged as exploitative conduct that is comparable to excessive pricing. In their joint report, the German and French competition authorities concede the possibility that excessive data collection by dominant undertakings could constitute an exploitative abuse of dominance.[16] Moreover, discussing the potential abuse of dominance by social networks, a report by the Monopolkommission—an independent expert group advising the German government on competition policy—suggests that 'when such companies collect data excessively and curb the ability of users to limit such data collection', this could potentially amount to an exploitative abuse.[17] The question is whether the current case law and practice on excessive pricing is able to capture excessive data collection as an abusive practice. While there is a theorical possibility for considering personal data as the 'price' users pay in exchange for accessing services, applying the case law on excessive pricing seems difficult. This is partly because it would require an estimation of the monetary value of the data provided and a comparison of this value with the cost of providing the services.

A. EU Case Law and Practice on Excessive Pricing

Commission decisions and CJEU case law on exploitative conduct, including excessive pricing, are very sparse. The Commission has addressed only a handful of cases on excessive pricing, several of which were annulled on appeal by the European Union (EU) courts.[18] Despite this, in the landmark *United Brands* case, the CJEU clarified some of the requirements and held that a dominant undertaking may abuse its dominance by 'charging a price which is excessive because it has no reasonable relation to the economic value of the product supplied'.[19] This has been the guiding principle on excessive pricing.

The CJEU employs a two-stage test and underlines the need to determine the following:

[16] See Autorité de la Concurrence and Bundeskartellamt, *Competition Law and Data* (2016) 24–26 <https://www.bundeskartellamt.de/SharedDocs/Publikation/DE/Berichte/Big%20Data%20Papier.pdf?__blob=publicationFile&v=4>.

[17] Monopolkommission, 'Competition Policy: The Challenges of Digital Markets' (Special Report No 68, 2015) para 326.

[18] See Case IV/26699 *Chiquita* decision of 17 December 1975 OJ L95/1; Case IV/28.851 *General Motors Continental* decision of 19 December 1974 OJ L29/14; Case IV/30.615 *British Leyland (BL)* decision of 2 July 1984 OJ L207/11; Case COMP/C-1/36.915 *Deutsche Post AG* decision of 25 July 2001 OJ L331/40. Of these, only the *BL* decision was upheld by the CJEU. See Richard Whish and David Bailey, *Competition Law* (9th edn, OUP 2018) 741.

[19] Case C-27/76 *United Brands v Commission* ECLI:EU:C:1978:22, para 250.

> Whether the difference between the costs actually incurred and the price actually charged *is excessive*, and, if the answer to this question is in the affirmative, whether a price has been imposed which is either *unfair in itself or when compared to competing products*.[20]

Accordingly, in the first stage, one needs to demonstrate that the price is excessive in relation to the economic value. However, the economic value of a service/product is not self-explanatory. In this regard, the CJEU highlighted that excessiveness could be assessed objectively by comparing 'the selling price of the product in question and its costs of production, which would disclose the amount of the profit margin'.[21] The idea behind this approach is that the price imposed by the dominant undertaking should allow for 'a reasonable margin' of cost-plus profit. Accordingly, the margin is seen as excessive if the dominant undertaking generates too much profit.[22] This approach is known as the price–cost test.

One challenge in applying the price–cost test is determining the appropriate standard to assess whether the gap between the actual price and the cost is substantial enough to be considered excessive. The CJEU recognizes the difficulty of estimating the economic value or the costs of a product and is open to alternative methods of showing excessiveness.[23] One such alternative is to use a comparator price. Comparisons could be conducted between the contested price and the price charged by the dominant undertaking over time or in neighbouring markets.[24] Another possibility is to compare the prices charged by the dominant firm and those charged by other firms in the same market or in other markets.[25]

Comparisons could also be made between the prices charged by the dominant undertaking in different member states. In a case referred to the CJEU for a preliminary ruling, the Latvian Competition Authority argued that the royalty rates charged by an authors' association, AKKA/LAA, in Latvia were excessive because they were between 50 and 100 per cent higher than the rates requested in other member states, such as Lithuania and Estonia.[26] The CJEU found this to be a valid method of determining excessiveness. Again, the decision does not provide an adequate answer regarding the relevant threshold for the contested price to be considered excessive in light of the comparator. Thus, competition authorities

[20] ibid para 252 (emphasis added).

[21] ibid para 251.

[22] Case C-177/16 *Autortiesību un komunicēšanās konsultāciju aģentūra/Latvijas Autoru apvienība v Konkurences padome* ECLI:EU:C:2017:286, Opinion of Advocate General Wahl, para 18.

[23] Case C-177/16 *Autortiesību un komunicēšanās konsultāciju aģentūra/Latvijas Autoru apvienība v Konkurences padome* ECLI:EU:C:2017:689 (*AKKA/LAA*) para 49.

[24] See *General Motors Continental* (n 18). Also Pinar Akman, 'The Role of Exploitation in Abuse under Article 82 EC' (2009) 11 Cambridge Yearbook of European Legal Studies 165, 171.

[25] Massimo Motta and Alexandre de Streel, 'Excessive Pricing in Competition Law: Never Say Never?' in Arvid Fredenberg and Niklas Strand (eds), *The Pros and Cons of High Prices* (Swedish Competition Authority 2007) 36.

[26] *AKKA/LAA* (n 23) para 9.

have a 'margin of manoeuvre' with respect to the methodology used to determine excessiveness.[27]

The second stage entails determining whether the price is 'unfair in itself or when compared to competing products'.[28] In assessing whether a price is 'unfair in itself', one needs to go back to the price–cost test and ask whether the excessive price bears 'no reasonable relation to the economic value of the product'.[29] The question is whether the price–cost-based assessment for unfairness is the same as in the first step or whether it involves something more. According to Whish and Baily, 'unfairness is something beyond excessiveness'.[30] This seems to be the line taken by the Commission in *Scandlines*, after the latter complained that the port charges at Helsingborg were excessive and in violation of Article 102.[31] While the Commission determined that the fees exceeded the costs, they were not considered to be unfair.[32] In so doing, the Commission emphasized the importance of the value of the product to the buyer (demand side) as follows:

> even if it were to be assumed that there is a positive difference between the price and the production costs exceeding what Scandlines claims as being a reasonable margin (whatever that may be), the conclusion should not necessarily be drawn that the price is unfair, provided that this price has a reasonable relation to the economic value of the product/service supplied. The assessment of the reasonable relation between the price and the economic value of the product/service must also take into account the relative weight of non-cost related factors.[33]

Thus, the Commission seems to use different standards to assess the economic value of the product when assessing excessiveness (purely on cost–price comparisons and hence supply-side factors) and assessing economic value in relation to unfairness. With the latter, the Commission seems open to account for demand-side and non-cost-related factors (location in the case of ports). Alternatively, as some authors argue, 'unfair in itself' could be assessed by looking at the prices charged in the past on the same market by the dominant undertaking.[34] This test is particularly informative if the past price relates to a period before the undertaking became dominant.

Unfairness could also be examined in relation to a comparator, that is a price charged by competitors in the same market, a price charged by the dominant

[27] *United Brands v Commission* (n 19) para 251.
[28] ibid para 252.
[29] ibid para 250.
[30] Whish and Bailey (n 18) 738.
[31] Case COMP/A.36.568/D3 *Scandlines Sverige AB v Port of Helsingborg* decision of 23 July 2004.
[32] ibid paras 104–109.
[33] ibid para 228.
[34] Pinar Akman and Luke Garrod, 'When Are Excessive Prices Unfair?' (2011) 7 Journal of Competition Law & Economics 403, 419.

undertaking in a neighbouring market or in other member states, or even using an international standard.[35] In *AKKA/LAA*, the CJEU accepted a comparison of prices charged by the dominant undertaking in different member states as a valid method of assessing unfairness, provided that 'the reference Member States are selected in accordance with objective, appropriate and verifiable criteria'.[36] Specifically, the Court held that when a dominant undertaking imposes fees that are '*appreciably higher* than those charged in other Member States and where a comparison of the fee levels has been made on a consistent basis', this fee must be regarded as unfair and indicative of abuse.[37] It is only indicative in that the undertaking can justify the differences 'by relying on objective dissimilarities' between the situations of the Member States that have an impact on costs.[38] The question is, when is the difference between the rates *appreciably* high enough to be regarded as unfair?

In *AKKA/LAA*, the Court acknowledged the lack of a 'minimum threshold' for determining 'appreciably higher' rate but indicated that the difference must be both significant and persistent—not just temporary or sporadic.[39] Despite this, assessing unfairness remains a complex, even potentially 'daunting, if not, impossible task'.[40] Moreover, distinguishing between the excessiveness and unfairness tests is challenging in practice. In some cases, the two tests seem to merge into one, especially when estimating the product's production costs is difficult, and a comparator is used to determine both excessiveness and unfairness. In these situations, the assessment becomes circular. In fact, some scholars suggest that assessing unfairness is only necessary when a price–cost analysis is infeasible.[41]

Apart from the above two conditions, the case law on excessive prices seems to focus on markets with high entry barriers and super-dominance. Many firms highlighted in the case law and Commission decisions held positions of legal monopoly or were collective societies with de facto monopolies. This is justified because, in markets in which there are no barriers, excessive prices will normally attract entry and push prices down. This might be the reason some countries, such as the United States, do not see excessive pricing as problematic. For the purposes of this section, it is sufficient to refer to the burgeoning literature, which demonstrates the high concentration in key digital markets and the barriers to entry based on economies of scale and scope, as well as traditional and data-driven network effects.[42]

35 See ibid 419.

36 *AKKA/LAA* (n 23) paras 38–41.

37 ibid para 38 (emphasis added).

38 ibid paras 57, 61.

39 ibid paras 55–56.

40 David Evans and Jorge Padilla, 'Excessive Prices: Using Economics to Define Administrable Legal Rules' (2005) 1 Journal of Competition Law and Economics 97, 118.

41 See Motta and de Streel (n 25) 39.

42 See European Commission, Directorate-General for Competition, Jacques Crémer, Yves-Alexandre de Montjoye, and Heike Schweitzer, *Competition Policy for the Digital Era* (EU Publications Office, 2019); Jason Furman and others, 'Unlocking Digital Competition: Report of the Digital Competition Expert Panel' (2019) <https://assets.publishing.service.gov.uk/media/5c88150ee5274a230219c35f/unlocking_digital_competition_furman_review_web.pdf>.

Moreover, when it comes to competition on privacy, the dysfunctional equilibrium makes it difficult for companies to attract users by offering a greater level of privacy than that offered by the dominant undertaking.[43] In light of these considerations, the following paragraphs will focus only on whether excessive data collection could be abusive under Article 102 based on the two-step test.

B. Excessive Data Collection in Light of the Case Law and Practice

At the centre of this issue is whether and when data collection should be considered 'excessive'. As noted above, excessiveness is to be assessed using the price–cost test, that is comparing the price with the cost of supplying the product/service. In relation to digital services, such as Facebook and Google Search, this test requires that one determine the cost of providing the service (access to the social network or search engine) and the price charged to use the service. Regarding the latter, given that users do not pay monetary prices, the data they are required to provide could be considered as the price/consideration they exchange to access these services. Applying the excessiveness requirement would mean that if there is a disproportionate difference between the cost and price (here, the amount of personal data), the collection should be considered excessive. Relying on the case law, the European Data Protection Supervisor (EDPS) has suggested that exploitative abuse may occur if '*the "price" paid through the surrender of personal information* [is] ... considered *excessive* in relation to the *value of the service consumed*'.[44] Robertson proposes a similar approach, suggesting that as part of the first step in the test, an assessment should be made to establish 'whether there is a reasonable relationship between the amount of data' collected and 'the economic value of the digital service the users receive'.[45] The second step would then evaluate 'whether the amount of data collected is excessive in absolute or relative terms'.[46]

This notwithstanding, applying the price–cost test to personal data is a difficult, if not impossible, task. First, determining production costs is not easy, and determining excessiveness in many digital markets is even harder, partly because these services are not provided on a per unit basis. What is the cost of providing access to a social network or a search engine? What is the cost benchmark to be employed to assess excessiveness? The multi-sided nature of many digital services further

[43] See more in Chapter 4.

[44] EDPS Preliminary Opinion, *Privacy and Competitiveness in the Age of Big Data: The Interplay between Data Protection, Competition Law and Consumer Protection in the Digital Economy* (2014) 29 (emphasis added).

[45] Viktoria Robertson, 'Excessive Data Collection: Privacy Considerations and Abuse of Dominance in the Era of Big Data' (2020) 57 Common Market Law Review 161, 175.

[46] ibid.

complicates the assessment of the costs and profit margins in relation to the different sides of the market. While many of the leading digital players boast high profit margins, often indicative of excessiveness, profit data is typically presented at an aggregate level. Consequently, it becomes unclear which costs are associated with specific products and in which markets the margins may be deemed excessive. Additionally, determining excessiveness requires one to estimate the monetary value of the data collected for comparison with costs; at present, this is next to impossible.

Second, even if one were able to estimate the cost of providing the service and the monetary value of the data collected, it would be difficult to rely on a cost-plus approach to assess excessiveness (and unfairness). For example, in the *Scandlines* decision, although the Commission estimated the cost of providing port facilities, it declined to use the cost-plus approach because this would not reflect the economic value of the port service due to its location. Similarly, the economic value and attractiveness of a digital service offered at zero price may vary depending on different factors: in the case of social networks, the size of the network and the functionalities offered; in the case of search engines, the speed and relevance of the search results; and so on. The question, then, is whether these factors need to be considered and how. Thus, the price–cost test seems unworkable in assessing the excessiveness of data.

One could argue that the assessment might be made at a more general level. A report by the German Monopolkommission indicated the possibility of assessing excessiveness (and unfairness) in relation to personal data collected by a dominant social network as follows:

> The potential for abuse to be caused by excessive data collection is not necessarily based on a provable breach of the law, but on the unbalanced nature of the service provided by the internet provider (in this case, for instance facilitating social interaction opportunities) and the service provided by the users in turn (facilitating access to personal data) ('exploitative abuse'). Abuse in the relationship between the service provider and the users can also be considered if—as with a number of social networks—the service is provided within a multi-sided relationship (e.g. because data are commercialised without any specific factual relationship with the service provided to users).[47]

Although it is possible to assess excessiveness (and unfairness) in theory, the task remains difficult in practice. The question is, how does one assess the 'unbalanced' factual relationship between the service and the data provided by users? This will raise the same challenges as above in relation to the price–cost test, as one cannot

[47] Monopolkommission (n 17) para 329.

conduct the assessment based on abstract concepts of 'service provided by the internet provider' and the data that users provide in return. Sanctioning behaviour based on such abstract concepts would also introduce unpredictability. Moreover, given that the amount of data provided by the user may differ depending on usage and privacy preferences, the analysis of whether the relationship is factually unbalanced might need to be conducted for each user. This would be impractical, to say the least.

An alternative method of assessing the excessiveness of data could be to use a comparator—for example, data collected by competitors or a comparable competitive market.[48] Again, there is the theoretical possibility of using a comparator to determine excessiveness and unfairness, but the practicality is questionable. First, apart from the conceptual challenges of using a comparator to determine excessiveness,[49] finding an appropriate comparator could be difficult. This is particularly so because, as noted above, the amount of personal data collected by different digital services may vary depending on not only the functionalities but also the intensity of usage by the user. Even if one can estimate the amount of personal data collected by the dominant undertaking and the comparator service(s), it is difficult to assess the excessiveness of one data set against the other. The data collected by the social networks may be the same in amount but different in kind—for example, in terms of sensitivity or even value. Even if the data sets are comparable, how does one factor in the different functionalities and value for the consumers of these services? The fact that the dominant firm collects more data than its rivals may simply be the result of the presence of more functionalities in the dominant firm's product that consumers value. Thus, although the theoretical possibility of assessing excessiveness exists, it is questionable whether competition authorities have the ability and resources to conduct this analysis in practice. The second-stage test of 'unfairness' faces similar challenges.

This leaves us with the question of whether data privacy rules could be used to assess excessiveness and unfairness. This flows from the argument that competition law is 'open to normative influence from other fields of law' and that data privacy can serve as a benchmark for determining excessive data collection.[50] Seeking normative guidance from other areas is not unusual, particularly when competition law lacks the necessary tools to determine excessiveness. For example, the Commission has used a standard set by an international standard-setting body as a

[48] Marco Botta and Klaus Wiedemann, 'EU Competition Law Enforcement vis-à-vis Exploitative Conducts in the Data Economy Exploring the Terra Incognita' (Max Planck Institute for Innovation and Competition Research Paper No 18-08, Max Planck Institute for Innovation and Competition 2018) 44; Nicholas Economides and Ioannis Lianos, 'Restrictions on Privacy and Exploitation in the Digital Economy: A Market Failure Perspective' (2021) 17 Journal of Competition Law & Economics 765, 804.

[49] Motta and de Streel (n 25) 36.

[50] Francisco Costa-Cabral and Orla Lynskey, 'Family Ties: The Intersection between Data Protection and Competition in EU Law' (2017) 54 Common Market Law Review 11, 31.

benchmark to assess whether the fees charged by financial institutions were excessive.[51] Given that competition law lacks its own standard for determining the fair ratio between the price and the economic value of the services, the Commission sought guidance from an international standard.

There are also instances in which competition authorities used another field of law as a benchmark to condemn certain conduct. In *Allianz Hungária Biztosító*, the CJEU resorted to domestic law to analyse the competitive impact of a vertical restriction imposed by insurance companies on insurance brokers.[52] The domestic law prohibited insurance companies and their brokers from being affiliated, and the Court found that such a prohibition was relevant in assessing whether the vertical restrictions constituted a restriction by object under Article 101. In this instance, competition law sought normative guidance from national legislation, which regulates how the car insurance market should operate, in determining whether the agreement conformed to the proper functioning of such a market.

In the same fashion, given the difficulty of determining excessive data collection, competition law could seek guidance from data privacy rules. Highlighting this point, a joint report by the German and French competition authorities indicates the possibility of using 'data privacy regulations ... [as] a useful benchmark to assess an exploitative conduct'.[53] In this regard, the data minimization and the purpose limitation principles could be particularly informative. The former requires that personal data be 'adequate, relevant and not excessive in relation to the purposes for which they are collected and/or further processed'.[54] The latter underlines, inter alia, the need for a specific and explicit purpose for the collection of personal data.[55] Together, these principles can provide guidance in assessing whether the data collected goes beyond the minimum necessary for achieving the purpose (ie excessive) and, thus, constitutes an abuse of dominance under Article 102. The CJEU has recently affirmed that competition agencies can consider violations of data privacy rules when assessing if the behaviour of a dominant undertaking constitutes abuse,[56] a topic further explored in Section V.

Nevertheless, resorting to data privacy rules is not without challenges. First, it is questionable whether using data privacy rules to assess both excessiveness and unfairness meets the two-step test in the case law. At best, this becomes circular. Importantly, the added value of incorporating privacy into competition analysis is that companies can strive to provide protections beyond those guaranteed under

[51] Case COMP/39.592 *Standard & Poor's* decision of 15 November 2011.

[52] Case C-32/11 *Allianz Hungária Biztosító Zrt v Gazdasági Versenyhivatal* ECLI:EU:C:2013:160, para 47.

[53] Autorité de la Concurrence and Bundeskartellamt (n 16) 25.

[54] Regulation (EU) 2016/679 of the European Parliament and of the Council of 27 April 2016 on the Protection of Natural Persons with Regard to the Processing of Personal Data and on the Free Movement of Such Data, and repealing Directive 95/46/EC OJ L119/1 (GDPR) Article 5(1(c)).

[55] ibid Article 5(1(b)).

[56] *Meta Platforms v Bundeskartellamt* (n 14).

data privacy rules.[57] Against this background, if a breach of data privacy rules is used as a benchmark for assessing excessiveness and unfairness, the effect of using competition law would be to restore the level to the one set by the rules. If so, the value of using competition rather than data privacy rules to address the problem is less evident. In these situations, the use of data privacy rules may be better suited to such cases.

Using data privacy rules is also important resource-wise, given that competition law enforcement—particularly Article 102 and excessive pricing—is more resource-intensive and time-consuming than data privacy enforcement. The Commission's failure in defending excessive pricing cases before the EU courts reflects the challenges of sanctioning excessive pricing. Given the additional difficulties associated with personal data, it seems unlikely that competition law will provide effective and timely redress for harm resulting from excessive data collection. Thus, insofar as the determination of excessiveness primarily depends on violations of data privacy law, competition law should take a backseat role.

This does not imply that competition law is irrelevant when it comes to excessive data collection in violation of data privacy rules, especially when such breaches have an impact on the competitive process. For example, excessive pricing can affect the competitive process when it is used as a constructive refusal to deal or to prevent parallel trade.[58] Similarly, the data collection practices of dominant undertakings that breach data privacy rules can have far-reaching consequences in the competitive process. One such instance might arise if, for example, the breach helps secure a dominant position or further entrenches an existing one (see Section V.B). This means that exploitative practices involving a breach of data privacy rules could be factored into competition analysis if they also affect the competitive process; that is, they are exclusionary. Moreover, as the subsequent section demonstrates, the case law on unfair trading conditions appears more suited to addressing concerns related to excessive data collection.

IV. Unfair Privacy Terms as an Abuse of Dominance

Key digital markets and gateways are dominated by a handful of players with business models that rely on the monetization of personal data. Moreover, such markets are characterized by strong network effects, which tend to lead to the winner-takes-all effect. These two factors might create lock-in for users, which firms might use to exploit users by forcing them to accept far-reaching privacy policies than could be expected in situations of effective competition. The question is to what degree terms and conditions affecting privacy and personal data

[57] See Chapter 4, Section IV.A.
[58] See *Deutsche Post* (n 18).

can be considered as exploitative abuses under Article 102, which prohibits 'unfair trading conditions' (sub-paragraph A) or making the conclusion of a contract conditional on acceptance of 'supplementary obligations' unrelated to the contract's subject matter (sub-paragraph D). Would it be considered an abuse of a dominant position if a company makes the use of its service conditional upon users providing the company with extensive permission to use their personal data?

These questions carry particular significance because the case law relating to excessive pricing seems fraught with uncertainties and practical difficulties, thereby complicating its application to personal data and privacy. Some of these challenges could be mitigated by resorting to unfair terms and shifting the focus from purely 'excessive' data collection to the broader context. The courts could consider, for example, the terms and conditions of data processing more generally, considering the amount and kind of personal data collected, how the data are used, who the data are shared with, the information provided to users, and the choices users have in relation to their data.

A. EU Case Law and Practice Regarding Abusive Unfair Terms

In recent years, fairness has become a recurring theme in the speeches of Commissioner Vestager. In her speech entitled 'Fairness and Competition', Vestager indicated how competition ensures a 'fair deal' for consumers whether that be 'a better price, or a wider choice of products ... better quality, whatever that means to them—whether it's a more reliable car, or *a social network that protects their private data better*'.[59] The reference to the use of data by social networks clearly shows the Commission's openness to the idea that issues related to privacy and the use of personal data, including the fairness of privacy policies, may attract scrutiny under competition law.

Multiple reports and scholars have pointed out the possibility that certain dominant undertakings' privacy terms and conditions—such as forcing users into agreeing to expansive usage of their personal data or the unreasonable expansion of the data use policy—could constitute exploitative abuse through the imposition of unfair terms under Article 102.[60] Moreover, in its widely publicized *Facebook Germany* decision, the Bundeskartellamt held that if 'a dominant company makes the use of its service conditional upon the user granting the company extensive permission to use his or her personal data', this can be considered as exploitative and unfair terms.[61] The question is whether there is support for prosecuting such practices in the case law of EU courts.

[59] European Commission, 'Fairness and Competition' speech by Commissioner Vestager at GCLC [Global Competition Law Centre] Annual Conference (25 January 2018) (emphasis added).
[60] See Monopolkommission (n 17) para 310; Botta and Wiedemann (n 48) 61.
[61] Bundeskartellamt, 'Background Information on the Facebook Proceeding' (2017) 4.

Unlike the case law on excessive pricing, which follows a purely technical approach and presents formidable methodological and practical challenges, the case law on unfair terms and conditions seems to be more flexible. This is because the case law employs normative concepts and the assessment takes the form of balancing different legitimate interests at stake, using the proportionality test.[62] This test is outlined in the *Belgische Radio en Televisie (BRT) v SABAM* judgment, in which SABAM (an association of Belgian authors and publishers) required some authors to assign all copyrights, both present and future, to the association. The clause also allowed SABAM to retain the rights for five years following the termination of association membership.[63] The CJEU found the clause to be unfair and in breach of Article 102.[64]

In so doing, the Court underlined that the assessment of unfairness and abuse needs to be conducted considering all the relevant interests, balancing the requirements of maximum freedom for members to dispose of their work and effective management of their rights by the association.[65] The Court also indicated the need to consider the association's objective, which was to protect the rights and interests of the right holders. Considering these factors, the Court found the clauses unfair because they imposed obligations on members that were not absolutely necessary for the attainment the objectives, thereby encroaching unfairly upon the members' freedom to exercise their copyright.[66] The test seems to insist on two related aspects: 'necessity' and 'disproportionality'.[67]

Similarly, in *Tetra Pak II*, the General Court (GC) confirmed the Commission's decision that contractual clauses between Tetra Pak and its customers were unfair. This is because the clauses 'went beyond their ostensible purpose' of protecting Tetra Pak's commercial interest and were 'wholly unreasonable in the context of protecting public health'.[68] The clauses pertain to machines leased by Tetra Pak and prohibited customers from adding accessory equipment, modifying or removing parts, or moving the machine. Moreover, the clauses required customers to notify Tetra Pak about any technical improvements and to transfer any associated intellectual property rights to Tetra Pak.[69] The clauses were found to be unfair and abusive.

In *GEMA III*, the Commission, relying on *BRT v SAMBA*, analysed whether the terms arising from a collecting society's statutes were in breach of Article 102.[70]

62 See Robert O'Donoghue and Jorge Padilla, *The Law and Economics of Article 102 TFEU* (2nd edn, Hart Publishing 2013) 846–60.
63 Case C-127-73 *Belgische Radio en Televisie (BRT) v SV SABAM and NV Fonior* ECLI:EU:C:1974:25.
64 ibid para 12.
65 ibid para 8.
66 ibid para 15.
67 See Case IV/29.971 *GEMA Statutes* decision of 4 December 1981 OJ L94/12 *(GEMA III)* para 36.
68 Case T-83/91 *Tetra Pak v Commission* ECLI:EU:T:1994:246, para 140.
69 Case IV/31043 *Tetra Pak II* decision of 24 July 1991 OJ L72/1, para 123.
70 *GEMA III* (n 67).

The Commission identified two critical factors to find a clause abusive: indispensability/necessity (ie whether the clause is 'absolutely necessary' for effective protection) and 'equity/disproportionality' (ie whether the clause unduly limits the copyright holders' freedom to dispose their work).[71] Accordingly, a contractual clause is deemed abusive if it is not indispensable or if it is disproportionate. In *GEMA III*, the Commission found no abuse as the contested clause was 'indispensable to the protection of all beneficiaries' interests' and 'not excessive' in relation to this objective.[72]

In light of the above tests, certain contractual clauses were found to be abusive because they lacked a legitimate objective and aimed to exploit customers. In *Tetra Pak II*, clauses that forbade customers from attaching additional parts or relocating the machines were found to be unfair and abusive. This is because they had 'no connection with the purpose of the contract and ... deprive[d] the purchaser of certain aspects of his property rights'.[73] A clause stipulating an initial lease term of nine years was also seen as excessive, as this duration was either equivalent to or exceeded the machines' lifespan.[74] The Commission further dismissed Tetra Pak's defence that such restrictions were necessary for technical and public health considerations.[75] Both the GC and the CJEU confirmed the Commission's decision.[76]

In *Amministrazione Autonoma dei Monopoli di Stato (AAMS)*, the GC confirmed the Commission's decision, which held that AAMS, the owner of a wholesale distribution network for cigarettes, abused its dominant position by 'making access to the network conditional upon the firms accepting unfair terms'.[77] Specifically, the Commission determined that clauses requiring quality inspection and control of foreign cigarettes were unnecessary and unjustified.[78] Moreover, the GC dismissed AAMS's defence that the clauses 'were necessary to protect its commercial interests' and to prevent overloading its distribution network.[79] In both *Tetra Pak II* and *AAMS*, the clauses did not pass the necessity/indispensability test.

In other situations, while contractual clauses may serve a legitimate purpose, they disproportionately impact the trading partner to such an extent that the latter may forfeit a right they would otherwise have under competitive conditions. This is exemplified in the contractual clauses of collecting societies, where specific limitations on copyright holders' rights are necessary for effective rights management. The *BRT v SABAM* decision is one such example, where even though

[71] ibid para 36.
[72] ibid paras 47, 53.
[73] *Tetra Pak II* (n 69) para 107.
[74] ibid para 140.
[75] ibid para 119.
[76] Case C-333/94 P *Tetra Pak v Commission* ECLI:EU:C:1996:436
[77] Case T-139/98 *Amministrazione Autonoma dei Monopoli di Stato (AAMS) v Commission* ECLI:EU:T:2001:272, para 76.
[78] Case IV/36.010-F3 *AAMS* decision of 17 June 1998 OJ L252/47, para 46.
[79] Case T-139/98 *AAMS* (n 77) para 79.

some restrictions were legitimate, the clause demanding the assignment of all copyrights, including a five-year exclusivity period following an author's withdrawal from the association, was deemed excessive relative to the stated objective. Similarly, in *Tetra Pak II*, the clauses not only lacked a legitimate objective but also unduly restricted the customer's 'right to dispose of an asset in his property or even to transfer its use'.[80]

Thus, the application of Article 102 to unfair contract terms involves, first, an assessment of whether the contractual clause is 'absolutely necessary' in view of the object of the contract. If the answer is positive, the court proceeds to the second test, that is whether the term is reasonable or proportionate considering the legitimate interests of the dominant undertaking, its trading parties and, ultimately, consumers.[81] If the answer to one of these questions is negative, the term is deemed unfair and abusive.

In *Duales System Deutschland (DSD)*, the Commission reiterated these tests and further elaborated on the second test. According to the Commission, unfair commercial terms under Article 102(a) exist 'where an undertaking in a dominant position fails to comply with the principle of proportionality'.[82] The assessment of proportionality is to be conducted considering the object of the contract, the terms of the contract, and the justification for those terms. In this specific instance, DSD was the owner of a comprehensive packaging collection and recycling system. The Commission had to assess a contractual clause, which required DSD's customers to pay a licensing fee 'in respect of all of the packaging distributed' in Germany 'bearing the Green Dot mark'.[83] The clause was found to be disproportionate and unfair because the fee was dependent solely on the use of the mark on their packaging, forcing customers to pay the same amount even if they made no use of DSD's collection service or if they used it only for some of their packaging.[84] Both the GC and the CJEU upheld the Commission's decision.[85]

In the context of digital markets, the Commission has applied these tests in the *Google Android* decision and the ongoing investigations into Apple and Facebook. In *Google Android*, the Commission evaluated Google's anti-fragmentation agreement with original equipment manufacturers (OEMs). This agreement prevented device manufacturers, who wanted to integrate the Play Store or Search on their devices, from marketing any device operating on a rival Android OS, known as Android Fork. The Commission determined that these anti-fragmentation obligations amounted to an abuse of dominance.[86] This is because they made access to

[80] *Tetra Pak II* (n 69) para 123.
[81] O'Donoghue and Padilla (n 62) 853.
[82] Case COMP D3/34493 *Duales System Deutschland (DSD)* decision of 20 April 2001 OJ L166/1, para 112.
[83] ibid para 100.
[84] ibid paras 102 and 113.
[85] Case T-151/01 *DSD v Commission* ECLI:EU:T:2007:154; Case C-385/07 P *DSD v Commission* ECLI:EU:C:2009:456.
[86] Case AT.40099 *Google Android* decision of 18 July 2018, para 1011.

the Play Store or Search contingent upon acceptance of an auxiliary obligation that was unrelated to the primary services offered. In its assessment, the Commission weighed multiple factors. These included the relevance of the additional obligation to the main contract, whether such stipulations left device manufacturers with no alternative but to accept the auxiliary obligation to access the service or product, and the degree to which this obligation could stifle competition.[87]

Central to this discussion is the Commission's conclusion that the anti-fragmentation obligations are not necessary to the licensing of the Play Store and the Search app.[88] These obligations 'do not naturally nor, in commercial practice, belong to a contract for licensing Android app stores or generic search apps'.[89] Furthermore, even if one were to consider that some of these restrictions might serve a valid purpose (such as ensuring interoperability and curbing fragmentation, as Google has contended), the Commission determined that these restrictions exceed what is necessary to achieve such aims. Addressing concerns about interoperability, the Commission pointed out the extensive nature of these obligations, which constrain the strategic choices of hardware manufacturers across their entire device range, not just those devices where the Play Store and Google Search app are pre-installed.[90]

Furthermore, Google's subsequent readiness to provide hardware manufacturers with an alternative agreement, which permits OEMs to produce Android-incompatible devices under a third-party brand, validates that Google could have adopted measures less restrictive than the originally phrased anti-fragmentation obligations.[91] The Commission also dismissed Google's concerns about potential reputational harm and the freeriding issue, pointing to the presence of less restrictive contractual and licensing terms that could fulfil these goals.[92] As such, the Commission deemed the anti-fragmentation obligation both disproportionate and not objectively necessary. This conclusion was later upheld by the GC.[93]

The Commission also applied the legal test based on unfair terms in the *Facebook Marketplace* case. The investigation centred around Meta's terms and conditions, which allowed it to utilize data acquired from rival providers when they advertise on Facebook or Instagram. This data was then leveraged to compete against them in sectors where Facebook operates, such as classified ads, subsequently benefiting Facebook's Marketplace.[94] In its statement of objection, the Commission preliminarily concluded that Meta abused its dominant position in

[87] ibid.
[88] ibid para 1019.
[89] ibid para 1020.
[90] ibid para 1021.
[91] ibid paras 1162 and 1185.
[92] ibid paras 1178–83.
[93] Case T-604/18 *Google and Alphabet v Commission (Google Android)* ECLI:EU:T:2022:541.
[94] European Commission, 'Commission Sends Statement of Objections to Meta over Abusive Practices benefiting Facebook Marketplace' (19 December 2022).

the market for personal social networks and national markets for online display advertising on social media by imposing unfair trading conditions.[95] According to the Commission, these unilateral terms and conditions 'are *unjustified, disproportionate and not necessary* for the provision of online display advertising services on Meta's platforms'.[96] The Commission reached a similar conclusion regarding Apple's app store terms restricting app developers' ability to inform iPhone and iPad users of alternative music subscription services at a lower price ('anti-steering obligations').[97] These cases underscore the significance of case law concerning exploitative conduct, particularly the case law on unfair terms, for digital markets.[98]

These decisions show the less technical nature of abuse-of-dominance cases based on proportionality, which tend to consider the different interests at stake. Overall, fairness under Article 102 is assessed with regard to (1) whether the clause has a legitimate objective other than to exploit the consumer; (2) whether the clause is capable of achieving the legitimate goal (effective); (3) whether there are less restrictive but equally effective alternative means to achieve the goal; and (4) whether the clause is proportionate, in the sense that the benefits are not outweighed by its exploitative effect on the trading party in question.

The less technical nature of the proportionality-based assessment might imply that data privacy issues could be more readily accommodated within the case law concerning unfair trading conditions, as opposed to those dealing with excessive prices. This is because the test discussed here allows for a broader evaluation of various interests, compared to the more rigid price–cost test used in cases of excessive pricing. Moreover, proportionality is a well-established principle under EU law, including in the field of data privacy, and can easily be adapted to privacy terms and conditions.

The suitability and appeal of the case law on unfair terms to privacy-related practices is further strengthened by recent cases involving Facebook and Google for exploitative abuse by imposing unfair privacy terms. In its widely publicized decision, the Bundeskartellamt found Facebook to have abused its dominant position in the market for social networks by imposing unfair privacy terms and conditions

[95] ibid.

[96] ibid (emphasis added).

[97] European Commission, 'Commission Sends Statement of Objections to Apple Clarifying Concerns over App Store Rules for Music Streaming Providers' (28 February 2023).

[98] One might contend that many of these practices bear closer resemblance to product design choices rather than conventional contractual limitations. In this context, there are concerns that the Commission's interference with product design decisions of undertakings is inconsistent with the CJEU case law, which sets a high bar for intervention. For instance, Colomo (n 15) argues that one way the Commission bypasses this stringent threshold is by framing exclusionary practices as exploitative. This concern is evident in the *Facebook Marketplace* and *Apple* cases, where the initial investigations appeared as exclusionary practices but shifted to exploitative focus when the Commission issued its statement of objections.

on users.[99] Similarly, in its investigation involving Google's proposed implementation of the 'Privacy Sandbox', the UK Competition and Markets Authority (CMA) alleged that the plan to remove third-party cookies from the Chrome browser 'may amount to an abuse in the form of the imposition of unfair terms on consumers' as this might restrict their ability to manage their data in alignment with their individual privacy and targeting preferences.[100]

B. Privacy-Related Exploitative Practices in Light of the Case Law

In light of the case law above, one could identify data and privacy-related practices that could fit into exploitative abuse under the case law. The subsequent subsections delve into two such practices: restrictions on users' choice to limit usage of their data and restrictions on users' ability to share their data with other entities.

The above discussion on the case law of EU Courts regarding abusive terms demonstrate that restrictions on customers' choice play a crucial role in assessing the unfairness of terms. For example, in *Tetra Pak II*, the CJEU held that terms by dominant undertakings that limit a customer's ability to dispose of an asset they control (or own) constitutes abusive. In the context of data privacy, similar concerns might arise when firms in a dominant position limit the ability of users to dispose their data as they wish. This could potentially occur when a dominant company deprives users of their ability to control or limit how their data is used by the undertaking. The *Facebook Germany* case falls under this category, where Facebook was found to have abused its dominant position in the German market for social networks by depriving users ability to limit how Facebook uses their data.[101] However, restrictions of choice could also take the form of denying users the ability to share data with other entities.

This type of conduct has been a focal point in the CMA's investigation of Google's 'Privacy Sandbox' proposal. The proposal seeks 'to address privacy concerns by removing the cross-site tracking of Chrome users through third-party-cookies and other methods of tracking', replacing them with alternative tools.[102] By so doing, this practice limits the ability of publishers and third-party advertisers to track users across websites and use the data for targeted advertisement. In this regard, the CMA has indicated that this practice might constitute an exploitative abuse by

[99] See Bundeskartellamt, 'Preliminary Assessment in Facebook Proceeding: Facebook's Collection and Use of Data from Third-Party Sources Is Abusive' (19 December 2017); Bundeskartellamt, *Decision in the Administrative Proceedings of Facebook (6th Division B6-22/16)* (2019) paras 523–24.

[100] Case 50972 *Decision to Accept Commitments Offered by Google in Relation to Its Privacy Sandbox Proposals*, Competition and Markets Authority 11 February 2022 (CMA, *Decision to Accept Google's Commitments*) para 5.82.

[101] See Bundeskartellamt, *Decision in the Administrative Proceedings* (n 99) paras 523–24.

[102] CMA, *Decision to Accept Google's Commitments* (n 100) para 1.2.

limiting users' choice 'in terms of whether and how their personal data is used for the purpose of targeting and delivering advertising to them'.[103] Subsections 1 and 2 discuss whether these two practices could meet the test established by the CJEU regarding unfair terms.

1. Restrictions on Users' Choice to Limit Usage of Their Data: *Facebook Germany* Case

One area of concern on the intersection between privacy and competition law is the extent that far-reaching privacy policies by dominant undertakings could be captured as exploitative abuse. This can take the form of forcing users to provide excessive data or agreeing to more expansive usage of their data than could be expected in situations of effective competition. The Bundeskartellamt *Facebook Germany* case is a good example in this regard. The investigation concerns Facebook's terms in relation to data collected from third-party sources, that is websites that embed Facebook plug-ins (such as 'Like') or use other Facebook services (such as 'Facebook login'). These functions allow users to share the content of an external website on Facebook or log into a third-party website using their Facebook credentials. Simultaneously, they allow Facebook to track the browsing behaviour of users (and non-users) across third-party websites. This means that whenever a user visits websites with Facebook plug-ins, Facebook receives data about the visited websites, what the user did on those sites, the kind of web browser used, and data related to the user's device.

Moreover, Facebook's privacy policy permits the aggregation of user data from third-party sources, including data from its subsidiaries like WhatsApp and Instagram, with the data collected on the Facebook social network. Essentially, users must consent to Facebook's collection of their data from these third-party sources and the merging of these data with their Facebook accounts to use the Facebook social network. At the centre of the Bundeskartellamt investigation was the question of 'whether Facebook imposes unfair conditions on its users by making them choose between accepting "the whole Facebook package", including an extensive disclosure of personal data, or not using Facebook at all'.[104]

According to the agency, when access to the personal data 'has great relevance for the competitive performance of a company', its collection and use by a dominant undertaking is relevant not only for data privacy but also for competition law.[105] This relevance for competition law arises, for instance, if the dominant firm conditions the use of its service on the user granting the company extensive permissions to utilize their personal data.[106] In December 2017, the Bundeskartellamt

[103] ibid para 5.80.
[104] Bundeskartellamt, 'Background Information' (n 61) 2.
[105] ibid 1–2.
[106] ibid.

reached a preliminary conclusion that Facebook had abused its dominant position 'by making the use of its social network conditional on its being allowed to limitlessly amass every kind of data generated by using third-party websites and merge it with the user's Facebook account'.[107] In February 2019, the Bundeskartellamt concluded its investigation and ordered Facebook to stop combining user data from third-party sources without users' 'voluntary consent'.[108] The agency reasoned that the consent to combine user data from third-party sources cannot be deemed voluntary if it is a prerequisite to using Facebook's social network. For consent to be voluntary, Facebook must give users the option of preventing the collection and merging of their data from third-party sources with their Facebook account, without denying them access to its social network if they choose to reject such terms.[109]

Two points from the investigation require particular mention. First, this was the first case in which harm to data privacy was at the centre of a competition law investigation. Some of the consumer harms identified by the Bundeskartellamt included users' loss of control over how 'their personal data are used', the lack of choice over the merging of their data, and the 'violation of users' constitutionally protected right to informational self-determination'.[110] Second, the investigation resorted to data privacy law as a metric for assessing unfairness and abuse. In its assessment, the Bundeskartellamt found Facebook's data collection practices from third-party sources to be unfair in light of European data protection law and to constitute an abuse of dominance under German competition law.[111]

Following an appeal for interim measures by Facebook, the Higher Regional Court of Duesseldorf suspended the Bundeskartellamt's order, which was subsequently overturned by the Federal Supreme Court.[112] The Higher Regional Court seems to cite three reasons for suspending the order.[113] The first relates to the lack of adequate causal link between Facebook's market dominance and its data collection. The second addresses the absence of a causal link between the market dominance and the infringement of data privacy rules. The third pertains to the lack of competitive harm resulting from Facebook's practices. Despite these arguments, the Federal Supreme Court found that the concerns of the Regional Higher Court

[107] Bundeskartellamt, 'Preliminary Assessment' (n 99).

[108] Bundeskartellamt, 'Bundeskartellamt Prohibits Facebook from Combining User Data from Different Sources' (7 February 2019); Bundeskartellamt, *Case Summary: Facebook, Exploitative Business Terms Pursuant to Section 19(1) GWB for Inadequate Data Processing* (2019).

[109] Bundeskartellamt, 'Bundeskartellamt Prohibits Facebook' (n 108).

[110] ibid 4.

[111] See Bundeskartellamt, *Case Summary* (n 108) 7–8.

[112] See BGH (German Federal Court of Justice), decision of 23 June 2020—KVR 69/19. However, at the time of this writing, there was only a press release of the decision in German. So, the discussions are based on subsequent commentaries in English. See Natasha Lomas, 'Antitrust Case against Facebook's "Super Profiling" Back on Track after German Federal Rourt Ruling', *TechCrunch* (23 June 2020); Rupprecht Podszun, 'Facebook @ BGH', *D'Kart* (23 June 2020).

[113] See Rupprecht Podszun, 'Facebook vs. Bundeskartellamt' *D'Kart* (30 August 2019).

were unwarranted. The Federal Supreme Court affirmed Facebook's unquestionable dominance in the German market for social networks and that the imposed terms could constitute an abuse of such dominance. In this context, the Federal Supreme Court underscored that an abuse of dominance and its negative impacts for competition could take the form of a restriction of users' freedom of choice. In the *Facebook Germany* case, this relates to the lack of choice in terms of the collection of data from different sources and the combination of such data with user's Facebook profile.

Thus, the question is whether Facebook's terms to combine data across websites can be considered unfair and abusive under Article 102 considering the decisions from the Commission and EU courts. Interestingly, there are significant similarities between the factual and legal analyses in existing case law and the *Facebook Germany* case. In several decisions involving collecting societies, the proportionality test focuses on the extent to which the contractual terms may limit a legally protected right, such as copyright holders' freedom to dispose their work. In *Tetra Pak II*, the impact was on the customer's property rights. Similarly, at the centre of the Bundeskartellamt's decision is the extent to which Facebook's terms 'unreasonably encroach' on users' constitutional rights to information self-determination. Whether breaches of data privacy rules could constitute abuse under Article 102 is addressed in Section V. Here, the focus is, instead, on whether Facebook's terms can be considered unfair by restricting users' choice to dispose their data, considering the two cumulative tests established in the CJEU's case law: necessity and proportionality.

a) Necessity test

The first test focuses on whether the clause is 'absolutely necessary' in relation to the object of the contract. In relation to the *Facebook Germany* case, the question is whether the collection of data from third-party sources and its integration into users' Facebook accounts is 'absolutely necessary' to the object of the contract, that is the provision of an ad-supported social network. Given that users might have different preferences regarding the amount of data they are willing to share in return for targeted advertisement, determining whether Facebook's combination of data from third-party sources is objectively necessary for the provision of an ad-supported social network would be difficult. Thus, the assessment is a matter of judgment rather than precision, and such assessment can be made without resorting to data privacy law. But, at least in the EU, data privacy is a normative concept, and seeking normative guidance is not only justified but may also be necessary.[114] Accordingly, one could resort to data privacy rules—particularly the purpose limitation and data minimization principles—to assess whether the

[114] Costa-Cabral and Lynskey (n 50) 29.

combination of data from third-party sources is absolutely necessary for providing an ad-supported social networking service.

This seems to be the approach followed by the Bundeskartellamt. According to the agency, the collection and combination of users' data from third-party sources was neither necessary 'for offering the social network as such nor for monetizing the network through personalized advertising'.[115] This is partially because a 'personalized network' could substantially be built upon the user data gathered and processed during the operation of the social network.[116] The Bundeskartellamt's reasoning seems to be cognizant of data privacy norms in recognizing that, in light of Facebook's purpose of providing a personalized social network, the collection and use of data from third-party sources is beyond what is minimally necessary to achieve the purpose. This is particularly the case in relation to data collected from websites with Facebook plug-ins when these plug-ins are not actually used. The Bundeskartellamt also questioned the legitimacy of the very object of the contract, as it lacks support under Article 6 of the GDPR.[117]

In response to the request for a preliminary ruling, both the Advocate General (AG) and CJEU appear to support the Bundeskartellamt's stance that the combination of data from third-party sources is not objectively necessary to maintain a social network, even when considering the need for providing personalized and ad-financed services.[118] For example, the CJEU questioned Facebook's ability to rely on contractual necessity (Article 6(1(b)), or legitimate interest (Article 6(1(f)), or even consent (Article 6(1(a)) for combining data from third-party sources with users' Facebook profiles.[119] Regarding contractual necessity, the Court highlighted that the mere fact that a processing is useful for performance of contact, or that the processing is mentioned within the contract, is insufficient to justify said processing under Article 6(1(b)).[120] To invoke contractual necessity, the Court noted, Facebook must be able to prove that the processing is 'objectively indispensable' for performance of the contract. This means that 'the main subject matter of the contract cannot be achieved if the processing in question does not occur' or that 'there are no workable, less intrusive alternatives'.[121] In this context, while the Court acknowledged certain benefits of personalization and seamless integration between services such as Facebook and Instagram, it questioned whether the consolidation of data is genuinely indispensable for the provision of a social networking

115 Bundeskartellamt, *Decision in the Administrative Proceedings* (n 99) para 741.

116 Bundeskartellamt, *Case Summary* (n 108) 10. The Federal Supreme Court reiterated this idea, pointing out that Facebook failed to prove that its legitimate interests could not be adequately protected by limiting data collection strictly to the confines of the social network: Podszun, 'Facebook @ BGH' (n 112).

117 Bundeskartellamt, *Case Summary* (n 108) 10.

118 Case C-252/21 *Meta Platforms Inc v Bundeskartellamt* ECLI:EU:C:2022:704, Opinion of Advocate General Rantos; *Meta Platforms v Bundeskartellamt* (n 14).

119 *Meta Platforms v Bundeskartellamt* (n 14).

120 ibid para 99.

121 ibid paras 98–99.

service.[122] Essentially, this appears to reiterate the necessity/indispensability test under Article 102 concerning unfair terms.

Furthermore, the Court dismissed the argument that the combination of data could be justified based on legitimate interest. The Court acknowledged that advertising falls within the scope of legitimate interests.[123] However, considering the extensive nature of the processing and the fact that users reasonably could not expect their data from third-party sources to be merged with their Facebook profiles, the Court ruled that users' interests and fundamental rights override the operator's interest in personalized advertising that funds its operations.[124] The Court also questioned Facebook's ability to rely on users' consent to justify the processing considering the extensive nature of the processing as well as the lack of choice for users to provide separate consent to data collected on and off Facebook.[125]

While the final determination must be made by the referring court, the CJEU's finding that Facebook's data collection and combination from third-party sources is not objectively necessary for an ad-supported social network and breaches the GDPR will be crucial in judging whether Facebook's terms are unfair under Article 102. This lends further support to the Bundeskartellamt's position that the combination of data is neither legitimate (ie the contract's objective may be unlawful as it lacks legal basis under Article 6 of the GDPR) nor necessary for attainment the contract's objective. Thus, there are signs that Facebook's terms may fail to meet the 'necessity' test and could be deemed abusive under Article 102.

b) Proportionality test

Even assuming that the data from third-party sources is necessary for the object of the contract, the question remains whether Facebook's terms are 'reasonably proportionate' for achieving the objective. In *DSD*, the main reason for considering the contract term to be unfair and abusive was that DSD charged licence fees in circumstances in which its services were not actually used.[126] This was because DSD subsumed the fees for using the service into the fees for using the trademark, which had the effect that customers paid the same amount even when they used the DSD collection service only for part of their packaging. The same argument could be made regarding Facebook's practice. As the Bundeskartellamt investigation shows, the collection and merging of data from third-party sources with Facebook plugins happens even when the user does not make use of these functionalities. For example, this data aggregation occurs when a user simply views a site that contains an embedded 'Like' button, regardless of whether they click on it or not.

122 ibid paras 102–104.
123 ibid para 115.
124 ibid paras 117–18.
125 ibid paras 150–51.
126 *DSD* (n 82) para 113.

In this regard, Facebook promotes its plug-ins as tools that allow users to easily 'like' or 'share' website content on Facebook, which, in turn, allows Facebook to track the browsing behaviour of users. Thus, the tracking could be seen as the users' performance, in return for which they are able to use these tools. However, to the extent that Facebook tracks users even when they do not use the plug-ins, it can be argued, following the reasoning in *DSD*, that Facebook's practice is unreasonable because it forces performance from users even when its services are not actually being used or because it subsumes the use of its plug-ins with the use of the website more generally. Facebook's tracking even extends to non-users, which is quite invasive. To draw a parallel from the offline world, if Facebook tracking its users on third-party websites without using the plug-ins is akin to a shop owner charging customers merely for visiting their shop, then tracking non-Facebook users is akin to charging customers for visiting a shop next door. Thus, at least with regard to these terms, there is room for an argument that these tracking practices go beyond what is proportionate to achieve the objective of providing an ad-supported social networking.

Even in relation to the data collected after users have utilized Facebook's plug-ins, questions could be raised regarding the proportionality of Facebook's terms and conditions considering users' privacy interests. One significant concern involves users' ability to control the data that is collected and how it is utilized. Giving effect to this interest requires that users be adequately informed about how such data are collected and used. In this sense, Facebook's failure to sufficiently inform users and provide them with adequate choice can be seen as disproportionate in light of the users' interests. In *Sequential Use of Coupons*, the Commission analysed whether British Airways' (BA) terms on the sequential use of tickets—which required that passengers who purchase a cheaper, indirect-flight ticket use the coupons in sequence—were unfair.[127] In this case, a passenger who did not use the first ticket was prohibited from boarding the onward flight. The Commission dismissed the complaint on the grounds that BA did not hold a dominant position. However, it also noted that, even if BA had been in a dominant position, the contractual clause would not constitute abuse. The Commission's decision underscored the significance of two factors. The first pertains to the question of whether users are informed of the sequential use in advance. In this regard, the Commission referenced the decision by the UK Office of Fair Trading, which determined that such a clause is not considered unfair under the Unfair Contracts Directive if users are informed in advance about the sequential use.[128]

Second, the Commission highlighted the different measures consumers can take to safeguard themselves against such restrictions, for example, by purchasing

[127] The decision has not been published on the Commission's website but is discussed in O'Donoghue and Padilla (n 62) 856–58.

[128] ibid 857.

flexible tickets or tickets that allow for refunds.[129] The Commission also took into account other existing frameworks that safeguarded the user's interests, such as the possibility to board the flight in case of force majeure, or after a price recalculation, and the fact that users could still use the return flight.[130] This decision underscores that the adequacy of user information regarding terms in advance, ideally in compliance with the applicable rules, as well as the availability of alternatives to circumvent the terms, are key factors when assessing unfairness. This suggests that a contractual clause imposed by a dominant undertaking could be deemed unfair if users are not notified beforehand and if they lack alternative options that could shield them from such a clause.

Facebook's practice fits this analysis. The Bundeskartellamt investigation indicates that users were not adequately informed about their data being collected upon visiting a third-party website with Facebook plug-ins. The agency further highlighted that these practices breach EU data privacy rules, particularly the lack of effective consent under GDPR.[131] However, even if users had been informed, the issue remains regarding the absence of options or alternatives to prevent this data from being merged into their Facebook profiles, a viewpoint corroborated by the CJEU. To begin with, Facebook does not offer users such possibilities. Additionally, an individual who visits a website with Facebook plug-ins cannot escape tracking by choosing not to use the plug-ins or by adjusting their browser or device settings, as Facebook ignores such signals. Moreover, an individual cannot evade tracking by choosing not to join or to leave Facebook, as Facebook also tracks non-users. Consequently, the only way for an individual to avoid being tracked on third-party websites is to refrain from visiting websites equipped with Facebook plug-ins, which is impractical.

First, considering the extensive adoption of such plug-ins, one would have to abstain from accessing content across millions of websites. Moreover, individuals have no way of knowing in advance whether the website they are about to visit has embedded Facebook plug-ins. Once users visit a website, Facebook collects and then merges users' data with their Facebook profiles. Explaining the exclusion from the investigation of data collected within Facebook itself, the Bundeskartellamt referred to the possibility that users can exert 'considerable influence in the collection of their data by being mindful of "the way they use the network and the content they post"'.[132] However, users lack such control regarding the data collected from third-party websites.

The above analysis highlighting users' lack of options to escape Facebook's tracking on third-party websites is exacerbated by Facebook's quasi-monopoly

[129] ibid.
[130] ibid 858.
[131] Bundeskartellamt, *Case Summary* (n 108) 10.
[132] Bundeskartellamt, 'Background Information' (n 61) 1–2.

position in the German market for social networks. Additionally, the lock-in effects arising from identity-based network effects make it nearly impossible to avoid Facebook's tracking by switching to competing social networking service. Considering these factors, along with the fact that users are not informed about the terms in advance and lack alternatives both inside and outside Facebook to avoid such terms, a strong argument could be made that Facebook's terms may be considered unfair under Article 102. This implies that although any breach of data privacy rules would bolster the case for intervention via competition law, the assertion of abuse relating to Facebook's practices could theoretically be substantiated without necessarily invoking this infringement.[133]

This notwithstanding, considering whether a contractual term infringes upon a legally protected right is consistent with the CJEU's jurisprudence. In the *BRT v SABAM* decision, clauses in the collecting society's statutes were found to be unfair and abusive because they impaired members' freedom to exercise their copyright.[134] In *Tetra Park II*, contractual clauses were found to be unfair because they deprived customers of 'the very essence of the right of ownership'.[135] Thus, a clause, which has a legitimate objective, could be considered unfair if, having considered all the relevant interests, it 'unreasonably restricts' the trading partners from exercising a legally protected right.

Consistent with the EU case law, the Bundeskartellamt underlined the need for balancing users' data privacy interests against Facebook's interest in using data for targeted advertising. However, the terms seem to tilt the balance in favour of Facebook to the detriment of users' legally protected rights.[136] Thus, even if one accepts that Facebook has a legitimate objective in collecting data from third-party sources for advertisement, one could argue that the measure is disproportionate, as the gains from pursuing the objective are outweighed by the exploitative effects on users' legally protected rights.

In this regard, the Bundeskartellamt determined that 'the efficiencies in a business model based on personalized advertising do not outweigh the interests of the users when it comes to processing data from sources outside of the social network'.[137] Accordingly, Facebook's terms are seen as imposing unreasonable restrictions on users' constitutional right to information self-determination and their rights to privacy. An important consideration in this balancing act is the

[133] This is also the position taken by the Federal Supreme Court in overturning the interim measures imposed by the Higher Regional Court of Duesseldorf. The Court indicated that it was not decisive whether Facebook's terms were in breach of data protection rules and instead emphasized that the terms constitute abuse because 'Facebook does not give its users any choice.' See Maximilian Volmar and Katharina Helmdach, 'Protecting Consumers and Their Data through Competition Law? Rethinking Abuse of Dominance in Light of the Federal Cartel Office's Facebook Investigation' (2018) 14 European Competition Journal 195, 203.

[134] *BRT v SABAM* (n 63) para 15.

[135] *Tetra Pak II* (n 69) para 123.

[136] Bundeskartellamt, 'Preliminary Assessment' (n 99).

[137] Bundeskartellamt, *Case Summary* (n 108) 1–2.

availability of less restrictive alternatives to achieve the legitimate goal. In *Tetra Pak II*, the GC rejected Tetra Pak's defence that the restrictions on technical modifications and improvements were justified on public health grounds. In so doing, the Court referred to the availability of less restrictive mechanisms, such as disclosing all the technical specifications to customers.[138]

Similarly, one can point to less restrictive alternatives that Facebook could adopt to achieve its legitimate interests. One such alternative would be to refrain from tracking of non-Facebook users and limit the tracking of Facebook users only when 'Like' and 'Share' services are actively used. In condemning the excessive nature of the same data collection, the Brussels Court of First Instance noted that 'it is possible to provide social plug-ins that do not transmit any information before the visitor to the third-party website tries to make use of the social plug-in'.[139] Moreover, Facebook could respect users' choices not to be tracked, as indicated by their device or browser settings. Considering these less restrictive alternatives, one could argue that Facebook's terms unfairly encroach on users' fundamental rights to data privacy, as recognized under the TFEU and the Charter, and thus could potentially constitute unfair and abusive under Article 102.

2. Restrictions on Users Ability to Share Their Data: Google Privacy Sandbox and Apple's App Tracking Transparency (ATT) Prompt

While earlier concerns in competition law focus on expansive privacy terms as a form of exploitative abuse, recent trends have shifted the focus to practices that enhance users' privacy. From the outset, such practices may enhance users' privacy by limiting further sharing and usage of their data but may also raise competition concerns by depriving users' choice and limiting the ability of third parties from accessing data that is important for competition. This, in turn, raises difficult questions on how to balance privacy and competition interests. Two examples are particularly noteworthy.

The first is Apple's move to implement a feature called App Tracking Transparency (hereinafter the ATT prompt) involving the display of a window for users to consent to being tracked on various websites or mobile apps. Adhering to this notice is a precondition for websites or app developers to access the unique device identifier for advertisers (IDFA), which allows apps or advertisers to track users' activities across websites or apps for the purposes of targeted advertising.[140] This has led to a complaint in France, where a group of advertisers accused Apple of abusing its dominant position by imposing unfair trading conditions under Article 102(a).[141] The abuse stems from Apple's requirement that app developers 'use a

[138] Case T-83/91 *Tetra Pak v Commission* (n 68) para 139.

[139] *Willem Debeuckelaere v Facebook* Brussels Court of First Instance Roll Number 2016/153/A 66-7.

[140] Autorité de la Concurrence, '*Decision 21-D-07 of 17 March 2021 Regarding a Request for Interim Measures in the Sector of Advertising on Mobile Apps on iOS*', paras 5–17.

[141] ibid. See also Vincent Giovannini, 'The French Apple Competition & Privacy Case' (2021) 18 Competition Forum.

non-customisable prompt for obtaining consent from internet users, with the sole aim of dissuading users for giving them access to the IDFA'.[142]

Another example is Google's proposed plan for Privacy Sandbox. As noted above, the proposal aims to enhance users' privacy by preventing cross-site tracking of Chrome users through third-party cookies and related technologies. However, the practice generates competition concerns as it restricts the ability of publishers and third-party advertisers to gather data, thereby impacting their targeted advertising capabilities. In this regard, the CMA has indicated that this practice could constitute exploitative abuse by restricting users' choice regarding 'whether and how their personal data is used for the purpose of targeting and delivering advertising to them'.[143] The question is whether these practices can be considered unfair and abusive under Article 102 in light of the decisions from the Commission and EU courts.

As the discussions in Section IV.A show, the assessment on whether Apple and Google's actions can be considered unfair trading terms under Article 102 hinges on two cumulative tests: necessity and proportionality. Concerning the first test, the issue at hand is whether the removal of third-party cookies from Chrome and the implementation of the ATT prompt are 'absolutely necessary' in relation to the object of the contract, namely the provision of App store and Browser services. It bears mentioning that both initiatives aim to enhance users' privacy. The Privacy Sandbox aims to limit further sharing of users' data with third parties, whereas the ATT gives users more transparency regarding third-party tracking and grants users greater control over their data. Thus, both measures visualize and mitigate privacy concerns associated with cross-site tracking, which is a major privacy-intrusive practice.

In this context, unlike the terms that compel users to agree to expansive data usage in breach of data privacy rules (as seen in the *Facebook Germany* example above), which raise questions on the very object of the contract, the objectives of these privacy-enhancing measures could be seen as legitimate and, in the EU, even mandated. To some extent, this alignment of the measures with users' privacy reduces the normative influence of data privacy in competition assessment, particularly the reliance on violations of data privacy rules to determine abuse.

Thus, the assessment of whether Apple's and Google's measures are necessary for the object of the contract must be conducted considering other factors. This includes the nature of the service on offer and whether the implementation of the privacy-enhancing measures is indispensable (or mandated) for providing the service. In the French *Apple* case, the claimants argued that the ATT prompt is not a necessary measure to protect users' privacy.[144] This argument is based on two

[142] Autorité de la Concurrence, *Decision 21-D-07* (n 140) para 73 <https://competition-forum.com/the-french-apple-competition-privacy-case/>.

[143] CMA, *Decision to Accept Google's Commitments* (n 100) para 5.80.

[144] Autorité de la Concurrence, '*Decision 21-D-07*' (n 140) para 80.

points: first, in the EU, users' privacy is protected through the GDPR and ePrivacy Directive, which requires data controllers to ensure that their data processing complies with these rules. Relatedly, the claimants asserted that the ATT implementation goes beyond what is required under the GDPR and ePrivacy Directive. This is because it is the responsibility of the data controllers, namely app developers and websites, not Apple, to ensure compliance and obtain consent under these rules.[145] Given that Apple is simply providing software and does not act as a controller, the ATT prompt is seen as an overreach. Second, the notice provided through the ATT prompt does not allow users to provide informed consent because it does not contain the information required under Articles 13 and 14 of the GDPR.[146]

It is interesting to see how compliance (or lack thereof) with data privacy rules feature in this case and the Bundeskartellamt *Facebook Germany* case. In the latter, the fact that Facebook's terms were in breach of the GDPR was central in finding Facebook's terms unfair and abusive under competition law. In contrast, in the *Apple* and *Google* cases, privacy improvements and compliance with data privacy rules seem to be the drivers (justifications) for the alleged abusive conduct. Moreover, in the *Apple* case the argument from claimants is that the ATT prompt is unfair and abusive under competition law because it goes beyond what is required under the GDPR.

This notwithstanding, the necessity of the ATT prompt should be evaluated not only from a GDPR perspective but also in the context of Apple's commercial interests. Apple has long used privacy as its brand image and a way to differentiate itself from the predominant data-intensive approach of other Silicon Valley companies. Importantly, Apple has taken several concrete measures to enhance users' privacy, including data encryption on user iPhones and the implementation of intelligent tracking prevention (ITP) on Safari to identify and remove third-party cookies. Furthermore, as highlighted by the French Competition Authority's (FCA) investigation, privacy is a fundamental aspect of a high-quality App Store, as it ensures that consumers can download apps knowing that their data is protected.[147]

The objections raised by the claimants, based on the GDPR and ePrivacy Directive, do not seem particularly compelling either. While it is, indeed, true that the primary responsibility for ensuring compliance—including obtaining consent—resides with data controllers (in this case, app developers and websites), there is nothing in these rules that prevents software developers like Apple from implementing privacy-enhancing measures. In this context, the FCA, after consulting with the data protection authority, indicated that both the GDPR and the ePrivacy Directive urge software developers to consider data protection rights during the design and development stages of their products.[148] Such consideration

[145] ibid para 76.
[146] ibid para 78.
[147] ibid para 170.
[148] ibid para 60.

will aid data controllers and processors in complying with their obligations under these rules. Thus, Apple's implementation of the ATT prompt can be seen as a necessary measure, considering both its commercial interests and the existing legal rules on data privacy.[149]

The second test in the case law on unfair terms is a measure of proportionality. A contractual clause, which is necessary for the object of the contract, can still be found unfair if it is disproportionate/unreasonable, considering the legitimate interests of the dominant undertaking, its trading parties, and, ultimately, consumers. Pertaining to Apple's measures, a balance must be struck between Apple's interest in protecting users' privacy and offering a secure app store and users' interest in controlling their data, as well as the interests of app developers and advertisers in accessing data for advertising.

From the perspective of app developers and advertisers, a key argument is that the standardization of the notice undermines their ability to communicate their data collection policies to users in a manner they see fit.[150] Importantly, the ATT implementation restricts their ability to collect user data, which is crucial for targeting and measuring advertisements.[151] From the users' perspective, the ATT implementation is perceived as introducing an unnecessary layer of information and request for consent, thereby creating bad user experience in using apps.[152] Additionally, due to the negative impact on advertisement revenue, the ATT prompt may drive content into paid apps and thereby limit the accessibility of content to a small number of consumers who can afford them. Thus, the claim is that the costs from the ATT implementation are disproportionate in light of protecting the privacy of iPhone users.

According to the CJEU, a contractual clause can be considered disproportionate if it limits freedom/choice of the trading parties any more than necessary.[153] Similarly, whether the customers have the possibility to avoid the clause is another important consideration. In the case of Apple, the ATT prompt does not prevent apps and websites from tracking users across websites; it only informs users about the tracking and prompts them to actively consent to such tracking. Thus, it is only when users decline consent that apps and websites would not be able to track and collect data.

Furthermore, the ATT implementation does not seem to overly restrict app developers' ability to customize the notice and provide additional information. First, Apple gives app developers the possibility to determine when the ATT prompt is displayed to the user, whether at the point of app installation or at a later stage during the app usage.[154] Second, and importantly, the ATT prompt contains a

149 ibid para 147.
150 ibid para 83.
151 ibid para 86.
152 ibid para 84.
153 *BRT v SABAM* (n 63) para 15.
154 Autorité de la Concurrence, '*Decision 21-D-07*' (n 140) para 152.

customizable section, which app developers can use to provide additional information about their data collection and to possibly persuade users to reconsider their choice. Furthermore, app developers can use their own pop-up window to provide extra information either before or after the ATT prompt is shown to users.

In terms of the impact on users, the FCA underscored the importance of concise and standardized information on data collection to empower users to take control of their data. Given the information overload problem that users are facing, the standardization of the notice is likely to facilitate consumer choice.[155] This is because it forces apps and websites to provide the purpose of the data collection in a precise manner, typically in one complete sentence, and lets the user make an informed decision.[156] In fact, the standardization might also be beneficial to some app developers because it can help smaller players to comply with their obligation to provide clear information and obtain consent for tracking.[157] In this sense, one could argue that the ATT implementation strikes a fair balance between Apple's interest in offering a secure app store, users' interest in controlling who gets to access their data, and app developers' commercial interest in collecting data for advertisement.[158]

Given the substantial similarities between the French *Apple* case and Google's Privacy Sandbox, there is no need to repeat the above discussions on the legal tests for unfair trading conditions. However, there are a few differences that are important to highlight. The first difference is that unlike Apple's commercial interests, those of Google are built on collecting and monetizing massive amounts of data. Additionally, Google has a bad track record in protecting users' privacy. Thus, when applying the first test on whether the measures are objectively necessary in providing the service, questions can be raised on whether improving users' privacy is the real reason behind the Privacy Sandbox. This puts Google in a much more difficult position than Apple in convincing competition agencies, such as the European Commission, which is investigating the conduct, that the measures are not designed to protect its position in the advertising market but to enhance users' privacy.

Indeed, one could argue that the browser market is competitive, and Google's move should be seen as part of the competition among web browsers to introduce similar features, rather than to protect its market position. For example, browsers such as Firefox and Brave have embedded such technologies that allow users to prevent cross-site tracking through cookies and related technologies. Importantly, Apple has implemented the ITP, which prevents the cross-site tracking of users through third-party cookies and browser/device fingerprinting. Apple's Safari

[155] ibid para 159.
[156] ibid para 24.
[157] ibid para 64.
[158] ibid para 153 (noting that Apple's measure is 'neither excessive nor disproportionate' with regard to the interests of consumers and app developers).

implements ITP by default. Thus, the Privacy Sandbox, which also prevents cross-site tracking by default, could be seen as a response to this competitive pressure. Furthermore, treating such moves as not necessary based on previous track record on privacy and the company's prevailing business model would be counterproductive as it may deter companies from responding to consumer needs and aligning their business practices in a manner that respects users' privacy. Thus, the focus ought to be on the proportionality of the measures in light of the different competing interests and the availability of less restrictive mechanisms to achieve the goal.

In this regard, some of the measures in Google's proposed Privacy Sandbox seem disproportionate considering Google interest in protecting users' privacy vis-à-vis users' interest to control their data and the interests of publishers and advertisers to access data for advertising purposes. As noted above, an important consideration in the balancing exercise is the availability of less restrictive alternatives to achieve the legitimate goal.[159] From the perspective of users, the claim is that users' privacy attitudes and preferences are different. Thus, while some users may not like to be tracked, others, albeit a small portion, might be willing to allow some tracking in return for seeing more targeted and relevant ads.[160] Accommodating those preferences dictates that users who want to allow tracking should have the possibility to do so. This is also reflected when looking at other browsers that have implemented similar features. For example, although Apple's ITP prevents cross-site tracking by default, users have the possibility to consent to such tracking. Thus, whether users have the choice about whom and how much data to share is an important consideration in assessing the proportionality of the measure and unfairness of the term.

In this regard, the investigation by the CMA shows that Google's proposed implementation of the Privacy Sandbox, through the Federated Learning of Cohorts (FLoC) and Privacy Budget proposals, does not give users the option to share their data with third-party websites.[161] Thus, if Google proceeds to implement the Privacy Sandbox without giving users the option to enable the sharing of their data with third parties, the subset of users who prefer to see targeted ads in return for collection of their data might be harmed. Moreover, the CMA is concerned that, in its current form, the Privacy Sandbox obscures users' choices regarding their ability to control what ads they see and how their data is used to target ads.[162] Therefore, despite the CMA's acceptance of the commitments precluding it from taking infringement decisions, the agency held that the restrictions could amount to abuse of dominance through the imposition of unfair terms. The conduct is

[159] Case T-83/91 *Tetra Pak v Commission* (n 68) para 139.
[160] CMA, *Decision to Accept Google's Commitments* (n 100) para 5.80.
[161] ibid para 6.42.
[162] ibid para 5.82.

likely to harm consumers 'by preventing them from adjusting the level of privacy and targeting in line with their preferences'.[163]

The restrictions on users' ability to consent to tracking by third parties is also important from the perspective of publishers and advertisers. This is because by limiting access to data, the measure may foreclose competition in the advertising market and strengthen Google's already strong position. Thus, absent changes to the proposal, Google's measure disproportionately harms users' interest in controlling their data and publishers' interest in collecting data for advertising. In characterizing the proposal as potentially disproportionate and unfair, the CMA refers to less restrictive mechanisms Google could deploy to achieve its goal of enhancing users' privacy. These include giving users the option of sharing their data with websites under the FLoC proposal and allowing users, under the Privacy Budget proposal, to flex the amount of data shared with different websites or publishers.[164]

Ultimately, the assessment on whether terms restricting users' ability to share data constitute unfair terms under Article 102 is contingent on various factors, including the extent to which the measure is aligned with the commercial interests of the dominant undertaking and the nature of service on offer. Another important consideration is the existence of less restrictive alternatives, which include offering users a real choice in terms of continuing to share data and its amount with third parties. Furthermore, the discussions highlight the starkly contrasting ways that data privacy rules feature in competition law investigations, either as a metric for determining abuse, as seen in the Bundeskartellamt's *Facebook Germany* case, or as justifications for the absence of abuse, as demonstrated in the *Apple* and *Google* cases. The French *Apple* case introduces an additional twist in this interplay with the argument, albeit unsuccessful, that a privacy-enhancing behaviour might constitute abusive under competition law if it goes beyond what is required under data privacy rules. However, despite the contradictory ways that privacy interests have featured in these cases, the competition remedies sought seem to be positive for users' privacy.

In the *Facebook Germany* case, the measure sought is for the company to stop combining data from third-party sources unless it obtains voluntary consent. This means users should be given a real choice of declining consent without losing access to Facebook services, which is a positive development for users' privacy. Similarly, the manner in which the CMA has gone about addressing the issues is instructive in terms of how to reconcile privacy and competition interests. The commitments accepted by the CMA do not require Google to roll back the privacy improvements brought by the Privacy Sandbox. Instead, they focus on ensuring Google provides users with the option to share data with third parties. Further, the commitments demand that Google treat its services equally and refrain from using

[163] ibid para 5.84.
[164] ibid para 6.42.

the data for its own purposes.[165] This is an immense win for users' privacy, as the intervention by competition authorities has strengthened users' privacy more than even Google's initial measures. Importantly, the discussions show that competition authorities were able to address the competition concerns without necessarily derailing the potential privacy improvements.

V. Breach of Data Privacy Rules and Their Role in Assessing Abuse

As elucidated in Chapter 4, as personal data becomes a key resource in the provision of many digital services, data privacy rules take central stage in regulating the competitive process both as a competitive constraint and as a barrier to market entry. One implication of this development is that breaches of data privacy rules may have effects that go beyond the harm to fundamental rights and disrupt the competitive process, with potential implications for competition law. This raises an important question of whether, and to what extent, breaches of data privacy rules by dominant undertaking could constitute a breach of competition rules. This section addresses this question. In so doing, it starts by highlighting two instances where breaches of data privacy rules have featured centrally in the assessment of abuse of dominance and whether there is support in the EU case law for consideration of other legal rules in competition assessment. The section then proceeds to outline additional considerations needed for addressing breaches of data privacy rules as a form of abuse. These considerations are important to mitigate the risk of automatically equating data privacy infringements by dominant entities with breaches of competition rules.

A. Recent Developments in Light of the Case Law

The Bundeskartellamt *Facebook Germany* case is one instance where breaches of data privacy rules feature centrally in assessing unfairness and abuse under competition law. The Bundeskartellamt found that Facebook's data collection practices from third-party sources were unfair considering European data protection law and that they constituted an abuse of dominance under German competition law.[166] The conclusions were based on precedent from the Federal Supreme Court. This precedent held that the contract terms of dominant undertakings, which are incompatible with the laws regulating general conditions and terms of trade, constitute an abuse of a dominant position under German competition law if such

[165] ibid para 6.55. See also Chapter 4, Section IV.B.2.
[166] See Bundeskartellamt, *Case Summary* (n 108) 7–8.

terms can be linked to the company's dominance.[167] Following this precedent, the Bundeskartellamt used data protection rules in assessing the fairness of the terms. Reiterating that the aim of data privacy rules is to ensure that users have the ability to 'decide freely and without coercion on how their personal data are used', the Bundeskartellamt assessed 'whether the consent given by Facebook users is sufficiently informed' pursuant to Article 4(11) of the GDPR.[168]

The Bundeskartellamt held that users were not sufficiently informed about the collection of their data from third-party websites. To begin with, users could not foresee and expect that data generated in using websites and services other than Facebook could be combined with their Facebook profile.[169] As noted in Section IV.B.1, users' data from third-party websites was collected and combined with their Facebook profiles, even if they did not use Facebook's plug-ins or even when no Facebook symbol was visible on a website.[170] Additionally, even if they are aware, users are not given adequate opportunities to prevent the combining of their browsing data with their Facebook profiles. Facebook merges the data from third-party websites into the user's Facebook profile 'even if the user has blocked web tracking in his browser or device settings'.[171] The agency found that the practice harmed users' data privacy.

The Bundeskartellamt described the concrete harms as follows:

> The damage for the users lies in a loss of control: they are no longer able to control how their personal data are used. Facebook's users are oblivious as to which data from which sources are being merged to develop a detailed profile of them and their online activities. On account of the merging of the data, individual data gain a significance the user cannot foresee. Because of Facebook's market power users have no option to avoid the merging of their data, either. Facebook's merging of the data thus also constitutes a violation of the users' constitutionally protected right to informational self-determination.[172]

Accordingly, the agency held that Facebook's terms and conditions 'are neither justified under data protection principles nor are they appropriate under competition law standards'.[173]

Similarly, the Italian Competition and Consumer Protection Authority (AGCM) accused Google of abusing its dominant position by preventing users from exercising their data portability right under the GDPR. The investigation

[167] ibid 8.
[168] Bundeskartellamt, 'Background Information' (n 61) 4.
[169] Bundeskartellamt, 'Preliminary Assessment' (n 99).
[170] ibid.
[171] Bundeskartellamt, 'Background Information' (n 61).
[172] ibid 4.
[173] ibid 2.

was opened following Google's refusal to allow interoperability on its platforms, thereby inhibiting users from sharing their data with other companies. In this case, Google allegedly hindered interoperability with an app named Weople, a provider of data vault service, which allows users to store and generate value from their data. According to the Agency, Google's conduct might infringe upon users' right to data portability, as stipulated under Article 20 of the GDPR, thereby curtailing the economic benefits that consumers might derive from their data. Simultaneously, the purported abuse could hamper competition by limiting the capacity of alternative operators to develop innovative data-based services.[174] The Agency underscored the importance of the right to data portability for competition. Given that the right allows users to port their data and switch to rivals, it offers rivals the opportunity to exert competitive pressure on companies such as Google, which have built their dominance based on creating ecosystems reliant on the monetization of vast amounts of data.[175]

In both the Bundeskartellamt *Facebook Germany* and *Google Italy* cases, data privacy rules feature centrally in the competition assessment, functioning as a benchmark for determining unfairness and abuse. The question arises whether the jurisprudence of the CJEU supports such consideration of other legal rules. While rare, there are instances in EU law where the Commission and EU courts have referred to other legal norms to determine the legality of conduct under competition law. As noted in Section III.B, in *Allianz Hungária*, the CJEU resorted to domestic law in assessing the competitive impact of a vertical restriction imposed by insurance companies on brokers.[176]

Moreover, intellectual property (IP) law has long been used as a normative yardstick in competition law, particularly in assessing whether the rewards of the legal monopoly (eg licensing conditions) are concerns for competition law. In *AstraZeneca*, the CJEU held that where IP rights are acquired unlawfully, the rewards are not based on 'merits' and are, thus, considered abusive.[177] In this instance, whether the monopoly is acquired in compliance with the relevant IP rules provides normative guidance in assessing whether the rewards are legal under competition law. These examples illustrate that when competition law lacks the necessary tools to assess the legality of certain conduct, it seeks guidance from norms outside competition law, including other fields of law. In a similar fashion, data privacy rules and the rules governing unfair contracts could provide normative guidance in assessing whether terms and conditions that affect privacy and personal data constitute an abuse of dominance.

[174] Autorità garante della Concorrenza e del Mercato (AGCM), 'Italian Competition Authority, Investigation Opened against Google for Abuse of Dominant Position in Data Portability' (14 July 2022) <https://en.agcm.it/en/media/press-releases/2022/7/A552>.

[175] ibid.

[176] *Allianz Hungária* (n 52) para 47.

[177] Case C-457/10 P *AstraZeneca v Commission* EU:C:2012:770, para 47.

Indeed, in the *Facebook Germany* case, both the AG and the CJEU have offered a timely clarification of the role of data privacy rules in competition assessment. Specifically, they underlined that competition authorities can factor in breaches of data protection rules in examining whether a dominant entity's behaviour constitutes abuse under Article 102.[178] This is because the notion of abuse under Article 102 relies on whether a dominant entity employs strategies other than competition on the merits, and this assessment must consider the legal and economic context in which that conduct takes place.[179] As a result, it is critical for competition authorities to consider the entity's compliance, or lack thereof, to the GDPR when assessing whether the behaviour involves resorting to methods other than competition on merits.[180] However, CJEU seems to accord more importance to the GDPR's role for competition assessment.

In his opinion, AG Rantos suggested the assessment on non-compliance with data privacy rules must not be conducted 'in isolation but considering all the circumstances of the case'.[181] Further, he maintained that considerations on breaches of data protection should be conducted in an 'incidental manner'.[182] In contrast, the CJEU emphasized that the assessment on GDPR compliance could provide 'a vital clue' in establishing abuse.[183] Importantly, considering the critical role of personal data in the digital economy and Facebook's business model, the CJEU stressed that 'excluding the rules on the protection of personal data ... when investigating an abuse of a dominant position would overlook the reality of this economic development and could jeopardize the effectiveness of competition law within the European Union'.[184] This is an important recognition of the important role that data privacy rules play in regulating the competitive landscape. The question is whether a dominant undertaking's breach of data protection rules, in and of itself, is sufficient to constitute an abuse of dominance under Article 102 or whether additional factors are necessary.

Indeed, while the CJEU does not explicitly state, as AG Rantos does, that GDPR non-compliance should be 'incidentally' considered in assessing abuse, it does acknowledge that such consideration serves as one 'vital clue among the relevant circumstances of the case'.[185] Given these considerations, it is reasonable to argue that a mere violation of data privacy rules does not automatically establish an abuse of dominance under Article 102. This approach is important in reducing the risk of breaches of data protection by dominant undertakings being automatically

[178] *Meta Platforms v Bundeskartellamt*, Opinion of AG Rantos (n 118) para 23; *Meta Platforms v Bundeskartellamt* (n 14) paras 47–48.
[179] *Meta Platforms v Bundeskartellamt* (n 14) paras 47–48.
[180] ibid.
[181] *Meta Platforms v Bundeskartellamt*, Opinion of AG Rantos (n 118) paras 23–24.
[182] ibid para 24.
[183] *Meta Platforms v Bundeskartellamt* (n 14) para 47.
[184] ibid paras 50–51.
[185] ibid para 47.

considered as breaches of competition rules. Avoiding this pitfall is relevant not only in light of the different objectives pursued by such rules but also to prevent the risk stemming from dual application of rules to the same conduct, including the duplication of efforts. However, it is not entirely clear from both the CJEU judgment and AG Rantos's opinion what additional factors, beyond breaches of data privacy rules, must be present for a particular behaviour to be considered abusive under competition law. The following sections highlight two alternative considerations that need to be taken into account in determining whether breaches of data privacy rules could be considered as breaches of competition law.

B. Additional Considerations for Abuses Based on Breaches of Data Privacy Law

1. Establishing a Link between Dominance and Breach of Data Privacy Rules

One mechanism for limiting the undesirable outcome of automating breaches of data protection by dominant undertakings as breaches of competition law is to require that there must be a link between the infringement and the dominance. Although the case law from the CJEU on Article 102 does not generally require such a causal link,[186] the practice regarding unfair terms paints a slightly different picture.[187] The CJEU decisions on collecting societies are predicated on the underlying idea that such restrictions would not have been imposed under competitive market conditions. Thus, before breaches of data privacy rules could be sanctioned as exploitative abuse under competition law, it must be shown that the breaches are due to the dominance of the undertaking.

In its *Facebook Germany* decision, the Bundeskartellamt indicated that the unlawfulness of the terms and conditions under data privacy law did not automatically translate into a breach of competition law, recognizing the need for a link between the data privacy infringement and market dominance.[188] In its preliminary ruling, the agency did not sufficiently clarify this connection, a deficiency that the Higher Regional Court of Düsseldorf cited as a reason for suspending the Bundeskartellamt's order. In this regard, it is crucial to acknowledge that breaches of data privacy rules and the ensuing harms may not always be a consequence of market dominance. Companies without dominance can also engage in similar violations and cause privacy-related harm. Simultaneously, privacy breaches and harms are not monolithic—certain harms or breaches may be unique to companies with significant market power or a dominant position. The Bundeskartellamt's

[186] See *Continental Can v Commission* (n 2) para 27.

[187] See Case C-33/94 P *Tetra Pak v Commission* (n 76) para 27 (stating that 'application of [Article 102] presupposes a link between the dominant position and the alleged abusive conduct').

[188] Bundeskartellamt, 'Background Information' (n 61).

Facebook Germany case might be one such an example as there are factors that point to the existence of a strong link between Facebook's dominance and the breach of data privacy rules, especially in relation to the data collected from third-party websites.

The focus on data collection from third-party sources provides a foundation for demonstrating that Facebook's market power is not only limited to end-users but also extends to websites (industrial consumers). Facebook's dominance in relation to users makes it an unavoidable partner for many websites that want to increase engagement with their content. Facebook takes advantage of this dependency to impose unfavourable terms. Specifically, the fact that millions of websites are willing to use Facebook's plug-ins and allow it to track their visitors, at the risk of being held responsible for breaching EU rules, may be a sign of Facebook's market power vis-à-vis these millions of websites.

Websites must further agree to transmit data even when users do not make use of the functionalities and do not have Facebook accounts. In doing so, websites are providing access to their content on the condition that Facebook can track their visitors, which signals Facebook's market power vis-à-vis these websites. Moreover, an investigation by the Belgian Privacy Commission on a similar issue shows that Facebook's lack of transparency also extends to the information provided to websites. According to the investigation, Facebook does not provide websites with sufficient information about how its 'cookies and pixels' are used to systematically monitor the browsing behaviour of visitors of these websites.[189] All of these factors signal Facebook's ability to act independently towards not only consumers but also websites.

Another factor linking the breach and Facebook's market power is the extensive number of third-party sites and apps whose users Facebook tracks. According to Facebook's own admission in 2018, the 'Like' and 'Share' buttons were embedded across 11.5 million websites and viewed billions of times daily.[190] While this figure is just the tip of the iceberg, it illustrates not only Facebook's vast significance to websites but also its omnipresence on the web and the challenge users face to escape Facebook's tracking. In other words, the scale of adoption of Facebook social plug-ins makes tracking by Facebook 'practically unavoidable'.[191] The ubiquity of the tracking is further strengthened by the fact that users cannot prevent the data collection by abstaining from using the plug-ins or setting their preferences on their devices or web browsers. Thus, there are indications that, owing to its extensive scale and ubiquity, Facebook has become an unavoidable partner for both users and websites.[192]

[189] *Willem Debeuckelaere v Facebook* (n 139) 64.

[190] Facebook Letter Addressed to the UK House of Commons, Digital, Culture, Media and Sports Committee (14 May 2018) 2.

[191] *Willem Debeuckelaere v Facebook* (n 139) 69.

[192] See Australian Competition and Consumer Commission, *Digital Platforms Inquiry: Final Report* (2019) 1.

In light of the above discussion, one could argue that the primary factor causing users to lose control over their data and the subsequent violation of data privacy rules is intrinsically connected to Facebook's massive scale and pervasive presence on the web or its market power in relation to users and websites. For example, a judgment from the Brussels Court of First Instance highlights how Facebook's scale and ubiquity on the web have led to higher privacy risks both quantitatively and qualitatively. On the quantitative aspect, the Court indicated that 'the extent of the violations in question is massive: they do not only concern the violation of the fundamental rights of a single person, but of an enormous group of persons', affecting both Facebook account holders and non-users visiting websites featuring Facebook plug-ins.[193]

Several factors connect this quantitative dimension of the breach to Facebook's market dominance. Because of network effects, Facebook is the leading social network, with billions of users, all of whom are affected by the breach. Facebook exploits this power derived from network effects to coerce websites into allowing it to track non-Facebook users, who are also impacted by the breach. Facebook's scale of adoption by websites has a qualitative effect on users' privacy risks. The information collected across these millions of websites 'is frequently of a very sensitive nature, allowing, for example, health-related, religious, sexual and political preferences to be gauged'.[194] This, in turn, exposes individuals to greater privacy risks.

In summary, Facebook's dominance in relation to users makes it an unavoidable partner for many websites, leading to its ubiquity and scale on the web. Facebook leverages this dominance and dependency of websites to impose expansive terms on both customer groups regarding the collection of users' data. In this sense, the loss of control, the breach of data privacy rights, and the resulting heightened privacy risks are highly intertwined with Facebook's dominance. This suggests that the type of loss of control or breach of data privacy addressed by the Bundeskartellamt is less likely to occur with a player that lacks Facebook's scale and ubiquity. In other words, a small player may violate the data privacy of individuals (eg by not adequately informing users), but not on the same scale and effect as Facebook. Absent a large market share among consumers, websites would not see a reason to use the plug-ins of a smaller social network or would not do so on the scale of a large social network like Facebook.

With less integration by websites, fewer users are affected by the tracking, and the volume of information collected from these sites is reduced (with the content of the information becoming less sensitive), thereby preventing or lessening the quantitative and qualitative privacy risks. Even if websites recognize the benefits of using the plug-ins from a smaller network, they are less likely to agree to far-reaching terms allowing the social network to track users (and non-users) on the

[193] *Willem Debeuckelaere v Facebook* (n 139) 69.
[194] ibid.

website, even when users do not make use of the plug-ins (again, preventing or mitigating the quantitative and qualitative privacy risks). This shows that the data privacy breach and the resulting higher quantitative and qualitative risks are less likely to arise with entities that lack market power or have not been adopted on the same scale as Facebook.

In this specific example, one could argue that the breach of data privacy rules is highly intertwined with Facebook's dominance, particularly its scale and ubiquity across the web. Thus, to the extent that an adequate causal link can be established between the company's market dominance and the data privacy infringement, it can be used as a filter for preventing undue overlap between data privacy and competition law. This suggest that the analysis for establishing such a link must involve an examination of how the undertaking's dominant position and its adopted data policies have resulted in a lower level of data privacy than would have been present in the market before the emergence of the dominant firm.[195] However, this might not be an easy exercise in other instances. The following section proposes another consideration, based on the existence of an exclusionary element, for filtering breaches of data privacy rules that are of interest to competition law.

2. Exclusionary Element as an Additional Consideration

Another mitigating measure against automatically equating data privacy infringements by dominant entities to breaches of competition rules is to require that breaches of data privacy must possess an exclusionary element before being sanctioned under Article 102. The existence of an exclusionary element allows competition agencies to focus on breaches of data privacy rules that also affect the competitive process. Absent an impact on the competitive process, unfair contractual terms that breach data privacy rules should be left to data privacy regulation and rules governing unfair trading practices. This is consistent with the Commission Guidelines, which suggest resorting to exploitative abuses only 'where the protection of consumers ... cannot otherwise be adequately ensured'.[196]

Moreover, the suggestion to include an exclusionary element is consistent with the CJEU case law on unfair terms. In many of these cases, the terms had also some exclusionary effect. In both *Tetra Pak* and *AAMS*, the unfair terms not only exploited consumers but also denied rival firms enough customers to gain economies of scale and scope, thereby thwarting any substantial challenge to Tetra Pak's near-monopoly and AAMS's actual monopoly.[197] Similarly, in *DSD*, the licence fees effectively deterred users from using another provider for collecting parts of their

[195] Economides and Lianos (n 48) 806.

[196] See European Commission, 'Guidance on the Commission's Enforcement Priorities in Applying Article 82 of the EC Treaty to Abusive Exclusionary Conduct by Dominant Undertakings' [2009] OJ C45/7, para 7. Lars-Hendrik Röller, 'Exploitative Abuses' (BB-107-002 Business Brief, 2007) 13 <https://d-nb.info/1012903311/34>.

[197] O'Donoghue and Padilla (n 62) 853.

packaging. In other instances, the exploitative practices hindered parallel imports or discriminated against firms from other member states.[198] Thus, in most cases, the exploitative abuses reinforced the exclusionary abuses.

In light of these considerations, the main argument advanced here is that to the extent that the exploitative abuse under Article 102 is based on a breach of data privacy rules, it should be further ascertained that the conduct also has an impact on the competitive process. Given the central role that personal data plays in the value creation process, certain data privacy breaches are more likely to affect the competitive process than others. This is particularly the case where such breaches lead to an illegal acquisition of dominance or further entrench existing dominance. This section identifies and discusses two scenarios in which breaches of data privacy rules could have an exclusionary dimension. The first encompasses situations where the breach and the exploitative practice exert an exclusionary effect, for example by leveraging dominance through the repurposing of data collected in one area to strengthen market power in another or by impeding access to consumers through the denial of their data portability rights. The second scenario arises in situations where the breach and the exploitative conduct contribute to the acquisition of dominance in a relevant market.

These proposals are partially informed by the literature that highlights the need for a limiting principle when applying Article 102 to exploitative conduct. This need stems from the uncertainty and unpredictability that comes with the use of fluid standards, such as 'proportionality', 'excessiveness', and 'fairness'. Two proposals for addressing these concerns are especially relevant for this section. The first, which comes from Akman, suggests that for exploitative conduct to be abusive, it should have some exclusionary effect.[199] The second proposal, from Röller, advocates for limiting the application of Article 102 to 'gap cases', specifically targeting exploitative behaviour that leads to dominance.[200] The above-mentioned two instances, in which breaches of data privacy could generate exclusionary effect, correspond to these two proposals. The following subsections elaborate on these two aspects.

a) Breaches of data privacy law with an exclusionary dimension

Concerning the need for exploitative conduct to have an exclusionary dimension, Akman contends that 'mere exploitation does not demonstrate harm to competition', and without such harm, exploitation should not be prohibited by Article 102.[201] Moreover, Akman argues that exploitative conduct that lacks exclusionary element should be addressed under contract or consumer protection laws.[202]

[198] Nils Wahl, 'Exploitative High Prices and European Competition Law—A Personal Reflection' in Fredenberg and Strand (eds) (n 25) 64.
[199] Akman (n 24) 179.
[200] Röller (n 196) 13.
[201] Akman (n 24) 165.
[202] ibid.

While insisting that all exploitative abuses exhibit an exclusionary dimension might be excessive, such a requirement could serve as an important limiting principle, especially when it comes to exploitative practices rooted in violations of data privacy rules. This is primarily because of the difficulties of determining when data privacy breaches transform into exploitative abuse.

In this regard, it is worth mentioning that breaches of certain data privacy rules, such as the purpose limitation principle and data portability by dominant undertakings, are more likely to have exclusionary effects. This is because the purpose limitation principle, for example, aims to prevent data collected for a specific purpose from being used for another 'incompatible' purpose. In this sense, the principle has the effect of preventing dominant undertakings from leveraging their market power by unlawfully repurposing data collected in one market to gain a competitive advantage in another market. Similarly, the data portability right allows data subjects to take their personal data to another service provider, thereby reducing switching costs resulting from usage or technical difficulties. This right is particularly important for many digital services, such as social networks and search engines, where data-driven network effects—particularly those deriving from the advantages of scale and scope of data—can create barriers to entry.[203] This implies that where the exploitative practice is due to a breach of such rules, it is more likely to have an exclusionary dimension in the form of illegal leveraging by repurposing data collected in one area to gain market power in another area or preventing access to consumers by denying their right to portability.

Although not widespread, there are cases where these principles have informed competition law enforcement. For example, the Belgian National Lottery was found to have abused its dominant position by repurposing personal data, initially collected in the context of its legal monopoly in the lottery market, to promote a new betting product.[204] The Competition Authority held that personal details were not acquired 'following competition on the merits'.[205] Similarly, the French Competition Law Authority found that the cross-usage of data collected in one market as an input in another market resulted in a restriction of competition.[206] The agency deemed this cross-usage illegal as the database was not a result of 'any particular innovation' but was, instead, inherited from its past monopoly status, hence not based on competition on the merits.[207]

In both cases, the exclusionary effect of the data-related conduct was not evaluated considering a breach of data privacy but rather based on the fact that the data was acquired in the context of the firms' legal monopoly. However, similar

[203] See also Chapter 4, Section II.B.
[204] Cited in EDPS, *Opinion 8/2016 on Coherent Enforcement of Fundamental Rights in the Age of Big Data* (2016) 9.
[205] Cited in ibid.
[206] Autorité de la Concurrence and Bundeskartellamt (n 16) 31.
[207] ibid.

competition concerns could arise if the repurposing of the data occurs in breach of the purpose limitation principle. Specifically, one could argue that the repurposing of personal data by dominant digital platforms from one market to another—in breach of the purpose limitation principle—could potentially have an anticompetitive exclusionary effect.

The ongoing investigations by the Commission into the data usage of Amazon and Meta possess such dimensions. In Amazon's case, the Commission is investigating the extent to which Amazon acquires an unlawful competitive edge by repurposing non-public seller data that it collects from third-party traders through its role as the Amazon Marketplace operator for its retail operations. The Commission's preliminary conclusion is that this data repurposing allows Amazon to avoid the risks of retail competition and to leverage its market dominance in providing marketplace services to the retail markets, in violation of Article 102.[208] The Commission has arrived at a similar conclusion with Meta, accusing the company of repurposing data related to the activities of competing online classified ads services collected from its Facebook and Instagram to benefit its Facebook Marketplace. The Commission has reached a preliminary conclusion that Meta's terms and conditions, which authorize such data reuse, represent unfair trading conditions, in violation of Article 102.[209] To the extent that the data usage involves personal data, compliance with the purpose limitation principle can serve as a measure to determine whether the data use is legitimate or unfair. There are many instances of data use in breach of the purpose limitation principle, which raise similar leveraging concerns.

In launching its Buzz Social Network, Google automatically assigned all Gmail account holders a Buzz account unless they opted out. This led to private email contacts becoming publicly available as social network contacts. According to the FTC investigation, in some cases, such publicly available contact lists included 'ex-spouses, patients, students, employers, or competitors'.[210] Google was found to be in breach of its own privacy promises by 'using information provided for Gmail for another purpose—social networking—without obtaining consumers' permission in advance'.[211] The conduct was also in clear breach of EU data privacy rules, particularly the purpose limitation principle. Assuming that Google had dominance in the provision of email, one could view such conduct as amounting to illegal leveraging of the data that Google collected in one market (email services) to gain an illegal advantage in another market (social network). If Google had succeeded,

[208] European Commission, 'Commission Sends Statement of Objections to Amazon for the Use of Non-Public Independent Seller Data and Opens Second Investigation into Its e-Commerce Business Practices' (10 November 2020).

[209] European Commission, 'Commission Sends Statement of Objections to Meta' (n 94).

[210] FTC, 'FTC Charges Deceptive Privacy Practices in Google's Rollout of Its Buzz Social Network' (30 March 2011).

[211] ibid.

this should have raised a competition concern, as its dominance would not have been based on 'competition on the merits' but rather on conduct breaching data privacy rules.

The right to data portability is another consideration that can have significant implication for competition. As highlighted in Chapter 4, competition authorities are increasingly recognizing the role of data portability right as a means to control market power and avoid user lock-in, with positive effects on competition.[212] The implication is that disregarding the data portability right could lead to an illegal acquisition of dominance or further entrenchment of existing dominance, which needs to be considered in competition assessment. Fortunately, competition authorities have started to account for breaches of such a right in their assessment. As noted in Section V.A above, the Italian AGCM accused Google of abusing its dominant position by violating the users' data portability right under the GDPR. According to the authority, this conduct constituted a violation of users' portability rights but also an abuse of dominance because it obstructed access to the market and restricted competition.[213]

Overall, the fundamental approach of incorporating the violation of users' data privacy rules when assessing whether a conduct—either exploitative or exclusionary—qualifies as an abuse of dominance under Article 102 aligns with the CJEU's jurisprudence in *Allianz Hungária*. This perspective is further confirmed by the CJEU in the *Meta v Bundeskartellamt* case.

b) Breaches of data privacy law contributing to dominance

Another principle suggested for limiting the application of Article 102 to exploitative conduct is to focus on 'gap cases'. As articulated by Röller, an abuse case should pinpoint anticompetitive conduct leading to increased market power, in comparison to a counterfactual scenario, and 'the road to dominance' can be important in distinguishing pro- and anticompetitive conduct.[214] This suggests that if dominance is obtained through means other than competition on the merits, it is determinantal for consumers and needs to be condemned.[215] However, anticompetitive conduct leading to dominance is not covered by Article 102, as this targets firms that are already dominant. This creates an 'enforcement gap'.[216]

To close this gap, Röller proposes that the enforcement of exploitive conduct should primarily target behaviours that contribute to the acquisition of a dominant position. Röller argues that by concentrating on 'the road to dominance through anticompetitive behaviour, exploitative abuse cases are firmly grounded in the way markets work, rather than deciding on what is "excessive"' *ex post*.[217] This

[212] Case M 7813 *Sanofi/Google/DMI JV* decision of 23 February 2016, paras 67–69.
[213] AGCM (n 174).
[214] Röller (n 196) 9.
[215] ibid.
[216] ibid.
[217] ibid.

proposal to link exploitative abuse with an exclusionary element has several advantages. Notably, it reduces the uncertainty resulting from using fluid concepts such as 'excessiveness' and closes the enforcement gap in Article 102.[218] Moreover, this link could serve as an important limiting principle for exploitive abuses based on a breach of data privacy rules. This implies that the enforcement of exploitative conduct under Article 102 could be used to discipline companies that have either acquired a dominant position or entrenched an existing dominant position through their disregard for data privacy rules.

The European Commission has started to recognize that breaches of data privacy rules may have a competition dimension. Commenting on the need for competition authorities to pay attention to possible breaches of data privacy, Commissioner Vestager indicated that

> Competition law enforcement cannot do the full trick, but neither can regulation because you need a competitive dynamic marketplace. You need innovation that is driven by competition. And this is why I would take such an interest in privacy, also because it shouldn't be a competitive edge for you that you completely disregard the need of each and every one of us to have privacy.[219]

The potential to gain unlawful competitive advantage through the disregard for privacy rules is particularly important in markets where personal data is a key input in providing goods and services. There are few examples of relevance here. In an article analysing Google's antitrust problems, Newman enumerates several illegal or 'bad acts' that Google used to strengthen its control over personal data and entrench its dominance in the search advertising market.[220] Among these bad acts, Newman mentions Google's controversial Street View Project, whereby Google accessed the communication of individuals transmitted via Wi-Fi hotspots in many countries, including the content accessed, their 'entire emails and URLs . . . as well as passwords'.[221] An investigation by the FTC found that this disregard was a deliberate software design decision, as such data was immensely useful for the success of Google Maps and self-driving cars.[222]

Newman asserts that this disregard for users' privacy gave Google an illegal edge over competing services, such as Apple Maps.[223] Even a company as resourceful

[218] ibid 10. However, this is not without its own problems. See Akman (n 24) 186 (recounting some of the dangers of focusing on the road to dominance, including the risk that one gets 'lost in the "mists of history"').

[219] David Brancaccio and Janet Nguyen, 'Europe's Top Antitrust Official: If There's No Regulation, "You Have Just the Laws of the Jungle and Not the Laws of Democracy"', *MarketPlace* (12 April 2018).

[220] Nathan Newman, 'Search, Antitrust, and the Economics of the Control of User Data' (2014) 31 Yale Journal on Regulation 401.

[221] In the Matter of Google Inc., Notice of Apparent Liability for Forfeiture File EB-10-IH-4055 (13 April 2012) 1–2.

[222] ibid.

[223] Newman (n 220).

as Apple had to suffer public backlash for its poor mapping product, which led to the resignation of the product manager in 2010. Google Maps is the leading navigation app by a wide margin, with more than 67 per cent of market share, with Apple holding only 11 per cent.[224] Assuming that Google Maps holds a dominant position in this market and that the breach involving Street View contributed to such dominance, this should raise a competition concern; clearly, this position was not acquired based on 'competition on the merits'. In such cases, the road to dominance becomes important and the exploitative conduct (ie the breach of data privacy rules) should constitute an abuse under Article 102, provided there is a strong link between the breach and the undertaking's market position. Adopting such an approach also brings Article 102 in line with the US concept of attempted monopolization.[225]

Newman further contends that Google's dominance in search advertising is sustained through several illegal practices, including the 2012 privacy policy change, which consolidated and linked all of its products to a single account, and Google's circumvention of Safari browser users' settings.[226] Further, Google's series of wrongful (illegal) acts to control user data forms 'part of a pattern of exclusionary conduct', which could give rise to antitrust liability under Section 2 of the Sherman Act, based on the 'bad acts' requirement.[227] In this context, Newman cites a precedent from several US courts where a series of illegal actions leading to monopoly power can cumulatively result in antitrust liability under Section 2 even if '[no] individual act was decisive in creating or maintaining the monopoly'.[228] Arguably, these illegal acts have assisted Google in strengthening and maintaining its monopoly in search advertising, enabling Google to control data across the internet while simultaneously denying competitors access to such data, thereby fulfilling the 'bad acts' liability requirement in Section 2.[229]

Insofar as this is valid and can be substantiated, it should also be condemned under Article 102. This stance aligns with the CJEU's jurisprudence that a

[224] Riley Panko, 'The Popularity of Google Maps: Trends in Navigation Apps', *The Manifest* (10 July 2018).

[225] Firms can be prosecuted under Section 2 of the Sherman Act if they (1) demonstrate a specific intent to monopolize, (2) engage in anticompetitive conduct to fulfil that intent, and (3) there exists a dangerous probability of success. However, there are many concerns with this approach. First, distinguishing between a genuine intent to compete and an intent to harm competition can be challenging. Second, it is often difficult to demonstrate a 'dangerous probability of success', which necessitates evidence that the practice either results in actual monopolization or comes close, as seen in a near-monopoly market share. In the EU, these concerns are somewhat mitigated since there is no need to prove intent, nor is there a requisite to exceed the customary 50 per cent market share to establish dominance. See Milton Handler and Richard Steuer, 'Attempts to Monopolize and No-Fault Monopolization' (1980) 129 University of Pennsylvania Law Review 125.

[226] Newman (n 220) 436–41. In the EU, Google's conduct was found to be illegal by the Article 29 Working Party and DPAs in five other member states.

[227] ibid 441.

[228] ibid 440. For EU discussions on this subject, see Chapter 3, Section IV.

[229] ibid 441.

dominant firm must not strengthen its position using methods other than those falling within the scope of 'competition on the merits'.[230] As noted in Section V.A, EU competition law is open to influences from other legal norms and the CJEU has confirmed that data protection rules could serve as benchmarks in determining what constitutes 'competition on the merits'.[231] In fact, during its investigation of similar practices in the advertising market by Google, the Commission emphasized the need to consider user privacy protection in accordance with the relevant rules, especially the GDPR, in the competition assessment. Specifically, the Commission highlighted the need for data privacy and competition rules to 'work hand in hand to ensure . . . a level playing field in which all market participants protect user privacy in the same manner'.[232]

This is encouraging but must also be complemented by the emergent thinking advocated in Chapter 3. It was demonstrated there that the case law from the CJEU, particularly 'the totality of the circumstances' standard, allows competition agencies to account for the synergic effects of a pattern of conduct, which in isolation may not be harmful but could, in combination, be detrimental to competition. This approach should also extend to abuse cases that are predicated on violations of data privacy regulations or other legal norms that contribute to the acquisition of a dominant position. This implies that while individual breaches, when considered separately, may not lead to dominance or constitute abuse, collectively they may meet the necessary threshold for intervention under Article 102.

Overall, the main argument is that the existence of an exclusionary element should be a key consideration in filtering breaches of data privacy rules that are relevant for competition law. The above discussion highlights a few instances in which breaches of data privacy law may have an exclusionary dimension, which should serve as a triggering factor for competition law scrutiny. Essentially, when data privacy breaches are considered in competition assessments, the focus ought to be on those that have a competitive dimension by excluding competitors from the market or contributing to the acquisition or maintenance of a dominant position.

VI. Implications for the Interface

The potential for EU competition law to address exploitive abuses such as excessive data collection or unfair privacy policies could have significant implications for the interface between data privacy and competition laws. First,

[230] See Case 85/76 *Hoffmann-La Roche v Commission* ECLI:EU:C:1979:36, para 177.
[231] *Meta Platforms v Bundeskartellamt* (n 14) para 48.
[232] See European Commission, 'Commission Opens Investigation into Possible Anticompetitive Conduct by Google in the Online Advertising Technology Sector' (22 June 2021).

competition law interventions can complement and reinforce data privacy by addressing some of the privacy risks and externalities from excessive data collection and lack of transparency on data use. As noted in Chapter 2, the practice of accumulating and aggregating user data from different services gives rise to emergent privacy risks in the form of overexposure of the individual and loss of practical obscurity.[233] The more data the entity accumulates on the individual, the more exposed that individual becomes, and the easier it is to suppress their capacity to make free choices. The chapter further illustrated that the current data privacy rules are not well suited to address these emergent privacy risks, that is risks that may not be attributed to, and exist independently of, individual processing operations. In this sense, prosecuting dominant players for excessive data collection and unfair privacy policies can address some of these emergent privacy risks.

The Bundeskartellamt's *Facebook Germany* case exemplifies this argument. The Bundeskartellamt ruled that Facebook had abused its dominant position by forcing users to agree to the combination of data from third-party sources (third-party websites and Facebook subsidiaries) with their Facebook profile. The agency then ordered Facebook to stop the combination unless users were given a genuine choice, including the possibility of refusing the combination of their data. In effect, the order restores data silos, preventing Facebook from combining data from third-party websites and its subsidiaries or imposing additional costs for the combination of data by soliciting 'voluntary consent'. Given that the combination of data across services is the main cause of emergent risks, such measures preventing the combination of data or increasing the costs thereof would be invaluable in mitigating privacy risks identified in Chapter 2, such as the overexposure of individuals and the loss of practical obscurity.

Second, and relatedly, lack of transparency on data use generates market externalities, thus hindering effective competition in the realm of data privacy. This issue is partly related to the phenomenon of dysfunctional equilibrium. This equilibrium is the result of companies' lack of transparency, which fosters a sense of cynicism among consumers, who perceive the act of reading privacy policies as an unrewarding. This, in turn, discourages newcomers from adopting more protective policies and clearer disclosures to attract users because users do not reward such behaviour, leading to a privacy-deficient equilibrium.[234] Essentially, the lack of transparency on data use creates externalities not borne by the culprits and

[233] See also Samson Esayas, 'The Idea of 'Emergent Properties' in Data Privacy: Towards a Holistic Approach' (2017) 25 International Journal of Law and Information Technology 139.

[234] Joseph Farrell, 'Can Privacy Be Just Another Good?' (2012) 10 Journal on Telecommunications & High Technology Law 251, 259.

discourages newcomers from offering transparent policies and privacy-friendly services.

In this regard, treating opaque data collection and use as an abusive practice could compel firms to absorb the externalities from the 'dysfunctional equilibrium'. Returning to the Bundeskartellamt *Facebook Germany* case, the investigation shows that Facebook did not provide adequate information on the combination of data from third-party sources with their Facebook profile, rendering the consent obtained to such processing as uninformed. Consequently, this was deemed as an abuse of dominance under competition law. Hence, Facebook is penalized for its lack of transparency by being barred from combining data unless users provide voluntary consent. The competition remedy, which forbids data combination without voluntary consent, attaches a cost to the lack of transparency, thereby ensuring that Facebook internalizes some of the costs. This might mitigate the tendency of newcomers to learn that they are not able to attract sufficient demand by providing clear, privacy-friendly policies.

Third, the discussion of the Bundeskartellamt *Facebook Germany* decision shows how dominance in a market is closely associated with higher quantitative and qualitative privacy risks. Thus, the establishment of dominance justifies—and can serve as a trigger for—imposing the enhanced responsibility regime discussed in Chapter 2. This means that data protection authorities (DPAs) can leverage the existing work of competition authorities in imposing enhanced responsibilities, which, in turn, enhances the efficient use of resources in the application of the rules. The increased risks from dominance further justify the decision to anchor the enhanced responsibility in the special responsibility regime for dominant undertakings under competition law.

Finally, discussions in Section V above show that breaches of data privacy rules could help competition law assess the legality of conduct, either when data privacy is a competition parameter or when personal data is relevant to competitive performance. This could result in convergence between breaches of data privacy and competition rules. The Bundeskartellamt's *Facebook Germany* decision illustrates this convergence, where a breach of data privacy rules informed the finding of abuse under competition law. The decision also highlights the exclusionary nature of breaches of data privacy rules, which, in this instance, gave Facebook an 'unlawful competitive edge over its competitors'. Put simply, to the extent that personal data is central to the value creation process, breaches of data privacy rules have implications that extend beyond breaches of fundamental rights and can disrupt the competitive process. This suggests that, at least in some instances, data privacy rules could serve as a metric to determine what constitutes an 'unfair term', 'normal competition', or 'competition on the merits'.

VII. Conclusion

This chapter has analysed whether unfair terms relating to personal data and privacy and excessive data collection by dominant undertakings constitute abuse under Article 102. The chapter started by exploring how the DMA's data-centric provisions could address some of these privacy-related practices and clarify the role of competition law. The discussions reveal that competition law remains crucial in tackling privacy and data-related practices of dominant undertakings. This includes curbing excessive data collection and ensuring a broader range of choices concerning user privacy. Having surveyed the case law on Article 102, the chapter further demonstrated the difficulty of fitting excessive data collection into the case law for excessive pricing, particularly considering the technical nature of the test (based on price–cost margins). Although it is possible to use personal data as the 'price' users pay in exchange for access to services, applying the test would require an estimation of the monetary value of the data provided and a comparison of this value with the cost of providing the services. This is difficult to determine for many digital services, primarily because most services are not provided on a per-unit basis. In addition, the multi-sided nature of many digital platforms complicates the assessment of costs and profit margins in relation to the different sides of the market.

The chapter maintains that, to the extent data privacy rules are viewed as a benchmark for assessing excessiveness, the case law on unfair contract terms is more suitable. This is because resorting to unfair terms shifts the focus from purely 'excessive' data collection to the broader context, looking at how users' personal data and privacy are addressed in the terms of service and privacy policies. Moreover, the case law on unfair contractual terms is based on normative concepts, such as proportionality, which are already familiar to data privacy law. This approach makes it possible to carry out a broader assessment of the different interests than the more rigid price–cost test employed for excessive pricing. The discussion further demonstrated how restrictions by dominant undertakings on users' choice to limit usage of their data and on users' ability to share their data with other entities can be captured under the case law on unfair terms.

In this regard, the discussion shows that even if the terms are not in breach of data privacy rules, they can still be deemed unfair and abusive under Article 102. Furthermore, the chapter explored the extent to which breaches of data privacy rules could constitute abuse of dominance. This discussion emphasized the need for a limiting principle based on an exclusionary element. In other words, when considering data privacy breaches in competition assessments, the emphasis should be on those with a competitive dimension that involve excluding competitors from the market or acquiring a dominant position.

Next, the chapter highlighted the implications for the interface between competition law and data privacy law. First, prosecuting companies for excessive data collection and unfair privacy policies can reinforce data privacy law by addressing some of the emergent data privacy risks resulting from data accumulation and the externalities resulting from a lack of transparency in data use. Second, the discussion of the Bundeskartellamt *Facebook Germany* decision shows how dominance in a market is closely associated with higher quantitative and qualitative privacy risks. This justifies the imposition of enhanced data privacy responsibilities on dominant companies and the decision to anchor the enhanced responsibility in the special responsibilities under competition law. Finally, data privacy rules could provide normative guidance in assessing the legality of conduct under competition law, particularly when data privacy is a competition parameter or personal data is of great importance for competition.

8

Regulating a Complex Economy

Beyond the Atomistic and Either/Or Approaches

I. Harnessing Complexity in Data Privacy Law and Competition Law

The digital economy is marked by increased complexity, as exemplified by the multiplicity of actors and their interactions. This increased complexity is largely underpinned by the commercialization of personal data. The quest to accumulate extensive and diverse data sets is driving organizations to expand into novel product sectors and to acquire entities with rich troves of personal information, leading to the emergence of multi-product ecosystems. These ecosystems generate value by bringing together multiple actors and markets and fostering a web of economic interactions. Moreover, personal data plays a crucial role in linking the different markets, enabling personalization of both production and distribution. The multiplicity of actors and the web of economic links generate feedback loops and lead to outcomes characterized by non-linear and emergent effects. These are the defining features of complex systems.[1]

Despite this complexity, the mindset that permeates current regulation, especially in data privacy law and competition law, still relies on a primordial model that emphasizes discrete units of analysis, targets additive rather than emergent and non-linear effects, and assumes actors to have static roles.[2] This model is reflected in two approaches to the application of data privacy law and competition law, both of which create enforcement challenges.[3]

The first challenge stems from the atomized approach used to apply both legal regimes, namely their reliance on isolating a specific component as the target of regulation when dealing with a system comprising several components. The

[1] Steven Johnson, *Emergence: The Connected Lives of Ants, Brains, Cities, and Software* (Penguin 2001).

[2] See Samson Esayas, 'The Important Role of Emergence in Conceptualizing the Challenges of New Technologies to Private Law' (2023) 31 European Private Law Review 779; Nicolas Petit and Thibault Schrepel, 'Complexity-Minded Antitrust' (2023) 33 Journal of Evolutionary Economics 541.

[3] In the context of competition law, the lack of an appropriate framework to understand this increased complexity has led to under-enforcement in cases dealing with digital markets. See Ioannis Lianos, 'Mind the (Institutional) Gap: Digital Economy, Competition Law and the Toolkit Approach' (Fall 2022) Network Law Review. Similarly, assertions characterizing data privacy law as 'a dead letter' denote its shortcomings in addressing the harms associated with the commercialization of personal and big data. See Bert-Jaap Koops, 'The Trouble with European Data Protection Law' (2014) 4 International Data Privacy Law 250, 250.

Data Privacy and Competition Law in the Age of Big Data. Samson Y. Esayas, Oxford University Press.
 DOI: 10.1093/oso/9780198891420.003.0009

application of data privacy rules is predicated on the ability to identify and isolate the individual processing operations based on a specific purpose and distinct legal basis and attribute the data to a particular processing operation. Similarly, the application of competition rules focuses on identifying the relevant product/service markets and assessing the impact of conduct within this zone. This approach rests on the assumption that there are well-delineated processing activities based on specific purposes (data privacy rules) and well-delineated relevant product/service markets (competition law perspective). Chapters 2 and 3 showed that this atomized approach poses significant challenges to the application of both sets of rules, given the complexity and shifts entailed by the commercialization of personal data and big data.

From a data privacy perspective, the book highlights two shifts: the tendency to process personal data for a panoply of purposes and to aggregate data across these processing activities. This introduces a level of complexity that is absent when entities process personal data for only a handful of purposes and in siloes. Closely related to these changes, and vitally important for competition law, is the shift from offering single products/services to offering ecosystems comprising several integrated products/services, where personal data plays a central role in coordinating activities across the different markets. These developments give rise to two key challenges in the application of data privacy law and competition law, one institutional and the other substantive.

The institutional challenge relates to the difficulty in isolating the different processing activities and relevant markets in the face of comprehensive ecosystems made up of multiple products/services often interconnected through data. These shifts complicate the attribution of individual data to a particular processing operation and competition harms to a relevant market. The substantive challenge pertains to the inadequacy of the atomized approach in addressing emergent privacy risks from the totality of processing operations and emergent competitive harms from multiple, systematic practices in seemingly different (yet interconnected) relevant markets within the comprehensive ecosystem. These risks are 'emergent' in the sense that they may exist independently of, and hence may not be attributed to, individual processing operations or a relevant market.

Another notable challenge stems from the prevailing either/or mentality in the application of data privacy law and competition law. Data privacy law and competition law are frequently perceived as two separate regimes, each pursuing distinct objectives, differing in their material scope, and addressing different types of harm. Thus, the conventional approach has been to treat them separately.[4] This either/or approach is also reflected in the practices of the Court of Justice of the European Union (CJEU) and the European Commission. Both have indicated

[4] See Wolfgang Kerber and Louisa Specht, 'Synergies between Data Protection Law and Competition Law' (2021) 56 <https://ssrncom/abstract=3977039> accessed 10 February 2024.

that privacy-related concerns are considered outside the ambit of European Union (EU) competition law.[5] However, maintaining this either/or mentality becomes increasingly challenging when faced with the burgeoning commercialization of personal data. While there is improved understanding of the growing intersection between the two regimes in recent years,[6] this is still nascent. Questions persist about how to forge synergies between the two fields that leverage the strengths of each legal regime. This requires that areas for coordination between the two sets of rules be identified and systematic ways to work across these regimes be developed.

To this end, Chapters 4–7 outline the intersection points between data privacy law and competition law both from an empirical and a normative perspective. Empirically, the commercialization of personal data has led to increased attention to personal data and data privacy in competition assessments, thus increasing the points of intersection (whether convergent or conflictual) between the two sets of rules. Competition authorities have started to recognize that the accumulation of personal data can give rise to market power by creating barriers to entry. Relatedly, facilitating access to data is seen as a measure to address some of the competition concerns in digital markets where there are data-related barriers to entry. Conversely, leading digital platforms are increasingly invoking privacy improvements as a justification for potentially anticompetitive practices, such as restricting third-party access to user data. This raises important questions about the intersection between data privacy law and competition law, including the limits imposed by data privacy law and how to balance privacy and competition interests. Moreover, as users hand over more and more of their personal data to access digital services, data privacy has begun to attract attention in competition law as a non-price competition parameter.

This increased attention to personal data and data privacy also bears normative implications. It elevates the importance of data privacy rules in the competitive process, both as a competitive constraint and as a source of barriers to entry. Furthermore, these developments, especially the recognition of data privacy as a non-price competition parameter, open competition law up to increased normative influence from data privacy law. In light of these interactions, maintaining the either/or mentality becomes increasingly challenging and misses opportunities for synergy.

This book calls for the recalibration of these laws for a complex economy, emphasizing a holistic, systems-level perspective that addresses emergent harms and leverages the strengths of each legal regime. In so doing, the book underscores the importance of three insights from complexity science: (1) its use of a system-level unit of analysis, (2) its emphasis on interconnections that lead to non-linear and

[5] See Case C-238/05 *Asnef-Equifax v Asociacion de Usuarios* ECLI:EU:C:2006:734; Case M.7217 *Facebook/WhatsApp* decision of 3 October 2014.

[6] Case C-252/21 *Meta Platforms Inc v Bundeskartellamt* ECLI:EU:C:2023:537.

emergent outcomes, and (3) its adoption of a polycentric approach to navigating such complexity.[7]

II. Towards a Holistic and System-Level Analytical Framework

One of the primary insights from complexity science applicable to data privacy and competition law is the need for a system-level analytical framework. This need is driven by the characterization of the digital economy as an interlinked network of organizations, technologies, consumers, and products.[8] Rather than being confined to a single market, sector, or industry, these elements exist as part of a broader business environment spanning multiple sectors and markets.[9] This portrayal of the economy generates challenges where the analytical framework for applying the law demands that the components of such systems be broken down into isolated parts. As emphasized in Chapters 2 and 3, a systemic issue arises in competition law and data privacy law due to their focus on isolating a specific unit—a relevant market or a distinct data-processing operation—even in the context of complex systems comprising several interrelated components. This atomistic approach overlooks system-wide (emergent) risks.[10] In this sense, using the lens of complexity science and emergence enables a deeper understanding of the *modus operandi* of competition law and data privacy rules. It shows their application to be atomized in nature and exposes the hidden similarities in the mechanics of their application.

Furthermore, the lens of complexity science and emergence sparks the proposal for a system-level analytical framework. Specifically, Chapters 2 and 3 insist that the absence of a system-level analysis can introduce institutional challenges in the application of both sets of rules. Indeed, the atomized approach fails amidst the inherent complexity, obscurity, and emergent risks posed by the multitude of processing operations, markets, and their interactions. From a data privacy perspective, the practice of collecting personal data for a panoply of purposes and aggregating data across operations blurs the lines between the different processing activities. It also complicates the attribution of individual data to a particular processing operation, making it difficult to enforce the rules. Similarly, from a competition law perspective, the emergence of multi-product ecosystems, interconnected

[7] Gregory Gundlach, 'Complexity Science and Antitrust?' (2006) 51 Antitrust Bulletin, 19.
[8] ibid 19.
[9] ibid.
[10] See also Mark Lemley and Feldman Robin, 'Atomistic Antitrust' (UC Hastings Research Paper, 2021) 1 <https://ssrn.com/abstract=3793809> accessed 10 February 2024 (noting that 'Antitrust is atomistic: deliberately focused on trees, not forests. It pays attention to the consequences of individual acts alleged to be anticompetitive').

through personal data, blurs the boundaries between what were once distinct relevant markets, complicating the attribution of competitive harms to a specific relevant market.

Thus, this book proposes a system-level analytical framework, based on a holistic approach. For example, to help address some of the challenges to data privacy law, the book draws from the special responsibility regime under competition law where companies with a dominant position bear special responsibility and are subject to closer scrutiny than other firms. The book argues that data privacy law would benefit from a similarly tiered framework that imposes enhanced responsibilities based on a holistic view of processing activities and data-aggregation practices. The enhanced responsibility regime would be crucial in mitigating the challenging task of delineating the boundaries between the distinct processing operations and in addressing some of the emergent privacy risks.

From a competition law viewpoint, a holistic, system-level approach might be applicable in different contexts. First, since the main challenges are associated with the mechanics of market definition, a holistic approach could be applied in defining the relevant market and assessing market power. In this regard, the discussion showed that initiatives to define markets and establish dominance at the ecosystem level can go a long way towards addressing some of the challenges associated with the atomized approach and emergent competitive harms. This would allow competition authorities to consider multiple practices and the cross-market effects of such practices, which is often difficult to do under the atomized approach. Relatedly, competition policy and enforcement ought to incorporate notions of power that transcend a specific relevant market, thus acknowledging power dimensions that arise at the industry and ecosystem levels. This may entail considering novel dimensions of market power—such as panopticon power and architectural power—and devising metrics to quantify these powers.

III. Accounting for Emergent Effects and Positional Power

The second insight from complexity science concerns the importance of understanding a system's essential features. Complexity science provides us with the tools to describe a system's components, the interactions between components, and the significance of features such as feedback loops, non-linearity, and emergence.[11] In this regard, both Chapters 2 and 3 underscored the need to address emergent risks in the application of data privacy law and competition law.[12] Chapter 2, in particular, discussed the need to recognize the emergent privacy risks that arise when

[11] Gundlach (n 7) 19.

[12] For discussion of the role of emergence in other legal domains, such as intellectual property and tort law, see Esayas (n 2).

entities process personal data for a wide array of purposes and combine data across different processing activities. These include, but are not limited to, overexposure of the individual and loss of transparency, accountability, and practical obscurity. Similarly, Chapter 3 showed that the atomized approach to defining relevant markets may potentially overlook emergent competitive harms stemming from multiple and systematic practices in seemingly separate relevant markets within the comprehensive ecosystem.

The discussion in both chapters further underscored the considerable obstacles present in current data privacy law and competition law when tackling emergent risks. This issue stems from the assumption inherent in the atomized approach that if each processing operation or behaviour within a specific relevant market is compliant, then the data privacy rights of individuals or risks to competition are not in jeopardy. Such logic prompts one to ascribe the properties of the constituent parts—in this case, compliance—to the system as a whole. However, this approach could potentially overlook emergent risks resulting from the interaction of these parts, leading to a fallacy of composition. In this context, the discussions in Chapters 2 and 3 have demonstrated that the whole (ie the totality of processing operations and multiple, systematic practices across ostensibly different relevant markets within the comprehensive ecosystem) may display features (risks) that are absent in the constituent parts.

Using the lens of emergent properties reveals that the attribution challenges in complex systems with several interacting components can be partially mitigated by considering the system as a whole. In the legal context, this implies giving legal recognition, where possible, to the whole (emergent risks). From a data privacy perspective, the book has underscored the need for a holistic approach that recognizes the emergent privacy risks that exist independently of, or in combination with, privacy interests in individual processing activities. Similarly, Chapter 3 exposed the need to recognize emergence in competition law, particularly when assessing anticompetitive effects and abuse of dominance. This demands that competition law be receptive to the prospect that disparate practices, which individually do not meet the legal standard, may generate anticompetitive outcomes that warrant intervention when considered together. Concurrently, the discourse on a holistic approach to the assessment of anticompetitive effects and abuse should embrace the potential benefits stemming from system-wide practices—systemic efficiencies. In this regard, the book emphasizes the flexibility of the existing EU rules to cater to emergent risks and holistic approaches.

Using the lens of emergent properties, the discussion aimed to show the substantial similarities in the mechanics of application of EU data privacy law and competition law, leading to a systemic problem common to both legal regimes. It showed how the concept of emergent properties might offer a unifying framework to help understand the challenges posed by big data when enforcing both data privacy law and competition law. There are two particularly important takeaways from the discussion of emergent properties in this context. First, while the principle of addressing 'one thing at a time' is often a useful guide, it may be insufficient in a world where the boundaries between one thing and another are unclear. Importantly, data privacy law and competition law must acknowledge that the sum of fully compliant behaviours may still engender non-compliant conduct or actions that deviate from the intended spirit of the law.

Furthermore, another insight from the focus of complexity science on system components and their interaction is the need for competition law to consider new forms of power stemming from managing interconnections within the ecosystem. In this regard, the discussion in Chapter 3, Section IV.B, illustrated how interconnections within the system, together with feedback loops, give rise to new types of positional power (such as panopticon power) that are not adequately addressed in competition law. Furthermore, as shown in Chapter 4, current methods for assessing market power and associated metrics often fail to capture the impact of behaviour on agents other than producers and consumers. This includes those acting as data producers and workers, who contribute to the socio-economic value of the ecosystem. Thus, the recognition of data privacy as a non-price parameter and the increasing attention to practices that harm privacy reflects a step towards embracing complexity, recognizing the potential harms faced by consumers as data producers, and mitigating some of the adverse effects of new forms of positional power derived from managing interconnections.

IV. Beyond the Either/Or Mentality and Towards a Polycentric Regulatory Approach

Complexity science also offers valuable insights into the appropriate methodologies for analysing and designing regulatory systems capable of effectively navigating complex economic landscapes. One key insight relevant to the discussions in this book is that the complexity of the ecosystem economy calls for a polycentric regulatory system. This involves establishing a network of legal regimes that interact and complement each other, along with a system for collaboration among different centres of legal authority.[13] A 'mix-and-match' approach is suggested, one which would combine diverse institutional mechanisms that transcend the boundaries of different legal domains and the jurisdictions of different regulatory authorities.[14]

The call for a polycentric approach aligns well with the central argument of this book, which emphasizes the need to move beyond the either/or mentality and embrace a holistic approach that draws on the perspectives of both data privacy law and competition law. This coordinated approach is particularly important in light

[13] Ioannis Lianos, 'Polycentric Competition Law' (2018) 71 Current Legal Problems 161.
[14] ibid 200.

of the increased convergence and tensions arising from the commercialization of personal data. However, its effective implementation requires an understanding of the points of intersection between the various legal fields and the potential areas of collaboration. This book, especially Chapters 4–7, contributes to a polycentric approach and effective enforcement of both data privacy law and competition law by exposing the points of intersection, identifying the appropriate legal regime to deploy depending on the situation, and highlighting areas for cooperation between the two fields.

More specifically, the discussions throughout this book pinpointed four key areas for collaboration between data protection authorities (DPAs) and competition agencies. First, DPAs could assist competition agencies when data privacy is a competition parameter or when conduct affects players competing on data privacy. As noted in Chapter 4, DPAs could help identify the relevant dimensions of privacy competition in light of the EU data privacy principles. They could also contribute to assessing what constitutes a reduction in data privacy, as discussed in Chapters 4, 5, and 7. Second, cooperation could be necessary when competition agencies scrutinize or enforce personal data-related measures. The role of DPAs would be to assess how these measures affect users' data privacy and collaboratively design and implement strategies to address these concerns, as discussed in Chapters 4 and 7. Chapter 4 provides an example of cooperation between the UK competition and data protection authorities involving Google's Privacy Sandbox proposal. The DPA was involved in assessing the proposal's impact on users' privacy, as well as the effects of the commitments, exemplifying successful collaboration.

Third, joint efforts are essential when violations of competition law are connected to personal data and user privacy, as observed in the Bundeskartellamt *Facebook Germany* case. In such scenarios, DPAs could contribute by assessing how the conduct under scrutiny impacts users' data privacy and determining whether it constitutes a breach of EU data privacy rules. They could also suggest effective measures to alleviate privacy concerns. Finally, breaches of data privacy rules concerning companies wielding market power or in a dominant position could also benefit from coordinated efforts. Competition authorities could contribute, for example, by establishing market power and dominance. This could then be used by the DPAs to evaluate the validity of consent in light of the power imbalance (as per Recital 43 of the General Data Protection Regulation (GDPR)) or to impose enhanced responsibility, as noted in Chapter 2.

This book emphasizes that the interface between data privacy and competition rules, if complemented by a coordinated approach, presents a unique opportunity to enhance the effectiveness of both sets of laws. Competition law can enhance the efficacy of data privacy rules by tackling macro-level harms to data privacy in the form of privacy fixing, reductions in choice from mergers, or exploitative and exclusionary practices related to privacy. Relatedly, the incorporation of data privacy as a non-price competition parameter incentivizes companies to turn data privacy into a competitive advantage by offering even higher levels of privacy than those guaranteed under the rules.

Similarly, data privacy law can provide competition law with the necessary tools and normative guidance needed to address new forms of anticompetitive conduct through data- and privacy-related harms. For example, as explained in Chapter 4, consulting data privacy rules could make it easier for competition authorities to identify and detect the relevant dimensions of privacy competition. Chapter 5 further clarified that these dimensions of privacy can aid in formulating a theory of harm based on privacy degradation and identifying potentially harmful conduct. Additionally, the discussion in Chapter 7 showed that breaches of data privacy rules could help competition law assess the legality of conduct when data privacy is a competition parameter or when personal data is relevant to competitive performance. The Bundeskartellamt's *Facebook Germany* decision exemplified this insofar as a breach of data privacy rules informed the finding of abuse under German competition law. The decision also highlights the exclusionary dimension of breaches of data privacy rules, which gave Facebook an 'unlawful competitive edge over its competitors'.[15] Thus, at least in some instances, data privacy rules could serve as a metric to determine what constitutes an 'unfair term', 'normal competition', or 'competition on the merits', a position recently endorsed by the CJEU.[16]

Finally, data privacy can draw on competition law when dealing with privacy risks associated with market power. The discussion of the Bundeskartellamt *Facebook Germany* case shows how dominance is closely associated with higher privacy risks, both quantitatively and qualitatively. Thus, the establishment of dominance justifies—and can serve as a trigger for—imposing the enhanced responsibility regime discussed in Chapter 2. The increased risks from dominance further justify the decision to anchor the enhanced responsibility regime in the existing special responsibility regime for dominant undertakings under competition law.[17] Building the holistic approach on an existing and tested framework also ensures methodological soundness. Moreover, it allows data privacy law to leverage the existing work of competition authorities in imposing enhanced responsibilities. For example, a finding of dominance under competition law could be used as a trigger for imposing enhanced responsibility. This, in turn, would enhance the efficient use of resources and alignment in the application of the rules. Similarly, scaling data privacy responsibilities based on the scale and scope of data-processing operations could partially mitigate the disproportionate disadvantage that data privacy rules place on smaller entities.

[15] Bundeskartellamt, *Case Summary: Facebook, Exploitative Business Terms Pursuant to Section 19(1) GWB for Inadequate Data Processing* (2019) 11.

[16] *Meta Platforms Inc v Bundeskartellamt* (n 6).

[17] See Orla Lynskey, 'Grappling with "Data Power": Normative Nudges from Data Protection and Privacy' (2019) 20 Theoretical Inquiries in Law 189 (suggesting a similar framework for addressing 'data-power').

V. Final Remarks

The commercialization of personal data and big data has unlocked enormous social and economic benefits for businesses, individuals, and the public. But, as shown throughout this book, they also pose significant challenges linked to data privacy and competition policy. More generally, the challenge lies in balancing the economic benefits of the commercialization of personal data and the resulting harms to privacy, while still maintaining a healthy, competitive environment. Getting the balance right is no easy task. However, the argument made in this book—that data privacy law and competition law be applied holistically—could go a long way towards ensuring that the benefits of the commercialization of personal data are not trumped by the risks to data privacy and the competitiveness of markets. Any effort to address the challenges needs to be backed by collaboration across legal domains and a willingness to explore new territory, drawing on other disciplines, where necessary, to inform application of the rules.

In this respect, the book draws on insights from complexity science and emergent properties to understand the challenges faced by the current rules and to suggest solutions to address these challenges. The opportunities are endless, and future research could explore an emerging body of literature that applies agent-based models and scenario analysis in competition law to examine the impact of economic behaviour within ecosystems.[18] These tools enable the modelling of agent diversity and foster a deeper comprehension of uncertainty, emergent properties, and non-linearity that may occur in complex systems. Of particular importance to this book is the degree to which such models enable measurable reductions in non-price parameters of competition, such as data privacy.[19]

The application of a complexity science lens to the discussion underscores the need for both competition law and data privacy law to reconsider their objectives in light of the complex economic landscape. For instance, there are suggestions that data privacy law should re-evaluate its primary objective of granting individuals control over their data.[20] A glaring issue in the current paradigm of information control is the heavy dependence on consent to legitimize data processing. Koops contends that this approach has failed for two main reasons: the limited choices available to users and the absence of viable alternative business models.[21] These factors resonate with the discussions in this book about the role of competition law in ensuring that users have choices regarding their privacy. Furthermore, the added layer of complexity (marked by a multitude of actors and an intricate web of interactions) complicates the idea of informed consent, making it somewhat

[18] Gundlach (n 7) 20; Petit and Schrepel (n 2) 26.
[19] Ioannis Lianos, 'Reorienting Competition Law' (2022) 10 Journal of Antitrust Enforcement 1.
[20] Koops (n 3) 251.
[21] ibid 251–52.

illusory. Consequently, there are growing appeals to reimagine data protection, by pivoting from a control-centric model to a model emphasizing responsible data use or by abandoning consent as a legal basis entirely.[22]

There are even stronger calls for competition law to reconsider its objectives. This is primarily because the current methods for assessing market power and associated metrics often fail to capture the impact of behaviour on agents acting as data producers and workers, who contribute to the socio-economic value of the ecosystem. To address this, there are suggestions that the aims of competition law should be redefined to incorporate broader concerns, including the impacts on privacy, labour conditions, and sustainability.[23] This is an area of active research, and several changes are already underway on both legislative and enforcement fronts.

On the enforcement front, the European Commission has undertaken to amend the guidelines on horizontal cooperation and the enforcement priorities under Article 102. The Commission's amendment of the guidelines for Article 102 is particularly noteworthy as it highlights the challenges of applying the effects-based approach amidst strong network effects and winner-takes-all dynamics prevalent in digital markets.[24] This is a positive step towards complexity-orientated antitrust. Of particular importance is the Commission's note on the role of competition law in ensuring consumer choice, which ultimately contributes to the attainment of broader societal objectives, including maintaining plurality in a democratic society. In this context, it underscores the need to seriously consider the role that smaller competitors and product diversity can play in the competitive process in relation to digital markets. As demonstrated in Chapter 5, the consumer choice approach is favourable for accounting non-price parameters, including data privacy. Once put into action, it paves the way for broader consideration of data- and privacy-related harms under competition law. The increased attention to data privacy and associated harms in competition law is vital in addressing concerns in data privacy law, especially the lack of choice. It ensures the availability of viable alternatives and helps prevent dominant companies from compelling users to consent to extensive data collection.

On the legislative front, the enactment of the Digital Markets Act (DMA) is a response to some of the limitations of contemporary competition law in addressing harms from digital platforms. The DMA is noteworthy in that it addresses the new dimensions of power derived from managing interconnections but also tackles

[22] See Corien Prins and Lokke Moerel, 'Privacy for the Homo Digitalis: Proposal for a New Regulatory Framework for Data Protection in the Light of Big Data and the Internet of Things' (2016) <https://ssrncom/abstract=2784123> accessed 10 February 2024.

[23] Ioannis Lianos, 'Competition Law for a Complex Economy' (2019) 50 IIC-International Review of Intellectual Property and Competition Law 643. Julie Cohen, 'Law for the Platform Economy' (2017) 51 University of California Davis Law Review 133.

[24] Linsey McCallum and others, 'A Dynamic and Workable Effects-Based Approach to Abuse of Dominance' (2023) 1 Competition Policy Brief 2.

important data privacy considerations. There are multiple legislative initiatives targeting digital players, which have an impact on the competitive landscape. These include the Data Act, the Digital Services Act (DSA), and the Artificial Intelligence (AI) Act, to name just a few. Especially relevant to the discussions in this book is a trend observed in these legislative initiatives, particularly in the DSA and the AI Act, towards a tiered approach to regulation, where basic obligations apply to all actors, with additional, enhanced obligations tailored for specific actors. As discussed in Chapter 2, data privacy law stands to gain from adopting a tiered approach. These developments, however, add another layer of complexity that requires careful consideration. With the proliferation of new regulations targeting digital players, including the DMA, there is an even more pressing need to understand the interaction among these emerging laws. Creating a platform for institutional collaboration is the true essence of a holistic approach and is fundamental to achieving synergistic outcomes.

Index

For the benefit of digital users, indexed terms that span two pages (e.g., 52–53) may, on occasion, appear on only one of those pages.

References to notes are indicated by a note suffix after the paragraph number, for example: C9P22 n.9

Tables and figures are indicated by an italic *t* or *f* following the page number.